CYCLESCAPES OF THE UNEQUAL CITY

Cyclescapes of the Unequal City

BICYCLE INFRASTRUCTURE AND UNEVEN DEVELOPMENT

John G. Stehlin

University of Minnesota Press
Minneapolis
London

Parts of chapter 2 were published as "The Post-Industrial 'Shop Floor': Emerging Forms of Gentrification in San Francisco's Innovation Economy," *Antipode* 48, no. 2 (2016): 474–93; copyright John G. Stehlin; *Antipode* copyright Antipode Foundation Ltd. Parts of chapter 3 were published as "Regulating Inclusion: Spatial Form, Social Process, and the Normalization of Cycling Practice in the USA," *Mobilities* 9, no. 1 (2014): 21–41; reprinted by permission of Taylor and Francis Ltd. Different versions of chapters 2 and 4 were published as "Cycles of Investment: Bicycle Infrastructure, Gentrification, and the Restructuring of the San Francisco Bay Area," *Environment and Planning A* 47, no. 1 (2015): 121–37; reprinted by permission of SAGE Publications; copyright Pion and its Licensors; DOI: 10.1068/a130098p.

Copyright 2019 by the Regents of the University of Minnesota

All rights reserved. No part of this publication may be reproduced, stored in a retrieval system, or transmitted, in any form or by any means, electronic, mechanical, photocopying, recording, or otherwise, without the prior written permission of the publisher.

Published by the University of Minnesota Press
111 Third Avenue South, Suite 290
Minneapolis, MN 55401-2520
http://www.upress.umn.edu

Printed in the United States of America on acid-free paper

The University of Minnesota is an equal-opportunity educator and employer.

25 24 23 22 21 20 19   10 9 8 7 6 5 4 3 2 1

Library of Congress Cataloging-in-Publication Data
Names: Stehlin, John G., author.
Title: Cyclescapes of the unequal city : bicycle infrastructure and uneven development / John G. Stehlin.
Description: Minneapolis, MN : University of Minnesota Press, 2019. | Includes bibliographical references and index. |
Identifiers: LCCN 2018039744 (print) | ISBN 978-1-5179-0380-0 (hc) | ISBN 978-1-5179-0381-7 (pb)
Subjects: LCSH: City planning. | Cities and towns—Growth. | Bicycle lanes—Planning. | BISAC: SOCIAL SCIENCE / Sociology / Urban. | POLITICAL SCIENCE / Public Policy / City Planning and Urban Development. | SOCIAL SCIENCE / Social Classes.
Classification: LCC HT165.5 .S764 2019 (print) | DDC 307.1/216—dc23
LC record available at https://lccn.loc.gov/2018039744

For Cathy, who always hoped I would be a writer

CONTENTS

Introduction: Vehicle for a New City ... ix
1. The City and the Cyclescape ... 1
2. The Bicycle and the Region in Post-Crisis America ... 19
3. Everyday Practices and the Social Infrastructure of Urban Cycling ... 53
4. Gentrification and the Changing Publics of Bicycle Infrastructure ... 85
5. Institutional Power and Intraclass Conflict over Complete Streets ... 111
6. Bicycle Sharing Systems as Already-Splintered Infrastructure ... 141

Conclusion: Notes on a Passive Revolution in Mobility ... 173
Acknowledgments ... 189
Notes ... 193
Index ... 279

INTRODUCTION

Vehicle for a New City

In the heart of San Francisco's historically Latino Mission District, just off the neighborhood's central axis of Twenty-fourth Street, lies Balmy Alley, the city's longest-running and most iconic mural alley. Balmy Alley's internationally recognized murals depict the history and politics of the Mission. Alongside murals commemorating the United Farm Workers' struggles and denouncing the "dirty war" in El Salvador in the 1980s are several that center on the politics of urban development. One of the most recent murals in this genre, *Mission Makeover*, captures a new common sense about what bicycles mean in today's city. Painted by young artist Lucia Ippolito and her father, Tirso Araiza, *Mission Makeover* juxtaposes parallel scenes of a neighborhood in the throes of advanced gentrification. On the left, icons of the Mission that Ippolito and her father knew: low-rider cars, a Muni bus, and the heavy hand of the police visited on two youths of color who are posing with a pit bull. On the right, parallel, exaggerated vignettes of gentrification: moving vans unloading furniture into renovated Victorian houses; a policeman sharing a Starbucks latte with a rich woman and her show dog; and perhaps most notably, white hipster youths on bicycles and hanging out on stoops, their eyes and ears glued to smartphones (Figure 1). These two scenes depict the same geographical space but reveal starkly different social worlds, worlds separated by race, class, gender, age—and mobility.

On two afternoons in the summer of 2012, I dropped by while the mural was still in progress and volunteered to help Lucia paint—with marginal success—while we chatted about how the Mission has changed. I was especially interested in the bikes in the mural and what she envisioned by including them. It wasn't the bicycles that were new, she said— her father and his friends, longtime Latino residents of the Mission, also

Figure 1. Detail of the "new" Mission from *Mission Makeover* mural (in progress) by Lucia Ippolito and Tirso Araiza, 2012. Photograph by the author.

ride bikes. But their meaning was different. She recounted a debate with her father:

> When I was actually painting the hipsters on the wall, I made one of them Black. And my dad . . . was like, "You need to make the guy white," and I was like, "Why?" And he said, "Because they *are* white."[1]

She noted that she could have included Latino youth on lowrider bicycles to represent the "authentic" neighborhood as well. But in the stark dichotomy between the two sides, the bicycle functions as what Melody Hoffmann calls a "rolling signifier," symbolizing an urban space where race, class, and social life are in flux.[2]

For many bicycle advocates and enthusiasts, this would seem counterintuitive for a number of reasons. Bicycles are the cheapest and most accessible form of mobility, and poor people should stand to benefit the most from being freed from the burdens of car ownership. Improvements in bicycle infrastructure are formally public, and in principle shared by all residents, regardless of race or income. People of color have absorbed the majority of the harms of the automobile era, from the highway construction that destroyed their houses to the exhaust that promotes their asthma; rolling back the effects of automobility should be a matter of justice.[3] These arguments are true, and yet they fail to grapple with *how* bicycling has been incorporated into highly unequal processes of urban growth now flourishing in the United States.

The Changing Meanings of Urban Bicycling

Not long ago, riding a bicycle in the city meant some kind of lack: of class or caste status, manhood, or a driver's license. Now it symbolizes progress itself (Figure 2). In the 1990s, caricatures of urban bicycle riders included hippies, broke college students, drug dealers, and the homeless. Today, one could add hipster, yuppie, or "techie" to the list. A beat-up bicycle laid on its side in front of a liquor store used to symbolize gritty urban life, perhaps a seedy corner, while today bikeshare stations in front of new condos now convey an altogether changed city. What material forces underpin this rapid shift in the "chain of equivalences" the humble bicycle calls forth?[4]

Figure 2. Absolut Vodka billboard in the upscale Condesa neighborhood of Mexico City, March 2018. Photograph by the author.

This book offers one explanation. It traces the shifts in the significance of bicycling from a critique of car-dominated American culture to a medium of urban economic competitiveness, environmental politics, and intercity policy circulation. The incorporation of bicycle infrastructure into the production of urban space has not occurred simply because of a commonsense idea that cycling is an environmental or social good to be encouraged. Instead, advocates have worked tirelessly over the past twenty years to get cycling taken seriously as a mode of transportation, a positive contribution to public life, and a way to reduce carbon emissions. Over the same period, city leaders have searched for a new framework for economic growth that is less vulnerable to globalization, less carbon-intensive, and (it is hoped) less alienating. These sets of actors have found each other in the street and its remaking.

In this way, the bicycle links everyday practices and broad structural changes together at what Neil Smith called the "new urban frontier."[5] Smith used this term to trace the discourses of Manifest Destiny elites invoked to justify the often-violent gentrification of New York City's Lower East Side in the 1980s and 1990s. Narratives of recapturing the city today are more likely to express a no-less-colonial tone that treats the frontier as a laboratory for making better places. In these laboratories, the struggle for hegemony is waged in part through mobility practices and the infrastructures that support them, and these struggles remake urban space itself. In this sense, *mobility* is, to borrow from Stuart Hall, a modality through which differences such as race, class, gender, and the division of labor are lived, and a medium through which the "social tectonics" of gentrifying space become visible.[6]

In this book, I show how bicycling and other low-carbon, "human-scale" mobilities have become symbols and vectors of the urban "renaissance" that has in many ways hardened these differences.[7] I also show, however, that the bicycle can bridge potential antagonisms, allowing people whose daily lives are extraordinarily different to commune over a shared way of moving through space. I celebrate these moments, even as I recognize that they are for the most part fleeting. They are fleeting because the story I am telling involves the reconquering of central cities by the wealthy as places of home, work, and cultural life. The emergence of divergent mobility regimes—one pertaining to the livable, decarbonizing urban core, the other to car-dependent edges and interstices—raises both environmental and ethical questions about the future of the sustainable city.

Although cycling remains marginal overall in American urban life, it looms large in certain imaginaries of the urban future. This is because the promotion of livability and sustainable development, handily symbolized by the bicycle, gets things done. Cities in search of economic growth now invest in bicycle infrastructure in order to trade directly on this image, hoping to attract members of the elusive "creative class," the firms they start, and the salaries they spend, with livable streets as part of the allure.[8] Bicycles get things done *materially* as well—they help people move flexibly in urban space without creating car traffic, adding to transit burdens, or requiring much in the way of services. Like contingent and flexible work, contingent and flexible mobilities like bicycling have always been a necessity for poor people, but they now contribute to the "buzz" of the creative city as well.[9] As bicycle infrastructure becomes another valuable amenity in the urban portfolio, however, the bicycle fails to meet what many justifiably see as its emancipatory potential.

The bicycle activists, livability advocates, mayors, planners, and everyday cyclists I discuss in the following chapters are all guided by a sense that a two-wheeled city should be a dignified and inclusive place for all. They are not blind to the problems cities face, most of which dwarf bike lanes. But in pursuit of what Stephen Graham and Simon Marvin call "the integrated ideal," they also work in the context of pervasive "capitalist realism," in which private profit not only disciplines planning efforts but also furnishes their most powerful justification.[10] Moreover, advocates working on sustainable mobility improvements tend to focus on small-scale, quickly achievable interventions in "placemaking."[11] While this focus is pragmatic, it nonetheless reinscribes local and regional patterns of uneven development. The argument of this book is that this actually works against the broader goal of building livable and sustainable cities for all and betrays the limits of the current mainstream political imagination.

Vehicle for a New City

The current wave of enthusiasm for bicycling in the United States, which began in the 1990s, has significant parallels with the far larger "bike boom" of the 1970s. Rooted in a similar moment of environmental awareness and social radicalism, the ideological roots of today's bike culture depicted cycling as a daily act combating ecological degradation, suburban alienation, and geopolitical conflict over oil. Critical Mass, an anarchic carnival against the car-dominated world, epitomized this tendency with the rallying cry of "One Less Car." Originating in San Francisco in 1992, Critical Mass would go on to spread virally across the world.[12] A more normative but equally powerful vision can be found in a 1989 UN paper that hailed the bicycle as a "vehicle for a small planet."[13] Such enthusiasm within development discourse for the democratization of mobility fueled the spread of global NGOs like Bicycles for Humanity and World Bicycle Relief throughout the 2000s. However, distinct from the 1970s boom, the bike culture that emerged in this period was fundamentally *urban*. Today's bicycle advocates frame cycling as a way to transform the city, rather than escape it.[14] This urban focus is critical to how advocates came to engage with remaking city streets themselves and win a seat at the planning table. Ironically, what looked in the 1990s like an "anti-systemic" movement would in the space of two decades claim its crucial role in improving the functioning of the capitalist city.[15]

Part of what made the difference was investment, as the official completion of the interstate highway system in the early 1990s created new funding sources for bicycle infrastructure. In 1991, the Intermodal Surface Transportation Efficiency Act devolved power over nonmotorized transportation to the local level and launched an unprecedented increase in federal bicycle and pedestrian spending on projects like bike lanes, greenways, pedestrian crossings, and so on.[16] Though bicycle and pedestrian funds remain only roughly 1 percent of total highway spending, annual obligations, channeled through states, counties, and localities, rose more than twentyfold in real terms, from $22.9 million in 1992 ($39.2 million in 2017 dollars) to over $970 million in 2017. Total spending over this span of years exceeds $13 billion (in 2017 dollars) on over 36,000 individual projects.[17] Furthermore, these programs required participation from local bicycle advocates in project planning and implementation, leading to the formation of advisory committees that directly linked grassroots activists to the official mechanisms of city building.[18]

The results appear to support the "build it and they will come" approach now favored by leading bicycle advocates and researchers.[19] Between 2000 and 2015, seventy major U.S. cities saw an aggregate rise in bicycle ridership of over 75 percent.[20] Cycling's profile in cultural life has also risen dramatically: bicycle clubs, organized rides, and informal gatherings; bike shops, "bike kitchens," and bike-oriented businesses; and bicycling's presence in media and advertising have all flourished. On Bike to Work Day, which has dominated the bicycle advocacy calendar since 1994, mayors and other political leaders can be found in photo-ops astride bicycles, and some routinely cycle to work throughout the year as well. They celebrate cycling not just for its environmental benefits but with the hard-nosed rhetoric of economic development. As Chicago mayor Rahm Emmanuel put it, "You cannot be for a start-up, high-tech economy and not be pro-bike."[21] Bicycle infrastructure even played a rhetorical role in the fierce competition for the second headquarters of Amazon, the second-largest firm in the United States.[22]

Neither the burgeoning "bike culture" nor the modest realignment of federal transportation spending priorities can explain this growth in cyclists' numbers and status, however. Rather, the explanation lies in how these factors became entwined with dynamics of uneven development, particularly the reconcentration of economic and cultural centers of gravity into a small number of key city-regions. In other words, it concerns how bicycle activism and federal spending *took place* in very specific ways in certain cities. Bicycle enthusiasts and advocates have framed the city as their natural home, and for the first time taken on a decisive role in reshaping it. By doing so, they are crafting a persuasive vision for the American future at a time when the urban core has become the dominant horizon of urbanization and capital accumulation.[23] In other words, the bicycle has become a motif of the gentrifying city not by *fiat*, but because self-styled progressives participated in making it so. What is today sometimes called corporate "bikewashing," therefore, has many authors.[24]

The ascent of bicycling is not the simple struggle of popular activity against the automobile behemoth, though many see it that way. The politicization of cycling articulates with existing forms of social power, namely race, class, gender, and cultural capital, through which advocates gain entry into the rising bloc organized around more compact, multimodal, sustainable development. The relationships that grant advocates access to growth coalitions are politically contingent, however, and are constantly made and remade. They mobilize the practices of daily life itself as techniques for reshaping the city.

Why the Bicycle?

A guiding premise of this book is that the material and discursive space of the bicycle—what I call the "cyclescape"—is a field of struggle over what cities will become in the twenty-first century.[25] Following Doreen Massey, the cyclescape is a place "constructed out of a particular constellation of social relations, meeting and weaving together" in a spatial lattice that is constantly evolving.[26] The cyclescape is not simply defined by the spatial extent of bicycle usage or infrastructure, therefore, but a social practice as well, in the sense outlined by Henri Lefebvre: it unites places, representations, actions, and spaces that are both trivial and monumental.[27] To paraphrase Marx, people produce and shape space in practice, but never under conditions of their own choosing, and with varying degrees of expertise, political power, and control over resources. The production of space cuts in multiple directions, stabilizing the volatility of capitalist society as well as nurturing the potential for different forms of urban habitation.[28]

Hence, the bicycle is more than just an idea whose time has come but less of a revolution in mobility than its mythology holds. It is a vector along which new practices of mobility are developed and institutionalized even as they reinscribe well-worn forms of social division. The cyclescape is thus a "dense transfer point," in Michel Foucault's terms: a site of normative struggle as well as a motif of resistance (see Figure 3).[29]

With this guiding orientation, I open outward onto processes beyond bicycling and mobility that are fundamental to understanding contemporary forms of producing capitalist urban sustainability. First, the mandate to attract capital—both "human" and economic—pushes cities to compete with one another on the basis of an ever-changing inventory of amenities. Bicycle infrastructures, especially bicycle-sharing facilities, have become a new arena of such interurban competition, woven into the "inter-referencing" of environmental governance strategies.[30] Second, contemporary ideas of "human capital" valorize a culture of flexibility, and bicycling enhances such flexible mobility within centrally located areas of the city without requiring large investments in mass transit.[31] Bicycle infrastructure has thus become a way for city leaders to support economic

Figure 3. Sidewalk graffiti in the Mission District, 2009. Photograph by Scott Beale/Laughing Squid. https://www.flickr.com/photos/laughingsquid/5283461938/ (accessed May 21, 2018).

development without increasing the carbon footprint or investing in expensive, debt-financed, and politically costly infrastructures. Lastly, competitive strategies on this basis focus investment strategically in key areas within the broader urban fabric, drawing political participation toward the submunicipal scale. A focus on neighborhood- or corridor-level "green" amenities meshes with this form of governance more generally and encourages intensified nodes of investment rather than broader redistribution—what Graham and Marvin call "splintering urbanism."[32]

No amount of individual or cultural drive to make environmentalism a part of daily life through bicycling would have resulted in the changes now underway without the political opening created by racialized disinvestment and subsequent gentrification.[33] Nor, however, is bicycling simply an expression of capital's long march "back to the city."[34] It is a practice that both addresses and reinscribes the contradictions of contemporary American urbanism. In this sense, much of the growing bike culture is an attempt to practice an emancipatory relationship with technology and place that is also entangled with capitalist efforts to remake the urban space economy. In what follows, these moments will be held in tension conceptually just as they are materially in daily practice. In many ways, therefore, in the words of disgraced American cycling star Lance Armstrong, "It's not about the bike."

Sites and Positionality

This book draws most directly on research conducted in the San Francisco Bay Area, as well as in Detroit, Portland, and Philadelphia, between 2011 and 2018. But it also invokes questions that interested me long before the research for this book began.

I was introduced to tinkering with bikes in 2002 by friends loosely involved in anarchism and the anti-globalization movement. They lived in collective houses packed with underemployed, mostly white youth in the majority–African American city of Richmond, Virginia, and cycling was a practical extension of a general anti-corporate politics. Like many in my generation of so-called millennials now known for their urbanophilia, after graduating from college in 2004 I moved to an older, disinvested, but "up-and-coming" neighborhood: the largely African American streetcar suburbs of West Philadelphia. There, ramshackle Victorian houses rented cheaply, there was a strong do-it-yourself vitality among a mostly white sub-/counterculture, and bicycles were ubiquitous. Though I owned a car, I used a bike for almost all tasks from commuting to grocery shopping, and almost every person in my group of friends did the same. Many of us also would likely not have lived in this area popularly considered "dangerous," at the edge of the university district, were it not for our bicycles, which allowed us to cover a lot of ground without depending on cars, transit schedules, or walking home late. Our mutual visibility contributed to a countercultural camaraderie in these spaces, while bicycles doubtlessly also made us more visible as *new* to mostly Black longtime residents.[35]

The whiteness of this social world ran counter to my experiences at work, as a mechanic at Via Bicycle, the longest-running bike shop in central Philadelphia. By the early 2000s, the nearby historic Italian Market neighborhood was a hub of immigration from Mexico and Central America. Largely by word of mouth, our shop had become the go-to location for Spanish-speaking cyclists who worked at local restaurants and job sites. Due to theft, damage, and cost concerns, they often used inexpensive bicycles from Walmart and Target that needed near-constant repair and were quite distant from the urban cool of the "fixie" trend. We also served longtime low-income residents of downtown Philadelphia, many of them Black, as well as white, middle-class residents who arrived in the area's first burst of gentrification in the 1980s. A growing clientele, however, were young white students, artists, and service workers, the storied "hipsters" who were flocking to gentrifying, cosmopolitan neighborhoods in urban cores throughout the country.[36] In other words, the shop was not a reflection of a unified bike culture but a hub of multiple cycling practices and social realities.

When I moved to Oakland in 2008, I found myself in familiar circumstances. The places I visited and the people I interacted with on bicycles were new to me (and the weather was more conducive to year-round cycling), but I intuitively understood the *how* of being a new resident and moving through space by bicycle. I was not alone in this. Few of the many punk, outsider, artist, student, and/or nonprofit workers I met who rode bikes had grown up in the city of Oakland. For these friends and acquaintances—most of them also white—from nearby suburban cities like Santa Rosa or Walnut Creek, as well as cities and suburbs in the Houston, Philadelphia, Boston, or New York metropolitan areas, bicycles were simply how one moved through the city. It was the unquestioned tool of our urban environment, suiting a way of life cultivated in gentrifying spaces as well as signifying a broader opposition to the car.

The growing visibility of bicycling in gentrifying areas supports an emerging commonsense notion that it is a white, bourgeois activity.[37] Yet this claim ignores the countless people of color continuing to use bicycles on a daily basis, for a variety of livelihoods that sustain the urban social and material fabric. Who are the food deliverers, day laborers, dishwashers, and recycling collectors, disproportionately people of color commuting and working by bicycle, if not cyclists? Who are the veteran bicycle messengers, many of them people of color, whose aesthetic roots lie with West Indian immigrants in 1980s New York, if not cyclists? Who are the middle-class people of color and working-class whites alike who ride bikes, if not cyclists? In other words, how could a practice so manifestly diverse be understood in such a limited way? I argue that this is more than just an ideological trick but is rooted in geographical political economy.

In taking on these questions, I situate myself *within*, not outside, the process of racialized gentrification itself, a position true of many gentrification researchers.[38] While I interrogate cycling as a new mode of urban whiteness, I also take seriously the line between analyzing and reifying.[39] I argue that the narrative of bicycling's whiteness is constructed in support of an economic narrative that flies in the face of abundant evidence to the contrary. At the same time, while cycling has increased substantially among people of color over the past two decades, this growth is often framed a-spatially, as though mobility practices are only selected ideologically rather than shaped geographically.[40] In the face of these erasures, bicyclists of color have claimed their own visibility.[41] But these groups, with some exceptions, have tended not to be included in the ascendant political bloc of bicycle advocates. My goal in raising these critiques is not to damn today's bicycle movement but to splash my own eyes, and those of my fellow cyclist-advocates, with cold water, in hopes of lowering the bicycle from its pedestal and setting it "back on the ground."[42]

Map of the Argument

Chapter 1 introduces the conceptual framework that guides the book. It focuses on the intersection between processes of gentrification, the infrastructural basis of urban mobility, and dynamics of neoliberal regional restructuring. The transformation of streets, as a way of reshaping mobility patterns at the submunicipal scale, has only recently become a key dimension of the gentrification process. As the middle and upper classes take over the urban cores of metropolitan areas across the country, providing nonautomobile infrastructure is increasingly critical to avoiding traffic congestion and a rising ecological footprint. This has brought mobility change to the center of environmental governance in cities across the United States, with strategies ranging from bike lanes and greenways to bus rapid transit, light rail, and transit-oriented development, and supported by federal grants, local bond measures, cap and trade funding (in California's case), and carbon offsets.[43] Bicycle infrastructure is a particularly inexpensive—and thus attractive—element of this broader strategy.[44]

In the second chapter, I outline the basic contours of the last thirty years of urban restructuring in the San Francisco Bay Area, where I did the majority of my qualitative research, as well as Philadelphia and Detroit. First, I argue that the regional reorganization of race, class, and the division of labor has in many cities fueled the growth of an increasingly white and affluent population in the areas now seeing the greatest investment in bicycle infrastructure. These populations also form the political constituency for bicycle infrastructure, in part because the proximity of live, work, and play—for well-paid white-collar workers—renders cycling a logical mobility choice. Central cities have become hubs of face-to-face, "creative" economic activity, prompting commentators and consultants to link the urban ecology of innovation to changing mobilities in particular.[45] These dynamics have cascaded "down" the urban hierarchy, such that even less affluent cities experience affordability crises and outward pressure on working-class populations, particularly those of color. In short, the growing popularity of bicycling among the "new middle class" reflects what we might call the "Europeanization" of America's race–class geography, with suburbanization increasingly working class and the central city rapidly gentrifying.[46] Second, I outline a planning initiative in each city that reflects the new urban innovation paradigm to demonstrate the centrality of bicycling to the institutions organizing the production of space. The following chapters then step backward and trace how this state of affairs came about.

The third chapter examines bicycling as an urban spatial practice. It explores the politicization of mass bicycling as a tool to remake the city, as well as the "infrapolitics" of daily cycling in a city built for cars. The roots of contemporary bicycle politics lie in Critical Mass, an anarchic "organized coincidence" of bicycle activists disrupting commute traffic that has spread throughout the world as a technique of protest.[47] This chapter contextualizes the Critical Mass phenomenon, and its many offshoots, as part of the wider spatial practices of cycling in gentrifying space, drawing on evidence from San Francisco, Oakland, and Detroit. The rhythms of these practices play a key role in shaping the spatial patterns and aesthetics of contemporary gentrification, as well as the experience of urbanity itself.

The fourth and fifth chapters examine the shift in bicycle politics toward increasing involvement in the planning and implementation of physical infrastructure. This involves the formation of bicycle-oriented "infrastructural publics" and their imbrication with the institutions (both official and unofficial) of the municipal state.[48] They reveal moments of struggle over what streets—and by extension the city—will become, and bicycle advocates have waged these battles with increasing sophistication by promoting the economic value of bicycle infrastructure. Chapter 4 shows how grassroots activists in San Francisco's Mission District, a rapidly gentrifying working-class Latino neighborhood, in the mid-1990s forged the case for the economic value of bicycle infrastructure initially as realpolitik rather than ideology. They quickly made influential allies within San Francisco's growth machine, which has championed placemaking as a growth paradigm in the decades since and shaped national institutions that reinforced this common sense. This narrative, now preeminent in advocacy, erases the ways that some forms of development now celebrated actively harm the urban poor and working class, many of them bicycle users.

The fifth chapter traces the contemporary influence of this narrative on bicycle planning and civic leadership in Oakland. The now widely accepted idea that bicycle infrastructure promotes economic growth lubricates the machinery of official planning, activates translocal expert networks among planners, and enjoys broad support in rapidly gentrifying areas. But the rollout of this planning paradigm in Oakland reveals some of the political contradictions of the bike movement as well. For instance, in rapidly gentrifying North Oakland, bicycle infrastructure plans generate vocal opposition. This opposition often comes not from the residents most threatened by gentrification, however, but from business interests and residents concerned about parking and traffic. Fights over the street become fights over the balance of forces between factions of the middle class with distinct and often mutually conflicting infrastructural dependencies. At the same time, in neighborhoods of color beyond the gentrification "frontier," bicycle infrastructure projects lack a local support base, resulting in contests between community interests and the municipal state.

The sixth chapter examines the phenomenon of bikeshare, which scales up some of the contradictions detailed in previous chapters. Bikeshare systems—public-private partnerships that provide fleets of bicycles organized in a network of digitally connected docking stations and rented on a short-term basis—have spread from Europe to cities across the United States and the world. These systems are spearheaded by powerful networks of policy transfer, particularly between mayors and planning departments in transnational alliances, and are implemented as part of "innovation"- and sustainability-oriented growth strategies. While publicly available, they are subjected to the discipline of financial sustainability, which sharply limits their extent and reinforces the uneven development of mobility. I focus on the San Francisco Bay Area, Detroit, and Philadelphia and explore the ways that advocates have attempted to steer bikeshare planning toward more equitable outcomes, often with quite remarkable success. However, in the long term, without dedicated resources and a more muscular role for the public sector, such systems will tend to trace and amplify existing patterns of gentrification.

Although this book is not directly oriented toward policy intervention, the conclusion offers some normative claims regarding the present and future of bicycle advocacy. It first traces three potential trajectories evident in contemporary bicycle politics. The first is the appropriation of practices of mass bicycle riding by young Black and Brown "wheelie" crews in cities like Philadelphia and Oakland, which shapes a new generation of bicycle riders in a way quite distinct from Critical Mass. The second is the shift in bicycle advocacy toward more general road-safety initiatives coalescing around Vision Zero, a zero traffic deaths paradigm that has become the newest "fast policy."[49] This welcome decentering of bicycling, however, comes with an increased dependence on racialized policing techniques, potentially exposing people of color to increased danger in the name of safety. The last is the phenomenon of GPS-based, venture capital–funded "dockless" bike and scooter sharing systems that "disrupt" the traditional dock-based networks by promising increased flexibility at a lower cost. These are part of a shift toward mobility as a service and the urbanization of broader trends in platform capitalism.[50]

The lifestyle-oriented and business-friendly framing of cycling has led bicycle advocates away from the urban progressive Left. While some bicycle advocates have made common cause with racial- and economic-justice organizations working on affordable housing, ending racist policing, and community-based economic development, these alliances have been both minimal and long overdue. More critically, they occur in a context in which uneven development steadily erodes potentials for greater racial and class diversity in cycling. Thus, in what follows I use the bicycle as a lens with which to apprehend some key aspects of the massive shifts at work in today's American city. I also hope to show that we may equally have to zoom back out from the bike lane to the metropolis in order to confront its contradictions.

CHAPTER ONE

The City and the Cyclescape

"The bike wars are over, and the bikes won," declared Janette Sadik-Khan, New York City Department of Transportation chief under Mayor Michael Bloomberg, in a March 2016 column for *New York Magazine*. The piece, excerpted from her recent book *Streetfight*, outlined a series of high-profile battles from 2010 to 2011 over bicycle infrastructure in Brooklyn, including a particularly acrimonious fight over a protected bikeway in the wealthy neighborhood of Prospect Park West. "None of the bike-lane opponents' predictions has come to pass," she wrote. "City streets have never been safer, more economically thriving, or offered more transportation options than they do today."[1] Sadik-Khan, a superstar in the increasingly high-profile world of bicycle planning, went on to chair the National Association of City Transportation Officials (NACTO) and serve as a principal at philanthropic consultancy Bloomberg Associates.[2] How did the ostensibly "progressive" bike movement come to idolize a billionaire mayor and a cohort of planners who presided over the solidification of New York as a "luxury city"?[3] What led bicycle politics to settle on a reinvigorated urban capitalism as proof of winning the "bike wars"?

In the period straddling the Great Recession, cities across the United States massively expanded their bicycle networks. Organizations like NACTO and PeopleForBikes built sophisticated policy networks and now enjoy strong followings among mayors and planners.[4] Since 2010, over fifty cities added bicycle sharing systems, short-term rental services that provide public access to bicycles that are electronically locked to docking stations.[5] Beginning in 2016, "dockless" bike sharing using smartphone apps became a multibillion-dollar industry in China and by 2018 were joined by several Silicon Valley firms and launched both bikes and small electric scooters in a number of American cities. Bicycle commuting rates,

2   THE CITY AND THE CYCLESCAPE

while still below 1 percent of commuters nationally, have leapt upward in dozens of cities (Tables 1 and 2). The National Household Travel Survey estimated that in 2009 12.8 percent of Americans eighteen and over used a bicycle at least once during a representative survey week, up from 6.8 percent in 2001.[6] While bicycle sales have remained steady since the 1990s, manufacturers have expanded their "urban" product lines, selling commuter-specific bicycles that embrace a cosmopolitan aesthetic informed by the cycling cultures of Northern Europe.[7] Most important, the reasons that advocates now give for investing in bicycle infrastructure are often quite far from the environmentalist pieties and anti-corporate sentiments

Table 1. Top 20 Cities in Bicycle Commute Share (of 70 Largest Cities), 1990–2015

	Bicycle commute share (%) 1990	2015[a]	Change (%)	Population rank 1990	2015
Portland, Ore.	1.2	6.4	452	29	27
Minneapolis, Minn.	1.6	4.3	165	36	46
Washington, D.C.	0.8	4.0	428	19	24
San Francisco, Calif.	1.0	4.0	320	14	14
Seattle, Wash.	1.5	3.8	149	21	21
Tucson, Ariz.	2.8	2.9	5	30	33
Oakland, Calif.	1.1	3.1	182	33	45
New Orleans, La.	0.9	3.0	227	23	51
Denver, Colo.	0.9	2.3	170	25	23
Sacramento, Calif.	1.9	2.1	13	35	35
Philadelphia, Pa.	0.6	2.1	261	5	5
Honolulu, Hawaii	1.2	2.0	61	37	55
Boston, Mass.	0.9	1.9	116	20	22
Pittsburgh, Pa.	0.4	1.7	316	34	63
Tampa, Fla.	0.9	1.4	55	38	54
Chicago, Ill.	0.3	1.6	458	3	3
Austin, Tex.	0.8	1.5	90	26	11
Albuquerque, N.M.	1.2	1.4	19	32	32
St. Paul, Minn.	0.5	1.6	221	39	67
Anchorage, Alaska	0.5	1.2	167	41	65
Los Angeles, Calif.[b]	0.6	1.2	96	2	2
New York City, N.Y.	0.3	1.0	242	1	1
Houston, Tex.	0.3	0.5	46	4	4
70 largest cities	0.6	1.2	93		
Total United States	0.4	0.6	50		

[a] 2015 figures are five-year aggregates from 2011 to 2015. Rankings are composed of the 70 largest U.S. cities in 2015.
[b] Los Angeles, New York, and Houston are included for reference as large cities; their bicycle commute ranks are 24, 27, and 47, respectively.
Source: Steven Manson, Jonathan Schroeder, David Van Riper, and Steven Ruggles, IPUMS National Historical Geographic Information System, Version 12.0 (database) (Minneapolis: University of Minnesota, 2017). http://doi.org/10.18128/D050.V12.0.

Table 2. Top 20 Metropolitan Areas in Bicycle Commute Share (of 50 Largest), 1990–2015

Metropolitan Area	Bicycle commute share (%) 1990	Bicycle commute share (%) 2015[a]	Change (%)	Population rank 1990	Population rank 2015
Portland, Ore.–Vancouver–Hillsboro, Wash.	0.6	2.4	285	27	24
San Francisco–Oakland–Hayward, Calif.	1.1	2.0	81	4	11
Sacramento–Roseville–Arden-Arcade, Calif.	1.8	1.8	1	26	28
San Jose–Sunnyvale–Santa Clara, Calif.[b]	1.1	1.8	70	4	35
Seattle–Tacoma–Bellevue, Wash.	0.5	1.1	115	14	15
New Orleans–Metairie, La.	0.5	1.2	132	32	46
Los Angeles–Long Beach–Anaheim, Calif.	0.7	0.9	29	22	2
Denver–Aurora–Lakewood, Colo.	0.7	0.9	22	2	21
Boston–Cambridge–Newton, Mass. (New Hampshire)	0.4	0.9	113	7	10
Minneapolis–St. Paul–Bloomington, Minn. (Wisconsin)	0.4	1.0	129	16	16
Phoenix–Mesa–Scottsdale, Ariz.	1.4	0.9	–38	20	12
Austin–Round Rock, Tex.	0.5	0.9	59	52	36
Tampa–St. Petersburg–Clearwater, Fla.	0.7	0.8	8	21	18
Washington, D.C.–Arlington–Alexandria, Va. (Maryland–West Virginia)	0.3	0.8	162	8	7
San Diego–Carlsbad, Calif.	0.9	0.7	–24	15	17
Chicago, Ill.–Naperville, Ind.–Elgin, Wis.	0.2	0.7	215	3	3
Philadelphia, Pa.–Camden, N.J.–Wilmington, Del. (Maryland)	0.3	0.6	93	5	6
Miami–Fort Lauderdale–West Palm Beach, Fla.	0.5	0.6	13	11	8
New York City–Newark–Jersey City, N.J. (New York–Pennsylvania)	0.2	0.6	152	1	1

continued on page 4

Jacksonville, Fla.	0.7	0.6	−11	47	41
Houston–The Woodlands–Sugar Land, Tex.[c]	0.3	0.3	6	10	5
Dallas–Fort Worth–Arlington, Tex.	0.1	0.2	26	9	4
Largest 50 metropolitan areas	0.4	0.6	56		
Total United States	0.4	0.6	50		

[a] 2015 figures are five-year aggregates from 2011 to 2015. Rankings are composed of the 100 largest U.S. metropolitan areas in the 2011–15 American Community Survey. Source: Manson et al., 2017.

[b] In 1990 San Jose–Sunnyvale–Santa Clara was included in the San Francisco–Oakland–San Jose MSA, so 1990 commute share and population rank for San Francisco–Oakland–San Jose are used. San Francisco–Oakland–San Jose would remain fourth in 2015 population estimates, just above Houston.

[c] Houston–The Woodlands–Sugar Land and Dallas–Fort Worth–Arlington are included for reference as large metropolitan areas; their bicycle commute ranks are 32 and 47, respectively.

that politicized cyclists claimed in the 1990s. Instead, consultants, advocates, mayors, and media all affirm that bicycling is good for business.[8]

Over the same period, gentrification became increasingly widespread throughout the United States, by some estimates affecting twice as many neighborhoods between 2000 and 2013 than in the previous decade.[9] After the Great Recession devastated housing markets at the urban fringe, homebuyers and large investors turned to central neighborhoods, while many cities' most promising economic recovery strategy has become the booming field of high technology, especially computer systems design. By 2017, home price levels in metropolitan areas like the San Francisco Bay Area, Portland (Oregon), and Boston exceeded their prerecession peaks (a year earlier than the S&P 20-City Composite Home Price Index), and the deepening affordability crisis in these areas is a matter of constant public debate.[10]

Meanwhile, concerns about the "suburbanization of poverty" have come to the fore even in booming regions, signaling that the model of extensive urban expansion that has predominated for well over a century is in crisis.[11] After the 2008 financial crisis, large numbers of Black and Latino first-time homebuyers found themselves stranded in car-dependent exurbs.[12] The resurgence of interest in cities has been accompanied by a mainstream dismissal of these exurbs, under a broad consensus that the age of the car–highway–suburb is past—in spirit, if not in actual practice.[13] For this way of thinking, the bicycle represents the future. It enables infill development without adding traffic congestion or carbon emissions, addressing in one stroke the economic and ecological imperatives of contemporary urban growth. Because of the obduracy of the existing built environment, and the regional scale produced by the regime of automobility, we might equally see the bicycle, following Antonio Gramsci, as a "morbid symptom" of a mobility interregnum.[14]

Vehicles for a New City

The discourse on bicycling that has shaped planners, policymakers, and urbanists is largely framed around its inherently progressive nature and its transformative implications for urban life. Critical Mass was particularly influential in endowing bicycles with both an implicit and explicit political message: another way of movement was possible (see chapter 3).[15] As a marginalized form of mobility, bicycling escaped regulations like licensing and taxation, aligning it with the anarchist-inspired political culture of the post-1960s Left.[16] This framing places bicycling alongside guerrilla gardening, graffiti, and skateboarding as acts of hacking the dominant code of the capitalist city.[17] Most important, because bicycling does not rely directly on fossil energy, it carries "an environmentalist message without a placard."[18]

With bicycling's growing influence on the liberal urban mainstream since the mid-2000s, the tone has shifted from this critique of the capitalist city toward how bicycling can support the American urban "renaissance" underway. A number of more journalistic case studies trace the growth of bike culture and its significance for environmental sustainability, economic vitality, and social renewal. In this genre, authors often have quasi-religious "conversion experiences" in renowned bicycling cities like Amsterdam and Copenhagen.[19] Blogs, "zines," and the broader counterculture have served as avenues for some of these ideas as well, further reinforcing cycling's underdog, "do-it-yourself" identity.[20] The titles themselves reflect the unbridled optimism of the moment: *Joyride: Pedaling toward a Healthier Planet*; *On Bicycles: 50 Ways the New Bike Culture Can Change Your Life*; and *How Cycling Can Save the World*, for example, position bicycling as a personal choice that has far-reaching positive impacts. Most important, this discourse emphasizes that the *city* is the bicycle's natural home, and the place where its transformative potential can be realized.

A more policy-oriented scholarly literature examines current trends in cycling and best practices in bicycle facility planning, with the goal of informing efforts to increase ridership.[21] As bicycle sharing becomes a main frontier of infrastructural investment and interurban competition, research has followed suit as well.[22] Organizations at all levels produce reports that circulate through the online channels of bicycle advocacy, from the national (e.g., the League of American Bicyclists, PeopleForBikes, and the Alliance for Biking and Walking) to the local and regional (the San Francisco Bicycle Coalition, Walk Oakland Bike Oakland, the Bicycle Coalition of Greater Philadelphia, and the Detroit Greenways Coalition, for example). Robust debates also increasingly take place online on sites like Streetsblog, Next City, and CityLab. A common feature of these forums is the circulation of infrastructural stories, particularly from Copenhagen, Amsterdam, and (increasingly) Bogotá.[23] These stories, though, are often abstracted from political economy and social context, which grants the designs themselves a quasi-fetishistic power.[24] By implication, with the right infrastructural treatments, and a little "urban acupuncture," the American city can thrive again.[25]

Recently, however, a growing cohort of scholars has critically examined the social, political, cultural, and institutional context within which this flowering of cycling has taken place.[26] This work has interrogated the racialization of bicycle advocacy and bicycle planning, which remains dominated by largely white, middle-class professionals whose activities reflect a narrow set of interests aligned with gentrification.[27] By contrast, scholars and activists like Adonia Lugo, Tamika Butler, and Olatunji Oboi Reed emphasize subaltern cyclists' invisibility to mainstream bicycle advocacy and their simultaneous overexposure to law enforcement and traffic violence, as well as the importance of the human infrastructure of collective learning that receives less attention than "world class" bicycle facilities do.[28] For this line of thinking, the bicyclist functions as what Melody Hoffmann calls a "rolling signifier," refracting in daily practice broader relationships of social power.[29] This symbolic dimension has led to pitched battles over infrastructure, with neighborhoods of color pushing back against what they see as an amenity that encourages gentrification.[30] Beyond imagery, the transformation of urban streets in the interest of "completeness" (better accommodation of cyclists, pedestrians, and transit) can materially exclude working people and the poor (both because such places become more expensive and because they crowd out industrial jobs), rendering these streets "incomplete" from the perspective of what Mimi Sheller calls mobility justice.[31] At the same time, the growing strength of advocates of color offers glimpses of new modes of solidarity that subvert the segregation of the contemporary metropolis.[32] These struggles all occur, though, within a broader urban political structure shaped by the hegemony of the automobile both at the scale of the corridor and that of the region.[33]

There have been a number of moments in recent years in which the implicit entanglement of bicycle infrastructure and gentrification has been made explicit. In 2010, Black parishioners in North Portland, the city's only African American neighborhood, protested a bike lane project as a "white lane," successfully altering the project and the process of community participation in planning.[34] The same year, in the D.C. mayoral primary, opponents of sitting mayor Adrian Fenty (who was Black) framed him as a supporter of "dog parks and bike lanes" who had abandoned his Black constituents.[35] In the African American neighborhood of East Austin, a resident told bicycle project coordinator Adrian Lipscombe (who is Black herself): "When the bikes came in, the blacks went out."[36] Thus, while a reactionary "bikelash" against bicycle planning driven by fear of change is a popular (and often accurate) trope, a parallel common sense has emerged about the role of bicycle infrastructure in exclusionary urbanism.

But humor broached the topic of cycling and gentrification largely before advocates did. The website *Stuff White People Like* listed bikes at 61, between the Toyota Prius and "Knowing what's best for poor people," while popular blogger BikeSnobNYC poked fun at the "Great Hipster Silk Route" of Kent Avenue in Brooklyn.[37] Beyond this, the silence of bicycle advocacy on questions of difference has been most forcefully contested by cyclists of color themselves. Pressure from groups like Black Women Bike in Washington, D.C.; Red, Bike and Green in Oakland, Chicago, and Atlanta; and Los Angeles's Ovarian Cycos, as well as concerted work within advocacy organizations in cities like Los Angeles and Chicago, forced the issue of the whiteness of mainstream advocacy at a time when its complicity with gentrification could no longer be ignored.[38] In response to such agitation, in 2013 the League of American Bicyclists appointed a council composed of high-profile advocates of color, the Equity Advisory Council, but it quickly disbanded, widening the contradictions of the moment.[39] At the same time, PeopleForBikes dramatically increased its focus on equity in bicycling, funding research into better practices for planning bicycle sharing systems.[40] Thus, in many ways, advocates of color have decisively shaped the terms of discourse today, creating the political space to launch their own initiatives, such as The Untokening and Equiticity, which challenge mainstream bicycle advocacy's tacitly pro-gentrification consensus. In a few short years, "equity" went from an occasional topic to an inescapable issue within the bicycle movement.

The contradictions that fuel these struggles have not been resolved. The current platform of American bicycle advocacy, with some deviations, holds to both promoting the economic benefits of bicycle infrastructure investment and affirming the need for greater equity. Growing attention is paid to the ways in which these come into direct contradiction through the process of gentrification, but this is a very recent shift. Furthermore, the contemporary celebration of streetscape changes as "urban acupuncture" tends to naturalize the neighborhood scale as the primary site of transformative action.[41] What emerges is a politics of urban mobility that rearticulates its radical influences into an ethos of liberal pluralism.

The entanglement of bicycle planning with urban development strategy over the past two decades was not simply an expression of the inherent value of bicycling, but neither was it imposed "from above" by what John Logan and Harvey Molotch call "the growth machine."[42] Rather, it was the contingent outcome of the interaction between the following: the articulation of subcultural cycling practices with processes of gentrification; the sociotechnical characteristics of bicycles and streets; and regional dynamics of political-economic restructuring and urban sustainability planning. The following sections will examine these elements in turn.

Gentrification, Daily Practice, and the Making of the Neighborhood Scale

In 1964 British sociologist Ruth Glass observed that "one by one, many of the working-class quarters of London have been invaded by the middle classes—upper and lower. Shabby, modest mews and cottages . . . have become elegant, expensive residences. Victorian houses, downgraded in an earlier or recent period . . . have been upgraded once again." Somewhat tongue-in-cheek, she called this process "gentrification."[43] In the 1960s and 1970s, this process was fairly sporadic, affecting a limited number of neighborhoods and cities, and was often treated with ambivalence by the local state.[44] But since the 1990s, gentrification has "scaled up," as globally connected investors redevelop disinvested neighborhoods for middle-class and elite residency at an unprecedented scale.[45] In the process, it has become a central plank of both urban economic and environmental policy at the local level.[46] "Livability" is the fulcrum of this link between the economic and the environmental, uniting the revaluation of *place* and a less carbon-intensive regime of *movement* through the transformation of the public realm, the street in particular.[47]

Gentrification constitutes "the class remake of the central urban landscape," the mechanism of which is the property market.[48] At its core is the "rent gap": the difference between present revenues from a given parcel of land—"capitalized rents"—and the *potential* rents that parcel could yield, given prevailing rents at the metropolitan level. When this gap is great enough, it exerts an economic compulsion on the owner to bring the parcel up to its "highest and best use" through capital investment, typically displacing the current occupants.[49] Strictly speaking, while gentrification only directly involves privately owned parcels, streets and other public places are key mediators of *localized* potential rents at the neighborhood scale. The quality and characteristics of streets as infrastructure become effectively "inherent" to the parcels in that they connect to the rest of the urban fabric.[50] Streets anchor urban practices, and even small-scale changes to their infrastructural characteristics allow new practices to flourish where they previously didn't, even changing perceptions of neighborhood desirability.[51] The reverse is also true: practices change the meaning and potential of streets, and they shape the kinds of amenities that generate value and spur further public investment.[52] These activities need not be *intended* to promote gentrification. "Marginal gentrifiers" — participants in but not leaders of the process — have become essential to the forms gentrification has taken, while larger, more powerful actors capture the lion's share of profits.[53] In other words, both "hard" and "soft" infrastructures (physical investments and everyday social practices) guide the reinvestment of capital to particular places and not others.

Many of these practices are inspired by writers who sought to recapture qualities of place that were eroded by suburbanization, midcentury high modernism, and the automobile. In *The Death and Life of Great American Cities* (1961), Jane Jacobs attacked contemporary planning orthodoxy, celebrating instead the "intricate sidewalk ballet" of ordinary residents in tight-knit neighborhoods as the foundation of urban vitality.[54] By the late 1970s, a new generation of planners, like Donald Appleyard, Peter Calthorpe, Kevin Lynch, Jan Gehl, and Allan Jacobs, was learning from thinkers like Jacobs and William Whyte, the urban struggles of the 1960s, and the emerging environmentalist movement.[55] These planners reinterpreted the city by claiming not just a sociocultural but an economic value for densely settled, vibrant, and diverse urban centers, and they slowly altered the normative basis for their line of work.[56] Over the same period, preserving and enhancing the qualities of place that Jacobs admired had become a potentially lucrative activity.[57]

Thus, the neighborhood is where leading forces in gentrification attempt to shape use-values — or "quality of life" — in ways that support increases in exchange-value. Property owners rarely settle for improving their own property by itself.[58] They enlist fellow rentiers, as well as the facilities of the state, in order to support redevelopment. As noted, this is most often considered in terms of making an area more attractive for investors.[59] Bicycling works at this level, reinforcing a sense of the neighborhood as a coherent place, which adds value to its "brand" (Figure 4). But improvements in accessibility can also be captured directly as rent, even if not all residents benefit from the accessibility premium they pay. Infrastructural improvements at the neighborhood scale are also easier for municipalities to undertake and easier for local actors to organize around. Thus, land markets capitalize as amenities the nominally public goods activists win, exerting upward pressure on neighborhood-level potential rents and prying the rent gap wider. This form of gentrification delivers tangibly positive qualities—better parks; more pleasant, human-scale streets; and bicycle infrastructure—leading some working-class neighborhoods to oppose the very improvements that in previous years they may have sought.

At the same time, gentrification depends on the prior devaluation of space through suburbanization, which was fundamentally a racial project that reallocated investment away from central cities.[60] From the perspective of urban elites, the revaluation of core neighborhoods adjacent to the central business district is its own justification. But "smart growth" ideas have given this justification an added power. The disinvested—but centrally located—neighborhoods to which poor people, immigrants, and people of color were relegated have become essential to the project of reducing carbon emissions by shortening and focusing trips. Bicycle infrastructure in this way fits both mandates, as part of a broader, "green" turn of gentrification, in which environmental improvements to previously polluted, traffic-choked, and/or disinvested areas are capitalized as amenities.[61]

The deeper implications are that practices like bicycling, once considered incidental urban capitalism, are now actually critical to its reproduction.[62]

Figure 4. Business-district promotional banner featuring a bicycle (top right), Baltimore Avenue, West Philadelphia, 2015. Photograph by the author.

We find a growth machine of an unusual sort, in which the exchange-value sought by property interests is somewhat dependent on grassroots actors' pursuit of use-value in urban space.[63] Investments in livability and sustainable mobility in residential neighborhoods have become fused to city–regional competitive strategies intended to leverage downtown quality of life toward growth in leading industries.[64] These amenities are part of the imagined "ecosystem" of competitiveness in the high-technology economy.[65] Meanwhile, while bicycle advocates do not usually directly benefit from gentrification per se, they frame their infrastructural demands in the language of the general interest and have convinced civic leaders and corporations that cycling is part of a "good business climate."[66] Bicycle infrastructure is therefore a key point of convergence between these interests, with powerful implications for the reorganization of capital investment across the metropolis.

Mobility Infrastructures and Social Space

A key contention of this book is that race, class, and gender are durably articulated with mobility practices in urban space.[67] For instance, the image of the bicycle has shifted from a vehicle of last resort (signifying racialized urban poverty) to a symbol of *choosing* a cosmopolitan, less carbon-intensive life (making visible the return of the largely white middle class). But the shift goes beyond image. Rather, the materiality and spatiality of the body–bicycle–infrastructure ensemble forms the basis for how certain bicyclists come to be seen while others remain "invisible" but nevertheless present. This highlights the importance of the bicycle as a technological object, its relationship to the physical infrastructures of urban mobility, and its intersection with spatial patterns of social division.

From the 1950s onward, as private, dispersed transportation by automobile became a national norm, urban mass transportation in turn became "differentially racialized" by its association with inner-city poverty.[68] The bus in particular was marked by race, signifying sluggishness, confinement, and a fundamental lack of freedom, fit for "captive" rather than "choice" riders.[69] Bus service is consistently threatened by austerity, while investment is on the rise in light rail and other systems intended to attract a predominantly white, middle-class ridership.[70] Moving through urban space is thus an important site where difference is *made* both materially and affectively. Crucially, the bicycle signifies a rejection of the car, associated with the exclusionary white suburbs, but also freedom from the inefficient, crowded bus. For "choice" bicycle users, cycling also performs an imagined lost urbanity, in a way that is more visible than the well-worn shoes of a pedestrian or the transit pass in the wallet of a subway rider. The bicycle and the complete street are the "appropriate technologies" for the contemporary urban renaissance.[71] This points to the experiential dimension of cycling and the rider's relationship to the machine and the street, a key thread in contemporary thinking on bicycling.[72] Speed, flexibility, bodily awareness, and urban "flow" are strong themes in this work. The figure of the cosmopolitan urban cyclist today (Figure 5, for example) increasingly represents a cyborg version of Walter Benjamin's *flâneur*, a quintessentially modern (male) subject who wandered the bourgeois city, consuming it with his eyes.[73] Much like Michel de Certeau's pedestrian, these new cyclists evade the rigid, hierarchical ordering of urban space, seeking experience and pleasure while recapturing fundamental freedom of mobility (see chapter 3).[74] The accessibility, simplicity of use and repair, and minimal regulation that enable this freedom have always existed as a necessity for the poor but have become an *option* for the new middle class. From this perspective, the freedom narrative of automobility is inverted: drivers are not freed by their purchase, they are trapped in it; bicyclists are freed by their machines, not confined by poverty to a lower class of mobility. The shifting sociotechnical meanings of cycling thus have very concrete material outcomes in urban space.

For the above reasons, bicycles are often framed in contrast to what Mimi Sheller and John Urry call "automobility": a large-scale sociotechnical system that encompasses the production, distribution, and consumption of cars and related support networks, as well as their cultural, environmental, and political dimensions.[75] This system is characterized by its "coercive flexibility": automobility enables and *enforces* the vast geographic dispersal of zones of home, work, and leisure. Automobility is also fundamentally a metabolic system, depending on and requiring the utilization of massive flows of metal, concrete, plastic, and fossil energy to move people and goods through space.[76] From this perspective, automobility is an ecologically destructive, and totally avoidable, way of organizing both human and nonhuman life.[77]

A key part of this sociotechnical system is the *technology* of the street. The configuration of the roadway—an arrangement of concrete, asphalt, paint, metal signage, traffic signals, electrical cables, storm drains, and (sometimes) planted greenery—enables certain forms of movement while restricting others, all through technical means.[78] The "hydraulic" nature of the automobile street—which prioritizes flow—speeds up the circulation of capital, allowing goods and people to course through the city's arteries more quickly.[79] The "obduracy" or "intransigence" of this configuration

Figure 5. Flyer for Public Bikes, a manufacturer of contemporary, urban-oriented bicycles, distributed on the UC Berkeley campus in spring 2015.

exerts a hold on the present even when there is broad agreement that it must change.[80] The automobile street instantiates the social order and even underpins notions of self and nation.[81]

Bicycle politics focus on fostering ways of life that counteract this malevolent ecology, particularly through complete streets: streets that include all users through new design standards. Bicycling, walking, and transit have become part of urban climate initiatives as well, although climate tends more often to form the backdrop for such plans; specific carbon accounting involving these mobilities is rare, though somewhat more common for transit.[82] But the politics of complete streets have a more complicated relationship to automobility than many observers realize. On one hand, they seek the return of the street as a social space—what we might call "slow urbanism." On the other, they claim the greater efficiency of designs that de-emphasize the car, in functional terms (showing the space efficiency of bicycles versus cars, for instance) and on economic grounds (in arguments about the "high cost of free parking" and the greater propensity of cyclists to spend on daily goods).[83]

Shifting the organization of the street, however, involves confronting durable norms of expertise that favor the automobile.[84] For bicycle planners and advocates, the conflict between car-oriented traffic engineering and bicycle–pedestrian planning is one of flow versus place (see chapter 5).[85] But in political-economic terms this flow-place conflict refracts a deeper contradiction: between the infrastructure required for the circulation of commodities and labor power (which reduces turnover time in the production process) and the investments that enhance site-specific exchange-values (which allow landowners to command rents).[86] As they argue with increasing persuasiveness for the value that livability brings to place, its advocates—often knowingly—cast their lot with the *rentier* class. To the extent that livable places also facilitate a less carbon-intensive way of life, the *value* of ecological renewal is partially captured by this class.[87]

Bicycle advocates have not always been so focused on infrastructure, and the strategy of changing the technical characteristics of streets has often provoked acrimonious intergenerational debates among advocates.[88] But the turn toward infrastructure does not just represent the changing of the guard. It reflects a sense, shaped by the rise of urbanism, that the struggle for complete streets is the struggle to improve and transform the city itself, by shifting travel behaviors away from cars.[89] In other words, contemporary advocates think of bicycle facilities as not for people who bicycle today but for people who do not yet bicycle.[90] This means that the production of infrastructure has a *normative* dimension, with the planetary future at stake. Complete streets are not simply about meeting existing demand through technical innovations but about transforming practices and thus subjectivities themselves.[91]

Socio-spatial Restructuring and Environmental Governance in the American City

Following the economic crisis of 2008, infrastructural experimentation that had been brewing at the neighborhood scale surged to become a municipal and even a metropolitan priority. While many cities drew up comprehensive bicycle plans in the 1990s, in the 2010s advocates devoted great effort to innovating, demonstrating, and testing new designs, particularly models for complete streets imported from Amsterdam and Copenhagen. Following Jamie Peck and Nik Theodore, these models have become a key "fast policy" applied to individual corridors and, less commonly, adopted as a guiding principle for street design throughout a given city. But advocates still grapple with messy local realities. Translating these infrastructure models to American streets, particularly with a resistant bureaucratic establishment, involves elements of "policy entrepreneurship" and participatory technocracy in which not all elements of the European model travel.[92] In "muddling through," American advocates have found that the symbolic value—both economic and environmental—of complete streets in many ways takes precedence over other features of Northern European urbanism like (relatively) coordinated planning, more balanced transportation investment, and a substantial welfare state.[93] The symbolic value of complete streets is rooted in their capacity to *redeem* the American city, which urbanists and (increasingly) policymakers see as having been wrecked by the automobile.

What city is to be redeemed, however? For adherents to the livability discourse, the car and the highway violated the idealized convivial urban fabric of the early twentieth century. But highways were also fundamentally racial projects.[94] They destroyed livelihoods, housing units, and property values; increased health hazards; and reinforced already existing segregation. Cities used Federal Highway Administration funds for "slum clearance," flattening dense, multiracial working-class neighborhoods like West Oakland, the Bronx, and Miami's Overtown, which confined people of color to areas with declining investment, including in mass transit.[95] Easy transportation by automobile further facilitated capital flight from central cities, while Federal Housing Administration policies buttressed segregation by favoring single-family homes in racially restricted greenfield developments.[96] The combination of the car, the single-family house, and the quiet suburb shaped the *aspirational* economy of the middle class, which depended on constantly extending the urban footprint and expanding roadway capacity.[97] The *scale* of the American metropolitan region is not pregiven but is a material artifact of how whiteness was invented through suburbanization.[98]

The push to make urban places less car-dependent also speaks to a broader process of restructuring currently underway in the most dynamic metropolitan areas, as the extensive "Fordist" metropolis gives way to the intensive, "post-Fordist" region. The "seesaw" motion of capital has partially reversed, with investment flooding back into urban cores as part of a new "spatial fix," alongside the concomitant displacement of the working class and people of color to the suburbs.[99] While the process is still very uneven both within and across regions, some places have begun to demonstrate a "European" morphology, with wealthy centers and poor *banlieues* at their edges—with the exception that the "banlieues" are tract homes rather than high-rises.[100] Moreover, movements for "urban quality" that emerged at the nadir of the central city now supply the ideas that fuel its renaissance, and the few places that successfully resisted the urbicidal twentieth century are now victims of this success.[101] There is a mutually constitutive logic at play. Without the influx of population and investment, there would be no momentum behind efforts to reshape mobility, but without different ways of getting around, the class remake of central cities would create intolerable congestion. The "complete streets" paradigm is, in this sense, the neighborhood-scale complement to regional-scale, political-economic restructuring. Within these processes, bicycling is in fact quite marginal, even as it becomes inordinately visible as a potential solution.

Sustainable urban development initiatives, what have been called the "new urban politics of carbon control," intensify these pressures by telescoping climate policy to the local level and turning decarbonization into competitive strategy.[102] Since the 1987 Brundtland Report on sustainable development, a wide range of actors has begun to see cities as the only settlement form adequate to the challenge of climate change.[103] In the United States, municipal governments (and in some places metropolitan planning organizations, or MPOs) have taken tentative steps toward reducing emissions from car trips, such as encouraging greater density in urban cores and around mass transit; promoting cycling, walking, and mass transit use; and shifting away from minimum parking requirements for new developments.[104] Some of these plans—such as the Washington, D.C., Metro's Purple and Silver lines or high-density multifamily housing near existing transit in Dublin, California—involve "retrofitting" suburban areas. But the areas that planners see as critical to meeting these goals, which have existing transit and multifamily housing, lower car usage, and substantial brownfield development potential tend primarily to be working-class neighborhoods in the urban core. Ironically, they are often already "green" by virtue of the low incomes of their residents.[105] The upshot is that market-based, low-carbon urbanization initiatives compound the pressure these areas already face from more conventional gentrification forces, with the added frame of sustainability, which in *urban* politics supersedes contestation even in the United States.[106]

Bicycle infrastructure also shores up cities' competitive stances toward each other. Becoming the next Amsterdam, the next Portland, or the next New York in terms of bicycle infrastructure has surged upward on the list of competitive urban strategies, in part at the urging of advocates. Such amenities are now framed as part of the competition for "talent."[107] Cycling no longer signifies cultural rebellion or a vehicle of last resort but the entrepreneurial subject.[108] Thus, the flexible, enterprising posture of the city and the individual converge through the bicycle and the infrastructure provided to support it. And advocates' strategic arguments about the value of bicycling—for commercial vitality, a productive workforce, and attracting jobs—have become nostrums of urban economic policy.[109]

It is crucial to maintain a nuanced approach here. Bicycling is not an expression of neoliberal*ism*, but the selective adoption of bicycling as an "institutional fix" is a key element of neoliberali*zation*, a process that often combines contradictory elements into an unstable ensemble.[110] This should not imply that the "livable" or ecological turns of urban capitalism are strictly functional for capital. Given conditions of austerity, plus the mandate to reduce cities' ecological footprint through market-friendly solutions, the possibilities for change are circumscribed but the latitude for *experimentation* is quite wide. Bicycling meets these requirements of neoliberal sustainable urbanism: bicycle infrastructure is cheap, bicycling reduces car usage, and the push for better cycling conditions comes from the very people cities need to attract in order to survive.[111] With the suburban ideal rejected by the new bourgeoisie, bicycles reflect and enact a new urban vision that has displaced it. A sanitized version of the city, constructed from a pastiche of European references and saturated with a localist romanticism inherited from Jacobs, with a dash of managed grit, constitutes the "fantasy city" of the contemporary urbanite.[112]

The implications of these dynamics for metropolitan-level spatial justice are not encouraging. Jurisdictional fragmentation is an obstacle to more redistributive regional planning. Small, wealthy cities can shield themselves from change, while underresourced cities are under pressure to encourage growth, even at the cost of social, economic, and environmental equity.[113] From this perspective, since the long half-century of automobility strangled investment in all other forms of mobility, the turn toward active transportation would constitute a just correction of resource allocation. Equally, a reversal of the urbicidal patterns of twentieth-century growth, and a renewal of dense urban places, would appear to serve the interest of justice. But the renewal of places is not equivalent to the restoration of the *capabilities* withheld from people of color and the working class through the past eighty years of urban policy.[114] The houses and streets they called home may return to glory without them.

The *value* claimed by bicycle and livability advocates is manifold: it encompasses safety, health, ecological well-being, *and* economic prosperity. However, once fragmented from a broader Left politics of the city, bicycle advocates' pragmatic decisions to ally with business interests have developed into a mature narrative of cycling as a *necessary* component of urban competitiveness.[115] Such ideas have become an essential element of the capitalist city as it reinvents itself in the twenty-first century. In other words, the neoliberalization of bicycling practice is not a strategy imposed from above, nor is it a fait accompli.[116] Rather, it reflects the entanglement of attempts at emancipatory practice with the realities of a metropolis fragmented along lines of race, class, nativity, and the division of labor.

In particular, the trajectory of bicycle politics in the United States demonstrates the rise of what we might call "participatory technocracy."[117] By this I mean the processes by which critiques of the car-dominated city achieve traction by building popular support among the new urban middle class for "better" technological fixes. Crucially, this does not take place in a temporal or spatial vacuum. Instead, urban space acts as a site where new spatial practices are worked out, new infrastructural arrangements are created, and changes are debated and contested. These processes in turn reshape urban space and create new relations of mobility and belonging. The next chapter explores how bicycling practices at the political and social margins set this process in motion.

CHAPTER TWO

The Bicycle and the Region in Post-Crisis America

The past thirty years have seen the beginnings of a sea change in the geography of work, residence, and mobility in cities across the United States. Though the effects have been highly uneven, as urban cores surge ahead as vanguards of the "new economy," deep changes in regional political economies have created fertile conditions for the surge in cycling and its political visibility. In turn, these changes play a critical role in shaping what investing in bicycle infrastructure means as an urban strategy. They have also expanded the roles of nonprofits, foundations, and think tanks in generating and circulating urban policy.

This chapter analyzes processes of metropolitan restructuring currently at work across the United States and the way they manifest in a set of dialectically opposed forces, spatially concentrating professional workforces and their residences on the one hand and dispersing working class residents, particularly Black and Latino, to increasingly diverse suburbs on the other. I focus particular attention on the San Francisco Bay Area, Philadelphia, and Detroit, as well as on key institutional efforts to channel investment in the "knowledge" economy toward the urban cores of each region. Though it was never the goal of the bicycle movement, bicycle infrastructure has become a key element of these strategies, which seek to attract the "talent" and high-tech investment city leaders are convinced they need to remain competitive.[1] Bicycle infrastructure is an inexpensive, interstitial solution that is well suited to materially "obdurate" metropolitan cores, where there are deep obstacles to overhauling mobility relations.[2] This has brought the progressive politics of nonmotorized mobility into alignment with more forward-looking factions of capital seeking a long-term "spatial fix" and a renewed competitive advantage rooted in a more livable public realm, a more prosperous city, and a more sustainable material base.[3] This regional restructuring, promoting both concentrated investment in centrally located tech clusters and increasing suburbanization of low- and middle-wage employment, unevenly shapes the possibilities for accessing work without the means of a private automobile.

Post-Fordism, Smart Growth, and the Bicycle

At the start of the 2010s, with the country still reeling from the worst economic crisis in eighty years, urbanists had much to celebrate: the mortgage meltdown, which ravaged suburbs and exurbs (as well as many cities) was seen as a guilty verdict on sprawl, and the time of the city was at hand.[4] Many urban areas saw a "back to the city" movement at warp speed: the rapid reurbanization of capital investment as well as high-income population, rising traffic congestion, and corresponding efforts to improve mobility infrastructure in urban cores. These dynamics are not limited to regions undergoing intense housing crises, like the San Francisco Bay Area, Los Angeles, New York, and Seattle, where high demand is evident even in marginal areas. Cities like Philadelphia, Cleveland, and Detroit show signs of simultaneous gentrification and abandonment at a fine spatial grain in their cores, as well as increasing diversity (ethnoracial and economic) in inner-ring suburbs. These inner-ring suburbs and emerging working-class exurbs, often with poor transit connections, both impose significant transportation burdens and are politically and infrastructurally challenging to retrofit, due to the dispersal of employment, amenities, and housing.[5]

Culturally, life in the urban core—formerly the dreaded "inner city"—is now widely celebrated as an antidote to the ecological and social pathologies of suburban sprawl. Livable cities are now celebrated as the most successful economic paradigm, not just because of a concentrated consumer market but increasingly because of their *productive* advantages.[6] Smart growth and New Urbanism, allied sets of principles focused on dense, walkable, and transit-oriented housing development, have achieved increasing currency since the 1990s, increasingly as an infill solution.[7] After decades of prioritizing unspoiled "wilderness," environmental discourse has partially refocused on intensive development in cities—even what David Wachsmuth and Hillary Angelo call "gray" sustainability, which reduces emissions but doesn't look "green"—as a way to combat greenfield expansion.[8] In this context, gentrification became the template for both economic recovery and climate change action, and the efforts of bicycle, pedestrian, and transit advocates to improve public mobility, already in motion in the 1990s, attained a new significance.

These dynamics play a growing role in shifting urban policy toward a program of "carbon control" and climate urbanism.[9] Over the course of the 1990s and 2000s, smart growth principles found expression in the EPA and HUD; Maryland's land use policies; the urban growth boundary in Portland, Oregon; and various advocacy organizations ranging from the Natural Resources Defense Council to the Sierra Club.[10] In the United States, California is a distinct leader in this field: in 2008 it began setting regional greenhouse gas emissions-reduction targets to be implemented by metropolitan planning organizations (MPOs) by coordinating transportation and land use.[11] These programs are intended to induce development with transportation investments—particularly in walking, bicycling, and transit—in designated areas.[12] From the perspective of urban political economy, these leading paradigms of smart growth repurpose ad hoc gentrification patterns—piecemeal and "voluntary" infill development—as a new regional development model.

Bicycle infrastructure is by no means dominant within the smart growth paradigm, which centers on aligning housing and mass transit at a regional scale, but within its local complement, the "complete streets" planning model, bicycles are key. Complete streets reorganize the existing right-of-way to promote walking, bicycling, and transit usage, by widening sidewalks, adding pedestrian refuges, creating protected bikeways and bus priority lanes, and reducing automobile capacity overall.[13] The purpose of these efforts is to create successful places, in environmental (including health), aesthetic, and economic terms. Bicycling in part enables the repurposing of existing street infrastructure in a flexible, low-cost manner; extends the access range of existing mass transit infrastructure without dependence on automobiles; and, if widely adopted, permits significant increases in density without corresponding traffic congestion.

The usefulness of the bicycle as a technological correlate to land-use intensification has granted it increasing credibility in the mainstream of urban infill development. Furthermore, bicycle infrastructure is now a default centerpiece of improvements in environmental quality, such as the reuse of derelict rail lines as greenways, which directly contribute to land development opportunities as well as concerns regarding "environmental" or "green" gentrification.[14] In this respect, what Theresa Enright calls "metromobility," a successor infrastructural framework for capitalist urbanization based on expanding regional transit systems, finds its complement in "velomobility" as a strategic tool to overcome the obduracy of the built environment by connecting more people to these systems.[15] This has the effect of widening the radius of accessibility to mass transit stations, potentially contributing to higher property values in the process.[16] Like smart growth, but at a localized scale, complete streets operationalize gentrification as a climate change mitigation tool.[17]

At a broader level, this is an expression of the ongoing breakdown of the regional scale that was produced by mass automobility, suburbanization, and highway construction under the postwar settlement characterized as "Fordism."[18] While it is not automatic, the proliferation of mobility solutions to the reurbanization of capital illustrate Neil Smith's theory of the "seesaw" motion of differentiation and equalization of profit within the region.[19] This motion produces new subregional spaces of concentrated capital investment in high-wage specialized manufacturing, professional and technical services, and financial activities, with corresponding high returns to property ownership. These spaces, which tend to feature new construction certified by Leadership in Environmental Design, green roofs, transit access, and other environmental amenities, are also more sustainable when considered in isolation.

As densification policies begin to actively constrain the geographic extent of investment, working-class livelihoods on the periphery may grow more precarious and ecologically untenable.[20] Meanwhile, bourgeois livelihoods in resurgent urban cores flourish within a more concentrated, intensive scale of firm clustering and housing development.[21] Industry sectors within which workers performing nonroutine tasks that require face-to-face interaction and command a high wage increasingly co-locate in space, driving high land prices, while support functions are performed by firms scattered in lower-cost areas.[22] The upshot is that certain kinds of non-car home–work linkages receive infrastructural support, becoming easier and even intuitive for those segments of a racialized division of labor that command high wages and salaries. In urban cores, the bicycle is worked into dominant developmental narratives in ways inconceivable even a decade ago. In the same stroke, car-based commutes often become difficult, time consuming, and geographically scattered for those on the losing end of labor market segmentation.[23] In other words, the "coercive flexibility" of the car is likely to be unevenly attenuated within the region through the deepening of the smart-growth development paradigm.[24] In places where smart growth is stalled or unevenly deployed, the environmental and accessibility premium of "ecological enclaves" is potentially even greater.[25]

Institutions and the Circulation of Post-Automobility

A key component of these shifts is the role of non- or quasi-governmental institutions, both as repositories of knowledge (and power) and as nodes in a circuit of knowledge production. Here again, we find a growing convergence between livability advocacy and economic development narratives, and a shift in the center of gravity of bicycle advocacy toward this position.

While the League of American Bicyclists, founded in 1880, is still a major actor, since the 1990s new organizations have emerged with the goal of expanding the funding available for bicycle infrastructure as well as directing its use. PeopleForBikes was formed in 1999 by American bicycle manufacturers—led by Trek—and retailers interested in more direct involvement in national bicycle policy, and has pressured for increases in federal funding (such as the Transportation Alternatives Program), bicycle access to public lands, and favorable trade and tax policies.[26] At the state and local level are bicycle advocacy organizations, who are collectively assembled as the national Alliance for Bicycling and Walking.

A second institutional nexus also reflects this urban shift. For one hundred years, roadway design has been governed by the American Association of State Highway and Transportation Officials (AASHTO), a group representing officials at the state level and providing technical assistance, including the setting of standards for highways, air, railroads, public transportation, and water. Historically, AASHTO has served as the repository of automobile-centric road design, particularly level of service grades that evaluate traffic flow in terms of delay to cars, applying highway standards to local streets.[27] In response, Elliot Sander, commissioner of the New York City Department of Transportation, founded the National Association of City Transportation Officials (NACTO) in 1996 to address the fact that "the large central cities had virtually no meaningful political or technical relationships with each other." Since the late 2000s, NACTO has taken the lead not just on designing bicycle facilities but in "building cities as places for people, with safe, sustainable, accessible and equitable transportation choices that support a strong economy and vibrant quality of life."[28] It also contributed to forming the Transportation Research Board's Large Cities Committee, and it created new expertise-sharing relationships with European city networks.[29] Particularly under Janette Sadik-Khan, NACTO became a key pivot in the network of actors reframing street design toward specifically *urban* priorities: the making of economically successful places (see chapter 1). Bicycle infrastructure is a core goal of NACTO's activities and a key element of its *Urban Street Design Guide*, a manual of standards that competes with AASHTO's "Green Book" for hegemonic expertise.[30]

These efforts mesh well with a rising tide of institutions focused on "placemaking." Not all placemaking initiatives take bicycling as a central focus, but they all reiterate similar narratives regarding the value of reducing accommodations for automobiles. One key nexus in this realm is the collaboration between the Project for Public Spaces and the Brookings Institution on the Anne T. and Robert M. Bass Initiative on Innovation and Placemaking. The Project for Public Spaces, a veteran in the "placemaking" field that emerged from William Whyte's research for *The Social Life of Small Urban Spaces*, provides consulting expertise on making successful urban places across the world. Brookings, a venerable liberal public policy think tank, has taken an increasingly urban turn in recent years, with a city-focused economic development strategy in the vein of Richard Florida and others who assert the urban roots of dynamic economies.[31] The Bass Initiative follows previous Brookings work on "innovation districts," which accorded a key role to changing mobility through building walkable and bike-friendly places. Notably, this work traces the "metropolitan revolution" to the ideological impasse at the federal level following the Great Recession and champions the "natural" pragmatism of cities.[32]

In short, the city has emerged as the ideological center of gravity, and field of institutional expertise, in both mobility and economic development policy. This has forcefully entwined progressive efforts to create better urban *use-values* with efforts by city leaders and capital alike to revive urban *exchange-values*.[33] More important, it has aligned capital, expertise, and political power behind the task of restoring the central city as the hearth of twenty-first-century capitalism.

Centripetal Core, Centrifugal Metropolis

The restructuring of American metropolitan economies from the 1980s to the mid-2000s has been described as a condition of "job sprawl," with the core cities of most metropolitan areas losing employment to suburban job centers.[34] The San Francisco Bay Area was exemplary in this regard, with large migrations of the Black and Latino working class drawn by job growth, inexpensive housing, and increasingly cheap credit to suburban and exurban areas.[35] In the aftermath of the 2008 crisis, researchers observed two related phenomena: the stalling of job sprawl in response to weak investment and the increasingly suburban character of poverty and housing foreclosure.[36] Many places saw not only the slowing of the outward march of employment but a turn back toward the urban core, particularly in rising sectors such as information, management, finance, and professional, scientific, and technical services.[37] These sectors rely on face-to-face contact, nonroutine labor, and tight agglomeration, reducing sensitivity to land price in the interest of accessing pools of skilled workers, and are characterized by high wages overall.[38] A relatively small cohort of places became the "winner-take-all" cities that Richard Florida has recently identified as an "unforeseeable" flaw in his "creative class" thesis.[39] Their fortunes created a new template for growth, and this template included the bicycle in unprecedented ways.

The Division of Labor and the Metropolitan Economy

Despite radically different growth rates, the Detroit, Philadelphia, and Bay Area regions reveal some shared trajectories (see Maps 1–3 for the shape of each region). Each place, however unevenly, illustrates a pattern common to many contemporary metropolitan areas: the shift to "services," which encompass high-wage sectors like professional and technical services, finance, and real estate as well as moderate- to low-wage industries like health care, education, retail, and food service.[40] The core industry of the San Francisco Bay Area since the 1960s is the high-technology sector.[41] This is the root both of the region's dynamism and its volatility.[42] Though there is some advanced manufacturing, most high-tech work in the region is grouped with the professional, scientific, and technical services sector, which together with health care and social assistance, manufacturing, retail trade, and accommodation and food services made up just over half of the region's jobs in 2015. These sectors display substantially different trajectories, wage levels, and representation by race and ethnicity; earnings by race and ethnicity are also deeply unequal (Tables 3 and 4).[43] These patterns hold for occupations as well, which categorize the type of job, rather than the industry sector. Between the 2005–2009 and 2011–15 five-year American Community Survey (ACS), the core metropolitan statistical areas (MSAs) of the San Francisco Bay Area saw a marked increase in both professional and service occupations, amid overall strong growth (Table 5).[44] San Francisco and San Jose added large numbers of managerial workers and service workers, while more area working-class cities like Richmond, South San Francisco, and Hayward added mainly service employees. The strength of the region's growth is reflected in a stunningly low unemployment rate, which dipped to 3 percent for the region in May 2017 and below 3 percent in San Francisco proper.[45]

In the Philadelphia area, similar patterns obtain. The city proper has added both service and managerial workers since 2009, particularly with the rapid growth of the education and health care sectors in University City while shedding other occupations like manufacturing, despite efforts to anchor new production facilities at the Philadelphia Navy Yard and elsewhere along the old industrial waterfront.[46] Inner-ring suburbs shifted toward service occupations as they became more Black and working class, while the gentrified areas proximal to the central business district (CBD)

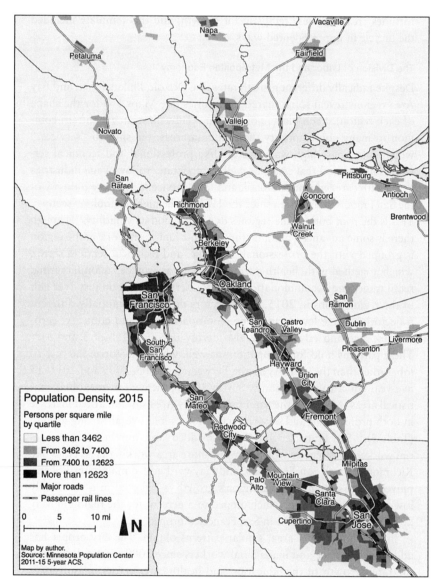

Map 1. Geography and population density in the Bay Area, 2015. BART runs in the center of the freeways from Oakland to Walnut Creek and San Leandro to Dublin and is not visible at this scale.

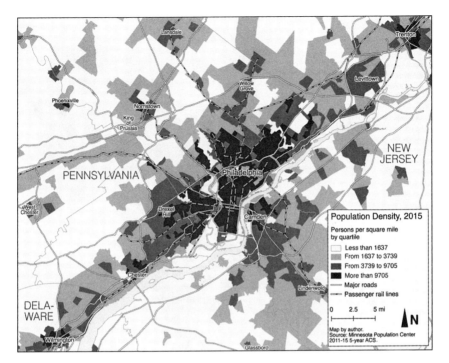

Map 2. Geography and population density in the Philadelphia region, 2015.

that are dominated by professional occupations expanded outward into contiguous, poorer Black neighborhoods in South and West Philadelphia, as well as white working-class strongholds in the inner Northeast along the elevated subway line. The basic spatial pattern of the region, a strong diagonal belt of working-class neighborhoods following the Delaware River through Philadelphia to Trenton, persists. The main difference is that high-income professionals have retaken more of the city itself.

The spatial divergence between growing and declining areas in the Detroit region is perhaps most extreme. Detroit was ravaged by the Great Recession, and in 2012 it became the largest American city ever to declare bankruptcy. While the region shed a small number of workers, numbers within the city itself collapsed utterly: across all occupations, the number of employees living in Detroit proper fell more than 25 percent.[47] However, though manufacturing has receded throughout the region since its peak in the 1950s, suburban R&D clusters have grown substantially, promoted by industry groups and attracting foreign capital.[48] Closer in, recent developments have accentuated the historical antagonism between downtown and "the neighborhoods." In 2011 Quicken Loans moved its headquarters

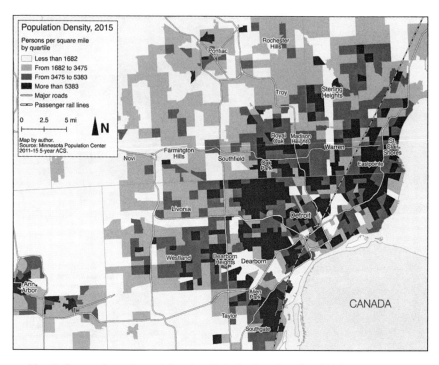

Map 3. Geography and population density in the Detroit region, 2015.

and twelve thousand jobs to downtown Detroit, prompting a building boom that has begun to lure (mostly white) professionals back to the city center for the first time in a generation.[49] Quicken's CEO, Dan Gilbert, leads the city's growth machine, with substantial support from local philanthropic institutions, and together these actors have poured capital into development projects along the city's central corridor, Woodward Avenue.[50] Other firms have followed this surge. In late 2017 Ford announced it would relocate its autonomous vehicle research division to the bustling hipster neighborhood of Corktown, and by 2018 office vacancy rates in the suburbs had surpassed the central city.[51] In general, central areas within the city show significant increases in job density in the professional and technical sector, but job growth in suburban clusters remains stronger. Thus, Detroit as a region remains biased toward suburban growth, with glimpses of a new logic emerging within select parts of the urban core.

Gentrification and Residential Change

These transformations influence the residential patterning that shapes local places. The San Francisco Bay Area is perhaps an extreme example

Table 3. Employment and Monthly Earnings by Race and Ethnicity in the San Francisco Bay Area, Philadelphia, and Detroit, 2015

	San Francisco Bay Area		Philadelphia		Detroit	
	2015 Q4 employment	Average monthly earnings (in dollars)	2015 Q4 employment	Average monthly earnings (in dollars)	2015 Q4 employment	Average monthly earnings (in dollars)
White	1,499,366	9,858	1,702,281	6,083	1,238,170	5,581
Asian	860,786	8,235	136,133	5,879	69,458	7,032
Latino	728,151	4,503	171,087	3,592	60,162	4,264
African American	203,066	4,991	433,373	3,419	286,345	3,528
Two or more race groups	82,992	6,726	26,870	4,111	22,068	3,913
Native Hawaiian/ Pacific Islander	19,996	4,865	1,482	3,938	787	4,431
American Indian or Alaska Native	9,067	4,865	3,418	3,963	4,581	4,109
Total	3,403,427	7,894	2,474,641	5,409	1,681,569	5,217

Source: United States Census Bureau Quarterly Workforce Indicators. Averages for Bay Area and Philadelphia are weighted by job counts per regional subdivision. All census racial groups are non-Hispanic to yield 100 percent totals when Latinos are added.

but is by no means unique. The explosion of the tech industry since the mid-1990s and the corresponding boom in the urban cores of San Francisco, Oakland, and San Jose has occurred alongside the massive outmigration of working-class residents of color from these areas to inner-ring suburbs like Hayward as well as new exurban developments to the east and northeast.[52] The foreclosure crisis, which devastated Black and Latino households in particular, was acute in these exurbs, while in areas of the core home prices rebounded, quickly eclipsing previous peaks.[53] Meanwhile, growth controls in Silicon Valley, where the tech economy is growing most rapidly, externalize the housing requirements of the industry both to suburban residential developments and gentrifying working-class neighborhoods of San Francisco, Oakland, and East Palo Alto.[54]

These changes are reflected in regionally uneven incomes at multiple scales. One is the broad resegregation of the region into booming cores and burdened suburbs, with belts of exclusion in between, while at a much finer grain are the neighborhood-level "social tectonics" that maintain social distance despite physical proximity.[55] Between 2009 and 2015, both per capita income and median household income fell slightly across the Bay Area. These measures rose in San Francisco, Santa Clara, and San

Table 4. Top Job Sectors, Wage Rates, and Ethnoracial Concentration in the San Francisco Bay Area, Philadelphia, and Detroit MSAs, 2000–2015

Urban areas	Top sectors in 2015	Jobs in Q4 2015	Change 2000–15 (%)	Average monthly wage ($)	Change 2000–15 (%)	Ethnoracial concentration	Share of workforce (%)	Share of sector (%)	Ratio (%)
San Francisco Bay Area (including San Benito County)	Health care and social assistance	450,337	71.6	5,901	15.2	Black	6.0	10.1	168
	Professional, scientific, and technical services	417,935	27.2	12,293	8.9	Asian	25.3	32.9	130
	Manufacturing	316,372	−29.0	11,774	12.4	Asian	25.3	35.7	141
	Retail trade	301,773	1.3	3,825	−14.4	Latino	21.4	28.6	134
	Accommodation and food services	295,252	50.5	2,478	4.5	Latino	21.4	32.3	151
	All sectors	3,403,427	10.5	7,894	9.0				
Philadelphia–Camden–Wilmington	Health care and social assistance	451,537	48.4	4,815	13.5	Black	17.6	29.7	169
	Retail trade	270,580	−1.4	2,995	2.5	Latino	2.0	2.8	144
	Educational services	242,794	16.0	5,095	11.6	White	68.7	76.6	112
	Professional, scientific, and technical services	202,913	25.8	9,293	25.6	Asian	5.5	9.6	175
	Manufacturing	170,248	−36.7	6,629	12.3	Latino	2.0	3.0	153
	All sectors	2,474,333	9.1	5,409	12.1				

Detroit–Warren–Dearborn	Health care and social assistance	241,683	38.2	4,656	11.3	Black	17.0	23.5	138
	Manufacturing	223,219	−38.1	6,658	9.6	Latino	3.6	4.2	117
	Professional, scientific, and technical services	186,219	11.4	7,927	13.4	Asian	4.1	9.1	220
	Retail trade	185,390	−14.0	2,928	−2.9	White	73.6	77.2	105
	Accommodation and food services	136,265	33.7	1,781	13.8	Black	17.0	22.0	129
	All sectors	1,681,569	−6.7	5,217	6.5				

Sources: EHD Quarterly Workforce Indicators for Q4 of 2000 and 2015, extracted from https://ledextract.ces.census.gov/static/data.html. All employment and wage data are for full-quarter stable employment. Inflation calculated using regional indicators: 1.47 for Northern California (http://www.dir.ca.gov/OPRL/capriceindex.htm), 1.483 for the Northeast region (https://www.bls.gov/regions/mid-atlantic/news-release/consumerpriceindex_northeast.htm), and 1.288 for the Detroit region (https://www.bls.gov/regions/midwest/data/consumerpriceindexhistorical_detroit_table.pdf). Ethnoracial is calculated as a ratio of the group's share of the sector to the group's share of the workforce as a whole, and it is calculated only for groups making up more than 1 percent of the workforce.

Table 5. Occupational Changes and Median Wages by Metropolitan Statistical Area, 2009–15

	San Francisco/San Jose			Philadelphia			Detroit		
	2011–15 employees	Change from 2009 to 2015 (%)	2011–15 median wage	2011–15 employees	Change from 2009 to 2015 (%)	2011–15 median wage	2011–15 employees	Change from 2009 to 2015 (%)	2011–15 median wage
Management, professional, and related occupations	1,549,177	14.2	$80,881	1,198,545	6.7	$61,491	709,481	3.3	$60,250
Service occupations	532,775	19.7	$20,949	491,392	12.3	$20,091	335,836	-1.0	$15,721
Sales and office occupations	687,081	-3.4	$36,607	700,460	-7.3	$32,379	464,669	-8.6	$28,648
Natural resources, construction, and maintenance occupations	205,302	-9.7	$38,081	197,348	-10.9	$42,237	127,839	-15.1	$40,486
Production, transportation, and material-moving occupations	250,003	4.0	$31,510	274,281	-3.1	$31,365	266,395	-3.5	$31,308
Total	3,224,338	8.2	$47,941	2,862,026	1.4	$40,639	1,904,220	-2.9	$35,412

Sources: Manson et al., 2017, 2005–2009 and 2011–15 Five-Year American Community Survey estimates. Median wage for the Bay Area is a weighted average of regional subdivisions.

Table 6. Housing Price Movements by City, 2011–16

City	Median sale price, all houses, 2016	Change 2011–16 (%)	Median rent price per square foot, 2016	Change 2011–16 (%)
Philadelphia	$150,965	14.6	$1.25	2.3
San Jose	$764,625	63.7	$2.38	33.2
San Francisco	$1,166,125	65.0	$4.08	39.8
Detroit	$33,500	62.0	$0.80	–8.3
Oakland	$555,625	71.8	$2.59	48.1

Source: Zillow, available at https://www.zillow.com/research/data. Medians for 2011 and 2016 calculated for January–June. 2011 prices adjusted by 1.07, based on BLS inflation calculator available at https://www.bls.gov/data/inflation_calculator.htm.

Mateo Counties, however, as well as for white and Asian households everywhere, while falling in counties with large exurban areas, like Solano and Contra Costa, and for Black and Latino households. Cities deeply tied to the tech economy, like San Francisco, Sunnyvale, and Cupertino, saw substantial gains, while Vallejo (which declared bankruptcy in 2012), Antioch, and Fairfield registered losses. In some neighborhoods of San Francisco, Oakland, and San Jose, which encompass some of the richest and poorest households in the entire region, the median household income of non-Hispanic whites is now *triple* that of Black- or Latino-headed households. Meanwhile, inflation-adjusted home sale prices and rental prices per square foot in San Francisco, Oakland, and San Jose leapt upward between 2011 and 2016 (Table 6), and working-class neighborhoods in transition like the Mission District are now widely known as playgrounds for the arriviste elite.[56]

Regional change in Philadelphia has been significantly more heterogeneous, in part due to slower growth overall. While Philadelphia is not one of gentrification's "superstar" cities, it has absorbed some overflow from New York's superheated market, gaining a local reputation as the "sixth borough."[57] At the MSA level, Philadelphia's home sale prices increased modestly and offered rents barely at all. However, since the Great Recession, housing starts within the city have reached new peaks and suburban construction new lows, spurred in part by developers taking advantage of the ten-year tax abatement on new construction adopted in 2000.[58] The region's booming downtown has seen a surge in condominium development and new office construction, and gentrification has spread outward from outposts in Society Hill and near the University of Pennsylvania in West Philadelphia.[59] At the same time, some parts of deeply disinvested, majority-Black North Philadelphia continue to lose population, as do older industrial cities on the Delaware River. As of 2016, Philadelphia still had the highest poverty rate of all large cities in the United States, with poverty rising in suburban areas and holding steady in the urban core.[60] Philadelphia's Black population continues to grow in inner-ring suburbs to the north and southwest (bordering the areas within the city with large Black populations), as well as relatively prosperous Black middle-class enclaves just inside the city's northern limits. Gentrification, ongoing suburbanization, and abandonment thus proceed together, sometimes in quite close spatial proximity.[61]

Meanwhile, Detroit's housing market utterly collapsed in the 2008 recession, but between 2013 and 2016 it rebounded somewhat, despite persistent poverty, abandonment, and tax foreclosure.[62] In May 2016 Detroit had a median house price of just $32,000, but this was up sharply compared to what it was before the bankruptcy. Median rents fell but remain very heterogeneous, considering the city's vast size and predominantly single-family housing stock. Rents in the newest residential buildings in the city's booming greater downtown—known as "the 7.2," for its 7.2 square miles—range from 33 percent to 150 percent higher than the city median.[63] Development plans along Woodward Avenue include the Little Caesar's Arena and surrounding "live-work-play" district; the Brush Park neighborhood, where genteel, restored Victorian houses sit alongside new condos and vast lots under redevelopment; and the burgeoning tech cluster in New Center. At the same time, large swaths of the city continue to undergo abandonment, while zones of gentrification beyond the core are much less numerous, smaller in area, and significantly less wealthy; they cluster near large institutions and prosperous suburbs.[64] Select neighborhoods beyond the 7.2 have seen intensive development plans led by philanthropic capital, but much of the city is essentially designated for abandonment, and one common measure of municipal government performance in these areas is the blight demolition rate.[65] Nevertheless, a rising discourse of Detroit as a "comeback city" has placed it in the cultural spotlight for the first time in decades. Not surprisingly, the allure of the gritty "urban frontier" (often plied by young artists and hipsters on bicycles) feeds this narrative.[66]

The Changing Commute

Such changes in spatial structure have substantial implications for possible travel patterns. In general, core areas surrounding dominant regional CBDs have much greater accessibility by transit to jobs, but these are also locations where rising housing costs have displaced—directly or by exclusion— lower-wage workers.[67] With the return of capital and high-wage work to regional cores, therefore, higher-income in-migrants reap the benefits of transit density and access to services that in earlier decades offset the disadvantages of living in the underinvested central city. Despite the narrative of a "return" to the city, between 2002 and 2015 central places in the Bay Area, Philadelphia, and Detroit regions did not see a rise in the overall proportion of workers *both living and working* in core cities, reflecting the fact that "job sprawl" remains a dominant metropolitan dynamic. Thus, the rise of cycling since 1990 is not the result of a realignment of home and work across the population as a whole but is that of a specific subset of the division of labor located in urban cores. These are places that are gentrifying rapidly in many cities, with highly paid workers in professional occupations crowding out service workers, who also depend on proximity to the CBD and often walk or bicycle to work. In this way, gentrification increases the proximity of home, work, and other services, enabling a slower, more pleasant, and more flexible mode of travel, while also increasing competition for this privilege. By the same token, with rapid growth comes traffic congestion and overtaxed transit, increasing the advantages of walking and cycling. In general, the infrastructure to support these mobilities is oriented toward downtown workers and tourists, facilitating commutes at normative hours to and from the central business district and key destinations (if not always within the congested CBD itself). These CBDs are even more likely to be the principal locations of "world-class" infrastructure like protected bike lanes, which require more demand, investment, and political will to be viable, further concentrating advocates' political focus. Meanwhile, cars become obligatory burdens, and already long commutes grow for the economically precarious.[68] This can be seen, following Doreen Massey, as the "power-geometry" of time–space *elongation*.[69]

As planning efforts in the San Francisco Bay area move fitfully away from automobility, public transportation infrastructure remains fragmented, underinvested, and straining at full capacity alongside soaring traffic congestion. More recent development near "edge city" job centers—some of them, ironically, situated near BART and CalTrain regional rail networks built to facilitate the inbound commute—lacks effective public transit infrastructure.[70] As a result, commutes are scattered throughout the region, but unevenly, with low-wage workers traveling significantly farther for work in many outer areas.[71] Meanwhile, between 2000 and 2015 rates of cycling to work have risen fastest in core cities like Oakland and San Francisco, as well as in areas of Berkeley and Palo Alto near the University of California and Stanford, respectively. In other places, cycling

Table 7. Mode Share Changes by Selected Cities in the San Francisco Bay Area, Philadelphia, and Detroit, 2000–15

	City	2011–15 total	2011–15: car, truck, or van	2011–15: car, truck, or van (%)	Change since 2000	2011–15: bicycle	2011–15: bicycle (%)	Change since 2000
Bay Area	San Jose	474,328	419,111	88.4	−2.3	4530	1.0	54.9
	San Francisco	468,350	201,892	43.1	−15.9	18883	4.0	103.3
	Oakland	192,725	123,589	64.1	−10.9	6024	3.1	155.6
	Fremont	84,307	70,553	83.7	−6.8	488	0.6	4.3
	Sunnyvale	75,018	64,145	85.5	−5.6	1307	1.7	137.6
	Hayward	70,638	59,357	84.0	−3.8	335	0.5	34.2
	Concord	59,060	48,148	81.5	−2.0	387	0.7	−35.0
	Berkeley	57,154	23,203	40.6	−23.2	4759	8.3	48.2
	Antioch	44,544	38,084	85.5	−4.7	194	0.4	92.7
	Livermore	43,835	38,294	87.4	−3.1	552	1.3	−7.4
	Mountain View	43,441	34,883	80.3	−7.4	2627	6.0	207.5
	Milpitas	32,233	29,581	91.8	−2.7	116	0.4	−20.4
	Palo Alto	31,312	22,280	71.2	−11.8	2886	9.2	63.8
Detroit	Detroit	207,868	170,437	82.0	−4.3	1083	0.5	228.3
	Warren	56,741	53,608	94.5	−1.7	168	0.3	73.8
	Livonia	46,738	44,372	94.9	−1.3	99	0.2	195.7
	Royal Oak	35,053	32,676	93.2	−0.6	147	0.4	30.8
	Dearborn	34,111	32,236	94.5	−0.1	108	0.3	144.8
	Ferndale	11,440	10,275	89.8	−4.5	169	1.5	432.6
	Romulus	9,300	8,789	94.5	−0.9	N/A	N/A	N/A
	Inkster	8,557	8,076	94.4	0.8	N/A	N/A	N/A
	Hamtramck	6,284	5,495	87.4	−2.1	N/A	N/A	N/A
	Highland Park	2,687	1,971	73.4	0.2	N/A	N/A	N/A
Philadelphia	Philadelphia	625,993	36,9138	59.0	−4.9	12888	2.1	139.0
	Norristown	15,368	12,684	82.5	2.5	N/A	N/A	N/A

Drexel Hill	14,241	11,880	83.4	−4.4	33	0.2	12.9
Chester	11,127	7,619	68.5	−8.5	N/A	N/A	N/A
Yeadon	5,270	4,104	77.9	4.9	N/A	N/A	N/A
Conshohocken	4,978	4,249	85.4	−2.5	N/A	N/A	N/A
Lansdowne	4,888	3,418	69.9	−13.0	N/A	N/A	N/A
Doylestown	4,420	3,455	78.2	−9.8	N/A	N/A	N/A
Darby	3,562	1,991	55.9	−18.4	15	0.4	N/A
Camden (N.J.)	23,873	18,151	76.0	12.2	110	0.5	70.2
Collingswood (N.J.)	7,648	6,311	82.5	1.4	41	0.5	24.2

Source: Manson et al., 2017, 2000 Census SF1 and 2011–15 Five-Year American Community Survey estimates.

rates have remained fairly flat or declined, even in areas with improving infrastructure. At the same time, rates of car commuting have fallen, but again unevenly, dropping substantially in San Francisco, Oakland, Berkeley, and Menlo Park, but much less in a number of suburbs and even San Jose, the largest city in the region (Table 7). In the meantime, the *number* of car commuters increased overall, falling only in San Francisco and Alameda Counties.

With Philadelphia's slower growth, congestion has grown more slowly as well. Since the eve of the Great Recession, the share of workers traveling more than forty-five minutes to work ticked up slightly. Poorer, more transit-dependent parts of North and West Philadelphia greatly exceed the county average in commute time, and nowhere did it visibly decrease. Since 2000, rates of cycling have risen significantly in centrally located areas within Philadelphia, with little to no change in most suburban areas. Rates of driving also decreased in many parts of the region, but they remained flat and even increased in some smaller cities, likely reflecting the growth there of previously transit-dependent populations.

The Detroit region is overwhelmingly car-dependent even by American standards, and outside of a few select locations, car-less life exacts a forbidding penalty.[72] Predictably for a sprawling region with a profoundly disinvested central city, rates of driving to work are high and rates of cycling are uniformly low. The border suburb of Ferndale is the only city with a cycling rate above 1 percent, while areas surrounding Wayne State University and mildly gentrified enclaves near the CBD have rates surpassing 4 percent.[73] Rates of transit usage are similarly very low throughout the region and have even shown slight decline. The city lacks a fixed-rail transit system outside of the central business district, which has just six miles of track between the People Mover (1987) and the recently opened QLine on Woodward Avenue. Its bus system is both severely underfunded and subject to storied delays, although there have been significant improvements since 2012.[74]

It should be recalled, however, that data on cycling rates, even more so than other modes of transportation, yield limited understandings of how people travel and why. First, census data only show trips to work, which make up roughly a quarter of all travel, and obscure the role of bicycles in other realms of life, particularly social reproduction. Perhaps because of this, cycling in the United States appears disproportionately male. By the same token, with unemployment profoundly racialized, the cycling population visible through these statistics tends to be whiter and more steadily employed, obscuring the ways that poor people use bicycles to make do, increasing the range or ease of essential daily activities like accessing social services. Second, by measuring only the primary transportation mode used to get to work, these data also hide multimodal trips and varying travel habits, implicitly valorizing "pure" cyclists. Meanwhile, while there is evidence that bicycling is becoming more equal in some ways, this depends largely on data on noncommute cycling only available at the national and state level, such as the National Household Travel Survey.[75] Nonetheless, measurements of the effectiveness of local and regional cycling policy and infrastructure provision rely on these Census data. Other methods of counting cyclists at a fine spatial grain, such as ride surveys, are unevenly implemented and tend to be conducted during office–work commute hours at central locations.[76] Faced with these limitations, some researchers have constructed their own local survey data, but even these are relatively geographically limited.[77]

These figures represent only a snapshot of a large process, as the spatial mismatch between housing and jobs, and of wage and housing costs, follows uneven regional development. Plans for livable urban space, which designers, advocates, political leaders, and investors hope will realign housing, employment, leisure, and social reproduction to the neighborhood or corridor scale, are up against a dramatically uneven regional employment landscape. While bicycle advocates recognize the need to reach beyond their traditional base of white, highly educated professionals, the geography of the current cycling boom works against them.[78] Focusing on journey-to-work commuter cycling limits the scope of their efforts, skewing livability and sustainability planning efforts toward professional and technical workers whose employers value centrality and who can secure advantageously located housing in gentrifying areas. Meanwhile, for advocates and municipal governments alike, the political value of showcasing valued populations astride bicycles is enormous.[79] The real gains in bicycling in select areas of core cities must be seen in the context of vast, car-dependent regions in which the *possibility* of replacing trips by bicycle is supremely uneven in distribution.

Planning the Two-Wheeled City of the Future

Despite quite different regional mobility regimes, each of these cities has adopted bicycle infrastructure as a core element of their official planning practices. They moved beyond simply placing bicycle infrastructure wherever it is practical or politically feasible (though they do this as well) to incorporating bicycles into key focal points within the urban fabric, as part of strategies to promote denser, less car-dependent patterns of urbanization. In other words, these strategies do not only accommodate cyclists into street space. They appropriate cycling as a mechanism to shift—however modestly—the forms of urban growth, and conversely to make denser forms of growth more functional in practice. As a "mobility fix," in Justin Spinney's terms, bicycle infrastructure actually enables changes in mobility practices with only minor corresponding changes in urban form.[80]

Density plays a multifaceted role in these processes. At a basic level, the perceived economic costs of traffic congestion increase with bursts of development in urban cores.[81] By absorbing growth without traffic congestion, densely settled and transit-connected places are attractive models of *economically* sustainable infill, entirely apart from their environmental benefits. Much of the current impetus behind increasing density in transit-connected urban cores adds the goal of carbon regulation.[82] This is increasingly wedded to narratives of economic competitiveness within leading sectors that assert the value of dense urban space, replete with "third places," vibrant cultural life, and flexible mobility, for the "open innovation" on which contemporary capitalism depends.[83] As Bruce Katz and Julie Wagner of Brookings argue, "Talented people want to work and live in urban places that are walkable, bike-able, connected by transit, and hyper-caffeinated."[84] It would be an overstatement to argue that these three concerns—congestion, environment, and innovation—articulated primarily in academic and policy circles, account for both the popularity and political will behind building cycling infrastructure in core neighborhoods of select metropolitan areas. But bicycle infrastructure suits these larger economic and environmental goals in part because it is low-cost, minimally disruptive, and—perhaps most crucially—preserves the *flexibility* of the mobility regime.

Some circumspection is necessary here. Economic concerns are not the primary factor behind bicycle infrastructure plans, and not every bike lane has a business-friendly justification. Bicycle plans have a wide range of objectives, and an ostensible mandate to serve the city equally where possible, which is why a causal relationship with gentrification is challenging to show. Many projects are simply opportunistic, taking advantage of low traffic volumes, proximity to recreation areas, or scheduled repaving. The plans I detail below, however, show the logical and material convergence between bicycle planning and explicit economic development strategy.

San Francisco: Mobility and Innovation in the Technopole

Market Street is San Francisco's central thoroughfare, a complicated interface between two different street grids, with as many as one hundred buses and streetcars at rush hour vying for space with the fleets of taxis and rideshare vehicles that ply the CBD. From the northeast waterfront, it passes through the Financial District and the Powell Street high-end retail zone, then into the Mid-Market district adjacent to Civic Center before ascending into the Castro. Once a thriving entertainment and residential hotel district, Mid-Market suffered from deep disinvestment over the twentieth century, and its liquor stores, discount retailers, vacant storefronts, and soaring homelessness contrast starkly with the city's wealth and cosmopolitan image.[85] Conservative *San Francisco Chronicle* columnist C. W. Nevius has called Market between Sixth Street and Van Ness the city's "black hole."[86] It is also downtown San Francisco's last pocket of low-income tenancy, into which the racialized poor have been compressed by gentrification and redevelopment on all sides.

After decades of frustrated efforts, by 2017 changes to Market Street were in the making, under the aegis of the Better Market Street Project. This multiagency collaboration, spanning the better part of a decade, plans a far-reaching transformation of the corridor into a complete street and the "revitalization" and reclamation of its deteriorated public spaces.[87] It reflects the alignment of bicycle advocates, and other progressive urbanists, with the city's growth machine in a way that renegotiates its spatial forms and incorporates bicycles into the city's perennial "obsession" with remaking Market Street (see chapter 4).[88]

Market, long considered a key artery for bicyclists commuting to downtown office buildings, was designated by the 1996 Bicycle Plan as a bicycle route. But bicycles were not always part of the official vision for the street. The city's landmark "Transit First" policy dates to 1973, but in the intervening decades the efforts of the San Francisco Municipal Railway (Muni) to create more transit-priority corridors languished in what Jason Henderson calls a "mobility stalemate."[89] This left Market a clogged corridor where historically only the most intrepid cyclists ventured. By the mid-2000s, organizational ties between progressive mobility organizations like Livable City and the San Francisco Bicycle Coalition, think tanks like San Francisco Planning and Urban Research (SPUR), and allies on the Board of Supervisors had grown substantially (see chapter 4). Around this time, SPUR became a key institution supporting the integration of bicycles and pedestrians with transit and parking reductions, especially for Market Street.[90] This was in part achieved by the "infiltration" of key organizations by bicycle and livability advocates.[91]

The expansion of bicycle infrastructure on Market has been fitful, and solutions have been interstitial rather than comprehensive. In 2006 a political reaction led by anti-bike activist Rob Anderson won a standing injunction against new bicycle facilities, stifling bicycle planning just when bicycle rates were growing rapidly. Its removal in 2010, after a lengthy environmental review, unleashed an explosion of infrastructure (see chapter 4).[92] Beginning in 2010, an increasingly complicated array of protected bike lanes, automobile diverters, and green-painted "sharrows" (arrows indicating a shared bicycle-car lane) were installed, greatly improving cycling on the corridor, though the most protective infrastructure is located in the least congested areas. In 2013 a real-time bike counter, modeled on similar infrastructure in Copenhagen, was installed on Market at Tenth Street in the Mid-Market district.[93] That same year the Bay Area Bike Share system opened, with a number of key stations on Market Street that extend the range of the CalTrain system that serves the Peninsula. According to recent counts, Market Street now boasts the heaviest bicycle traffic of any street west of the Mississippi, with bicycles often outnumbering private cars during rush hour.[94] In 2017, after four years of study and a number of abandoned proposals, the Planning Commission announced a new design for the corridor, which would eliminate private car traffic and create a fully protected bike lane integrated into the sidewalk, in the model of the European cycletrack.[95] These changes are intended to complement other place-making efforts aimed at "positive activation" with "eyes on the street," to crowd out what are deemed antisocial uses of the street by the poor.[96]

These street changes articulate with new concepts of economic development that take *place*, rather than skills or firms, as their focal point. By the early 2010s, the Bay Area's high-technology industry was experiencing an expansion arguably more thoroughgoing than the 1996–2001 dot-com boom.[97] While large firms like Google, Facebook, Apple, and Cisco are clustered in the vast campuses of Silicon Valley, the sector has grown more quickly in San Francisco proper (and increasingly Oakland). This reflects an evolving logic within the industry. The shift away from suburban office parks in "nerdistans" like Palo Alto and Mountain View more properly reflects a spatial division of labor between established firms and small, dynamic, venture-funded startups that rely on the "untraded interdependencies" of dense social networks.[98] As the latter grow, and even larger firms expand their downtown presence, tech firms have displaced even traditional business services within the financial district.[99]

San Francisco's leaders have attempted to capitalize on this opportunity by extending the South of Market "technopole," which flourished in the first dot-com boom, into Mid-Market (re-christened "Central Market"), where they envision an ecosystem of high-tech firms anchored by a vibrant, livable public realm, in which mobility infrastructure is a priority.[100] Former

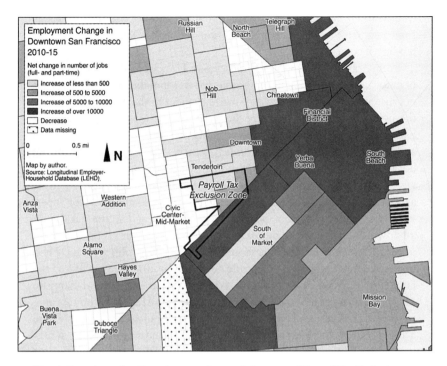

Map 4. Downtown San Francisco employment change and Payroll Tax Exclusion Zone.

Mayor Ed Lee summed up the ethos of the project by claiming, "You just don't feel innovative in suburban areas."[101] In 2011 the city outlined the Central Market Strategy, which identified a deep rent gap in office and retail that would require state assistance to close.[102] To steer growth toward the district, the Board of Supervisors also approved a six-year payroll-tax exclusion on new hires by firms in the district (Map 4).[103] The "anchor tenant" of the zone, Twitter, moved into a former furniture store at Tenth and Market Streets later that year, sparking a feverish boom on the corridor, with twenty-one tech and tech-related firms, including Yahoo, Square, Spotify, and Uber, adding more than thirteen thousand jobs in the area between 2011 and 2014.[104] Colloquially, the area is often now referred to as the "Twitterloin," in reference to the deeply impoverished Tenderloin neighborhood of single-room occupancy hotels nearby. A residential building boom followed these firms, with the area adding more than five thousand housing units from 2012 to 2016, with more than ten thousand units in the pipeline as of 2016.[105] Glittering renderings of new developments in

Mid-Market and its immediate surroundings dominate the imagery surrounding San Francisco's transformation, as well as narratives of its exploding income gap.[106]

In the transformation of downtown San Francisco into a "shop floor" of innovation-based capitalism, flexible, car-free mobility has been reframed not just as an amenity but as an integral element to the practices on which the new economy thrives.[107] By the early 2010s, various commentators had noted that a bicycle had become an essential accoutrement of the archetypal tech worker; as *Bloomberg* put it, "In the dizzy days of the dot-com bubble, sports cars emblazoned with Starship Academy stickers were the emblems of geek chic. Now . . . it's the one-speed bicycle known as a fixie that can cost as much as $2,000."[108] In 2012 the Board of Supervisors passed legislation mandating bicycle access and secure parking in all downtown office buildings of seventy-five feet or more, a measure supported by the Building Owners and Managers Association, which had opposed similar legislation a decade before.[109] In 2013 Lee celebrated the launch of Bay Area Bike Share by tying cycling to the city's dynamism: "It's no surprise that SOMA [the South of Market Area] is the hottest area of [Bay Area Bikeshare] bicycle use in all of San Francisco . . . that's where a lot of our technology workers and small business workers are working."[110] New high-end apartment buildings in the area now frequently tout the bike-friendly character of the corridor and even offer bicycle-specific amenities to residents.[111] In short, the kinds of infrastructural transformations long sought by bicycle and pedestrian advocates to improve quality of life are now essential to the discourse of the *economic* benefits of livability.

The deleterious effects of San Francisco's dizzying boom are now widely recognized.[112] Commentators decry the deep social gulf between the tech elite and working people in San Francisco's "*Blade Runner* kind of society."[113] Widely aired denunciations of industry leaders as anti-poor robber barons and the shuttle buses carrying "alien overlords" from gentrifying San Francisco neighborhoods to their Silicon Valley campuses have put tech ideologically on the run.[114] In this context, growth coalition stalwarts like SPUR and the Urban Land Institute, as well as upstart organizations like SF YIMBY (Yes in My Back Yard), argue for a relaxation of land-use regulations to encourage development, locating high housing costs as a San Francisco supply problem rather than a reflection of regional wage disparities and landlord power (though some also argue for aggressive construction of affordable housing).[115] Lamentations abound that superheated gentrification is causing San Francisco to lose its "cool" edge, as artists and other "creatives," as well as teachers, public employees, and even tech workers themselves, relocate to Oakland—if not to Los Angeles, Austin, or some other burgeoning tech hub.[116] By 2014, Oakland's gentrification was in full swing as well, buoyed by its proximity to the wealth generated by San Francisco and even capturing some of the tech industry itself. Unlike the "fortress urbanism" or "revanchism" of the 1990s, this new wave of urban development incorporates progressive notions of what makes cities vital, productive, and sustainable into a new, business-friendly synthesis.[117]

Philadelphia: University City and the Knowledge Economy

Philadelphia's knowledge cluster, the University City District, takes a more traditional form than San Francisco's, but performs a similar set of neighborhood "revitalization" functions. University City is organized not around a core axis of the city but a trio of universities—the University of Pennsylvania, Drexel University, and University of the Sciences—as well as the Children's Hospital of Philadelphia (CHOP), all of which are situated in West Philadelphia just across the Schuylkill River from the city center (Map 5). This Victorian-era streetcar suburb was deeply disinvested in the postwar era, and stark inequalities persist between its historically Black residents and the university-affiliated population. UPenn and Drexel launched the University City District in 1997 to address public safety and cleanliness issues, of particular concern to the roughly 50,000 students and 20,000 staff, and by extension the universities' competitive position. Early on, the District also became closely involved in the land market, coordinating small-scale gentrification in an area of prime Victorian housing stock and a well-preserved streetcar network, while committing to curtailing westward expansion into neighborhoods. Instead, the universities expanded eastward toward the old industrial waterfront and its vast railyards, as the Center City CBD expanded westward; today, they virtually meet at the Schuylkill River.[118]

The University City District's has moved beyond core BID functions to anchor an enormous expansion in technology and medicine, driven in part by growing partnerships with industry. Between 2002 and 2016, the district added over 13 million square feet of new real estate development, including 3 million in medical research, 3.3 million in office, 4.4 million in residential, and 2.7 million in instructional and lab space. Between 2010 and 2016 alone, over $4 billion in real estate was built.[119] The medical cluster continues to expand with the Roberts Center for Pediatric Research, the first of a four-tower CHOP campus on the Schuylkill waterfront, and UPenn's Center for Healthcare Technology, begun in 2017.[120] In 2010 UPenn also purchased a derelict DuPont facility just across the river and

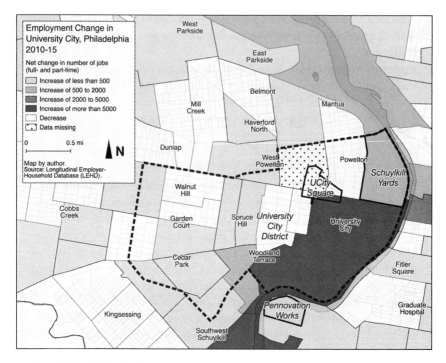

Map 5. West Philadelphia/University City employment change and development areas.

created the Pennovation Works campus, a tech incubator.[121] Vigorous office, retail, housing, and hotel development continues apace in University City, which is quickly becoming the city's second downtown, and even a new industrial cluster, as it extends down the old industrial riverfront to meet the former Navy Yards, also in the process of "incubation." The flagship project of the area is Schuylkill Yards, a massive twenty-year, $3.5 billion effort spearheaded by Drexel to create "a new neighborhood based on innovation," which the developer, Brandywine Realty Trust, claims "is not a corporate campus . . . but a fully-engaged ecosystem."[122]

Here we see the reappearance of themes from San Francisco's Mid-Market: the use of high-tech innovation to close a deep (largely commercial) rent gap and expand the city's business district, as well as its livability. The supportive infrastructure for these developments includes typical attractors like improved mass transit and highway access but also a completely revamped recreational trail along the Schuylkill, which has turned the largely ignored riverfront into a social center for the Center City and University City area. The largest new developments are accessible through a network of off-street trails and bicycle and pedestrian bridges, with the newly redesigned South Street Bridge boasting the highest volume of bicycle and pedestrian traffic of any bridge in Pennsylvania.[123] The district also has the greatest density of bicycle infrastructure in the entire city, as well as a historic streetcar system that fans out throughout the West Philadelphia area. As University City District president Matt Bergheiser claimed in a report on the area's progress:

> Schuylkill Yards, Pennovation and uCity Square are three focal points of commercialization and discovery, all tightly bound within a walkable, bikeable, transit-oriented neighborhood of eclectic food options, gorgeous Victorian homes and gathering spaces that spur the kinds of serendipitous collisions among creators and dreamers that are necessary for breakthrough innovation.[124]

If this is resonant of narratives circulated by Brookings thinkers like Katz, this is not simply because the ideas are "in the air." University City was the subject of a detailed study by the Bass Initiative, *Connect to Compete*. The research team argued that the clustering of innovative facilities was not enough: the district's leadership needed a holistic vision and the will to fully connect the district, particularly through walking, bicycling, and transit, into a seamless web of places destined to yield innovative leaps.[125] Here again we see the articulation together of human-scale mobility and high-tech agglomeration into a new logic of redevelopment.

Techtown Detroit and the "Degrowth Machine"

The innovation district boom is also in motion in Detroit, although the city struggles with much stronger headwinds. In the downtown business district, city and business leaders have shown great attention to "placemaking" strategies, as part of efforts to revive the quality of life in the area to complement employment expansion, primarily in traditional CBD functions, as well as residential development. These efforts display in classic form the interests of local business elites and rentiers in restoring qualities of place, particularly the pedestrian experience, in order to promote tourism and economic development. The city hired Project for Public Spaces in 1999 to help design the reestablished Campus Martius Park in the heart of the business district.[126] PPS returned in 2013 to consult on a "placemaking vision" for the entire Woodward Corridor through downtown, spearheaded by local growth machine leaders Rock Ventures, Illich Holdings, and the Downtown Detroit Partnership (DDP), to improve the public realm in conjunction with increasing investment. In PPS's Placemaking Vision for Downtown Detroit, bicycle infrastructure and "road diets" to accommodate bike lanes were suggested but not prioritized. The focus was mainly on public spaces to linger, appropriate to a downtown where until recently most workers retreated to the suburbs at the close of business. It also anticipated the arrival of the QLine light rail line—named for Quicken Loans, who bought the naming rights—running between the waterfront and the second downtown of New Center, three miles to the north.[127] With the launch in May 2017 of MoGo, the city's bikeshare system (also led by the DDP), in areas that connect to the QLine, bicycles have become a growing element of the downtown recovery strategy, but they still figure primarily as a consumer amenity, rather than a functional part of an economically productive cluster (see chapter 6). Many advocates, however, celebrate the delicious irony of the bicycle contributing to the Motor City's "comeback."[128]

Midtown (previously the Cass Corridor) is a focal point of the central Detroit boom, particularly in residential, mixed-use, and "flex-space" (multipurpose design and fabrication space) development (Map 6). The arrival of the QLine and the construction of the Little Caesar's Arena just to the south inaugurated a development boom that intensified previous pockets of countercultural and arts-related growth (including a community bike shop) in the derelict industrial spaces of the area. Between 2005 and 2015, $350 million was invested in over 1,000 units, more than half of them in multifamily market-rate developments. In 2015 the Midtown development pipeline, valued at over $700 million, contained over 2,800 units planned and underway, over 80 percent of them market rate (up from roughly 60 percent in the previous decade).[129] This clearly reflects the growing demand for centrally located space in the area. In Detroit as a whole, 2016 saw over 1,000 new building permits issued (leading the region), primarily in downtown, Midtown, and the riverfront, and between 2010 and 2015 the white population increased for the first time in decades.[130]

There is some evidence of a shift akin to San Francisco's toward envisioning mobility change as part of Detroit's competitive advantage. Techtown, founded by Wayne State's Office of Economic Development, General Motors, and Henry Ford Health Services in 2000, is the city's technology incubator just south of New Center. Another key institution in this area is the Detroit Creative Corridor Center (DC3).[131] Until recently, narratives about economic development from Techtown and the DC3 have not displayed the same level of focus on qualities of place as those in Philadelphia, for instance. This is beginning to change with the increase in bicycle and pedestrian infrastructure in the Wayne State area, and with new planning efforts focused explicitly on the role of public space in innovation.

Midtown Detroit, Inc. (MDI), which represents businesses and institutions in the Midtown and New Center districts, planned the Midtown Greenway to connect the area's educational institutions with bikeways to the waterfront, calling it "a critical piece of the overall strategy in rebuilding and reinventing Midtown Detroit, and will ultimately help breathe healthy life back into the community."[132]

MDI also hired veteran urban design and landscape architecture firm Sasaki Associates, which has a growing specialization in innovation districts, to conduct a site plan for Techtown. The result was a buzzword-laden and award-winning take on the role of place in innovation, with concepts like "Collaboration Cubes" and the "Brainstorming Grove" and "third spaces" like cafes and food trucks to "promote creative collisions," as well as a public realm with parks, traffic-calmed streets, and two new plazas. Fittingly, the goal of the plan is "Bring people out of their silos and cars."[133] Four years later, in 2017, there was scarce evidence of action on the plan, except for the elements that were already part of the Midtown Greenway. Nevertheless, the Sasaki plan's wish list reflects the ways that the "innovation district" frame, with a vibrant, walkable, and bicycle-friendly urban

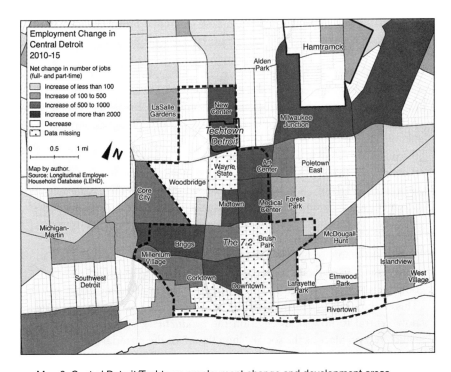

Map 6. Central Detroit/Techtown employment change and development areas.

realm as a "platform" for investment, has pervaded thinking about the role of place in economic development. In the broader city, continued abandonment yields a strategy of focused investment in density in some places alongside the withdrawal of services in others. This reality has given rise to what Seth Schindler has called "degrowth machine" politics, represented by the Detroit Future City plan.[134] The plan calls for an aggressive "right-sizing" of the city around higher-density nodes, some of which are separated by swaths of high-vacancy neighborhoods, and the withdrawal of services in sparsely populated areas, in order to create a network of "twenty-minute neighborhoods" within the city's vast 139 square mile perimeter.[135] Planners envision these neighborhoods as places where residents can meet all daily needs by bicycling or walking for no longer than twenty minutes. Their viability depends on nurturing markets in areas where they all but dissolved in the crisis.[136] When it was announced, the Detroit Future City framework received sharp criticism from community groups as a "gentrification plan" that would enrich large investors while demolishing neighborhoods that residents had struggled to maintain in the face of severe disinvestment.[137] But the plan reflects a broader common sense beyond the specifics of Detroit: that sociospatial proximity lies at the root of economic prosperity, and that human-scale ways of moving are integral to such proximity.

Across these very different places, we can see common threads emerging. The first is the unevenness of the centrifugal (outward) and centripetal (inward) pressures in each region, and how the post-recession economy partially stalled extensive urbanization in favor of infill development and "knowledge economy" functions in the urban core. The second common thread is the small rise in cycling to work as a visible manifestation of these shifts, which have affected different segments of the division of labor differently. The third is a policy response, which reveals the circulation of an emerging common sense regarding quality of life as essential to twenty-first-century economic competitiveness, which includes bicycle infrastructure as a normative dimension.

As Neil Smith argued, by the turn of the millennium gentrification had gone from a sporadic process affecting a select group of cities and neighborhoods within them to a core element of urban economic strategy.[138] This chapter shows a further shift, in which processes of gentrification are now central to how cities envision the *productivity* of their economies, which rely on place as the social "shop floor," or the material platform for "creative" capitalism.[139] Plans for restarting the engines of accumulation in "underutilized" areas of urban cores now incorporate cycling infrastructure as a key signal of livability, environmental rectitude, and economic dynamism. For the policy actors detailed above, bicycle infrastructure and the various knock-on effects it is presumed to have are part of a new form of productive urban space—the technopole—and support the everyday practices of a favored segment of the division of labor, though most of their plans remain aspirational and performative.[140] The upshot, for bicycle advocates and livability advocates more generally, is a finely grained dialectical tension between complicity with and cooptation into the growth machine. As David Harvey argues, the construction of place, as an important dimension of urban entrepreneurialism, enrolls disparate actors with contradictory interests and attachments to place into the process of capital accumulation. This is possible because place is multivalent, and not reducible to exchange-value alone.[141]

As capital courses through thriving sections of urban cores, those well positioned within the spatial division of labor, in whose image the city is being built, can take advantage of the accessibility this buys them and commute by bicycle to "innovation hubs" using world-class infrastructure. Through the same processes that brought privileged workers downtown, working-class residents must make do with car dependence in less well-connected places, and often more precarious employment. Furthermore, there is a certain myopia to narratives of livability that reject the sprawling suburb only scant years after such places came within the grasp of Black and Latino homebuyers.[142] The politics of reducing carbon emissions by acting through individualized mobility choices in this way elides the *group-differentiated* basis of postwar mobility apartheid.[143] The bicycle is both a vector and a symbol of this dynamic.

CHAPTER THREE

Everyday Practices and the Social Infrastructure of Urban Cycling

For as long as there have been bicycles, they have been used in both collective rituals and quotidian practices. Permeating this history are moments when these rituals, or practices, or both, have become fields of political action. The current political sequence that has raised the profile of bicycling began in the 1990s, with a rising tide of bicycle politics and a bicycle-oriented counterculture across the globe, a focal point of which was the Critical Mass phenomenon. In Critical Mass, cyclists took over city streets in a monthly "organized coincidence" as a statement of both their rights to the street and their opposition to petroleum capitalism, which durably marked the political meaning of the bicycle. Bicycles also steadily permeated everyday urban life among the largely white, middle class (or déclassé) counterculture, while the gentrification boom of the 2000s dramatically expanded their ranks. Cycling is now celebrated in the discourse on urban sustainability and touted as an economic benefit to cities where it is growing.[1] In the popular imaginary, the cyclist is no longer a radical environmentalist or social failure; instead, she is an urbane, ecologically responsible aesthete who zips from her stylish condo to the café and her creative workplace (Figure 6).

This chapter explores how the material and the symbolic come together in the practices of bicycling and how these practices become the grounds for multivalent claims to space, both in mass events and quotidian travels. Following James Rojas, it traces how the cyclescape is *enacted*.[2] In particular, it draws attention to the ways that the "infrapolitics" of bicycling solidify into formal platforms and durable spaces at some times, while remaining ephemeral at others.[3] At the same time, not all claims to space carry the same weight, nor do all cycling practices become politically legible. How these practices articulate with divisions along race, gender, and

Figure 6. The new "smart living by bike," as shown in *Momentum Magazine*, August/September 2010.

class influences their legibility. I examine three spaces of cycling practice: the collective ride, the individual path through space, and the social life of the workshop. These spaces tend to refract social relationships of power, but they often also reveal emergent moments of possibility.

Social Practices, Infrastructures, and Mobilities

Social worlds are composed of webs of interaction that are sustained by repeated practices. These webs act as a social infrastructure, linking actors in networks of varying length, density, and durability, but they are also embedded in space.[4] People and their relationships repurpose existing urban spaces into an improvised world of "intersecting fragments" and transmit meaning and practical knowledge.[5] The rhythm of the everyday makes such infrastructures relatively long-lasting, even if they do not become objectified in technological systems, or "hard" infrastructure. Following Michel de Certeau, the rigid urban order gives rise to endless tactical inventions that resist standardization. Bicycling is one such form of appropriation, analogous to de Certeau's idea of *le perruque*, in which the tools of this urban order are turned against it with the aid of a simple emancipatory technology.[6] But how these microscale "tactics" congeal into spatial "strategies"—or the shift from evading to exerting power—is central to what hard infrastructure gets built, where, and for whom.

This is a key issue for what has variously been called "DIY urbanism," "urban acupuncture," and "tactical urbanism."[7] In this context, the bicycle is an ethical tool for politicizing mobility, renouncing (or at least eroding) the world the car made and humanizing the street itself. The capacity to "do it yourself," however, is unevenly distributed along lines of race, class, and gender, and it strongly favors those who are already socially empowered, especially in places where state intervention is slow or nonexistent.[8] Most important, it appropriates the *territory* of the automobile in order to articulate a claim for a different form of urban life and mobility. This narrative of redemption tends to elide the racialized contradictions of gentrification, centering the bike–car binary as the fundamental antagonism in urban space. Many imagine the resolution of this antagonism as a matter of restoring the localized harmony of the neighborhood before it was destroyed by the automobile.[9] In this sense, the bicycle serves as the corollary technology to the local neighborhood as *the* authentic site of urban life.[10]

The specific technical qualities of bicycles as extensions of human bodies matter for how they construct rider identities and materialize localized social relations.[11] They shape a cyclist's embodied relation to the built environment: the "affordances" of the sociotechnical system of body, bicycle, and road.[12] They also form part of the attractiveness of cycling for many people, including independence, flexibility, speed, and fun.[13] By the same token, the social relations through which bicycle users become "bicyclists" shape the meaning that these material objects have. This operates in part through what Pierre Bourdieu calls the "bodily hexis," in this case of the cycling body.[14] The flexibility and autonomy that the bicycle affords also grounds a mode of experiencing urban space akin to that of the *flâneur*, as described by Walter Benjamin.[15] While Benjamin's (male) *flâneur* roamed the boulevards of nineteenth-century Paris, consuming the bounty of commodities with his eyes, the cycling *flâneur* or *flâneuse*, in a society that has denigrated urbanity for the better part of a century, consumes the city itself. In other words, bicycling implies a more intuitive, intimate, and engaged relationship with urban space and a more authentic experience of the city, while retaining the flexibility and autonomy of both walking and driving.

Collective Riding as Appropriation of Urban Space

Cycling has gone through at least five distinct political waves since bicycles first emerged as a mass commodity in the late nineteenth century. By the mid-1890s, in the middle of the first bicycle boom, the League of American Wheelmen, the largest bicycle club in the United States, could boast more than one hundred thousand members. On July 25, 1896, five thousand cyclists assembled in the streets of San Francisco in support of the Good Roads Movement, the club's campaign for better street surfaces that ultimately "paved" the way for the car.[16] Susan B. Anthony and other feminists credited the bicycle with liberating women from dress codes and sexist limits on mobility.[17] In the 1930s some socialist groups saw cycling as a way to increase the health and independence of the working class.[18] By the 1960s and 1970s, many in the counterculture saw the bicycle as a solution to an impending socioecological crisis, but after World War II this gave way to mass motorization.[19] The Bike Boom of the mid-1970s, partially in response to the oil crisis, introduced a whole generation to a form of mobility that spoke to the issues of the day.[20] With this momentum, cyclists in cities like New York, San Francisco, and Los Angeles pressed for infrastructure improvements (and in Oregon won lasting funding for bicycling), but on the whole the zeitgeist didn't result in widespread adoption of cycling for transportation, or the transformation of city streets, as it did in parts of Europe.[21] It did, however, spur communities and nascent political constituencies to form around bicycle policy and planning.

After ebbing in the 1980s, bicycle politics rebounded in the 1990s with the emergence of Critical Mass, the mark of which continues to be felt both culturally and politically. Critical Mass began in 1992 with a small group of cyclists involved in the near-dormant San Francisco Bicycle Coalition , who spread a call via photocopied flyers—what they called the "Xerocracy"—for cyclists to reclaim city streets. They took their moniker from a documentary film about the practices of cyclists in Beijing, who would amass at busy intersections until their group was large enough to safely cross.[22] Since these beginnings, Critical Mass has met on the last Friday of every month in cities across the world, snaking through urban downtowns with chants of "Whose streets? Our streets!" and "We're not blocking traffic, we are traffic!" (Figure 7). Avoiding permits and formal organization, Critical Mass speaks to post-Fordist shifts in the logic of collective action toward the horizontal "swarm" rather than the vertical political structure.[23] The power of Critical Mass is simple: it does not demand a car-free city but instead enacts it. For founding member Chris Carlsson, Critical Mass is "a *prefigurative* demonstration," a precipitate of the primary political act—moving through the city by bicycle—rather

Figure 7. Critical Mass in downtown San Francisco, September 2012. Photograph by the author.

than a representation of it.[24] Bicycling in the city is inherently radical, but its politics only become *visible*, argues Carlsson, when "the creative eruption of Critical Mass proclaims these myriad isolated acts to the world as a shared act."[25]

Since its inception, Critical Mass has become the most globally recognizable form of bicycle politics, with monthly Critical Mass rides occurring in cities from Zurich to Kuala Lumpur.[26] In the United States, Critical Mass achieved its greatest notoriety during the "anti-globalization" and anti-war movements of the late 1990s and early 2000s, with a Critical Mass–inspired "Bikes Not Bombs" ride against the Iraq War aiding the shutdown of San Francisco in 2003. Bicycles were not only crucial logistical tools in these protests, they also symbolized what activists saw as a struggle against the petrocapitalist economy, exemplified by American intervention in the Middle East.[27] Critical Mass grew in part through the trans-local circulation of media through ever-wider internet networks, which have given it what Susan Blickstein and Susan Hanson call "scale-flexibility" that renders it "everywhere, locally," in the words of one Chicago participant.[28] Critical Mass is in this way a creature of the Internet Age, prefiguring both the networked activism of Occupy or the Arab Spring as well as the "swarm" logic of new military theory.[29] In short, Critical Mass is a networked and decentralized political aggregation—a "machine" in Gilles Deleuze and Félix Guattari's terms—that enacts a politics of everyday spatial practice.[30]

The identity cultivated by Critical Mass did not in practice include all cyclists. Although it is common for all kinds of people to join in as the ride passes, recollections from Critical Mass veterans and film footage reveal a largely white, progressive subculture for which San Francisco was (and remains) well known. The very first Mass was a collective commute back to the Mission from the financial district, and for many cycling represented a rejection of the alienation of the monotony and frustration of the car commute to the office. It was not uncommon that the inevitable conflicts with cars took on a racialized cast; one longtime participant told me that when he thought of Critical Mass he thought of a white cyclist blocking a Black limousine driver, an observation which corroborated my own experiences. Longtime participants also decry what they call the "Testosterone Brigade": thrill-seeking, aggressive cyclists who fueled sensational images of white male cyclists confronting drivers. For young, upwardly mobile urbanites, Critical Mass expressed a primary contradiction: the city's domination by the car, even though its seasoned veterans resisted this dualism.

Despite (or perhaps because of) its flair for disruption, Critical Mass legitimized bicyclists as a political constituency, putting city cycling on the political agenda while feeding the ranks of mainstream advocacy organizations (see chapter 4). As Dave Snyder, former director of the SFBC, put it, "Critical Mass forced the politicians to ask us 'what is it you folks want?'"[31] Through Critical Mass, and later advocacy for formal infrastructure, cyclists took their first steps as participants in the production of urban space, transforming a ludic insurrection into support for changing the built environment. At the same time, the success of bicycle advocates in the institutional sphere led them to further diverge from Critical Mass, eroding appetites for its tactics.[32] For many, in order for cycling to be *normal*, Critical Mass has to become irrelevant.

This "postpolitical" framing of Critical Mass extends beyond places where cycling has become widely accepted. In Detroit, abandonment and the roadway overcapacity that has followed seems fertile for reappropriation by bike without the need for political confrontation. As Detroit-based journalist Toby Barlow wrote in 2009, "Instead of raging against their cities' internal combustion machines, [cyclists] might consider a tactical retreat to the city that cars have pretty much abandoned."[33] When I participated in Detroit Critical Mass in 2011, a few hundred of us rode in high spirits in the late September rain, greeted with cheers from the people we passed: not a protest but "a party, with lots of audience participation."[34] We met after the commute time and away from downtown, to allow participants from surrounding suburban areas time to arrive after work, which led to the amusing sight of riders arriving by car for an ostensibly "anticar" gathering. More significantly, many participants represented Black neighborhood bike clubs like the East Side Riders and Grown Men on Bikes (G-MOB), who foreground community-specific health concerns and anti-violence education.[35] Sound systems mounted on their heavily decorated bikes and trikes provided musical accompaniment. These clubs have received growing media attention that underscores how Detroit's bicycle renaissance—at least in its formative years—has not been the typical story of young white in-migrants.[36] Instead, Critical Mass there reveals a complex articulation of different geographies of cycling practice, temporarily bridging the racialized urban-suburban divide that plagues the region by drawing together groups of cyclists who may rarely come in contact on a daily basis. It also prefigures the "fun" turn in collective riding.

Bike Party and the Postpolitical

Over the course of the 2000s, with the wane of bicycling as a method of direct action, Critical Mass came under fire as disruption for disruption's sake, fueling a search for less "confrontational" alternatives.[37] Even Critical

Mass members, who had avoided "leadership" roles, started SFCritical Mass.org in hopes of imparting group riding norms on less seasoned participants and dispel myths of a "class war" between cyclists and motorists.[38] In 2012, speaking at an event in San Francisco commemorating the twentieth anniversary of Critical Mass, Chris Carlsson said locally it felt like "the hole in the middle of a donut." Its practices had reverberated outward, leaving the center empty, a spent force enacting the same monthly routine. The "new kind of public space" Carlsson called for now reappears in mutations that depart from both the disruptive tactics of Critical Mass and overt politics entirely.

Over the course of the 2000s, a new wave of avowedly nonpolitical mass rides swept cities across the United States, marginalizing Critical Mass as a collective ritual. In northern California, the most established of these offshoots is Bike Party, which began in 2007 in San Jose and spread to the East Bay and San Francisco, where in its first decade it regularly saw five hundred or more participants.[39] From the start, Bike Party positioned itself in contrast to Critical Mass, and adopted an entirely different form of organization while creating a similar social space. Where Critical Mass

Figure 8. "Hella Big" Bike Party gathering in Oakland, April 2012. Photograph by the author.

has no leadership structure, Bike Party is conducted by a committee that sets the month's theme, plans and tests the route, produces media, and enlists volunteers to direct the ride. Bike Party also assembles on a Friday each month, but long after commute hours have passed, at a public place where it can amass without blocking traffic, and it makes several designated off-street party stops. Finally, Bike Party actively enlists police cooperation, despite eschewing a permit, and its organizers demand that participants follow the rules of the road as a courtesy to other road users.[40] This structure creates a space of cycling practice similar to that of Critical Mass but within a frame that prioritizes "fun."[41]

The Bike Parties I attended in 2012 and 2013 began with a trickle of riders at the designated meeting point around 7:30 in the evening, with participants milling around, organizers coordinating among each other, and volunteers distributing route sheets, maps, and spoke cards (Figure 8). Heavily decorated bicycles and tricycles arrived with high-powered sound systems and bright flashing lights. Some participants were dressed up according to the chosen theme, such as "Under the Sea" or "Lebowski Ride," while most just wore street clothes. Bikes tended to vary in quality and style, from fashionably disheveled "beaters" and sleek "fixies" to hard-core commuters, low-riders, and ordinary department store bikes.

As the departure time approached, the mingling acquired a direction, with organizers announcing the rules of the ride by megaphone:

- Stay in the right lane
- Leave nothing and no one behind
- Stop at red lights
- Ride straight, ride predictably
- Roll past conflict
- Ride sober
- Make some NOISE!!!

A crescendo of bells, horns, shouts, and clattering gears grew as the ride rolled out, led by the techno or hip-hop blaring from sound systems. Volunteers directed traffic at turns, sometimes enlisting the help of police at busy intersections. As we moved along, the act of riding itself provoked lively conversations and the sharing of intoxicants. Barks of "Bike Party!" prompted residents we passed to come to their doors and observe the sight, and riders went out of their way to sow good cheer when they did. People mostly observed the call to stop at lights, although stop signs were usually disregarded, with only an occasional scolding. Some riders nearly raced, while most rolled along in clumps at a leisurely pace. At designated stops, the revelry continued with multiple different dance parties, rolling taco stands, and bike-mounted barbecue grills. After the last stop, close to midnight, small groups of riders trickled away into the night, to go home or to continue their evening adventure. Even to a critical researcher, Bike Party is undeniable fun.

Bike Party's norms introduce possibilities not open to Critical Mass. Bike Party remains somewhat more open to the uninitiated, and I saw many riders whose presentation signified neither "activist" nor "bike nerd," the two main genres of Critical Mass rider. Bike Party tends toward less congested areas, and more than a few riders noted to me that it was "a

Figure 9. Bike Party was featured prominently in the May 11–17, 2011, issue of the *San Francisco Bay Guardian*.

way to see parts of the city you wouldn't see otherwise," tacitly assuming that participants don't come from these neighborhoods. The consciously nonconfrontational tone meant greater participation by families and any other riders who have no interest in potential melees with irate drivers, let alone police. The San Francisco Bike Party blog put the issue in terms of *respect*: "The number one complaint from the community against group rides is that we often run red lights.... As bicycle riders, we need drivers to respect our rights to share the road. However, in order to get respect, we must also give respect."[42]

This frame has won praise for Bike Party in the media, even the Left media typically sympathetic to Critical Mass. For the *San Francisco Bay Guardian*, "While the venerable Critical Mass ride—which marks its twentieth anniversary next year—seizes space on the roads, ignores red lights, and often sparks confrontations with motorists, Bike Party is a celebration that seeks to share space, avoid conflict, and just have fun" (Figure 9).[43] Accordingly, while still relatively white, Bike Party tends to be more racially diverse than Critical Mass, although they overlap significantly.

The gaze of respectability polices difference within Bike Party as well. In 2014, incidents of graffiti and physical conflicts prompted a racialized debate within East Bay Bike Party over how certain behaviors should be enforced—and by extension, who should be included. The group's Facebook page canceled the December ride that year with the following admonition:

> Despite concerted thought and effort over many months to more effectively communicate our values and reign [*sic*] in behavior counter to those values, we've experienced a general decline in civility at our bike parties, manifested by:
>
> - Riding into oncoming traffic, attacks on motorists
> - Property destruction / tagging
> - Threats directed at volunteers
> - Theft of bicycles and personal gear
> - Disregard for music volume limits in residential areas after hours
> - Offensive and exclusionary misogynistic music
> - Littering

Debates in the comments about the causes of the "breakdown in civility" at times shifted from coded language to overt racism, and themselves became a debate over the *places* that Bike Party traverses. One commenter wrote: "Once the 'hood' gets ahold of something it pretty much turns ghetto from there . . . sorry to say. I've noticed a drastic change in Bike party in the last few months I've attended. Routes particularly in the Oakland area tend to attract the wrong crowd." Another commenter responded with irony: "Don't worry everyone, bike party will return as soon as oakland is safely gentrified and the undesirables have been relocated to the less bike-friendly environs where they belong." Another post from a Black participant, worth quoting at length, read:

> Phixed Bikes Party- All music bikes welcome, all "Ghetto Trash" welcome, all Oakland Residents welcome, all Women and Female Identifying bike riders welcome, all LGBTQ Identifying People welcome, all Disenfranchised Souls welcome, all targets of police brutality welcome, all ***TRUE*** Allies welcome, all people disgusted by coded language welcome, all people who actually want to connect with new people welcome, all people who work for justice and equality welcome, all people who ride bikes by choice welcome, all people who ride bikes as a last resort welcome, all people who are not scared of East Bay natives welcome, all people who have never ridden in a group before welcome, all people who love getting sweaty welcome, all People of the First Nations welcome . . .[44]

These exchanges reveal Bike Party both as a site where race-classed norms of "bike culture" are made and contested and as a social formation implicated more broadly in the politics of space in a gentrifying city.

It is important not to overstate Bike Party's quiescence. The filling of city streets with bicycles, for any reason, briefly subverts the dominance of the automobile and points toward a different way of inhabiting the city. To this extent it is necessarily political.[45] The rolling celebration provokes exuberance and positivity, sentiments often lacking in the public discourse that frames cyclists as smug elitists.[46] As noted, the conscious avoidance of conflict makes the ride safer for youth and people of color. Considering Critical Mass's fraught relationship with the police, this would seem like a positive step. But avoidance of conflict is still no guarantee of safety in the context of racist policing; in August 2018 Black community bike organizer and East Bay Bike Party stalwart Najari Smith was arbitrarily arrested for "creating excessive noise," a move widely decried across the advocacy world but an all-too-common occurrence for less well known cyclists of color.[47] Such episodes reveal that the powerful critique of the city that Critical Mass issued needs to be deepened, rather than avoided.

Slow Roll to a New Detroit

In Detroit, Critical Mass has also been superseded by a massive, organized "fun" ride: Slow Roll. When I visited Detroit in 2011, Slow Roll was just a group of a dozen or so friends who rode around the city on Monday nights before alighting at a bar in the Woodbridge neighborhood near Wayne State. By the time I returned in 2016, Slow Roll had exploded, drawing thousands on a weekly basis in the summertime from throughout the Detroit region. Because of this runaway success, in 2015, after discussions with the police department, Slow Roll created a membership system in order to pay for permitting and police escorts.[48] A small, informal ride that had begun like Critical Mass or Bike Party had become a 501(c)(3) nonprofit with a board and membership dues, with rides facilitated by designated team members communicating over radios.

One immediately notable element of Slow Roll is its racial and geographic diversity. Like Critical Mass, it draws riders from across Detroit's white suburbs as well as the city's dozens of Black bike clubs, many of them based in neighborhood churches. Riding heavily customized and color-coordinated bikes and wearing matching vests covered with patches—on the model of motorcycle clubs—these clubs, with names like Peace Riderz, Detroit Westside Riderz, and Grown Ladies on Wheels (GLOW), give Detroit bike culture its distinctive image, as well as its sound. When Slow Roll passes through a neighborhood, residents gather on porches and cheer or dance along, and occasionally join in. But Slow Roll is not just a fusion of white suburbanites and Black Detroit; those who drove to Slow Roll were as diverse as the ride itself, and the bulk of participants, both Black and white, presented as middle class. At the conclusion of the ride, most participants lingered, congregating around food trucks, retailers with stands set up, and on some occasions an outdoor beer garden (though, being a Monday, the event does not become a raucous party).

Part of Slow Roll's appeal is the improbable success of a multiracial and cross-class weekly bike ride in the profoundly segregated city and region of Detroit particularly, and this has made Slow Roll a representation of a place in the midst of a comeback. In 2014 Slow Roll cofounder, Jason Hall, a charismatic, dreadlocked lifelong Black Detroiter, was featured in commercials for the Apple iPad. Commenting on Slow Roll's massive growth, over sweeping shots of masses of cyclists passing through industrial areas and iconic sites, Hall neatly captures the "Detroit Hustles Harder" spirit that has become the city's brand: "I didn't do this, *we* did this. It's something we built. We as a collective built this. And Detroit as a collective helped build this."[49] While Hall resists being characterized as the face of Detroit's bike culture, Slow Roll is a perfect storm of "bottom-up" branding, combining inspiring stories, authentic diversity in a deeply segregated region, and "buzz" surrounding Detroit's renaissance. As a testament to the demand for this kind of imagery, when I arrived at Slow Roll registration in 2016 and told a volunteer I was visiting from California, he asked wryly, "You're not here to make a documentary film, are you?"

From Constitutive Outside to Oakland Brand

The political significance of the ritual of collective riding is not limited to large and disruptive formations. In Oakland, collective riding practices articulated through what Katherine McKittrick calls a "black sense of place" have emerged as counternarratives to the marginalization of Black and Latino neighborhoods and cyclists amid the city's renaissance.[50] One such practice is the Scraper Bike Team, which originated among Black youth in East Oakland, appropriating local car culture, and rose to prominence in Oakland in 2007 with "Scraper Bike," a widely shared viral video.[51] Tyrone "Baybe Champ" Stevenson, one of the rappers in the video, founded the Scraper Bike Team as a formal organization the next year. Scraper bikes are brightly decorated and highly customized bikes, with oversized wheels that are duct taped and painted and jammed into small, scavenged bike frames, often decorated with candy wrappers and potato chip bags in a coordinated color scheme (Figure 10). Scraper tricycles carrying a stereo connected to a car battery for musical accompaniment are also common. Since around 2010, scraper bikes have been a fixture in Oakland's cycling image circulating through activist networks, vividly demonstrating affective attachments to place by cyclists who are rarely included in hegemonic visions of bicycling.

The Scraper Bike Team is not a mass ride like Critical Mass or Slow Roll, but it is a collective ritual of riding and a way of producing subjects and spaces. Its focus is on youth, rather than the city:

> The Scraper Bike Movement seeks to capture the creativity of youth living within dangerous communities. It gives them a positive outlet that is fun, educational, and promotes healthy lifestyles. The Scraper Bike Movement offers youth a sustainable group of peers that is positive and motivating. We want to expand and enlighten young peoples perspective on life through fixing and painting bicycles. Our goal is to support youth entrepreneurship and cultural innovation.[52]

When I conducted fieldwork with the Scraper Bike Team, the group was meeting at El Colectivelo, a community bike repair space in the basement of a Catholic Worker house in East Oakland.[53] On Saturdays, Scraper Bike Team members, mostly school-aged youth, congregated to assemble and decorate bikes, with help from Colectivelo volunteers like myself. Champ and his co-leader Reggie Burnett (R.B.) would hold a team meeting,

Figure 10. Scraper bikes lined up for maintenance and decoration at El Colectivelo in East Oakland, 2014. Photograph by the author.

initiating new members to rules like mandatory helmets, mandatory decorations, and keeping a 3.0 GPA. Following these meetings, the team would get in formation and set out on a winding ride with musical accompaniment through East Oakland's neighborhoods.

As with Slow Roll, the Scraper Bike Team has had an influence far beyond the neighborhoods where it began. The imagery of youth from hardscrabble neighborhoods riding customized bicycles in formation offers a redemptive narrative *and* a window into spaces of cycling practice that are largely invisible within mainstream bicycle advocacy. I happened upon a key moment in this process quite by accident. I arrived at Colectivelo one afternoon in June 2014 to volunteer and found a film crew shooting a commercial for the Levi's Commuter Jean, a bike-oriented "lifestyle" design (Figure 11). The crew had been following the Scraper Bike Team's online presence and found it to be an inspiring story that they wanted to document. The film crew, made up of young, white hipsters (who looked like me), spent a few hours filming repairs, decorations, and other activities going on in the cramped workshop and then followed the team on a

Figure 11. A sign posted during the filming of a Levi's advertisement at Colectivelo in June 2014. Photograph by the author.

ride. Several weeks later the video came out on YouTube.[54] In the video, Champ narrates a story about youth empowerment and keeping kids on the right path, over artfully shot views of Colectivelo's workshop. In slow motion, the team swerves back and forth across the street in formation, waving to people they pass, with a gorgeous soul dirge for the soundtrack.[55] It is a beautiful video. What it does not show, however, is that the Scraper Bike Team is performing *labor*, producing value for the Levi's brand and placing it on the side of authenticity, rather than rehearsing the same tired footage of white hipsters on bikes that is now ubiquitous in pop culture. The play of value, image, and affect that articulates these different segments of bike culture into an important site of encounter also reveals the shortcomings of a marketing-based appropriation of the scraper bike as a cultural form. This dynamic would emerge again during the launch of the Bay Area's bikeshare system (see chapter 6).

Occupying Bicycle Politics

The above implies that the overt politics and direct action of Critical Mass are waning as cyclists attain formal political strength. This is not exactly the case. Instead, Critical Mass exists as an archive of practices and know-how that can be called upon for purposes beyond those of bicycle advocacy. This became evident during the Occupy Wall Street struggles of 2011 to 2012, in which cyclists played an important role and drew on these practices. Occupy Oakland, for instance, was saturated by bicycles. Many participants arrived by bicycle, locking onto every conceivable location at Frank Ogawa Plaza in front of City Hall (rechristened Oscar Grant Plaza by Occupy Oakland), and bicycles were used at the camp for generating electricity, to collect supplies, and for reconnaissance of police positions during raids. During the general strike and shutdown of the Port of Oakland on November 2, 2011, hundreds of participants rode bicycles, which were tactically useful to confirm the location and strength of various pickets. Advocacy organization Bike East Bay even set up a bicycle valet parking area at Oscar Grant Plaza. In Portland, a novel mutation of Critical Mass also emerged, known as "Bike Swarm," which successfully defended Occupy Portland from eviction by the police.[56] As Dan Kaufman, a bike activist and participant, put it to me, the presence of bikes was "a tool, like a cavalry" supporting the encampment.[57] Bicycles were again prevalent within the Black Lives Matter demonstrations in Oakland in late 2014, ridden by militant Black youths in leadership roles. In other conditions, the bodily hexis of these youths would have slotted them as "hipsters," but here they were street tacticians in immediate, high-stakes situations—a far cry from the bourgeois lifestyle the bicycle often signifies today.

These instances are important to recall, because they work against the teleology of radical spontaneity giving way to institutional cooptation. In other words, Critical Mass is not a pure origin of authentic bicycle politics that has been corrupted but a collective political practice of making cycling subjects. As bicycles continue to play a role both in the resurgence of Left politics *and* the commodification of urban space, these contradictory elements are likely to produce new configurations.

Machines for Urban Living

It would be incorrect to locate the meaning of urban bicycling today in these collective rituals alone, because, as Carlsson suggests, quotidian mobilities form the bedrock of practices from which the above collective rituals emerge. However, this everyday cyclescape is not simply a field of action common to all cyclists; bicyclists in particular subject positions *produce space* in the interstices of a built environment in constant flux. Through these interstitial practices, some bicycle users may evade visibility, while others seek it out, in order to assert claims to space. In doing so, their practices articulate with processes of political economy and state territoriality in ways that re-signify the bicycle itself. In this respect, bicycling is not just a favored practice among gentrifiers, as many have noted.[58] It also shapes the corresponding forms and practices of neighborhood change, forming an increasingly normalized part of the corpus of the contemporary middle-class urban everyday, making bicycling also a site where difference is (re)produced.

Unseen Geographies

In the 1990s and 2000s, bicycling formed a growing part of the lives of new residents of formerly working-class neighborhoods, who moved there for the excitement and freedom of the city, packed into old single-family houses to save money on rent, and left behind their cars in the process.[59] Many of these riders would become the first generation of Critical Mass. Susan King, the Sunday Streets coordinator for Livable City (see chapter 4), described being converted by practicality, rather than politics: "When I moved to San Francisco in 1989, I moved to the Upper Haight, and I very quickly started racking up parking tickets that I couldn't pay. . . . So I think it was 1994, I lost 2,000 pounds in one day. I sold my car and I never looked back." The experience of marginality in urban space strongly shaped King's political outlook, but cycling also simply made sense.[60] LisaRuth Elliot, a longtime bike activist and member of the planning committee for the Critical Mass twentieth anniversary, echoed this sentiment: bicycling was "just my life," a cheap and easy way to get around.[61] Bicycling allows autonomy and flexibility—independence from transit timetables and fixed routes, but also from traffic and parking. Because of its implicit environmental politics, the bicycle enables the rider to daily enact the *choice* of rejecting the ecological catastrophe of automobility.[62]

Cycling produces space, and acts as a lens into it. The material qualities of bicycles themselves elicit this orientation. They do not shield the rider from the weather, from injury due to collisions, or from the gaze of other road users. They cost their riders energy and impose risks, meaning distances measured in bicycle time vary between individual levels of effort, and routes are selected flexibly for their ease and safety. This is a matter of interpretation that may change on a daily basis. Nevertheless, they also afford different social practices than other modes of mobility, which is why cycling can never be reduced to the individual experience of bicycling, but must be considered as socially embedded. On a bicycle, I often make eye contact, nod or occasionally wave at other cyclists, some of whom I see frequently and others I've never seen before, as well as pedestrians and people on the street. Bicycling charts urban time, tracing the rhythms of change in the built environment: I ride through neighborhoods and see houses under renovation, houses for sale, condos under construction, new cafes opening, old establishments closing, new bike lanes being striped, new bike racks installed, and bike shops opening or closing. This is not to say that other ways of getting around blind one to these details. But there is something irreducible to the practice of space, and the combination of the attention required—equal to driving, and significantly more than walking or riding the bus—and exposure to place—equal to walking, but more than driving or transit—that gives bicycling its peculiar qualities.[63]

Bicycles remain visible when not in use. Unlike walking or transit, they must be parked, but unlike driving, because bicycling remains relatively marginal, where and even *how* they are parked can be revealing. Where things are happening, bikes appear. Avant-garde cultural events like punk shows, art openings, poetry readings, and panels of radical thinkers, taking place at warehouse spaces, communal houses, and dive bars, create clusters of bicycles parked outside. They are stacked and locked to each other, affixed to stop signs, fences, and racks, or brought inside and awkwardly piled among each other. Outbuildings, in-law apartments, basements, and garages host makeshift repair areas and even welding shops. Those with more repair experience open their garages as impromptu bike shops (Figure 12). These clusters of bicycles signify a distinct kind of presence in a given

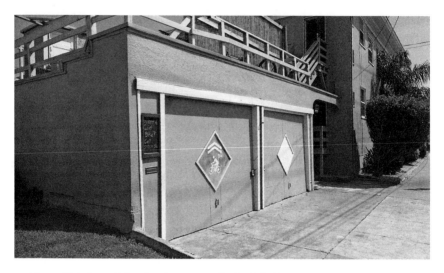

Figure 12. Informal bike shop in a garage in North Oakland. Photograph by the author.

place, and demonstrate evidence of activity and excitement. In these fertile spaces of "nowtopian" experimentation, the alignment between cycling and urban *métis,* or knowhow, is consistently being made and remade.[64]

"Red Lines in Our Heads"

Bicycling also serves as a way of accessing previously "neglected" places. "Discovering" neighborhoods is often framed as best done by bike, which is presumed to yield more authentic engagement with urban space.[65] Of course, one person's discovery is another's longtime home, a divide that typically cleaves along race-class lines. In spaces shot through with power, bodies out of place become uniquely visible through the body-machine nexus in which race is a central element. For example, on a sunny afternoon in 2011 in southwestern San Francisco, a Black youth roughly my age called out to a group of us—all white—cycling back from the beach: "Oh man, y'all are all the way out here now?" We weren't "out there" as residents, but the meaning required no translation: for him, we were far from the natural habitat of white cyclists like Valencia Street in the Mission District. Hence, racialized uneven development, whether appearing as gentrification or disinvestment, endows the cyclist who glides through space with what Sherry Ortner calls "surplus antagonism."[66]

Key to cycling in zones of gentrification is a fleeting relationship to spaces that are racially coded as dangerous. Here the material characteristics of the bicycle intersect with race, class, and gender in complex ways. The bicycle enables a more rapid pace and lessened exposure to danger (both perceived and real) than walking. By the same token, on a bicycle one moves slowly and visibly enough, without the metal and glass casing of a car, that social interaction is still possible. In dozens of informal conversations, friends, acquaintances, and interview subjects have expressed the sense that the neighborhood near where they live is "sketchy," but they can pass through quickly without problems when on a bicycle. One interviewee put it to me particularly poignantly, regarding these kinds of cognitive maps: "The marker of West Oakland is maybe a moving target, as people change mental maps where we draw red lines. We all have red lines in our heads. The bike changes these red lines." In other words, the bicycle is not just grafted onto what George Lipsitz calls a "white spatial imaginary"—it reshapes it.[67] At the same time, many déclassé white youths, the "marginal gentrifiers" or "shock troops" of gentrification, are renters who depend on "naturally" affordable (disinvested) housing, even if their poverty is a stage in the life course rather than a structural condition.[68] They fan farther out into less expensive neighborhoods, only to soon face the same pressures. Moving by bicycle extends their range and increases their locational flexibility, but it also renders them visible as new, and potentially an omen of gentrification to come.

This understanding of spatial danger articulates with gendered perceptions of safety as well. One young white woman I knew rode her bike one block to the local corner store, rather than walk and increase her exposure to men on the street.[69] Nor are all who have affirmed to me feeling safer cycling in "dangerous" spaces white, either. As Jenna Burton, leader of the Oakland Afrocentric bike organization Red, Bike and Green (RBG), put it to me, "My bike is my only security blanket, getting from the BART station home, or from A to B, I'm like, 'If I'm on my bike, chances are no one can catch me.'"[70] This same distrust of certain spaces, however, deters cycling by residents of color in neighborhoods with high crime rates, even as the bicycle is an essential tool for white in-migrants in these same places. Burton described Black men and women from East Oakland driving their bicycles to Lake Merritt to participate in RBG events, rather than riding there through the neighborhoods near where they lived. They did so not just out of fear of cars but concern about the neighborhoods themselves.[71]

I do not belabor these points for ethnographic texture alone. They are critical to explaining why the bicycle feels novel in urban space, even if it is not: it is the middle-class bicycle user, often—white—who is novel. This subject could not become visible in the same way without the bicycle. In the same stroke, this subject also becomes visible as part of a new mode of urbanism, a *flâneur* for the postindustrial city. This cyclist-as-*flâneur* provides a key point of attachment for the commodification of some cycling practices—in certain places—while others remain invisible.

Publicness as a Commodity

Whether "the most civilized conveyance known to man," a "vehicle for a small planet," or "one less car," the bicycle has been imbued with virtue at multiple levels.[72] This virtue creates a powerful ideological pivot between practices of sustainable and ethical consumption and a political economy that *requires* place-based consumerism. With the rise of bicycling as an urban practice has come the growing recognition of urban cyclists as a valuable market with distinct aspirations.[73] The urban market can be roughly divided into three groups. The first is the fixed-gear or "fixie" style: simple, often colorful single-speed bikes associated with youth culture, whose use in cities was pioneered by West Indian bicycle messengers in New York in the 1980s. The second encompasses utility bicycles modeled in various ways on bicycles common in Northern Europe, which offer an upright riding position, fenders, a rack, and often a dynamo-powered light system. A third, rapidly emerging market is the resurgent BMX ("bicycle motocross") scene popular with Black and Latino youth (see Conclusion).

One company adeptly filling the second niche with transportation-specific bicycles is Public Bikes, part of a flock of new firms serving the commuter market (see chapter 1, Figure 5). Founded in 2008 by Rob Forbes, a scion of the Forbes family, Public Bikes sells relatively inexpensive, well-appointed commuter bicycles in crisp, bright colors. They feature a relaxed riding position, simple gearing, integrated fenders, a chainguard, and a rear rack; higher end models offer an integrated lighting system. Public also provides fleets to companies like AOL, Mozilla, Square, Clif Bar, and the Gap for employee use. Cloud computing firm Rackspace offers Public bicycles to its employees "to reinforce its progressive, innovative culture to attract top tier talent, especially with younger software engineers who appreciate the urban lifestyle" (see chapter 2 for more on this phenomenon).[74] Their advertising showcases all the trappings of gracious urban living, featuring stylish men and women at farmer's markets, cafes, industrial lofts, and sleek offices. Like Forbes's previous venture, Design Within Reach, Public Bikes taps the market for intelligently designed products.

Beyond commodity fetishism, however, Public reveals important aspects of how bicycles are considered as consumer products. The pithy slogan found on its business cards—"Mass Transit for One"—shows an orientation toward individual mobility that is endemic to the contemporary politics of the bicycle. Here publicness is more than just a marketing mechanism. It references real desires, already manifested in the spatial practices discussed above, for a more socially and environmentally responsible form of everyday mobility.[75] Here bicycles are fetishistically imbued with the power to make a public:

> Our vision is that more of our urban streets and sidewalks get reclaimed for walking and biking, and that our public spaces are developed for better human interaction and conversation. We'd like to see a closer personal connection between residences with shops, parks, cafes and libraries. We'd like to see streets safe enough for kids and old folks to get around on foot or on a bike. The quality and usage of our public spaces is the measure of the success of our democracy. This is why we call ourselves PUBLIC. We want to help in our own way.[76]

This is firmly in keeping with the contemporary valorization of socially minded, small-scale entrepreneurialism and the view of automobility as fundamentally a design problem. The fact that Public is not public is not just ironic. The individualized consumption of "publicness" as an amenity vividly illustrates what Steven Graham and Simon Marvin call the "residualization" of the collectively funded public realm itself.[77]

A broader irony of the bicycle as a consumption item that conveys local social connectedness and environmental awareness is the fact that bicycles are global commodities with a nonnegligible carbon footprint.[78] A vast production cluster anchored in Taiwan and Singapore and extending into coastal China, Thailand, Vietnam, Indonesia, and Cambodia, with production and component assembly facilities in the Czech Republic and Portugal as well, accounts for over 90 percent of bicycle imports to the United States.[79] With the growth in electric pedal-assisted bicycles, GPS-based bicycle navigation technologies, and "dockless" bikeshare systems, the electronic component elements (and thus rare earth metal content) of bicycles is likely to increase as well. While bicycles pale in comparison to other modes—even transit—in total carbon emissions per mile over the life cycle, the sense that they are more "local" is largely an artifact of their adoption in the practices of producing the neighborhood scale of mobility.[80]

The Cycling Workforce and Its Others

As cycling's profile grows, the amount of advocacy work that goes into staging middle-class professionals in ordinary office clothing on bicycles grows as well. One key opportunity for this is Bike to Work Day. Bike to Work Day is one of the oldest annual rites of bicycle advocacy, and the biggest day in the calendar of every bicycle advocacy organization in

America since it began in 1994. Occurring in the middle of May, designated by the League of American Bicyclists as National Bike Month, Bike to Work Day is a massive publicity opportunity, a day when more Americans cycle to work than any other, and probably the only day of the year when mayors and council members in many cities ride together to City Hall. Bike to Work Day festivities are organized by local and state-level advocacy organizations and thus vary widely, but in Oakland, Bike East Bay's activities include "Energizer Stations" where volunteers flag down cyclists headed to work, handing them bags of snacks, stickers, and outreach literature; a festive pancake breakfast at City Hall, with speeches from politicians, booths set up by sponsors, and free all-day valet parking coordinated by local bike shops; demonstrations of new bicycle infrastructure or similar amenities; and an evening after-party with food, beer, live music, and other festivities. Bike to Work Day does not just celebrate what existing cyclists already do but creates an institutional and social setting for creating new bicycle commuters. As such, it has an ethical and pedagogical orientation that says, "You could do this every day." Informal and formal intra-office competitions during Bike Month, increasingly using digital platforms like Strava and Love to Ride to track miles ridden, exemplify this orientation. With the rise of human capital narratives of the value of bicycling (see chapter 2), this attains even greater importance as a mandate for the city itself, and Bike Month activities focus more intently on facilitating commutes in the urban core than ever before.

Like Critical Mass, these rituals condense and politicize existing daily practices. But they also raise the question of the limits to the figure of "cyclist" that Critical Mass and Bike to Work Day, in their own ways, help to create, and what kinds of subjects can become visible as cyclists. In the political struggle to transform the city, the urge to be valued tempts advocates to narrow their definition of who they represent. This manifests concretely in attempts to encourage (and sometimes to mandate) compliance with safety rules—helmet use, the use of lights, classes on safe riding, and so on—from populations receiving outreach. More subtle forms, though, discourage advocates from seeing as cyclists people whose riding practices differ from the norms advocacy has promoted. Emily Drennen, a former project coordinator at the Municipal Transportation Agency and author of a foundational report on Valencia Street (see chapter 4), described this fracture within bicycle practices and their representation: "There are two classes of cyclists: the bikes that have always been there and the induced biking. The induced bikers are now more attractive [from a policy perspective]. These two worlds don't even come together. People haven't even counted them [the former]."[81] These two "classes" of cyclists do in fact come together, however, when advocates attempt to address issues of racial and economic inequality, but they do so under conditions of deeply unequal relations of power and expertise.

One example is the involvement of community-based cyclists of color like the Scraper Bike Team in more formal advocacy efforts. The power of the Scraper Bike Team image to convey Oakland authenticity, detailed above, has led to a growing role in planning efforts led by Bike East Bay to support bicycle infrastructure in East Oakland, a low-income, predominantly Black and Latino neighborhood with a number of high-speed, car-dominated corridors. In 2013 Reggie Burnett (R.B.) began working for Bike East Bay on outreach in East Oakland, where there are historically very low membership numbers, low official cycling rates, and low political will as a result, but also numerous cycling injuries and a desperate need for safer streets.[82] The Scraper Bike Team has become a conduit for bicycle planning efforts in these areas where local political allies are scarce on the ground. But during these outreach efforts, R.B. and other team members, as young people of color on bikes, face unwelcome contact with the police even as well-known public figures in the area.

Bike to Work Day is one example of this collaboration. In 2014, instead of riding downtown on Bike to Work Day to observe the festivities as I had in the past, I rode seventy blocks east, away from downtown, to the corner of Bancroft Avenue and Havenscourt Boulevard, where Bike Easy Bay was facing opposition to a bike lane. There, R.B. and a friend were manning a Bike to Work Day Energizer Station, a first for that area of East Oakland. A handful of commuters and kids riding their bikes to school stopped by and partook of the free snacks, but by and large there were few cyclists, perhaps a dozen, when compared to the hundreds who pass more centrally located stations. Many passersby on foot asked what we were doing and remained quizzical when R.B. explained. As he noted wryly, it was odd to be talking about biking to work in a neighborhood where many people don't even have jobs, so he liked to call it "Bike to School and Work Day."

The difference between the central nodes of bike culture and the Havenscourt area was not just one of geography and density of destinations. Cycling practices in East Oakland also elicit different relationships to space and law enforcement. After I had been there for a while, R.B. mentioned that he had seen the same police car roll through the intersection several times. He then turned to me and said, "If you weren't here they would have harassed us by now, but they're probably like, 'Oh, there's a white guy with them, it's cool.'" He and his friend laughed. I asked him if the police frequently harassed him. He shrugged and said,

"They think we're up to something." Indeed, after a couple of hours there, I headed downtown to check in with other advocates. When I caught up with R.B. later, he told me that the police car had stopped on its next pass after I left. This sequence of events highlighted, in compressed form, the unevenness of how cycling practices provoke contact with police power based on race, class, and gender. With low-income African American male youth framed as idle and dangerous, riding a bicycle becomes evidence not of ecological rectitude but a threat to order.[83] This casts the discipline Champ showed with the Scraper Bike Team in a different light: as a matter of safety having little to do with collisions with cars. As Chema Hernandez Gil, former community organizer with the San Francisco Bicycle Coalition, told me, the reason he teaches the rules of the road in poor communities is that they can reduce youth of color's exposure to police violence. Where marginal gentrifiers pursue new forms of life, here the bicycle serves a more urgent goal: the evasion of what Ruth Wilson Gilmore calls the "group-differentiated vulnerability to premature death" that shapes collective futures in East Oakland.[84] Sometimes these two groups of cyclists even occupy the same spaces.

Therefore, it must be recalled that the bicycle per se is not on its own an indication of gentrification. Poor and working-class people in neighborhoods of color have used bicycles for decades. The recoding of the bicycle from a marker of urban poverty to a symbol of value has not eroded its racialization but instead worked through it, both rendering invisible and overexposing the mobilities of the subaltern residents of rapidly changing cities.[85] Subaltern cycling issues a challenge to bicycle advocacy: to accept as political practices that do not fit the pattern set by dominant bike culture.[86]

Workshops as Nodes in Alternate Networks of Urban Life

No space is as critical to how cycling cultures have developed over the past two decades in the United States as the bike shop. Bike shops have always served both as places to purchase needed goods or conduct repairs and as social spaces in which cycling practice is shaped and expertise transmitted.[87] But in many places, with the urban bike boom has come a new kind of bike shop that is linked to the politicization of the bicycle and the valorization of cycling as ethical action.[88] Community-based, cooperative, and do-it-yourself bike shops like the Bike Kitchen in San Francisco, Colectivelo and Cycles of Change in Oakland, BiciCocina in Los Angeles, the Yellow Bike Project in Austin, Back Alley Bikes in Detroit, the Community Cycling Center in Portland, and Neighborhood Bike Works in

Philadelphia are focal points for local bicycle communities. These spaces foster control over personal mobility, democratize repair expertise, and anchor a specifically urban cycling world. Many host programs through which youth can earn a bike by learning to build one, lead adult classes in bike repair, and offer access to bins of cast-off parts for repairs. Volunteers often learn skills that they use when starting their own bike shops, both for-profit and nonprofit, making evident a tighter link between the "diverse economies" of the community bike world and the small, entrepreneurial but still socially minded bike shop.[89] Spatially, these bike shops require what we might call "use gaps," or what Jane Jacobs called "new ideas in old buildings": centrally located areas with relatively depressed rents that reduce financial pressure.[90] Ironically, this leads cooperatives to those same places targeted by capitalists' search for profitable rent gaps. These critical elements of the urbanization of bike culture also shed light on the contradictory nexus of value, difference, and place within which they are entangled.

One example is the Bike Kitchen in San Francisco. Founded in the Mission District in 2002 by Oberlin graduates, the Bike Kitchen was an anchor of the early 2000s neighborhood bike culture and a space from which many other shop founders emerged.[91] Like many kindred projects, San Francisco's Bike Kitchen was originally located in a neighborhood with depressed rents, an industrial area in the eastern portion of the Mission District that was undergoing rampant loft conversion. It began under the wing of CELLspace, an avant-garde artist collective and performance center, where volunteers began hosting bike repair efforts once a week in the parking lot, and the massive space allowed for the storage of spare parts and supplies while keeping costs low. In 2006 the organization obtained nonprofit 501(c)(3) status and moved to the Mid-Market area for two years, before moving back to be "in the Mission with our community," as co-founder Evangeline Lowrey put it.[92] At that point, it struck up a deal with Citizens Housing Corporation, an affordable housing developer, who built retail space around the Bike Kitchen's needs in a mixed-income, mixed-use development just a block from the CELLspace.

This was not the story I expected when I began my research into the Bike Kitchen. I imagined an organization hounded by rising rents that forced them to choose between a social justice mission and political-economic realities. Instead, I found a community bike shop with security of tenure but its clientele of working-class cyclists dwindling in the face of gentrification pressure. CELLspace was not as fortunate. It struggled to pay rent, even taking an interest-free loan from the Bike Kitchen, and in 2013, just months after hosting the twentieth anniversary celebration of

Critical Mass, it folded and the building was sold to a developer.[93] Whether in San Francisco, East Hollywood, East Oakland, or midtown Detroit, bike kitchens, like other nonprofits, tend to be in the path of development and must secure protection from the land market to survive. "Bike kitchens," as community bike shops are often colloquially known, have also tended to spin off other local shops, increasing the density of bike culture networks in a given place.[94] Metropolis Cycles, in the hip Corktown neighborhood of Detroit, was founded by two former volunteers at Back Alley Bikes, Midtown's bike kitchen.[95] Volunteers from the Bike Church, a program of Neighborhood Bike Works, launched Firehouse Bicycles on bustling Baltimore Avenue in West Philadelphia in 2001; where previously it was an "outpost," it is now an anchor of a rapidly gentrifying commercial strip. Box Dog Bikes, a worker-owned cooperative in San Francisco where I worked part-time as a mechanic from 2009 to 2015, was started in 2004 by young college graduates who had been volunteers in campus bike cooperatives and at the Bike Kitchen.[96] Like the Bike Kitchen, they found a space in the Mission where most of them lived, in an area that had largely escaped the first wave of gentrification in the late 1990s. With a year of proverbial "sweat equity," austerity, and refurbishing used bicycles, the shop was profitable and co-owners were able to pay themselves and afford health insurance.[97] The customer base in the early years of the shop was primarily young people just out of college, who knew each other from restaurants, bars, and shops in the neighborhood, as well as low-income cyclists who lived nearby. Box Dog was even credited as part of the area's revitalization by the *San Francisco Bay Guardian*: "If you want to create the perfect neighborhood, do it yourself."[98]

Ten years later, the shop had been thoroughly transformed. The clientele, like much of the Mission District, had grown visibly more affluent, and by 2012 Box Dog was no longer selling used items or keeping up a free community workbench as before, concentrating instead on new bike sales, broader product lines, and boutique parts and accessories. These changes followed shifts in customers' ability to pay, as well as the requirements of financial sustainability, particularly for worker-owners, as "the need to pay rent became more and more real as [they] got older."[99] By 2015, fewer employees remained in the Mission, living instead in more distant neighborhoods of San Francisco and the East Bay. The neighborhood was now festooned with restaurants, cafes, clothing boutiques, art galleries, and new condominiums.

Even traditional for-profit shops have taken on a narrative of urban improvement. Like San Francisco, Oakland has seen a similar surge in new bike shops, concentrated in and adjacent to zones of gentrification.

Manifesto Bicycles was located on an emerging commercial strip in North Oakland that is exemplary of Oakland's boom, where light-industrial spaces and construction suppliers give way to a hip cafe, a hair salon, a macaroni-and-cheese restaurant with two locations, and a record store. The shop's website puts their mission in bold terms:

> Manifesto is located in the beautiful city of Oakland. Our shop promotes customization, recycling and the spread of urban bike culture. Manifesto likes art, music, and skateboarding. Manifesto likes DIY. Manifesto likes small business and local products. . . . Manifesto believes in bicycles. As an extension of the rider, bicycles are a form of self-expression. There is a simple joy that comes with riding a bike and experiencing a city at street level. We believe bicycles are more important than ever because they are practical, low-cost, and nonpolluting. And that the camaraderie shared by groups of cyclists in cities can be a powerful force for change. . . . Join the movement. We are Manifesto.[100]

Here lies a central premise of urban cycling ideology, a thread connecting bike culture's lineage in Critical Mass to a localist ecology of small-scale ethical capitalism.

This redemptive framing for urban bike culture carries a racialized edge, particularly when counterposed to less salubrious businesses. Before the website was overhauled in March 2014, the "Who We Are" section affirmed:

> We are: a couple of Oaklanders who decided to open a different kind of bike shop. We are: part of a growing bike shop cartel—operating under the assumption that more bike shops in a city is a good thing. We are: looking forward to a time when every neighborhood has a local bike shop instead of three nail salons.[101]

Statements like this do not issue from conscious racism against the kinds of businesses operated and frequented by people of color (particularly women), but from a stance against the mainstream and a celebration of sustainable local businesses that is inseparable from the displacement of what came before. But in 2018, succumbing to rising rents and competition from online sales, Manifesto closed its doors.

The bike shop itself, however, is not simply the expression of an internally homogeneous in-migration of new residents, because bicycles are used in diverse ways across the "gentrifier" vs. "resident" binary. Thus it is a site where belonging is negotiated across difference, largely through a "hidden transcript" that hinges on the bodily hexis of bicycle and rider.[102]

Brian Drayton, a Black bike shop owner active in building networks of advocates of color, described being "treated like an unwanted customer" when entering an unfamiliar shop.[103] While a number of new bike shops have opened in the course of Oakland's surge in bicycling, two Black-owned bike shops in North Oakland/South Berkeley closed; one was reopened by a white former employee only to close again. Drayton described Bikes 4 Life, a West Oakland institution consciously oriented around racial justice, as rent-burdened and likely serving more hipsters than members of the neighborhood's Black community. And beyond the gentrifying core, many low-income neighborhoods of color in Oakland have no bike shops at all. When we spoke in 2013, Drayton was working on getting a bike shop up and running in the poor, predominantly African American city of Richmond. He described a visit from a white homebuyer, who had recently moved to the area and who told him, "When I saw the bike shop I knew everything would be all right."[104] His shop has since closed. Najari Smith, another activist at the intersection of cycling and Black empowerment, opened Rich City Rides, now central Richmond's only bike shop. If planners' hopes for transit-oriented development in Richmond come to fruition, Rich City Rides, which has a consciously cooperative and community-focused approach, might also be threatened by ensuing rising rents.

This chapter has argued that bicycle users produce space and in doing so produce a lifeworld—or the "cyclescape."[105] This way of producing space occurs both through political ruptures and quotidian rhythms, both of which are rooted in spatial practice. These practices are linked through the circulation of knowledge, rumor, habit, and "feel for the game" through situated networks connecting nodes in space.[106] These collectivities in motion are organized loosely around a uniquely user-modifiable form of mobility—the bicycle—but are neither uniform nor determined by it. Rather, they refract the race-class geography of urban spaces in flux, and the "social tectonics" of gentrifying space and urban abandonment alike.[107]

Political ruptures like Critical Mass have a complicated relationship to the popularization of cycling, embodying a tension between radical disruption and the normative claims for inclusion. On one hand, with the slogan "We Are Traffic!" Critical Mass showed that traffic could be a social experience, if society were organized differently. On the other hand, it revealed an invisible collective of cyclists claiming safer inclusion in existing traffic patterns, which perform a critical role in the reproduction of capitalism by transporting the commodity of labor-power to the site of its use. The second of these claims has had a more lasting effect. Critical

Mass didn't transform the city into a post-capitalist paradise but was key to forming a class of city-dwelling cyclists who claim a right to be part of traffic.

Conversely, the practices that produce the cyclescape infiltrate the urban fabric, articulating these claims in the spaces of the everyday. In effect, they produce a shadow geography, an enacted city beyond the automobile. As this geography becomes more durable, the implicit politics of the bicycle inform a normative valorization of this alternate everyday cyclescape, and political efforts to expand and enhance it. Many practices, such as the alternative economy of the community bike shop, make claims in a different register of value from that of capital, but the lingua franca of urban capitalism exerts a magnetic pull on these claims, particularly when articulated to powerful actors.

The chapters that follow elaborate how these claims to belonging intersect with the role of the state and the apparatus of planning in building hard infrastructure. The results are increasingly "premium ecological enclaves" where the conditions for human thriving are concentrated spatially rather than distributed across place and difference.[108] The mainstreaming of bicycle politics is part of a broader process of rescaling, which subjects and spaces count as worthy of focus. The figure of the cyclist, effaced of overt racialization but irreducibly implicated in the white spatial imaginary, becomes the pole around which political claims to infrastructure are organized and which values signified.

CHAPTER FOUR

Gentrification and the Changing Publics of Bicycle Infrastructure

Over the course of the first decade of the twenty-first century, bicycle infrastructure planning underwent a massive shift. Before the mid-2000s, the cities that stood out as bicycling hotspots tended to be relatively small cities and college towns rather than large urban centers.[1] By the next decade, bicycle infrastructure had become a key pillar of both environmental and economic policy for all cities, even famously car-choked places like Los Angeles and Houston. A number of threads contributed to this shift. Out of the politics of everyday life detailed in chapter 3 emerged a mission to transform the street itself. This forced bicycle activists and advocates to contend with the obduracy of the built environment and the apparatus of urban development. In the process, however, the substantive stakes of bicycle politics have narrowed from an indictment of urban capitalism to the celebration of the value of "complete streets" that include all road users. The bicycle has become a signifier of an urban dynamism that is increasingly profitable, leading to a focus on successful corridors as models to emulate. Advocates and policymakers now commonly argue that investment in bicycle infrastructure leads directly to higher property values, thriving commercial districts, and a healthier, more dynamic workforce. Moreover, they argue, bicycle infrastructure does this on the cheap: no other investment in sustainable mobility is as inexpensive per mile.

In contemporary American cities, the flip side of this economic dynamism is rising inequality, expressed spatially as gentrification. Working-class districts in close proximity to dynamic urban core neighborhoods have become prime targets for high-wage in-migration, and the ensuing property speculation both directly and indirectly displaces existing residents. Bicycling—of the kind visible to policymakers—has taken root neither in elite strongholds nor poor, marginalized areas but in gentrifying neighborhoods near urban cores and transit nodes that are becoming wealthier and whiter.[2] These areas have also seen the greatest investment in bicycle infrastructure.[3] Thus, when infrastructure arrives in working-class neighborhoods, many existing residents see it as serving more affluent in-migrants, making bicycle infrastructure planning politically fraught in ways that take advocates by surprise. In North Portland, where black community activists decried "white lanes" as tools of gentrification, cyclists bore the brunt of blame for rapid demographic change in the area.[4] In 2010 Washington, D.C., mayor Adrian Fenty, young, technocratic Black politician and noted supporter of bicycle network expansion, lost a reelection bid in which the opposing campaign used coded language of "dog parks and bike lanes" to brand Fenty as a promoter of gentrification.[5] In Austin, Texas, a Black resident of East Austin told bicycle program project manager and UT doctoral candidate Adrian Lipscombe, "When the bikes came in, the blacks went out."[6] Though bike lanes do not cause gentrification in isolation, support for bicycle infrastructure comes from the same social bloc that gentrification empowers and makes visible in urban space: young, mostly white, upwardly mobile professionals. And the economic contributions that bicycle advocates now celebrate are the product of the reworking of race, space, and capital.

This chapter analyzes one suggestive case in the making of this new common sense. It traces how bicycle advocacy networks played a key role in transforming Valencia Street in San Francisco's Mission District into a more bicycle-friendly corridor (see Map 7). In the late 1990s, the Mission District was a low-income, majority-Latino neighborhood already experiencing early waves of gentrification; it also formed the heart of the countercultural bicycle community. Through a contentious process spearheaded by the San Francisco Bicycle Coalition (SFBC), and drawing strength from Critical Mass, advocates won a "road diet" for Valencia Street in 1998 that removed a car travel lane and added bike lanes and a center turn lane. The result was a lower-speed "complete street." This change coincided with a massive surge in gentrification as the dot-com boom of 1996–2001 reached its crescendo. Retrospective studies seemed to validate the idea that the road diet contributed to the corridor's increasing vitality. Crucially, however, this narrative was not simply the "bike-washing" of gentrification by outside actors but was promoted by bicycle advocates themselves. Success in the Mission District led to the formation of new alliances with powerful institutions of the city's growth machine, particularly San Francisco Planning and Urban Research (SPUR), cemented by an emerging focus on livability.[7]

CHANGING PUBLICS OF BICYCLE INFRASTRUCTURE   87

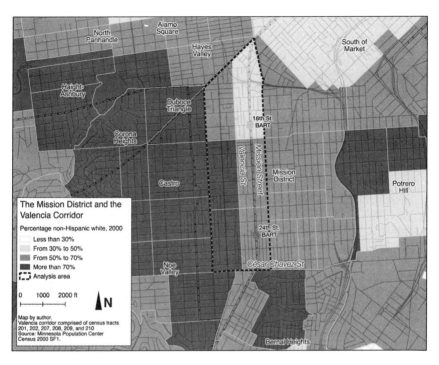

Map 7. Valencia Street in the Mission District, showing tracts analyzed in Table 8.

Valencia Street highlights the transformation of the relationship between the politics of mobility and post-Fordist urban capitalism, in which qualities of place rather than capacity for traffic flow have become a city's most valuable asset.[8] As C. W. Nevius, conservative columnist with the *San Francisco Chronicle*, put it: "Rather than fat-cat developers promoting ugly skyscrapers, the demand is coming from young techies who work here or in the Silicon Valley and want to preserve the feel of unique neighborhoods."[9] Such claims reveal how the "livable" turn of planning now furnishes gentrification's dominant spatial forms.[10] In particular, the Valencia Street experience gave advocates powerful lessons about how to argue for bicycle infrastructure, particularly in conditions of what Mark Fisher called "capitalist realism": the absence of foreseeable alternatives.[11] Moreover, the reorientation of the street around qualities of place brings the "three E's" of sustainability (economy, environment, and equity, the last of which is often a junior partner) together at the scale of the corridor, reinforcing uneven development not just in its economic but also its environmental dimensions.[12]

Over the past two decades, the association between bicycle infrastructure and gentrification has become more durable, especially as turning the tide of automobility, which began as a grassroots project to improve quality of life, finds support at the highest levels of the local business community and its ideological backers in the press.[13] The circumstances that allowed bicycle advocates to take such a central role in the production of space were not structurally given but politically contingent. They depended on an articulation of interests between bicycle advocates pursuing infrastructural improvements, other organizations working toward livability goals, a wave of progressive political victories, and leadership within the business community and the planning apparatus with a vision of more sustainable growth in the urban core.[14] Meanwhile, the interests of bicycle advocates have directly benefited from the gentrification process that grows their base of support in the "new middle class" and ensures their seat at the planning table.[15] Involvement with planning has drawn bicycle advocates into tighter relationships with other extra-state actors like nonprofits, think tanks, consulting firms, and online media, which have come to play an increasingly critical role in the production of urban space. This process of what Jason Henderson has called "progressive-neoliberal hybridization" has articulated bicycle advocates into the urban growth machine as symbolically central but ultimately junior partners.[16]

Infrastructural Publics and the Splintering of Collective Consumption

The transformation of Valencia Street and the empowerment of the SFBC as a major political actor can be seen as part of a longer trajectory of political activism in San Francisco oriented around preserving qualities of place against unrestrained development.[17] Whereas historically such efforts tended to be defensive, Valencia Street shows advocates on the offensive in a process that both articulated with and ultimately fractured the city's Left political culture.[18] Bicycle advocates took a grassroots position within a heterogeneous progressive bloc, storming the gates of official street planning and taking on the political machine of development-friendly mayor Willie Brown. Ultimately, though, while the progressive bloc foundered, bicycle advocates built lasting alliances with rising powers within the growth machine, with the goal of transforming the infrastructural basis of growth itself.

The struggle to remake the street is, in general terms, about determining the spatial form of what Manuel Castells calls "collective consumption," or what David Harvey terms the "consumption fund": the public use-values provided by the municipal state as a support for the accumulation process.[19] Bicycle advocates seek to convert streets designed over the course of the twentieth century to exclusively facilitate the flow and storage of automobiles into streets that accommodate bicycles by using specific infrastructure. In other words, the purpose is to modify the technology of the street.[20] In the "one less car" vernacular of bicycle advocacy, this change is seen as inherently progressive. But use-values are multivalent. In the case of Valencia Street, these improved use-values would become part of a shift in the exchange-value of the neighborhood as a place, though they in principle benefited any existing residents who used bicycles and were not priced out. Ironically, progressive (even leftist) bicycle advocates provided the most powerful arguments for this process. In the process, their position shifted from grassroots activism to what Sergio Montero and Oscar Sosa Lopez call "expert-citizens" who mobilize technical expertise and political credibility to link technocratic planning to grassroots "civil society."[21]

At issue is that the collective consumption of the street is mediated through vehicles. While there is a tendency to view mass transit as "public" and automobility as "private," vast public subsidies go into the making of streets with specific affordances that prioritize automobiles. These streets are no less objects of collective consumption. This raises the ways in which collective consumption is "splintered," in Stephen Graham and Simon Marvin's terms.[22] This splintering occurs along two dimensions. The first divides collective consumption along lines of "infrastructural publics," or the political constituencies of specific forms of mobility infrastructure. In other words, within the same spaces, infrastructures are splintered by mode of mobility.[23] In this case, the SFBC became the central node of the social bloc that supported bicycle infrastructure—the institutional home of the "expert-citizen"—through the process outlined in this chapter. The second dimension divides collective consumption along scalar lines, fragmenting the urban fabric into unevenly developed spaces. The collective city, or what Graham and Marvin call the "integrated ideal," which under growing austerity is unrealizable at the scale of the city or region as a whole, is scaled downward to the neighborhood level. Here, mobilized publics advocate for tangible improvements to local use-values—or what Castells terms "neighborhood quality."[24] These two vectors of splintering underpin the political and economic divergence between distinct zones of the urban fabric based on infrastructural organization. Localized use-values that are won through struggles for improved services tend to be capitalized into land values and housing prices, leading to what Richard Walker terms "redistributive rents": the rent gradient created through state-led—and even civil society-led—infrastructure provision.

In the case of Valencia Street, the infrastructural public of bicycle advocacy made a convincing case that the improvement of neighborhood use-values for bicycles, which reduced use-values for cars through technical means, was not just a victory for urban quality but also increased the economic productivity of the street. Moreover, it was an inexpensive intervention that advocates asserted had positive knock-on effects. The case was buttressed by broader shifts in urban political economy toward the valorization of place and the "light" touch of the municipal state, often with expert-citizens taking the lead. This is reflected in the growing "tactical urbanism" or "urban acupuncture" narratives through this same period, which hold that small-scale, flexible interventions—like needles in the skin of the city—are quicker, more democratic, and potentially more effective than long-range, deliberative planning.[25] But the neoliberal context is also critical: the neoliberalization of collective consumption reframes public goods as state expenditures with "multiplier effects," treating service provision not as the correction of a market failure but as an investment in a market solution. Thus, bicycle infrastructure was not so much an expenditure on a deserving constituency but an investment in economic progress.[26] In Michel de Certeau's terms, the political sequence outlined below details how bicycle advocates operating tactically began to reorient strategically around the interests of urban competitiveness.

A New Street for a New Public

The years 1997–2003 were a critical period for bicycle advocacy in San Francisco. They spanned the explosion of Critical Mass as a disruptive force, the concomitant growth of the SFBC, and their collective push to transform Valencia Street. They also saw the professionalization of the SFBC and its alliance with fragments of the growth machine, chiefly SPUR (see chapter 2). These events occurred within the political conjuncture of a rising tide of progressive mobilization against the pro-growth Brown regime amid the spectacular transformation of the city during the "dot-com" boom and its permanent realignment with the "New Economy."[27] The predominantly Latino Mission District, where Valencia Street is located, saw a surge of investment and thousands of evictions, including those of non-profits, community organizations, artist collectives, and other broadly progressive entities.[28] These threats to the grassroots tightened the SFBC's alliance with the broader left in the 1990s.[29] But by the mid-2000s, the success of Valencia Street had in part pushed them in the opposite direction: toward partnerships with more "enlightened" fractions of capital on the rise. As a result, the Mission is now both the epicenter of San Francisco's bicycle culture and the epicenter of its struggles over gentrification.

The Valencia Street "Road Diet"

In 1995 the San Francisco Department of Parking and Traffic (DPT) released a draft of the city's first bicycle plan. The plan was developed in conjunction with the SFBC and the newly formed Bicycle Advisory Committee, a citizen advisory board composed primarily of veteran bicycle advocates, per the guidelines of the Intermodal Surface Transportation Efficiency Act (see chapter 1). The plan identified key bicycle routes through the city (based on existing suggested routes in the General Plan) and trip attractors and generators like educational institutions, major employers, and retail corridors. It laid out a route map, a numbering system, and a prioritization schedule for improvements to these routes.[30]

The final plan was approved by the Board of Supervisors and released in 1997. From the perspective of seasoned cyclists and bicycle advocates, however, it was far from complete. Some criticized the plan's ignorance of Latino cyclists, others the omission of the African American Bayview entirely. Many also took issue with the plan's neglect of routes that San Francisco's cyclists had already claimed in practice, Valencia Street in particular.[31] Despite four lanes of car traffic, Valencia was a "desire line" for cyclists traveling downtown from the Mission District, which was quickly becoming the hub of the city's bike scene.[32] The street itself was also a place claimed by the counterculture, in contrast to Mission Street one block to the east, which remained a working-class Latino commercial corridor. The plan listed Valencia as a suggested route, and while it had considered bike lanes, it ultimately did not recommend them in the interest of political expediency.[33] As Dave Snyder, SFBC director at the time, put it, "[Valencia Street] always was a priority, it just wasn't necessarily reflected in the bike plan because the bike plan at the time was a crock of shit." He attributed this to the city's lack of institutional experience with bicycle planning.[34]

In light of this inadequacy, the SFBC and its allies began laying the groundwork for the road diet that would turn Valencia Street into a more livable street. In doing so, they went up against the entrenched practices of the DPT and the Planning Department, which like many such entities throughout the United States had prioritized efficient automobile flow through the postwar era.[35] For example, at a public meeting in 1997, the head of the DPT vowed that there would be bike lanes on Valencia "over [his] dead body."[36] The bureaucratic strategy of following the path of least resistance in the creation of bicycle infrastructure did not square with the hard political work many bicycle advocates wanted. With municipal actors loathe to court political turmoil, the initiative fell to the SFBC.[37]

Thus, a parallel planning process began in 1996, spearheaded by volunteers loosely organized by the SFBC, which hired volunteer Mary Brown as membership coordinator. Brown recalled it as a "young person scene": "environmentally-tinged," "scrappy," and white, composed of déclassé artists and nonprofit workers who filled the abundant cheap apartments and houses in the neighborhood.[38] She described this world as a very close-knit community, in which chances were good that she would know nearly any cyclist she encountered on the street.[39] This social bloc formed the infrastructural public for transforming Valencia Street, and its emerging leaders would become the city's new expert-citizens.

The SFBC was fully committed to the road diet plan, though there was no precedent available to follow. They had not done measurements or run traffic models; they simply knew that a lane of car traffic had to be removed to make room for bicycles. Cadres put flyers on bikes they saw parked throughout the area to solicit other volunteers and distributed information at Critical Mass, the center of the bicycling subculture in the city at the time. They also began conducting outreach and collecting signatures from churches and neighborhood associations, but they focused specifically on merchants, who Brown and Dave Snyder worried would be the most recalcitrant parties if not contacted early. But once initial concerns were allayed, the two were surprised at the extent of support from the Mission Merchants Association, given that the corridor was lined with auto repair shops, filling stations, and other car-oriented businesses, and some merchants were opposed to changes that could affect car traffic. Nevertheless, though some businesses (like ostensible allies Valencia Cyclery) did not want to sour relations with their fellow merchants by being the first to sign on to an unpopular measure, once one leading establishment lent support, a "herd effect" set in and the majority joined.[40]

With these efforts in motion, the critical conjunctural moment came unexpectedly in July 1997. Mayor Willie Brown moved to crack down on Critical Mass (according to rumor, because it impeded his limousine one evening), calling it "the height of arrogance" and ordering the SFPD to come ready with "hats and bats."[41] The situation quickly devolved into a police riot, and a memorable image of the melee showed a police officer's knee holding a white woman's head, complete with bicycle helmet, to the ground.[42] The SFPD arrested 105 participants and impounded dozens of bicycles, though all charges were eventually dropped. This massive show of force galvanized San Francisco's bicycle community and even strengthened

Critical Mass, which grew in size the following month in response.[43] It also created a political opening that the SFBC, with only two full-time employees and about a thousand members at the time, could step into and make claims on behalf of San Francisco cyclists as a whole.

Up to that point, the SFBC had avoided any association with Critical Mass, although there was substantial overlap between the two groups, in the interest of political respectability. As Snyder put it in retrospect, "[We] decided that we would take advantage of all of the attention to spin the message that people are upset because the city actually has a bike plan but they're not implementing it well, it's just sitting on the shelf, they're not taking it seriously. 'Implement the bike plan'—that was our message."[44]

The importance of this turn cannot be overstated. In a 1997 interview with the *San Francisco Chronicle*, Snyder said, "If it weren't for Critical Mass, I don't think the politicians would understand the urgency of the issues we've been advocating for years. And if it weren't for us, Critical Mass would just be an amorphous ride causing a lot of trouble with no clear demands."[45] But after this point Critical Mass and the SFBC would slowly but decisively diverge.

Based on the SFBC's outreach and the urgency of the political moment, progressive supervisor Tom Ammiano and his allies Susan Leal and José Medina championed a resolution to implement the road diet on Valencia Street. The resolution authorized the construction of bike lanes on Valencia Street on a trial basis. At a hearing before the Board of Supervisors in 1998, more than one hundred cyclists packed the room in support of the road diet. Mary Brown described it as "Critical Mass in City Hall."[46] Affirming its support for public safety and environmentally sustainable transportation, the board unanimously adopted the resolution in October 1998 and repainting began shortly thereafter.[47] It also ordered the DPT to submit an evaluation of the trial, based on its effect on vehicular traffic, bicycle usage, and pedestrian safety (Figure 13).[48]

In 1999, the new head of the DPT, Stuart Sunshine, declared, "We are extremely pleased by the impact of the Valencia Street bike lanes," a striking shift for the organization.[49] Tom Radulovich, head of Livable City, quoting a colleague from the San Francisco Municipal Railway (Muni), called the shift in the DPT the "Valencia epiphany":

> The prediction was this was going to be terrible for businesses . . . and nothing happened! It slowly became a better street to bike on, you know, all the businesses were doing fine if not better, and everything just chugged along. So that created this understanding within the MTA that road diet works, and again road diet's a really cheap thing to do.[50]

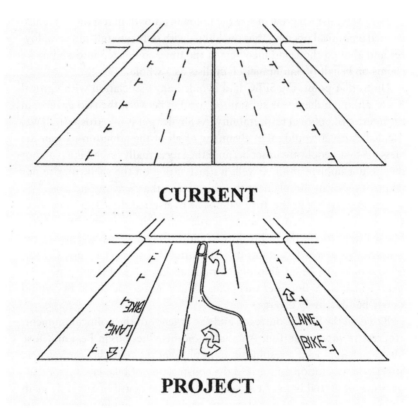

Figure 13. The Valencia Street road diet. From Michael Sallaberry, "Valencia Street Bicycle Lanes: A One-Year Evaluation," San Francisco Department of Parking and Traffic. http://industrializedcyclist.com/Valencia_bikelanes.pdf (accessed May 21, 2018).

The DPT's one-year evaluation, conducted as the "dot-com" boom was intensifying, found that cycling rates increased dramatically on Valencia Street, and all accidents decreased, including those involving cyclists.[51] It also hinted at the potential to expand the evaluation criteria, noting that the Valencia corridor was already by this point becoming a "destination" and observing the potential harmony between the road diet and commercial activity.[52] At the hearing to confirm the changes to the street, Supervisor Mark Leno declared the project a success, stating, "We need to build the whole network."[53]

Advocates took notice of the strong merchant support for the road diet. Celebrating the victory in December 1998, future SFBC executive director Leah Shahum wrote in the *Tube Times*, the SFBC's newsletter: "Bicyclists can't work alone. We need the support of neighborhood groups, merchants and everyone who has a stake in improving the area."[54] The Bicycle Advisory Committee Annual Report noted the following:

> Since adding the lanes, bicycle ridership has increased by nearly 2.5 times on this important corridor. Bike lanes often improve the attractiveness and safety of walking in a neighborhood. . . . Local merchants, restaurants, and other commercial establishments often benefit from increased business that bike lanes bring to their neighborhood. The Valencia Street bike lanes, for example, enjoy broad support from many local businesses, including the Mission Merchants Association.[55]

The SFBC honored the Mission Merchants Association at its annual Golden Wheel Awards—more of an offbeat fundraiser then than the gala it is today—in 1999, declaring it "an early, strong, and unwavering supporter" and "a model for other merchant groups in their insistence for safe streets for pedestrians and bicyclists as an important prerequisite for a healthy urban business climate."[56] Here the SFBC began to take explicit positions that would soon become hegemonic in bicycle advocacy more broadly.

The Economic Argument

The lesson that traveled most widely, however, did not come directly from bicycle advocates. A second study of the Valencia Street road diet, conducted by Emily Drennen, a public policy student at San Francisco State University and unaffiliated with the DPT, took up Valencia Street as a test case for the economic benefits of traffic-calming measures. While other cities had slowed down cars to enliven moribund business districts, Valencia Street was the first test case for the use of bicycle infrastructure to achieve this outcome.[57] Drennen used a qualitative business survey to zoom in on business owners' perceptions of street changes.[58] On the whole, out of 27 business interviewed, 65 percent reported a positive impact on business and would support further road diets; the remainder reported no effect or didn't know, with less than 5 percent claiming a negative impact.[59]

The rationale for the study reiterated the emerging advocacy common sense in a more concrete way, focusing on the way that slowing down the pace of traffic contributed to more local, sustainable consumer patterns. The study suggested that bicycle infrastructure could complement transit-oriented development and walkability as part of a complete urban economic strategy: "Traffic calming can increase residential and commercial property values, which attracts wealthier residents to the area (gentrification) and can increase retail sales and bring economic revitalization to a commercial corridor."[60] The study singled out bicyclists specifically as contributors to neighborhood vitality and claimed that providing infrastructure for cyclists would encourage local economic activity both directly (cyclists shop locally) and indirectly (bike lanes slow down traffic). The main goal of the study was not to promote gentrification but to allay the concerns of small business owners and support further economic impact studies in community outreach.[61] As Drennen put it to me when we spoke on the phone, "I had seen too many good projects get stopped by merchant groups at the last minute."[62] She saw her work as a tool to meet business concerns head on, instead of ignoring or minimizing them. But this was done in a way that framed bicyclists as agents of (positive) gentrification. The low cost of a car-free lifestyle, the study claimed, "increase[s] the amount of discretionary income [bicyclists] can spend on things other than transportation."[63] In other words, providing bicycle infrastructure means attracting consumers who make more small trips and have more to spend, sometimes called a "green dividend," an argument that has become a hallmark of bicycle advocacy.[64] This was not just speculation but a key part of the SFBC's advocacy efforts. The SFBC had conducted what Mary Brown called a "post-sell" strategy: during a month of intensive outreach after the road diet, members were encouraged to patronize businesses on Valencia. Advocates sold "bike bucks" to spend at local businesses and urged their members to shop with a helmet on to reveal their identities as users of the new infrastructure.[65] Thus, the positive outcomes that merchants identified in the study likely also reflected the way the SFBC *performed* these positive impacts after the road diet was completed.[66]

The study had no effect on the city's official evaluation of the project, which had already occurred, but it had a broad impact in the world of bicycle advocacy. Meanwhile, the SFBC's success on Valencia Street created momentum for future projects like Fell Street in the Haight District and Polk Street adjacent to the Tenderloin. According to Mary Brown, by the mid-2000s the internet was yielding study after study akin to Drennen's. "At the time we didn't realize how important it would be," she said, "but it was held up as a model for road diets. A lot of people from different jurisdictions would come and see it."[67] Despite a thin methodology, the Drennen paper would also become a convenient anchor for more sophisticated arguments in the future, as the bicycle advocacy world shifted toward capitalizing on the post-recession success of bicycle-friendly neighborhoods.

The Mission Transformed

The success of Valencia Street was inseparable from the context of a neighborhood that was rapidly gentrifying, and Valencia was the central axis of the Mission's "dot-com fever."[68] Still, according to Dave Snyder, few people involved in bicycle advocacy at the time anticipated the extent of the gentrification the next few years would see.[69] Still less was it conceivable that bicycle infrastructure could be related to the changes. At this time, the symbol of gentrification was still "young, latte-swilling, S.U.V.-driving dot-com millionaires" parking in the Valencia Street median.[70] Nevertheless, bike culture was an intrinsic element of the social world of "marginal gentrifiers" in the Mission (see chapter 1) and would prove important for future interpretations of Valencia's significance.[71]

The dot-com boom, despite its spectacular crash in 2001, set the stage for a continued round of growth in the Mission through the 2000s. The most visible commercial changes concentrated on Valencia Street. Through the first decade of the century, Valencia changed from a working-class light-industrial corridor with a Latino character and a strong punk and lesbian subculture to the spine of one of the most rapidly gentrifying areas in the Bay Area, lined with chic cafes, boutiques, restaurants, and bars that reflected deep demographic shifts in the neighborhood (see Table 8). The corridor now sits proudly at the center of the transformation of the Mission into the "hottest neighborhood for residential real estate."[72] By 2015, formerly low Mission rents were nearly matching the citywide median for one-bedroom apartments, even surpassing neighborhoods that had gentrified earlier, and by 2014 home sale prices, once below the San Francisco median, were frequently exceeding it.[73] By this time, talk of San Francisco's "affordability crisis" dominated the press, as gentrification strongly hit the middle class, squeezing even highly paid tech workers (especially if they lacked stock options).[74] The neighborhood is now the scene of pitched battles over large, market-rate housing developments amid a dwindling Latino working class.[75] While gentrification is affecting almost every neighborhood, the Mission's meteoric rise as a real estate hotspot and cultural center attracts disproportionate attention.

In addition to becoming a metonym for San Francisco's gentrification, Valencia Street became the center of the city's bicycle culture. The number of cyclists passing Seventeenth and Valencia at peak time nearly tripled from 2006 to 2015 (from 441 to 1,259).[76] Hundreds of new bike parking racks were installed within a half block of Valencia since 2000, including at least ten in-street "corrals" since 2010.[77] Eleven new bike shops were located on Valencia or within five blocks between 1999 and 2015.[78] A "green wave"—a series of traffic signals timed to thirteen miles per hour to slow traffic to bicycle speeds—was installed in 2011 (Figure 14). At peak commute times the bike lanes are routinely full.

Bicycling made its mark on real estate development as well. When 299 Valencia, a thirty-six-unit condo development at Fourteenth and Valencia, opened in 2012, its website portrayed a row of cyclists and advertised

Table 8. Demographic and Occupational Change along Valencia Street, 1990–2015

	1990	2000	2005–2009	2011–2015
Population	32,762	34,977	35,183	32,666
Population density (persons per sq. mi.)	41,051	43,691	43,948	40,221
Housing units	13,959	14,940	15,712	16,591
Vacancy rate	6.2%	3.5%	7.3%	6.7%
Renter-occupied units	87.9%	86.2%	78.8%	80.5%
Race				
White	36.7%	38.6%	46.7%	45.9%
Latino	43.4%	42.0%	34.3%	32.8%
Asian, Native Hawaiian, and other Pacific Islander	14.7%	12.1%	12.8%	14.0%
Black	4.3%	3.6%	3.1%	2.4%
American Indian and Alaska Native	0.7%	0.6%	0.3%	0.4%
Two or more races		2.6%	2.0%	3.9%
Business, finance, management, and professional occupations		41.7%	50.0%	57.0%
Bachelor's degree or higher	27.9%	39.4%	52.6%	56.9%
Median household income	$47,299	$64,099	$67,515	$70,617
Median home value	$529,071	$621,795	$818,491	$803,293
Median gross monthly rent	$1,011	$1,100	$1,092	$1,336
Median gross rent as a percentage of household income	28.3%	24.7%	27.0%	25.6%
Mobility				
Bicycle mode share	1.7%	5.8%	7.9%	8.6%
Walk mode share	7.8%	9.4%	11.2%	12.0%

Source: Manson et al., 2017 and Social Explorer tables based on U.S. Census (1990, 2000) and American Community Survey five-year estimates (2005–2009, 2011–15) for census tracts 201, 202, 207, 208, 209, and 210. Universe of owner-occupied units for 1990 is "specified." Universe of median gross rent is "specified" for all years. All monetary figures adjusted to 2015 dollars.

Figure 14. "Green wave" timed traffic signal on Valencia Street. Photograph by the author.

locally owned bike shops nearby as an amenity. Vara, built nearby in 2013 at Fifteenth and Mission, featured high-design bike racks and a fully apportioned bicycle repair station behind its imposing gates. Meanwhile, by 2015 SFBC was boasting over 12,000 dues-paying members and held a permanent seat at the planning table. Its membership remains concentrated in politically progressive and gentrifying areas of the city, with low membership numbers in the poorer outer neighborhoods to which working-class people of color are increasingly relegated.[79] If San Francisco, with the Mission District as its centerpiece, has earned a consistent place near the top of the hierarchy of bicycle-friendly American cities, a nearly recession-proof property market has cemented its reputation as among the most expensive.

Making Common Sense

The Valencia Street narrative was an early example of a broader shift in the ways that bicycle advocates justified their infrastructural goals. Drennen's study spoke the lingua franca of urban politics—economic development—toward which the advocacy world as a whole was moving. Since then the Valencia Street road diet has entered the official discourse of bicycle advocacy, from local bicycle coalitions to national organizations. It did not prove an iron law, but it formed a key element in a discursive shift in bicycle politics from the ethical to the economic realm, which was particularly strong in the mid-2010s.[80] From this perspective, the tenuous evidence and cautious statements of causality of the Drennen study have little importance. The circulation of the study cemented its credibility, with the gentrification of urban cores in the United States creating a set of conditions that reinforced its claims.[81]

From Strategy to Ideology

Drennen's study is now referenced in literature prepared at the highest levels of bicycle advocacy, although its careful wording has been eroded by reproduction. It appears in the widely circulated handbook *Protected Bike Lanes Mean Business*, produced by PeopleForBikes in 2013, which states simply that 66 percent of merchants saw increased sales.[82] The Smart Growth America website, under the "Economic Development" category, also claims that the Valencia road diet contributed to an increase in sales."[83] The theme of the 2013 Bike Summit in Washington, D.C., which convened advocates from across the country to lobby Congress, from policy to planning to community activism, was "Bicycling Means Business." At the summit, a consultant explained to attendees that "If you're not speaking traffic safety and economic competitiveness, then forget it."[84] Coverage of the summit supported these claims with another reference to Valencia: "On San Francisco's Valencia Street, two-thirds of the merchants said bike lanes had been good for business."[85] In general, arguments claiming the economic value of bicyclists often return to the Valencia Street road diet as a coda, though there is now a much larger menu of studies to draw from.

Clearly, the study had played a *tactical* role in the local politics of bicycle advocacy, at a time when it was hard for policymakers and business owners to believe that decreasing car traffic could benefit a commercial district economically. The SFBC's original goal in the road diet was not to promote local businesses or prove the economic value of cyclists; these were simply handy arguments. And in the study, Drennen's intent had *not* been to position bicycle infrastructure as a gentrification strategy; when we spoke she voiced concerns about the state of the bike movement on this score. Nevertheless, she affirmed that ubiquity had been her goal; she wanted to create a document that would circulate and make future planning efforts easier.[86] In this respect, through the study's circulation an opportunistic argument became a key strategy for the bicycle movement.

Infiltrating the Bureaucracy

Locally, the success of Valencia Street consolidated the SFBC's role as a representative of cyclists' interests and led the organization to collaborate with others in a new wave of infrastructural innovation in San Francisco. Most important, success in a few corridors gave the SFBC the opportunity to build alliances, the most immediate of which were with progressive supervisors who were broadly aligned against the Democratic political machine helmed by Willie Brown.[87] In 1999 the SFBC became a 501(c)(4) organization, which permitted lobbying and official political endorsements, and waded into electoral politics.[88] It worked hard for Mark Leno's reelection campaign for supervisor and in support of the creation of the San Francisco Municipal Transportation Agency (SFMTA) in 1999, which consolidated Muni and the DPT and became a powerful node of progressive planning.[89] A new cohort of progressive supervisors elected in 2000, including Chris Daly, Matt Gonzalez, and Aaron Peskin, led to further collaborations. Bike to Work Day in May 2001 even saw Mayor Willie Brown astride a bike on his way to City Hall, less than four years after he cracked down on Critical Mass.[90] By 2003, the SFBC was a pillar of the broad left coalition supporting Green Party candidate Matt Gonzalez's shoestring—but nearly successful—mayoral bid against Gavin Newsom, the chosen successor to the pro-development Brown regime.[91] After his victory, Newsom did not punish the SFBC for supporting his rival, instead appointing SFBC executive director Leah Shahum to the board of the

Metropolitan Transportation Commission, further incorporating the SFBC into the political fold.[92] As Shahum put it to the *Chronicle*, "These politicians want to look green, and there are only so many things they can do at the local level."[93] In these years, Dave Snyder recalled planning for bicycling in San Francisco shifting "from 'What if?' to 'How soon?'"[94]

The SFBC also cemented its position within a growing network of progressive planning nonprofit organizations and the foundations who funded this work. The link between the SFBC and SPUR, the region's preeminent progressive-capitalist planning think tank for over fifty years, was the first and tightest.[95] In 2001 Frankie Lee of SPUR declared the Valencia road diet proof that "if you build them, we will come," confirming SPUR's support for the SFBC's work.[96] And in 2001, to work on broader land-use issues, the SFBC formed a sister organization, Transportation for a Livable City (now Livable City), that was tightly coordinated with SPUR (whose director wrote its mission statement). The SFBC, SPUR, Walk SF, City Car Share (of which the SFBC was a fiscal sponsor), Congress for New Urbanism, the Housing Action Coalition (a traditional pro-development opponent of progressives in the realm of housing), and nonprofit developer Bridge Housing, as well as a number of local philanthropic insitutions, all found alignment around Livable City.[97] This network became a main pole of attraction for progressive planning in San Francisco. The SFBC also began actively to make extra-local connections in bicycle advocacy, sending staff to Amsterdam and the global cycling conference Velo Mondial in Montreal in 2000, and to the first National Bike Summit in Washington, D.C., in 2001.[98] The linkages between the SFMTA and these national and global networks of expertise, brokered in part by the SFBC, would continue to grow over the first decade of the twentieth century.

The Great Streets Project

The most serious challenge to bicycle infrastructure came, ironically, from state environmental law. Also ironically, this challenge strengthened the SFBC's linkages to dominant interests in the urban growth machine. In 2005 an already delayed update of the 1995 Bicycle Plan was rushed before the Board of Supervisors, exempted from environmental review, and approved. The updated plan recommended on-street parking removal, car lane reductions, and "sharrows" (shared car and bike lane markings) throughout the city, as well as the modification of level of service guidelines in accordance with San Francisco's long-standing transit-first policy.[99] In an archetypal case of "bikelash," in the name of the "majority" of citizens, local political gadfly Rob Anderson, filing under the name Coalition for Adequate Review (CAR), appealed the city's decision. He argued that the Board of Supervisors had illegally exempted the bicycle plan from environmental impact review, and that delays to cars would increase emissions.[100] The California Superior Court concurred, issuing an injunction in 2006 against any new infrastructure in San Francisco's public right of way, with the exception of "easily reversible" projects, pending a full review.[101] This stalled the implementation of an additional thirty-four miles of bikeways until 2010, when the injunction was lifted following an exhaustive 1,300-page, $1 million review.[102] Given the city's inability to even stripe new bike lanes, let alone more aggressive interventions, bicycle advocates focused on innovation and collaboration during the injunction, moving beyond bicycling to build even broader support for livability planning within city government, the private sector, and nonprofit affiliates.

The Great Streets Project, which focused on small-scale, reversible "tactical urbanism" projects allowable under the injunction, emerged from these collaborations. In 2002, the SFBC had formed the Market Street Committee along with SPUR, the Market Street Association, the Green Party, Walk SF, and Livable City to develop designs for a less car-dependent Market Street.[103] These collaborations led to the Great Streets Project, led by the SFBC, SPUR, and Livable City. The goal of the Great Streets Project was the "return of our city's streets to their rightful place as the center of civic life in this wonderful city by working with government, business, and neighborhood leaders to test, analyze and institutionalize placemaking."[104] It drew as well on broader expertise networks such as the Project for Public Spaces and superstar planners Gil Peñalosa of Bogotá and Janette Sadik-Khan of the New York Department of Transportation and Bloomberg Associates (see Introduction). These two revered practitioners brought in expertise on how to accomplish these feats and shaped the missions of organizations working within San Francisco.[105] Though this collaboration began before the injunction, the blockage of bicycle planning further broadened the SFBC's efforts.

From 2005 to 2009, the project developed streetscape plans for key mixed-use corridors in neighborhoods adjacent to San Francisco's core: Market Street, Valencia Street, Divisadero Street, Polk Street, and Van Ness Avenue, among others. Given the constraints of the injunction, plans focused on pedestrian improvements and beautification rather than on altering the public right of way, reinforcing the widened scope of bicycle advocacy that Valencia Street had launched.[106] In 2009 implementation of streetscape plans on several corridors began. Market Street received trial bicycle treatments, and the monthly Sunday Streets open streets event and the pavement-to-parks conversion (or "parklet") program both expanded. Improvements also included another lane reduction on Valencia, which widened the sidewalks between Fifteenth and Nineteenth Streets and added custom lighting, bike racks, unique sidewalk designs, and street furniture.[107] The Great Streets Project concluded in 2012, after completing changes to roughly a dozen corridors and, more important, institutionalizing organizational connections that would be critical to further changes to the city's streets. The project website announced its conclusion with the following:

> When the San Francisco Bicycle Coalition began the Great Streets Project back in 2009 [sic], San Francisco was a frustrating place for those of us wanting to make our streets safer and more enjoyable. Three years later we are celebrating dramatic improvements to bicycling, walking and transit. . . . Perhaps less obviously, we're also celebrating a City administration that feels inspired and empowered, more than ever, to find innovative ways to create great streets, and many new, unlikely allies in our quest to realize the potential of our streets as great places. Today, businesses and business groups are some of the loudest advocates for investing in creative improvements to our public realm. This is truly a new era![108]

These organizational changes cemented the emergent common sense that began with the "Valencia epiphany" regarding what the technology of the street is *for*, linking it to broader ideas circulating through transnational planning networks with increasing speed. As Tom Radulovich put it, "Somewhere between 2006 and 2008 it just tipped"; the bicycle and livability advocates had "won the argument."[109] One way the argument was won was by bringing in experts who were planners, rather than advocates, and could say to the bureaucracy: "We're your people, and we'll tell you how to do it."[110] Authority, in this framing, comes neither from hierarchical mandates from above nor political ferment from below, but horizontally, from "realistic" practitioners from other cities.[111]

The Great Streets Project also heralded what Radulovich called the "infiltration" of the city's planning bureaucracy by livability advocates like Ed Reiskin, who was appointed head of the MTA in 2011, and Cheryl Brinkman, SFBC affiliate and former director of Livable City, who joined the MTA board in 2010. The SFBC continued to contribute staff to the MTA thereafter. Through the efforts of the SFBC, Livable City, and other advocacy organizations, San Francisco's planning apparatus had been drawn into a global network of innovation in urban form, which as Sergio Montero notes is increasingly transmitted digitally through images, videos, and stories.[112]

As a temporary collaboration on small-scale projects among the city, various extra-state actors, and key "expert-citizens," however, the Great

Streets Project also revealed a great deal about the limits of tactical urbanism. Radulovich called it symptomatic of the "[Gavin] Newsom approach" in which "everything should be short-term, a pilot, and send out the press release, the glossy photos."[113] The obduracy of the built environment, and the daunting political commitment required to remake streets, speaks to the way "tactical urbanism," despite its roots in more radical milieux, reframes the neoliberal logic of austerity and flexibility as a virtue. Moreover, it represents the gentrification of insurgent urbanism. The informal interventions in urban space that achieve traction as public policy are practiced not by subaltern populations but by what Pierre Bourdieu called the "dominated fraction of the dominant class."[114] In other words, the apparatus of livability planning that developed over this period has been able to deliver tangible benefits—to particular actors in particular places—while the car-dominated city and region largely persist intact.

By 2016, the intensity of gentrification in the Mission, and the explosion in transportation network companies (TNCs) like Uber and Lyft, necessitated further tactical action on Valencia Street. A self-proclaimed "guerrilla safety" group calling itself SF Transformation (SFMTrA), a playful reference to the SFMTA, began a campaign to increase the safety of Valencia Street's bike lane, which had become a de facto drop-off area for TNC drivers. They glued flexible posts (akin to those used officially by the SFMTA) along the bike lane, and organized a number of "human chain" protests in which volunteers physically stood along the bike lane during the evening commute.[115] These actions pressed the Board of Supervisors and the SFMTA to install flexible posts on Valencia permanently in 2018.[116] The avatars of this "tactical urbanist" intervention were not even the scrappy bicycle advocates of yesteryear but well-connected advocates in San Francisco's urbanist scene whose efforts even drew a photo-op from mayoral candidate London Breed on Bike to Work Day in 2018.[117] One vocal organizer is a venture capitalist and investor in "dockless" bikeshare and scooter company Spin.[118] In short, the infrastructural public for bicycle facilities in San Francisco has entwined with the ascendant white-collar workforce demanding sorely needed roadway improvements, and Valencia Street is a key site of this entanglement.

Uneven Developments

The successes of streets like Valencia superseded nearby corridors that were not prioritized by politically active cyclists. One example is César Chavez Street. César Chavez crosses Valencia at its southern end, exits the Mission eastward via a harrowing tangle of freeway interchanges aptly named the "Hairball," passes through an industrial area and under another freeway, and emerges in the Dogpatch, a gentrifying cluster of converted warehouses at the formerly industrial waterfront. The 1996 draft of the bicycle plan identified César Chavez Street as a priority corridor and the Hairball as an especially dangerous site, and bicycle advocates were well aware of its dangers. But changing traffic patterns on such an industrial artery was not as simple as a road diet on Valencia, and the reasons were not just technical.

First of all, the prospect of improving César Chavez, which divides the gentrifying neighborhoods of the Mission, Mission Bay, and Dogpatch from the politically and geographically isolated African American neighborhood of the Bayview, did not mobilize politically active cyclists in the Mission the way Valencia did. Bayview residents compose only a small fraction of SFBC members, and at 1.4 percent, rates of cycling to work in the area are well below the city's average, while commuting by car is significantly higher. Nevertheless, as Dave Snyder put it, "I bet you could find a lot of people of color trying to navigate their way through [the Hairball]. You could get a lot more people who live and work between those neighborhoods to ride bikes if you made that safe."[119] Though there were periodic outreach efforts throughout the 2000s, bicycle advocates did not prioritize the Bayview District until relatively recently.[120] In 2012 the SFBC began partnerships with left-wing community organizations People Organized to Win Employment Rights (POWER) and People Organizing to Demand Environmental and Economic Justice (PODER, or "power" in Spanish) to conduct "bike builds" and giveaways of bicycles impounded by the police department in the Bayview. These were led by Chema Hernandez Gil, who was hired in 2012 as a community organizer.[121] Though these efforts were not especially focused on building support for infrastructure, when Hernandez Gil and I spoke in 2013, he hoped they would lead to a cooperative bike shop.

The changes to César Chavez envisioned by the 1996 plan were finally implemented in 2013, nearly twenty years later, as a result of local community organizations—mostly on the Mission District side—putting strong pressure on the city to make the street safer. The Bayview continues to be politically marginalized and cut off by freeways, however, even as it hemorrhages its Black population amid rising gentrification. This type of demand-based bicycle infrastructure provision, focused on normative notions of the commuter cyclist, tends to mirror processes of gentrification, which relies on support from favored populations to spur reinvestment.[122] The result is a fragmented infrastructural fabric. Twenty years after San Francisco's first bicycle plan, infrastructure still concentrates in the city's core.

My argument is not that cynical bicycle advocates have intentionally ignored under-served areas in favor of projects that serve gentrifying neighborhoods and put bicycling in the public eye. The development of bicycle infrastructure was pushed by the grassroots efforts of people for whom safe cycling is a priority. In low-income neighborhoods of color like the Bayview, where transit service is inadequate and activists are more concerned about police brutality, unemployment, discrimination, and disinvestment, this tone often falls on deaf ears unless incorporated into a broader, place-based program of justice and empowerment.[123] Indeed, in late 2017 the Cornerstone Missionary Baptist Church in the Bayview fought to have a new bike lane on Paul Avenue removed, because it had displaced some parking that parishioners depended on.[124] In Jason Henderson's typology of the mobility politics of San Francisco, this would firmly qualify as "conservative."[125] Yet the dependence of the church on abundant parking is symptomatic of the outmigration of Black San Franciscans and their weekly return to the neighborhood church from far-flung parts of the Bay Area. In other words, the simplified opposition between car and bike masks a more complicated politics of space and place.

Valencia Street was a touchstone for a new phase of bicycle advocacy, produced at the overdetermined intersection of the political rupture created by Critical Mass, its agile reinterpretation by the SFBC, and a progressive takeover of the city council that shook San Francisco's power structure.[126] This new phase departed from the older notion that cycling promotes more environmentally sustainable living through frugality. Instead, it reframed the income cyclists save by not owning and operating a car as an untapped resource that can support vibrant local economies and bicycle infrastructure as the mechanism for accessing this spending. This reflects a consumerist and urbanist turn in environmentalism more generally. It also implicitly parses bicycle users into those with disposable income and those who cycle out of poverty and valorizes the former.

By the end of the first decade of the 2000s, a growing institutional network helped the SFBC participate in sweeping changes to San Francisco's central thoroughfare: Market Street. The Better Market Street Project brought the ambitions of livability advocates into line with the most prized target of the city's development machine (see chapter 2).[127] Shifts within the SFBC and its relationships to other organizations, particularly SPUR, enabled it to pursue these converging interests with vigor. Pent up by the injunction and the glacial speed of the planning process, a burst of cycling energy following the 2008 financial crisis synchronized with a new wave of urban growth, with a city leadership at the helm that recognized the value of livability for leveraging accumulation. Livability, in this sense, links advocates' interests in more expansive use-values and city leaders' interests in increasing exchange-values. It also blurs the mission of advocacy between these two faces of urban space, while appearing to resolve their contradictions.

Rather than seeing the ubiquitous claims about the economic benefits of bicycle infrastructure as tenuous, overstating the far more modest arguments of Drennen and earlier advocates, we might instead understand them as cementing a discourse that no longer requires a referent. Bicycle infrastructure provision and gentrification have become so intertwined that causality is cumulative. The two are entangled in a reflexive process through which localized improvements to the public realm—which go beyond bikes but now include them—spur rising housing prices, attracting new residents who support further improvements. Arguments for the economic benefits of bicycle infrastructure connect claims made by bicycle advocates toward policymakers (who rarely have the luxury of ignoring the economic impact of any initiative) with urban boosters like Richard Florida, who has framed bicycle infrastructure as necessary to attract a high-value labor force and high-tech employers.[128] These narratives constitute what we might call, following Peck and Theodore, "fast ideology": a ready-made, mayor-friendly set of claims to progressive legitimacy perfectly suited to allaying the concerns of business districts about roadway changes.[129] They have become the bread and butter of bicycle advocacy's entry into the mainstream of urban growth politics.

A comparison to an earlier moment of planning intervention in the Mission illustrates the shifts set in motion during the period this chapter describes, particularly the valorization of "bottom-up" planning activity. The federal Model Cities Program, instituted in the 1960s in the wake of the devastation wrought by urban renewal, was designed to elicit greater citizen participation than preceding waves of planning.[130] In 1968 Mayor Joseph Alioto responded to the defeat of an urban renewal plan for the Mission with a Model Cities Program proposal to redevelop the neighborhood, and the Mission Coalition Organization was formed to organize citizen input. As in other cities, it articulated with other fractions of the popular defensive struggle against urban renewal to become much more than what was intended.[131] Though the organization dissolved after a brief period of action, it successfully defended the district from a plan similar to the ones that destroyed countless working-class neighborhoods of color across the United States and laid down a political culture that resisted development pressures from outside while promoting household renovations and Latino small businesses.[132]

The Valencia Street story is in many ways an outgrowth of this reaction to urban renewal, with the ironic consequence that gentrification has had at least as destructive an effect. On the one hand, it is significant that Valencia was not one of the Mission's main axes like Mission or Twenty-fourth Street, which are controlled by Latino-serving businesses, but a somewhat overlooked mixed-use corridor with auto service stations, furniture stores, small shops, and many vacant storefronts. It was also a space substantially imbued with subcultural practices, once called "America's only lesbian neighborhood."[133] The consciously grassroots efforts of bicycle advocates to transform Valencia Street did not overtly intend to change its "character," despite the fact that these activists represented an emerging white-dominated social bloc settling within the Mission. They were recognizably based within an activist community—though neither working class nor Latino—whose vision of quality of life did not represent, in Jacobs's terms, the threat of "cataclysmic money."[134] Because many Latino residents of the area used bicycles on a regular basis, it was also possible to frame bike lanes as in the *general* interest of the neighborhood as a whole, framed as a community.[135]

On the other hand, as Miranda Joseph argues, framing "community" as separate from the workings of capital obscures the way that they are intimately connected.[136] The forms of community-making the SFBC pursued after initial successes on Valencia Street did not simply place it in the camp of capital. Instead, it formed alliances with other elements—capitalists included—searching for a "transition urbanism" that worked to mobilize support for reasonable infill development within the existing urban fabric.[137] These alliances did not "destroy" community but articulated together fragments of the cycling, livability, and environmentalist communities to embark on new practices of urbanization.

The success of bicycle advocates in framing bicycle infrastructure as representing the general interest has not been universal. In 2013 a nasty struggle broke out between the SFBC and a group of merchants on Polk Street, a gentrified corridor nestled against tony Nob Hill northwest of downtown, regarding a bike project that would change the street's configuration—and in particular remove parking.[138] Polk's anti-bike merchants, aligned under the name "Save Polk Street," represented mainly older businesses and reacted in terror at any loss of parking on the corridor. They allied with local senior citizens, for whom cycling held little interest and who had accepted a framing of cyclists as dangerous scofflaws. Meanwhile, the SFBC and allied businesses on the corridor formed Folks for Polk, which put forward arguments similar to those made regarding Valencia Street. At the same time, one advocate I spoke to mused that Valencia was actually limiting as a model, because it was so unique. At a public meeting in May 2013, I watched opponents of a Polk Street road diet openly accuse MTA staff of simply acting as an extension of the SFBC. They positioned themselves as populists defending local values against a marauding city bureaucracy, now ironically represented by the bicycle coalition.

The Polk Street example shows that battles that appeared to be "won" at the discursive level are still very much alive. If anything, the success of bicycle advocates at *partially* changing *some* streets has intensified the bicycle's role as what Michel Foucault calls a "dense transfer point" where wider ideological positions converge to contest its meaning.[139] In this sense, the contradictions of the "Valencia epiphany" are not simply given by gentrification. Neither has gentrification simply been "bike-washed." Instead, a condensation of conflicts over place, economy, and meaning, shot through with race, class, and intergenerational tensions, is refracted through debates over the purpose of the street itself.

CHAPTER FIVE

Institutional Power and Intraclass Conflict over Complete Streets

In the San Francisco Bay Area, the rhythms of economic growth and bicycle advocacy first synchronized for contingent reasons in the planning of Valencia Street. But the past decade has seen its lessons solidify into a powerful new orthodoxy. National and transnational organizations like PeopleforBikes and NACTO have synthesized lessons from Valencia Street, as well as New York, Toronto, Long Beach, and Minneapolis, into a ready set of narratives about the business benefits of investing in bicycle infrastructure. These arguments began in neighborhood commercial corridors but have become increasingly persuasive to major employers seeking "talent."[1] Influential San Francisco architect David Baker supports bike lanes in the South of Market area for openly "selfish" reasons: increasing property values and attracting a healthy workforce.[2] Beaverton, Oregon, announced a bicycle infrastructure project in what it calls "Silicon Forest," with the justification that "to attract new and younger talent as the Baby Boomer workforce retires, a location adjacent to bike and pedestrian facilities is a distinct competitive advantage."[3] The Valencia Street road diet was not the only exemplary corridor in this growing consensus, but it was a key proving ground and a retroactive "laboratory" that enabled the business case for bicycle infrastructure to become mobile.[4]

Beginning around 2011, a new, more extensive boom in the Bay Area surged far beyond San Francisco's borders.[5] Oakland's comparative affordability and accessibility began to attract large numbers of artists, young professionals, and tech workers, threatening to steal San Francisco's creative thunder.[6] By 2016, even Oakland's startup scene was drawing attention, as San Francisco began to succumb to its own success.[7] Transit-oriented development plans for the MacArthur and Lake Merritt BART stations, each with significant bicycle infrastructure components, anchor development throughout Oakland's downtown and wealthier northern neighborhoods. From this base of strength, growth has extended into historically disinvested and stigmatized areas of West and East Oakland, with bicycle infrastructure intertwined in complicated ways. Oakland has seen an explosion in bicycle use, with bicycle commuting increasing over 150 percent between 2000 and 2015 and the bicycling population roughly doubling between 2010 and 2015 alone.[8] This places it among the fastest-growing U.S. cities for cycling to work.[9] In 2007 the Oakland City Council adopted a renewed and updated bicycle master plan, and the city added almost fifty miles of bicycle facilities (over half of them bike lanes) between 2007 and 2015.[10] And in 2014, bicycle and pedestrian program manager Jason Patton told the *San Francisco Chronicle*, "In certain portions of Oakland, we can't keep up with what the public is asking for."[11] Bike East Bay (formerly the East Bay Bicycle Coalition) has seen a spike in membership, from under 2,000 in 2008 to over 4,500 in 2016. Armed with increasing numbers and the now commonsense association of bike culture with urban revitalization, advocacy groups like Bike East Bay and Walk Oakland Bike Oakland (WOBO) have made significant political gains. Like the San Francisco Bicycle Coalition (SFBC) in 1998, these organizations have intervened in the planning process and built allies in city government, steering infrastructure toward core membership areas and critical commute routes. This shift was confirmed by the launch of the city's first Department of Transportation (OakDOT), which reorganized the city's governmental structure to create a new agency helmed by experts steeped in the new logic of street planning, particularly "complete streets."[12]

The production of the material cyclescape in Oakland reveals deep race-classed cleavages stretching back to the wreckage wrought by redlining and urban renewal.[13] The resurgence of Oakland's livable core proceeds apace with the highly uneven transformation of West Oakland and the ongoing crisis of underinvestment in East Oakland. The often-contradictory aims of a progressive approach to complete streets—to both stimulate development and increasingly to mitigate displacement—unfold in historically racialized spaces. Oakland is in this way the "meeting place," following Doreen Massey, of processes operating at multiple spatial and temporal scales: the globalization of property investment; regional industrial restructuring and high-tech growth; local histories of Black prosperity and radical internationalism; and leading-edge currents in everyday mobility.[14] Its transformation raises important questions about how progressive efforts to remake cities into more livable and sustainable places have become

INSTITUTIONAL POWER, INTRACLASS CONFLICT 113

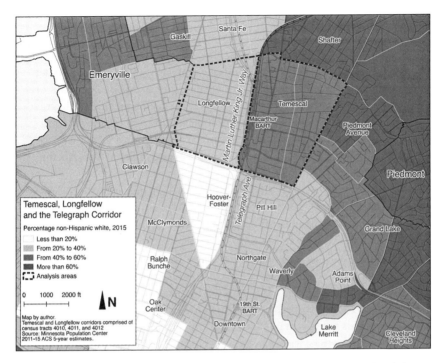

Map 8. The Telegraph corridor and the Temescal and Longfellow neighborhoods in North Oakland, showing tracts analyzed in Table 9.

entangled with histories of racialized dispossession, in which infrastructural change is a key factor.

This chapter focuses on the struggle to transform Telegraph Avenue into a more complete street (Map 8). Telegraph is the central corridor of North Oakland, which is divided by an elevated freeway that reinforced the midcentury color line in housing. It is both an arterial and a commercial corridor, passing through and dividing nodes of intensive investment and disinvestment alike. Along Telegraph, as well as other major corridors, Oakland's troubled past and possible futures are interwoven by mobility. The articulation of bicycle infrastructure planning with processes of gentrification is not a simple story of white bicyclists against longtime Black residents, however. Instead, it raises both the specter of racialized change and the durability of class power voiced in the language of populism. Both of these antagonisms are experienced and contested through infrastructural change, and they derive from the historical shaping of race and class in the city and region.

Racialized Infrastructures and Racialized Spaces

Urban space is not a container for race and class but a dynamic milieu that shapes how race and class are lived, and infrastructure is a key material force in forming this milieu. Oakland's incomplete transition to becoming a bicycle city, therefore, must be situated within a broader dialectic of economic, demographic, and infrastructural change. In particular, the trajectory of the "flatlands," a belt of working- and lower-middle-class streetcar districts situated between the industrial waterfront and the wealthy hills, was powerfully shaped by racist housing and highway construction policies in the postwar era.

World War II was Oakland's belle époque. War industries drew large numbers of workers, Black and white, from the South to shipbuilding, warehousing, and manufacturing hubs in San Francisco, Oakland, Richmond, and Vallejo. Due to housing discrimination, the West Oakland flatlands, already a Black working-class district with a homeowning proletariat and a small professional class, organized around the railroads and the port, absorbed the Black workers from this flow, who crowded into aging housing stock.[15] More prosperous residents moved northward and eastward in the flatlands while remaining confined by the color line, forming Black middle-class districts west of Telegraph Avenue in North Oakland and along East Fourteenth Street in East Oakland.[16]

The urban renewal period set the stage for the transformations now underway. Between the 1950s and the 1970s, the Nimitz, Cypress, and Grove Shafter freeways carved up West Oakland, destroyed thousands of homes, and separated the neighborhood from the rest of the city.[17] These freeways stretched into North and East Oakland, tracing the boundary between "yellow-lined" and "redlined" areas used by the Federal Housing Administration to underwrite mortgages, thus reinforcing segregation with zones of concrete where houses once stood.[18] The Bay Area Rapid Transit (BART) system, built to reinforce San Francisco's centrality in the suburbanizing region, blasted through Seventh Street, the commercial heart of what had been called "the Harlem of the West," and its elevated sections largely followed the freeways from there. At a political level, struggles over infrastructure formed a key part of Oakland's Black radicalism of the 1960s and 1970s, the center of which was the Black Panther Party.[19]

But the broader legacy of postwar redevelopment was the growing separation between downtown and surrounding neighborhoods.[20] From the 1970s to the 1990s, successive Black mayoral administrations used the Oakland Redevelopment Agency to focus on revitalizing the central business district, which had been abandoned by major retailers and the white political class.[21] Only with the 1996–2007 regime of Jerry Brown, Oakland's first white mayor in twenty years, did redevelopment attempt to bring residents back to the urban core. Brown's "10K Plan" sought to attract 10,000 new residents to downtown, which he envisioned as an "elegantly dense Ecopolis" accessible to BART.[22] The strategy became known as "Jerryfication," a barely concealed racial project that he contrasted to "slumification," eliciting opposition from a new wave of housing activists.[23] The focus remained on downtown; transit-accessible neighborhoods north and east of downtown remained auto-oriented and their BART stations surrounded by surface parking lots.

The transportation corridors laid down in the postwar era created lasting patterns of racialized disinvestment and political marginality, as well as the ideological justification for the necessity of redevelopment and gentrification today: the urgent need to encourage investment wherever possible. But they also sorted neighborhoods within the flatlands, such as in North Oakland, where the Grove Shafter Freeway separated moderately underinvested Temescal from deeper disinvestment to the west. Residents of Temescal had a front-row seat for the depredations of postwar urban development, but their neighborhood did not become one of Oakland's sacrifice zones. The result was a fragile white, middle-class hegemony in the neighborhood, shaped by a mistrust of large plans and the valorization of small businesses, modest houses, and an "urban village" atmosphere.[24] Temescal is indicative of the internal contradictions of late-twentieth-century whiteness.[25] It also highlights the tendency for gentrification to first hit moderately disinvested—or "yellow-lined"—areas, leaving the deepest portions of the rent gap to persist long into the process of gentrification.[26] In short, the flow of capital and middle-class whites back into the area has not reversed racialized patterns of devaluation in the built environment but taken advantage of them.

Making a New Telegraph Avenue

Temescal was one of the first neighborhoods in the Oakland flatlands to experience "organic" reinvestment without the impetus of state-led redevelopment. By 2010, in Oakland as a whole, whites, African Americans, Asians, and Latinos each comprised roughly a quarter of the population, with white numbers rising rapidly and the Black population on the decline since 1990. By this time, in North Oakland and South Berkeley east of the Grove Shafter Freeway, gentrification had created solid white majorities. Since the 1990s, white renters and home buyers have gradually expanded into Black middle-class strongholds west of the freeway, especially near

BART stations with access to San Francisco. Following the 2008 crisis, foreclosures swept these neighborhoods, followed by mass purchases by global investors.[27] With the revival and acceleration of gentrification in 2010–11, housing costs in San Francisco began their meteoric rise, and North Oakland offered a relatively affordable alternative, especially for young professionals seeking homes for purchase, while more marginal areas attracted artists, punks, and déclassé intellectuals.

Telegraph Avenue is the central axis of this celebrated revival. It runs northward from downtown Oakland to the UC Berkeley campus, connecting the CBD, the booming Uptown district (the focus of the "10K" plan), the slower-to-gentrify Koreatown–Northgate District (KONO), and the Temescal District, before passing into Berkeley to the north. Formerly a mixed-income, largely Italian neighborhood, Temescal is a thriving commercial center of eateries, cafes, and boutiques, where by 2015 single-family bungalows commanded median prices of over $900,000, surpassing the previous peak reached in 2007.[28] Between the transit-oriented redevelopment of MacArthur BART and a number of new multifamily buildings under construction in the area, by 2017 Temescal stood to add over a thousand new housing units in the near future.

Telegraph is also a significant divider of social space, a pattern that is reinforced by the Grove Shafter Freeway. The east side of Telegraph, which shades into the foothills and abuts the elite enclave of Piedmont, was a consistently majority-white, professionally employed stronghold throughout the postwar era. While the commercial district was severely disrupted by freeway construction, it never experienced the levels of disinvestment of other areas.[29] The Longfellow neighborhood on the west side of the freeway is mere blocks away, but the commercial strip along Martin Luther King Jr. Way, and much of the housing stock surrounding it, was thoroughly denuded by postwar redlining. Following the Great Recession, however, these neighborhoods became the "frontier" (Table 9).[30]

Within this context, the bicycle has taken hold. With easy access to BART, downtown Oakland, and the University of California, North Oakland more generally sees substantially higher rates of bicycle commuting than other parts of Oakland.[31] A study for the city's 1997 bicycle plan called North Oakland the "king of bicycling neighborhoods," and it represents the bulk of the gains that have propelled Oakland to sixth in the United States in bicycle-commute mode share.[32] Bicycle counts on Telegraph, the area's busiest cycling arterial, recorded 1,200 riders daily in 2011, despite the absence of bike lanes along its most heavily used stretch and the threat of "dooring" by passengers exiting parked cars.[33] The estimated mode share for bicyclists accessing MacArthur and Nineteenth Street

Table 9. Demographic and Economic Characteristics of the Longfellow and Temescal Neighborhoods in Map 8, 1990–2015

	Longfellow				Temescal		
	1990	2000	2005–2009	2011–15	1990	2000	2005–2009	2011–15
Population	5,496	5,709	6,152	5,987	6,396	6,439	6,066	6,706
Population density (persons per sq. mi.)	12,187	12,674	13,657	13,436	10,660	10,318	10,110	11,176
Housing units	2,453	2,475	2,682	2,772	3,232	3,276	3,719	3,396
Vacancy rate	8.6%	7.1%	8.6%	8.6%	7.1%	4.1%	7.8%	3.5%
Renter-occupied units	64.6%	67.8%	57.7%	69.4%	76.6%	76.1%	70.0%	72.7%
Race								
White	8.4%	9.2%	16.7%	31.4%	42.1%	43.2%	58.5%	48.5%
Black	81.4%	70.5%	56.6%	38.5%	37.2%	28.3%	14.0%	19.1%
Latino	5.0%	9.6%	7.1%	19.6%	7.9%	10.2%	12.6%	16.3%
Asian, Native Hawaiian, and other Pacific Islander	4.6%	6.3%	14.3%	5.7%	11.5%	12.2%	11.9%	10.8%
American Indian and Alaska Native	0.4%	0.3%	0.0%	0.2%	0.9%	0.6%	0.6%	0.1%
Two or more races		3.8%	3.8%	4.1%	N/A	5.0%	2.3%	5.2%
Business, finance, management, and professional occupations		33.4%	46.3%	47.2%		48.8%	50.3%	67.4%
Bachelor's degree or higher	12.1%	15.2%	28.8%	33.2%	37.4%	47.3%	61.9%	59.1%
Median household income	$31,619	$38,833	$40,762	$44,766	$43,199	$56,476	$52,555	$68,852
Median home value	$188,169	$226,901	$459,403	$358,100	$334,659	$394,737	$631,624	$595,250
Median gross rent	$814	$840	$978	$1,147	$950	$1,036	$1,155	$1,283
Median gross rent as a percentage of household income	33.5%	31.6%	36.3%	37.3%	33.3%	28.1%	31.6%	27.0%
Mobility								
Bicycle mode share	2.2%	2.8%	3.9%	5.1%	2.8%	5.0%	8.0%	11.1%
Walk mode share	5.3%	2.5%	4.4%	8.0%	4.7%	2.6%	4.9%	3.5%

Source: Social Explorer tables based on U.S. Census (1990, 2000) and American Community Survey (2005–2009, 2011–15) five-year estimates. Universe of owner-occupied units for 1990 is "specified." Universe of median gross rent is "specified" for all years. All monetary figures adjusted to 2015 dollars.

BART from home leapt upward from 8 percent and 6 percent (respectively) in 2008 to 14 percent each in 2015, and the ZIP code through which the corridor passes had the highest Bike East Bay membership density in the region as of 2012, matched only by South Berkeley to the north.[34] This ridership base has led to a bias toward North Oakland in planning efforts, recognized by the city as early as 1999.[35] The bulk of the mileage of in-street bicycle lanes is located near Telegraph Avenue, feeding downtown Oakland and access to BART, but Telegraph itself had none south of Fifty-seventh Street, the northern border of Temescal, until 2015. Throughout the North Oakland area, racially diverse populations use bicycles, but they are unevenly represented in advocacy. While areas along Telegraph Avenue are only roughly 30 percent white, just 13 percent of respondents to a 2013 Bike East Bay survey about bicycling conditions on Telegraph identified themselves as people of color.[36] In short, the political support base of bicycle infrastructure in the area reproduces the association between mobility improvements, gentrification, and the new, largely white middle class.

The Oakland Bikeways Campaign

As in San Francisco, bicycle and pedestrian advocates in Oakland play key roles in building the institutional infrastructure of livability planning. The timing and substance of the conjunctural moments of the process differ significantly, however. As discussed in chapter 4, in San Francisco, the political settlement over bicycle infrastructure emerged from a struggle between the countercultural Left, the SFBC, and the municipal bureaucracy, in which advocates assumed the role of constructing expert knowledge — becoming "expert-citizens," in Oscar Sosa López and Sergio Montero's term.[37] In Oakland's case, consensus essentially already existed between the municipal state and the professional advocacy organizations, particularly Bike East Bay and Walk Oakland Bike Oakland (WOBO), who were supported by new bases of expertise like the National Association of City Transportation Officials (NACTO) and San Francisco Planning and Urban Research (SPUR). Instead, conflict emerged between this coalition and the older class fraction of merchants, and the infrastructural public for bicycle planning came not from the countercultural left but from the rising professional stratum.[38] The conflict was essentially an intraclass struggle between social blocs — and generations — within the largely white middle class.

While the SFBC began as part of the broader Left, and was in part pushed into economic claims for pragmatic reasons, the Telegraph campaign began on well-established terrain that ideologically linked economic growth and nonmotorized mobility. New advocacy organizations were part of this shift. Bike East Bay is a membership-driven organization like the SFBC, representing cyclists in thirty-three varied, mostly suburban municipalities. In the early 2000s, the EBBC shifted to the "social movement" advocacy model, began to shed its "old white guy" culture, and hired René Rivera, a queer person of color, as executive director.[39] This included an alliance with the newer, more urbanism-focused WOBO, which had formed in the early 2000s explicitly in the interest of livable urban revitalization, informed by marketing, real estate, and the broader nonprofit world.[40] In 2014 SPUR opened an Oakland office with an explicit bicycle and pedestrian planning focus. Together, these three organizations have successfully forwarded a growth-based livability agenda that mobilizes expertise from broader advocacy networks in support of "world class" infrastructure.[41] This new common sense was evinced by the formation of OakDOT as well. Thus, much like the SFBC, Bike East Bay has engaged in the planning process beyond traditional lobbying and advisory roles.

In 2013 Bike East Bay and WOBO launched the Oakland Bikeways Campaign, designed to apply pressure on the implementation process for bicycle infrastructure on three particularly difficult corridors: Telegraph Avenue, 14th Street through downtown, and Park Boulevard east of Lake Merritt. The 2007 bike plan included all three of these corridors as candidates for road diets. The goal of the campaign was to get ahead of the city and present comprehensive, technically sophisticated street plans generated through mobilized member input. Out of this campaign, Telegraph Avenue emerged as the highest priority as well as the greatest challenge.[42] The effort to transform this arterial from a technology of automobile throughput to one of a convivial place would mobilize all of the discourses set into motion by the "Valencia epiphany."[43] But it was now aided by the popular understanding of cycling as a central feature of the urban renaissance, and in order to become a valued infrastructural public, bicycle advocates have sought to represent cyclists as a valuable customer base. But more traditional elements of the local merchants and property owners envisioned themselves as embattled victims of a city plan that would create intolerable congestion, despite their prosperity. Many of them saw value in bicycling, but only if bicycle infrastructure did not impinge on space devoted to cars. Thus debates over the shape of Telegraph took the form of an intraclass struggle fought out through mobility infrastructure.

Local Champions

These conflicts in fact divided the merchant class itself, with a number of new businesses on Telegraph ardently supporting bicycle infrastructure improvements. As the outreach campaign's coordinator, Bike East Bay's Dave Campbell compiled a list of friendly and "on the fence" businesses on the corridor, posted it on the campaign website, and encouraged members to shop conspicuously and wear helmets to show their support for bicycle infrastructure. The list of friendly businesses read as a who's who of the "New Oakland": cafes, taprooms and beer gardens, restaurants, and boutiques. At least 80 percent had opened since the Great Recession and served a clientele brought to their doors by gentrification.[44] Campbell also won the favor of the KONO and Uptown business districts to the south, both of which hoped to encourage activity on the less congested sections of the Telegraph that they represent, and explored forming the city's first Bicycle-Friendly Business District, a new certification offered by the League of American Bicyclists.

As part of his efforts, Campbell held several "Bike Talks" at various businesses on the strip in spring of 2014, encouraging Bike East Bay members to drop by, spend money, and get excited about improving bicycling on Telegraph. He wrote, in a blog post, "People bicycling are competitive shoppers to other modes already on Telegraph Avenue, and this with no current bicycle facilities. The installation of bike lanes on Telegraph is only going to increase the success of local businesses, as will making the street safer and more inviting for pedestrians and a better street for transit."[45] Over falafel at a Middle Eastern establishment on the corridor, Dave updated me on the state of the outreach: "People are amped, businesses not so much. Some are cool and do get it, but there's one of those for every ten neighborhood groups." He framed the political outcome he hoped for as a version of the performative "post-sell" that occurred on Valencia: "Ideally, Telegraph gets bike lanes, then Broadway says, 'What about us?' and then San Pablo says, 'What about us?'" In other words, an ideal result would be for local business owners to essentially bid for future infrastructure development after witnessing its success, creating a tacit business-advocacy coalition to pressure the city.

Temescal, where gentrification is most advanced, is also the most contentious choke point of the Telegraph corridor because of multiple bus lines, frequent deliveries to local businesses, and a high volume of traffic accessing the Grove Shafter Freeway. The Temescal–Telegraph Business Improvement District (BID below), which stewards commercial activity in the area, has carefully tended a bike-friendly image while simultaneously resisting changes to the street itself.[46] Nevertheless, with bicyclists ubiquitous in the district, the BID began taking tentative steps toward integrating bicycle infrastructure into the corridor's brand identity. Interest in accommodating bicycles grew from October 2011 onward, after a city of Oakland

Figure 15. In-street bike parking in the Temescal District, distinctively branded by the Temescal–Telegraph Business Improvement District. Photograph by the author.

traffic study showed that fewer than half of customers surveyed arrived by car. By April 2012, the BID was moving forward on an in-street bicycle parking facility—or "bike corral"—with distinctive branding, located in front of the wildly popular restaurant Burma Superstar (Figure 15).[47] Since then, two other in-street bike corrals were installed on the corridor.

Though this position would appear to support completing the corridor's transformation into Oakland's Valencia Street, prominent property owners had opposed prior efforts to change the street and continued to do so now. In 1998 bike lanes planned for Temescal, which would have removed a travel lane, were blocked by a lawsuit filed under the name Coalition to Save Telegraph Avenue by a local property owner and a traditional "vehicular cycling" advocate.[48] This history was also part of the reason for Bike East Bay's concerns about winning the favor of businesses and finding local allies.[49] But this time the discourse was not just a convenient palliative. Advocates had clearly absorbed the *economic* rationale for bicycle infrastructure as a primary goal—to contribute to the rebirth of the city. Also, because of business turnover, Patton expected the question of bike lanes to be "a very different conversation" from before.[50] The struggle over remaking Telegraph became essentially a clash of two localisms: one defensive, for whom planners represented an unaccountable local government; the other "visionary," but drawn toward the scale of the corridor.

Critical Mass for Planning

Advocates also harnessed the affective practice of riding itself. Bike East Bay organized social rides of the critical corridors, in which volunteers mapped street conditions, identified hazards, shared experiences, and debated designs for various street segments. I participated in these rides, along with a group of a dozen or so other members and several Bike East Bay staff. With detailed site maps from the city's planning department and collective experience riding the street, we embarked on two-hour journeys on each corridor. We surveyed existing conditions, choke points, danger zones, opportunities to change traffic flow, and existing uses—especially businesses—that could pose obstacles. Each ride ended at an eatery where, over a beer and a meal, we drew up on the maps the designs we had envisioned during the ride. As in planning efforts on Valencia Street, these practices mobilized affective neighborhood ties (including those of very recent arrivals) as part of a citizen mapping project in which the bicycle was not just an object but a tool. At the same time, these practices raise inevitable questions of what kinds of cyclists have access to the planning process in this way, what corridors receive this kind of focused attention, and why.

The subject of gentrification did not come up during the rides themselves, which focused on the technical characteristics of the street. During postride meals, however, when members of the group asked me about my research, all manner of comments emerged. I explained the various debates surrounding bicycle infrastructure and gentrification and awaited hostile reactions.[51] Instead, these advocates, who were almost all white and all middle class, wanted to talk about race, class, and bicycle infrastructure. A Bike East Bay member said that as a longtime Oakland cyclist he felt he saw all social groups represented out on the streets but then noted the homogeneity of our group. One volunteer expressed discomfort at the position that bicycle coalitions have been forced to take, often putting themselves on the side of business, developers, and neighborhood associations defending property values.[52] Nevertheless, as a group we often discussed elements like connectivity and access to downtown and leisure areas without reference to how these serve as amenities. In fact, regardless of the goals of the advocates involved, we were working toward establishing just these spatial relationships.[53]

These practices extended to "prefigurative" interventions in the street itself. Although the campaign partners anticipated serious opposition to any plan that reduced street parking or slowed traffic flow to install a full-fledged bike lane, Bike East Bay took a "maximalist" position, advocating "world class" separated cycle tracks for the entire length of Telegraph, including Temescal. On Bike to Work Day in May 2014, Dave Campbell set up a demonstration "pop-up" cycle track on Telegraph at Twenty-sixth Street for participants—and several council members—to try out, in an effort to build support for separated facilities along the entire corridor (Figure 16). It was a clever piece of "tactical urbanism," making headlines on Streetsblog and allowing cyclists—and, more important, elected officials—to experience what advocates saw as the future of Telegraph. At the same time, it was placed in a portion of the corridor where even peak-hour traffic is light, on an exceptional day for cycling. More work would be needed to make the shift from tactical appropriation of the street to its strategic reconfiguration.

Extra-Local Support

When NACTO brought its Cities for Cycling Roadshow to Oakland in April 2014, it pushed the Oakland Bikeways campaign to a new level. Beyond its role as a clearinghouse of information and a depository of best practices, NACTO has become a pedagogical tool for embattled planners within their own departments. In its mission to depose the more car-oriented standards of the American Association of State Highway and

Figure 16. "Pop-up" cycle track on Telegraph Avenue on Bike to Work Day, May 2014. Photograph by the author.

Transportation Officials (see chapter 1), NACTO both holds that cities should be planned differently in order to influence mobility change and promotes metrics beyond efficiency—particularly safety and economic growth—to inform alternative street designs.[54] At the scale of the municipality, though, this translates into reshaping key corridors in ways that make them more conducive to gentrification.

To convince planners schooled in the old ways, Oakland called on the authority of what Bruno Latour calls "long networks" of practitioners whose distance and epistemic commonality gives them authority.[55] The Roadshow brought in experts like New York's Ryan Russo (deputy commissioner of the New York Department of Transportation under Janette Sadik-Khan), Chicago DOT's Mike Amsden, and Boston's bicycle program director Nicole Freedman to share NACTO best practices on bikeway design with transportation engineers who were not yet inculcated in— or convinced by—the new hegemonic expertise in the field (see chapter 2). But businesses also formed a key infrastructural public mobilized by these efforts as well. The Roadshow included presentations and design charrettes, a test ride of existing infrastructure in Oakland, and a presentation from the California Department of Transportation, which had just endorsed the NACTO Urban Bikeway Design Guide. The timing was not arbitrary. Organizers hoped to convert the city traffic engineers whose support would be needed to relax the LOS standards on Telegraph in particular, and the

Telegraph Avenue project would "provide a unique opportunity for a peer review of alternative concepts by national experts in bikeway design to ensure that the project incorporates emerging best practices."[56] Also key was a presentation on the economic benefits of bicycle infrastructure to business leaders from districts along Telegraph and Fourteenth Street.[57]

NACTO concluded the event with a dinner open to the public, attended by advocates, academic researchers like me, representatives from other planning departments, and planners at the several consulting firms who contributed to the design guide. Guest speakers shared mostly hagiographic stories of their experiences in bike planning. Then-mayor Jean Quan extolled the city's green virtues, affirmed bicycle infrastructure and housing along transit corridors as "critical to economic development," and placed bicycle advocacy within the arc of Oakland's progressive history from the Pullman Porters to the Black Panther Party. After speakers from WOBO and Bike East Bay, Ed Reiskin affirmed that Oakland could be "ground zero for the next wave of biking." Throughout the event, speaker after speaker affirmed bicycle infrastructure as fundamental to a "world class city." To achieve the successes of its aspirational peers like San Francisco, Chicago, and New York, Oakland needed comprehensive bikeways.

The NACTO dinner revealed as much about the limitations of this new network of experts as about its growing strength, especially with regards to race and class. Not surprisingly, white faces dominated the crowd, which drew from the ranks of professional planning and consulting. It was primarily a cheerleading crowd as well, celebrating accomplishments and leaving some dimensions of bicycle planning conspicuously unexamined. Ryan Russo spoke, dismissing the "bikelash" in Park Slope as "a moment that every city has to go through" and a product of "the political chatter class"—implicitly dismissing all such concerns, whether from wealthy neighbors defending their privileges or poor communities threatened by gentrification. Similarly, Boston's Nicole Freedman celebrated the Hubway bikeshare's subsidy to low-income riders, but when asked how Boston justified the investments, she quoted Chicago Mayor Rahm Emanuel: "There is no way to be for a tech economy and not be for bikes, but more importantly 'Oh my god, every other city is doing this, we need to do it too!'" Meanwhile, other forms of expertise never entered the room. Bike East Bay offered free valet bicycle parking, common at many such events in Oakland. Amid the excitement and knowledge-sharing regarding Oakland's pedal-powered renaissance, R.B. of the Scraper Bike Team (see chapter 3), one of the few Black attendees, spent most of the event downstairs parking bikes, not upstairs meeting with the city officials who were drumming up excitement for Oakland's bicycle-powered renaissance.

Narrating the Contradictions of Growth

The city's initial plans for Telegraph Avenue surfaced tensions that are inherent in current practices of bicycle facility planning. These tensions articulate with the larger contradictions of intervening in the built environment to leverage quality of life into capital accumulation. They also revealed how debates about the cyclescape had shifted onto a discursive terrain dominated by economic concerns. This had contradictory effects. On one hand, support for robust bicycle infrastructure brings together a rising bloc of young in-migrants, a subgroup of planners won over to livability, "quality-of-life"-oriented grassroots organizations, key political figures, and, most important, small business owners whose establishments are cultural hubs of this social world. But on the other hand, older, more car-dependent residents, typically homeowners, who feared overflow from restricted parking supply, offered resistance to these plans, as did business owners, who saw their customers in the same light. The latter especially viewed the existing configuration of the street, especially the supply of parking, as critical to commercial viability, and they mobilized their economic power, which was in many ways waning, to block any changes.

The generalization of the "Valencia epiphany" helped the advocates' case significantly. When we spoke in 2013, Jason Patton was tentative about making an economic argument, though he did hint at that direction: "Bicycling supports local business. People are not bicycling to Walnut Creek to shop.... Beyond that, I think the lifestyle angle has a lot of potential, and you have companies choosing to locate in a particular place because they want a lifestyle that can attract high-quality employees." But at that time he saw Valencia Street as a unique situation that couldn't easily transfer to Oakland. While he did not use the Drennen study in his own outreach work in Oakland, he concurred that the economic role of bicycle infrastructure was now common sense among planners:

> [It] was one of the early [studies of the economic benefits of bicycle facilities], and so it circulated a lot, and then Valencia went through this massive transformation, and how much of that is the cause or the effect of the road diet, who knows? Because things were simply changing. And I think that if you already believe the argument you don't really care that maybe San Francisco is or isn't different from everywhere else.[58]

Max Hunter, Bike East Bay's membership and volunteer director at the time, echoed this convergence of economic and political interests, recalling that a local politician had surprised him by thanking him for his efforts in promoting economic growth.[59] Before the 2000s, when the relationship between bike culture, style, and gentrification solidified, such a statement would have been strange. Now advocates and planners at all levels regard it as common sense.

Street design options for Telegraph were completed in early 2014 and displayed at "open houses" in the Temescal area that spring. The form of public engagement was designed to minimize the adversarial nature of the traditional public meeting—but arguably also to insulate planners from contestation. At each open house, representatives from the consulting firms hired by the city to facilitate the meeting circulated around the room, explaining designs and possible modifications. Designs were displayed on easels around the edges of the room, while at the center were long tables with butcher paper, markers, and letter-size versions of the posters. Also on every table were copies of *Economic Benefits of Sustainable Streets*, a report from the New York Department of Transportation, and *Protected Bike Lanes Mean Business* from PeopleForBikes, both of which made the economic case for bicycle improvements that stretched all the way back to Valencia Street (Figure 17). While the posters covered several different elements of the street (like loading conditions, improved pedestrian crossings, and transit improvements), the bicycle element was the undeniable centerpiece of the project and its greatest political liability.

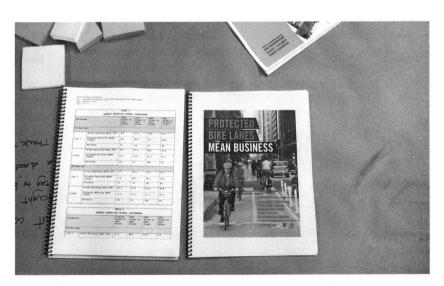

Figure 17. *Protected Bike Lanes Mean Business*, a report by PeopleForBikes, on a table at a Telegraph Bikeways Project open house, April 2014. Photograph by the author.

128   INSTITUTIONAL POWER, INTRACLASS CONFLICT

Explanations of the designs were firmly on the terrain of business. One poster framed the new design as a way to "Grow Business Without Growing Congestion": "Complete streets can help Telegraph Avenue's ongoing transformation from a place people just want to get *through* to a place they want to get *to*" (emphasis added). Another read, "New businesses are creating a more walkable, enjoyable environment for pedestrians on Telegraph Avenue, with new restaurants, cafes, bars, yoga and fitness studios, clothing shops, galleries, etc.," and held that bicycle volumes would stand to increase with business development. The presentation also touted bike lanes as a way to make the pedestrian realm safer and more pleasant, contributing in this way to the vitality of the commercial corridor as well. One poster featured a "word cloud" showing the most common responses to the question, "What streets in Oakland, the Bay Area, or anywhere in the world do you wish Telegraph Avenue more closely resembled?" Valencia Street was by far the most common response (Figure 18).[60]

The crowds at these open houses were quite homogeneous socioeconomically, and to a great extent ideologically as well. Nevertheless, there were moments of dissent, both muted and open. One African American woman who was not a part of the cyclist crowd noted that pedestrian improvements had been needed for "two, three, four decades," but are only being provided now. She did not raise the issue of gentrification frontally, but the subtext was that only with middle-class white people flocking to the area had road safety finally been placed on the agenda. The more dominant

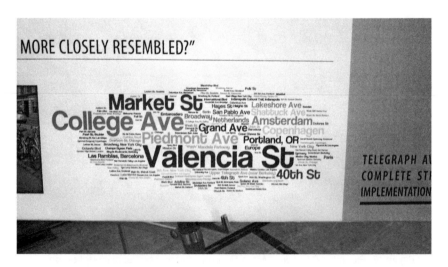

Figure 18. "Word cloud" of survey responses to ideal models for Telegraph Avenue. Photograph by the author.

voices among critics, however, emerged at the second meeting, in the heart of Temescal.[61] Almost as soon as the open house began, several people raised their voices in criticism, forcing reluctant facilitators to field questions, primarily on the issue of parking. One woman said, "You're talking about a solution where there's not enough parking. . . . We keep adding businesses without adding one space." She added, "We've never won once," although it was unclear what battles she was referring to. "You want less people driving," said another wryly, "but you want businesses to grow!" "Streets are important public places. Safe and comfortable can equal economically vibrant streets," the facilitator argued, adding, "Every time there's a new business there are more pedestrians." Another woman exclaimed, "People *live* here!" implying that loss of parking would reduce livability. Facilitators reiterated their interest in "balancing the needs of all users." Among a core of older white residents, suspicions persisted. One woman, a property owner, wondered whether the city was withholding badly needed repaving until the project was approved. Another, a twenty-five-year resident, had "heard about a lot of projects" that didn't happen over the years and doubted how real the plan was.[62] An older man asked, "What's next, our houses get torn down for new condos?"

Mistrust of city efforts and outside consultants was clear, but when opponents claimed that Oakland officials were already committed to the plan, they were basically correct. The chief of staff for Council member Dan Kalb, who represents the Temescal neighborhood, affirmed Kalb's support for the project and the opportunities it provided: "Some areas hit rock bottom and I want to be a part of building something new." Despite the outcry, only 5 percent of comment cards collected at the meetings were negative. "It was like a Soviet election," Parks joked.[63] Nevertheless, the vocal critics performed the roles of aggrieved locals "fighting City Hall," in Jane Jacobs's phrasing. Their internally contradictory perspectives cohered around a sense that the city was imposing a plan from outside and forcing existing residents to deal with the congestion resulting from gentrification, despite the fact that these residents directly benefited from owning property in one of the hottest real estate markets in the country. Dave Campbell called their counterproposal, a bike boulevard two blocks away that roughly parallels Telegraph as it passes through a residential neighborhood with no destinations, a "non-starter."[64]

The most outspoken critic was a man at the second meeting, who called out, "There's going to be a lot of neighborhood opposition. Have you looked at alternatives? Have you looked at how this will affect traffic flow and air pollution?" He was Robert Pratt, the veteran cyclist who had led the fight against bike lanes on Telegraph in 1998. Lane reductions, he argued, would cause congestion and reduce efficiency. Moreover, drawing on a standard vehicular cycling argument, he claimed that "segregated" facilities would eventually lead to the exclusion of cyclists from roadways without bike lanes. "There's an agenda being pushed here," he said. At the third open house, held at the Oakland Humanist Hall, Pratt was again in attendance. One attendee raised the 1998 lawsuit, hoping that the business community had changed its position since then. The facilitator replied: "A lot has changed with how bike/ped improvements affect businesses." Pratt responded, "The merchants are opposed to this!" This time a response came from somebody in the crowd: "Streets that are better for biking and walking are better for business!" to which Jamie Parks responded by citing the NYDOT study that had been again distributed to every table.

When I spoke to Pratt, he was suspicious that I would use my work to vilify the plan's detractors, and was clearly concerned that I was a devotee of the new, infrastructural wave of bicycle advocacy. To him, this was a fusion of Critical Mass, which he detested, Bike East Bay, whose politics he saw as "vindictive," and the city, which he claimed was imposing preordained changes to the roadway via the charade of a nominally public meeting. Regarding the CEQA suit, he said vehemently, "We used environmental law, like they do, to stop their arrogant scheme that causes congestion and in some cases reduces cyclist safety."[65] Here, the contradictions of the economic narrative of livability and the technological function of the street emerge in sharp relief through a populist motif. By identifying traffic-calming efforts on Telegraph as an outside imposition, Pratt and other vocal opponents attempted to rally those who had played a major role in crafting the area's image and nurturing its property market, and who feared the change that, ironically, their success had sown.[66]

When the final draft plans were unveiled at two public meetings in September 2014, it was bicycle advocates' turn to be angry. The plan divided Telegraph into three segments with different characteristics. The middle segment, in the heart of Temescal, the draft plan called for shared lane markings—"sharrows"—in the right lane.[67] According to this design, bicycles, sixty-foot articulated buses, and parking cars would compete for space, suddenly forced to coexist after remaining separated by bike lanes for thirty blocks in either direction. From the perspective of vocal cyclists at these two meetings, this solution was unacceptable. Several even hissed and jeered when the design was announced. Even beyond the controversial sharrows, the "maximal" proposal of protected cycle tracks was rejected in favor of bike lanes with a two-foot painted buffer and flexible posts but no protection from parking maneuvers. To one angry cyclist, this design was "radical for the 1990s" and "a missed opportunity for cycle tracks." "The city needs them, Telegraph needs them," he said. Dave Campbell voiced Bike East Bay's position: "Do you envision a future for Oakland where twenty to thirty percent of all trips are done by bicycle? Do you want people who are 'interested but concerned'?[68] Then you need cycle tracks." To bicycle advocates, the proposed street configuration would discourage new cyclists from using the street, which would be an enormous liability given the planned expansion of Bay Area Bike Share to the East Bay (see chapter 6). In other words, while established cyclists voiced their concerns based on their own experiences, the draft did not depict a street that could make new cyclists, the main goal of current advocates.

Moreover, it was a configuration that highlighted the contradictions of Telegraph's multiple functions in the broader Oakland street fabric. From a street performance standpoint, therefore, the only reasonable compromise—parking removal—was the only option outside of consideration. Because of entrenched merchant and property interests, the process pitted bicycles and public transit against each other for scraps of street space. As the facilitator put it, "We know that this isn't ideal. But from past experience and from outreach to businesses, we've heard concerns about the loss of parking." Within this situation of politically enforced scarcity, bicycle advocacy engages on the only front available by claiming the economic value of cyclists as both elements of a more human-scale flow of traffic and a valuable customer base that has gone ignored. While the frontal assault on parking, which some in Bike East Bay and WOBO hope for, is unlikely to happen, the political alignment of bicycle-oriented infrastructural change with a more comprehensive economic development strategy for the corridor is more or less secure, even if incomplete in this case.

In all of the debates about Telegraph Avenue, the street's ability to sustain livability through infill development without congestion was at stake. Telegraph represents the maturation of the Valencia epiphany: from a pragmatic bargaining chip used with dubious merchants to a sense that the bicycle is part of a larger, systemically integrated shift underway. The contest is ultimately about whose class interests will win out, refracted through the technology of the street as both a facilitator of movement and a place of belonging. The bicycle's position in this struggle is contingent, but it has been made necessary as advocates and policymakers have articulated it into the "chain of equivalences" that comprise the world-class city.[69] The circulation of the discourse inherited from Valencia Street did not simply part the waters for bicycle infrastructure to unfold over urban space unimpeded. Nor have widely endorsed NACTO planning guidelines simply altered how the technology of the street is produced. Instead, claims about the economic benefits of cycling widen the field of battle, running up against entrenched power and exposing competing fractions within the process of gentrification.

Epilogue

After disappointment in the design recommendations released in 2014, which removed separated bikeways from the final design, advocates regrouped and pushed for their return. Narratives in comments on Streetsblog were not just about the technical characteristics of the street but argued that Oakland's conservatism on street design belied its self-identification as a progressive city.[70] In December 2014, after further meetings before an angry, mobilized bicycle community, the City Council unanimously passed a plan that called for a road diet between Uptown and the southernmost part of Temescal, including parking protected bike lanes in the least congested stretch of Telegraph, between Nineteenth and Twenty-ninth Streets just north of the Uptown area (where the pop-up had been placed the previous year). Advocates celebrated this victory and the potential that the rest of the corridor would be revisited too.[71]

Part of the reason that this stretch of Telegraph is less constrained is that the area is poorer and much of the commercial strip has less traffic and lower parking demand. It has many older businesses serving low-income and/or immigrant residents, as well as a large amount of subsidized housing. At the same time, by 2015 the area was growing rapidly, with four major new mixed-used developments underway, plunging vacancy rates, new bars and restaurants, and the monthly arts and culture festival Art Murmur. The KONO community benefits district, formed in 2007, was also a firm supporter of bicycle infrastructure on Telegraph from the start. The business case for bicycle infrastructure was a decisive motivating factor, particularly the spectacular quality of the infrastructure demonstration. After the approval of protected lanes, KONO was clearly eager to host Oakland's foray into "world class" infrastructure, which they expected would "increase the sales for district businesses, according to several studies from around the country."[72] As Oakland bike advocate Chris Kidd put it, "Once other neighborhoods and business districts see the overwhelmingly positive outcome of protected bike lanes ... they'll start asking, 'Why don't we have those?' Putting a real-world example on the ground in Oakland is just the beginning."[73]

In early May 2016, just in time for Bike to Work Day, Mayor Libby Schaaf, Councilwoman Lynnette Gibson-McElhaney, KONO executive director Shari Godinez, René Rivera of Bike East Bay, and traffic engineer

Vlad Wladowski spoke at a ribbon cutting for the new protected bike lanes. Each of them affirmed the economic importance of the infrastructure, from Schaaf's celebration of Oakland as a "vibrant and sustainable city," to Gibson-McElhaney's anticipation of "increasing our commerce and livability" in her district, to Godinez's praise for the process, in which the city "[took] into consideration the concerns of our business owners. . . . It appears our business owners have embraced the biking community." Rivera looked forward to the lanes "bring[ing] new people to Oakland to explore KONO and Temescal and help them thrive." These statements summarized the new common sense of bicycle planning, as did Bike East Bay's exhortation to follow up as "good bike ambassadors": "It's time to try out Telegraph's bike lanes if you haven't already and stop by any of the unique businesses in the KONO Community Improvement District. The new lanes place you practically within arm's reach of many unique ethnic markets, restaurants, new night spots, art galleries, and of course First Fridays [Art Murmur]."[74] To be sure, economic revitalization is the bread and butter of political theater, so it is no surprise that a contentious project courting skeptical businesses would elicit these kinds of statements. At a deeper level, however, we can see how the seemingly technocratic terrain of sociotechnical change is shaped by the demands of fractions of capital whose power lies at different scales, all within a city dependent on a "good business climate."[75] In other words, the long itinerary from Critical Mass to the Telegraph Bikeways project is in part about redefining the infrastructural content of such a climate.

A Tale of Two Mobilities

The development of bicycle infrastructure in Oakland's core reinforces the spatial congregation of valued bodies and valued property, exposing the stark divisions between those zones of the city receiving heightened investment and those that appear to be discarded. While Oakland's bicycle master plan mandates network coverage throughout the city, most infrastructural investment, both in in-street facilities and parking, has concentrated in areas of high ridership, especially the north-south corridors connecting Berkeley and downtown Oakland.[76] The concentration of investment oriented toward the CBD contrasts sharply with the neglect of car- and bus-dependent East Oakland, where people on bicycles, primarily of color, face freeway-like conditions on surface streets and must often ride on sidewalks (Figure 19 and Map 9). Over 100,000 people—a quarter of the city's population and a third of its people of color—live in the flatlands east of High Street, but less than 1 percent of workers there commute

Figure 19. Sidewalk riding on International Boulevard in East Oakland, 2014. Photograph by the author.

by bicycle, and city bicycle counts show uniformly low numbers of cyclists east of Lake Merritt.[77] Along with fewer BART stations than Oakland's core, the number of cyclists connecting to BART is lower and has grown less rapidly than in North Oakland.[78] Meanwhile, since 2011 the number of bicycle facilities in East Oakland has increased somewhat, but so has political ambivalence about their value.[79] In neighborhoods where many people bicycle out of necessity, cyclists are stereotyped as "others": the poor, alcoholics, drug dealers, or outsider "hipsters," not ordinary working people (see chapter 3). The race–class articulation between bicycling and economic development that now holds sway in bicycle advocacy has less traction where many people bicycle out of need.

Since advocacy for bicycle infrastructure has depended on grassroots networks of cyclists that increase in strength with gentrification, in East Oakland, where white, middle-class in-migration has been slow, bicycle infrastructure appears as part of a suite of larger, top-down transportation projects. One example is the East Bay Bus Rapid Transit (BRT) project. AC Transit launched the project in 2001 with the goal of connecting San

INSTITUTIONAL POWER, INTRACLASS CONFLICT 135

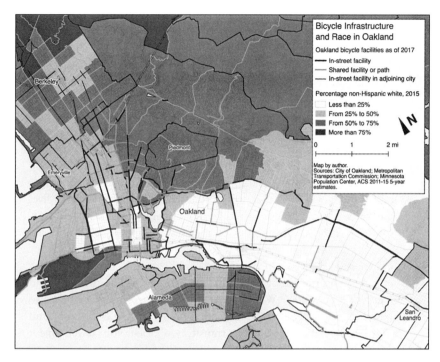

Map 9. Uneven development of bicycle infrastructure in Oakland. Note distinction between in-street facilities (black) and "sharrows" or off-street paths (gray) that do not require reallocation of road space.

Leandro to downtown Oakland via International Boulevard, then continuing to Berkeley via Telegraph, using stations in the center median and all-door boarding to reduce headways.[80] Construction of BRT began in 2016. The project will thoroughly transform the busy arterial, with some of the city's highest numbers of pedestrian and cyclist injuries and fatalities, by reducing travel lanes and parking in some areas and adding bike lanes through some of the corridor. BRT has been celebrated as a much-needed investment and an improvement to the mobility of the over 100,000 residents adjacent to the route.

As the project approached the final design stages in 2012, it met a backlash from street-front merchants along Telegraph, both in Temescal and in Berkeley, in part because the bike lanes planned as part of the project would have reduced parking.[81] In the end, AC Transit dropped the portion connecting to Berkeley because of these concerns, instead adopting a truncated plan for BRT through East Oakland alone.[82] As in 1998, merchant opposition had altered the process of reconfiguring street technology, stalling a wave of spatial reorganization intending to adapt Oakland's infrastructure to a less car-based mode of growth.[83] Merchants on International Boulevard in East Oakland, overwhelmingly small proprietors of color, were less successful in modifying the project. As part of the planning process, the city organized the Oakland Sustainable Neighborhoods Initiative (OSNI) to coordinate "equitable development," partnering with the Alameda County Department of Public Health, East Bay Housing Organizations, East Bay Asian Local Development Corporation, transportation justice organization TransForm, and Bike East Bay.[84] However, not unlike the merchants on Telegraph, business owners along International were also concerned about the impact of BRT construction. At a 2013 public meeting called by OSNI, attended by around seventy-five, most of them African American and Latino residents of the neighborhood, the loudest concerns were about what they saw as an insufficient business impact mitigation plan, which was to provide $20 million in funds for businesses disrupted by construction. As on Telegraph, the voices in the room were concerned about the outreach process, feeling that they had been taken by surprise.[85] While the AC Transit representative worked to allay their concerns, calling the mitigation plan "a living document" and a major opportunity ("Here's your transit, now orient your development on this transit"), many there regarded BRT with suspicion at best.

While the focus is on BRT, bike lanes have a complicated relationship to the project and could be politically vulnerable in the event of rising contention. More broadly, the more organized, wealthier, and largely white Temescal property owners were able to resist BRT not just because of their social power but because their gamble was likely to pay off: even without transit improvements, the area's property boom is secure. Moreover, wealthy neighborhoods are as likely to appropriate moral narratives of injury as any others, allowing them to shunt infrastructure interventions onto other places.[86] In other words, in the context of urban planning, the grammar of contentious politics has been detached from the social base of poor people and people of color who opposed midcentury urban renewal. The less organized, less politically connected residents of East Oakland face a much different scenario. The elements of BRT they see as unfavorable, accurately or not, come with much-needed investment and improved transit service, even if it spurs gentrification as East Oakland becomes the city's last relatively affordable "frontier." As the history of infrastructural investment in Oakland shows, politically marginalized residents do not easily or quietly weather the "creative destruction" that comes with such plans.

These processes underpin the vernacular identification of bicycle infrastructure with wrenching change. When talking to her membership, Jenna

Burton of Red, Bike and Green describes bike lanes in the following way: "Taking up this space is a reminder that new bike lanes obviously weren't built for you, because if they had been they would have been there a long time ago. But they're yours now and you aren't going anywhere."[87] This contestation of the racialization of infrastructure speaks to how investment in the cyclescape has been led by and served primarily white inmigrants to "up-and-coming" neighborhoods, creating a fraught political landscape for further expansion.

The renewal of Oakland's bicycle master plan (under consideration as of this writing) has raised the specter of gentrification anew. However, recognizing the fraught moment, their lack of local political support, and their responsibilities to spatial justice, planners ceded a substantial amount of control over the outreach process to community-based organizations like the Scraper Bike Team, Cycles of Change, and the East Oakland Collective. This yielded a set of conversations that were substantially different from the business narratives in North Oakland. Instead of excitement about a booming economy, residents looked coolly on "world-class" infrastructure and instead advocated broader practices of infrastructural care (more rapid repaving, glass cleanup, youth programming, and support for bike shops), with a healthy skepticism for what better infrastructure would mean for their communities. As one planner involved with the project put it, there was "not a lot of interest in fancy protected bikeways on major streets because of concerns for displacement."[88] This recalls Winifred Curran and Trina Hamilton's concept of "just green enough": material improvements to the urban environment that fall short of commodifiable amenities and benefit existing rather than future residents.[89]

Amid residential segregation along race–class lines, bicycle infrastructure becomes a physical reminder of the unevenness of municipal investment and an ideological motif that demonstrates the city's aggressive promotion of some neighborhoods and neglect of others. Advocates of bicycle-led revitalization ignore or minimize these histories at their peril. Gentrification in Oakland is directly tied to the co-production of race and space, within which people of color, particularly African Americans and Latinos, have consistently been on the losing end of infrastructural change. As in North Portland or Humboldt Park in Chicago, there is no reason for residents of East Oakland to see bike lanes, promoted by a movement with white leadership and associated with processes of gentrification, as any different.[90] At the same time, bicycle advocates have sought alliances with growth-machine actors like SPUR and translocal organizations like NACTO precisely because their position within the ensemble of urban power remains tenuous. This gives an outsize impression of the centrality of bicycle infrastructure to the gentrification process, while simultaneously broadening support among the young, liberal professional class for the urban transformations necessary for the city to remain competitive in the new economy.

As in chapter 4, it is important here to recall earlier moments in the restructuring of urban space in Oakland. The federal Model Cities program in the 1960s, which required "maximum feasible participation" in response to the destructiveness of the first wave of urban renewal, articulated together the very radical currents it was intended to demobilize.[91] Movements against the extension of the Grove Shafter Freeway in the 1970s and 1980s similarly galvanized political fragments in opposition to infrastructural racism.[92] More recently, in the 1990s, the Latino Unity Council in the Fruitvale neighborhood successfully transformed a plan for expanding BART into Fruitvale Village, creating a model for community-driven, affordable, transit-oriented development.[93]

Against this backdrop, mobilization around bicycle infrastructure planning in Oakland's neighborhoods looks quite different. The subtle passage of bicycle advocacy from a radical promotion of human-scale mobility to the vanguard of development discourse must be considered in terms of the historical commitments of the city. Up through the Brown administration, city leaders focused on the rejuvenation of downtown, first with office development and later with transit-oriented housing and entertainment clusters in the New Urbanist mold. Claiming the value of cyclists for localized patterns of neighborhood growth, on Valencia Street, Telegraph Avenue, or International Boulevard, appears to be a great departure from this tradition. However, presenting certain cyclists as key economic actors makes the neighborhoods they shape legible as investable spaces. This chapter has argued that these two dynamics are at this point almost impossible to disentangle.

By the same token, this turn was not automatic. Federal programs to increase active transportation are filtered through the priorities of states, master planning organizations like the Metropolitan Transportation Commission, and localities such as Oakland or San Francisco. These funds do not automatically conjure a politics that conjoins bicycle planning to economic development, any more than Model Cities automatically conjured Black radicalism in Oakland. Rather, they become points of struggle over how urban space is produced, and over what the role of the state and the polity as defined will be in that process. In places where they have yet to succeed, like Temescal, the discourse of the value of bicycle infrastructure has strengthened in the contest between two visions of capitalist growth.

In places like East Oakland, where bicycle advocates have yet to produce comprehensive infrastructure plans, significant resident skepticism can be explained in part by the race–class dynamics of how cycling has achieved prominence, along with a general distrust of plans emanating from the city. What appears self-evident now to both advocates and city officials—that bicyclists signal economic vitality—was in fact made through a discursive and material process to which gentrification was critical. In essence, it was not the aggrieved poor but the rising middle classes who mobilized around this wave of federal spending.

Therefore, the entanglement of bicycle advocacy with gentrification did not simply happen because middle-class and professional whites moved to disinvested urban cores and began bicycling. But as gentrification has accelerated, due mainly to forces beyond the bicycle, the framing of bicycle infrastructure as an economic development strategy has become increasingly persuasive, and cities now act upon this narrative in ways that do contribute to gentrification. What was originally a pragmatic approach to property interests with the power to halt the planning process is now a commonsense understanding within bicycle advocacy. An entire epistemic infrastructure connects national, regional, and local advocacy, design firms, and consultants via online "communities of consciousness."[94] Mayors draw on evidence from other successful cities, municipal bicycle-pedestrian planners bring in comrades from elsewhere to convince skeptical colleagues, and advocacy organizations import outreach techniques and materials from throughout the advocacy world. Local efforts draw on the authority of these long networks, while broader organizations depend on localized successes for evidence that cycling helps a city's bottom line. The sites where these claims achieve traction, however, are racialized landscapes undergoing rapid flux, places where the question of who belongs to the new city is answered with infrastructure. In this way, a new regime of livable streets is incompletely worked into the broader reorganization of urban space that Oakland is now pursuing.

The stakes of livable streetscaping become clear when considering what kinds of subjects already use bicycles in the areas of Oakland experiencing gentrification, compared to whose mobility the bike lanes anticipate. Just west of Telegraph Avenue, beneath the "MacArthur Maze," the various overpasses that connect the MacArthur and Grove Shafter Freeways, is an infrastructural netherworld within a stone's throw of some of Oakland's most rapid gentrification. Here dozens if not hundreds of people live in lean-tos, in tents, or out under blankets, between periodic clearances by the police. Among them bicycles are ubiquitous, enabling relatively rapid movement for people who cannot afford bus fare and facilitating the recycling of scrap metal through which many make do. Until 2016 the destination of these recyclers was Alliance Metals, a recycling center at the northern end of West Oakland. Living nearby as a graduate student from 2008 to 2012, I frequently watched recyclers negotiate complex traffic, speed bumps, road debris, and hostile drivers as they towed their cargo. No infrastructure has been installed to make these cyclists' daily rounds safer. No advocates seek these cyclists' opinions on where infrastructure should be located. Nobody courts the support of small business owners by touting the value of recyclers' discretionary income. In the context of contemporary bike culture, they are not "cyclists" but just people who use bikes, and their dilapidated machines are as likely to be stolen as trash-picked and cobbled together. These "invisible cyclists" do not appear as infrastructural publics.[95] In fact, they themselves constitute a "noxious use" to members of the local neighborhood association and have been a frequent topic of neighborhood meetings and online invectives alike.[96]

In 2014, the City of Oakland completed work on the West Oakland Specific Plan, a comprehensive plan for the West Oakland Redevelopment Area and the former Oakland Army Base supported by a $2 million federal grant.[97] A core mission of the plan was to reduce the environmental burdens experienced by current residents as well as in-movers to the numerous developments planned for this deeply disinvested industrial neighborhood. Public comment on the plan showed that residents were both supportive of better bicycle facilities and eager to see recycling operations like Alliance relocated.[98] The final plan did just this, relocating recycling facilities to the Oakland Army Base redevelopment site and reconfiguring major corridors as complete streets. Thus, bicycle infrastructure arrived just as Alliance Metals and no fewer than ten other recycling facilities disappeared from the area. Some of those who already used bicycles for their daily rounds likely saw their livelihoods further eroded by this change.

This sorting of cyclists into valued and devalued populations is a process without a single author. It is produced in a crucible of dramatic neighborhood change, the need to transform streets in order to enable more concentrated development, the politicization of the environmentalist dimensions of bicycle usage, and a history of racialized dispossession. In recent decades, bicycle advocates have made strong claims to mattering in urban space—to meriting the allocation of resources and arrangement of space into durable configurations that reduce the likelihood of their avoidable deaths. These claims have taken on an economic vocabulary that depends on an articulation of race, class, age, and geography that marks the ascendancy of certain cyclists as the city's future. But the political labor that it will require for advocates to make good on their claims to social justice, which go far beyond the bicycle, has only just begun.

CHAPTER SIX

Bicycle Sharing Systems as Already-Splintered Infrastructure

On a warm night in June 2017, I am riding a bikeshare bike along a quiet side street in Southwest Detroit, a low-income, dense, and lively Latino neighborhood just west of rapidly gentrifying Corktown. The street is quiet enough that I am the only traffic, and a group of Latino men in their teens and twenties plays a pickup game of basketball under a streetlight. The other side of the street is vacant. I pass by without interrupting the game, nodding wordlessly to the players. After I pass, one of the men yells, "White people!" the way one might call out, "Car!"—perhaps a mock warning directed at his friends, or a comment on the changing neighborhood. I do not stop to ask.

I turn at the next intersection and arrive at my destination: a shiny new station of MoGo, Detroit's bikeshare system launched in May 2017. This station, situated on a bustling corner adjacent to beautiful Clark Park, is the westernmost station in the MoGo system but lies at the easternmost edge of Latino Southwest Detroit proper. Across the street from the station is El Club, a hipster bar recently opened by a Los Angeles transplant, where I grab a slice of pizza and a beer while an indie rock band plays to a young, mostly white, alternative crowd. Leaving the bar, I get back on a MoGo and ride east toward the lights of downtown. Perhaps other patrons of El Club also arrived by bikeshare, but I don't see any. It is equally possible that the men I passed playing basketball are bicyclists or even MoGo users. Yet the man who called out attuned me to my position as what Melody Hoffmann calls a "rolling signifier" in this place, and the bike itself—a novel infrastructure investment spearheaded largely by downtown interests—matters for this performance.[1]

This chapter explores the ways in which bikeshare planning both challenges and reinforces the spatialization of race and class through an examination of systems in Philadelphia, Detroit, and Oakland. First, though planners envision bikeshare systems as a way to transform daily mobility, they are planned based on existing patterns of uneven development, both at the regional and the neighborhood level, which shape where networks can be efficiently deployed. This leads bikeshare facilities to cluster largely in central business districts and the gentrifying residential neighborhoods that surround them. Second, in the networks of policy experimentation, recognition of these inequalities has led to the construction and circulation of new models for increasing "equity" in bikeshare. Philadelphia has taken on the role of standard bearer in these networks, within which philanthropic institutions have played a key role in offsetting the costs of extending bikeshare beyond downtown. However, the *translation* of these models to other places is often selective, privileging spectacular elements like subsidized memberships rather than mundane funding issues that shape the geography of the resulting systems. The entanglement of bikeshare system planning with inequalities on the ground reveals the gaps between the now-dominant "equity" frame and questions of substantive spatial justice.[2]

In this respect, bicycle sharing systems amplify the contradictions of bicycle infrastructure provision outlined in the previous chapters. While bicycle users can and do ride anywhere and, once painted, bike lanes are largely costless, bikeshare-systems use purpose-built fleets that necessitate a dedicated network of docking stations and are operated (and sometimes owned) by independent providers under contract with the municipality. This raises the issue of efficient performance, because bikeshare systems require constant labor to manage and maintain, which subjects location decisions to expectations of demand and revenue generation. Because bikeshare systems are not federally obligated to act as public utilities, and indeed some are entirely private, extending their benefits beyond professional strata in gentrifying neighborhoods requires political will and supplementary funding, even in cases where they are municipally owned.[3] Overcoming the requirement of revenue neutrality enlarges the role that corporations and large institutions play in infrastructure provision, both as visibly branded sponsors and behind the scenes in planning and funding.[4] More broadly, bikeshare betrays a neoliberal shift away from comprehensive mobility access and in favor of efficiency.[5] At the same time, the bikeshare planning process creates openings, often unintentionally, in which conditions of uneven development can be politicized. Thus, in practice bikeshare planning demonstrates what Jamie Peck and Nik Theodore call the "institutional *and political* indeterminacy" of the outcomes of policy circulation and experimentation.[6] Nevertheless, the constraints imposed by a neoliberal framework of action are real, and they limit the social benefits, and redistributive potential, of such policy efforts.

Bicycle Sharing: From DIY Commoning to Platform Capitalism

Ironically, given their attractiveness to the contemporary urban growth machine, modern bikeshare systems originated in commoning experiments. For example, "first-generation" bikeshare, like Amsterdam's White Bike Plan proposed by the anarchist Provo group in 1965, were more like political statements, with freely distributed bicycles that quickly disappeared.[7] The "second generation" of coin-deposit bikeshare system with dedicated docks, such as Copenhagen's Bycyken, were launched in the 1990s in Scandinavia by municipalities themselves. The "third generation" in the 2000s introduced distinctive, purpose-built bicycles and electronic docking stations with computerized kiosks, accessible by on-the-spot credit card checkout or yearly subscription for unlimited short trips, with a membership tied to the user's bank card.[8] The most well-known early examples of this third wave are Paris's Vélib' (2007), Barcelona's Bicing (2007), and Montréal's BIXI (2009).

These technological shifts reflected the growing sophistication—and falling costs—of the digital technologies that power these schemes, as well as the equipment itself. Bikeshare is relatively inexpensive and simple to install (especially compared to other transit infrastructure), and is placed in the densest parts of already built-up urban areas to facilitate quick trips, increase transit access, and alleviate traffic congestion. To maximize system efficiency through the "network effect," stations in these systems are located in areas where they will be well utilized, such as in central business districts, near major institutions and entertainment destinations, and in close proximity to transit (Figure 20).[9] Many of these systems attract title sponsorships, often from advertising firms and banks, giving them revenue-generation capabilities for advertisers. Underscoring their sudden popularity among cities in Europe, the *New York Times* wrote in 2008 that there were "only two kinds of mayors: those who have a bicycle-sharing program and those who want one."[10]

Bike sharing first came to the United States as a pilot program during the 2008 Democratic National Convention in Denver, which was made permanent in 2010. Minneapolis and Washington, D.C., followed shortly afterward.[11] With the arrival of New York's Citi Bike system in 2013, which proved that bikeshare was good business rather than just a cosmetic investment in sustainability, bikeshare entered the mainstream of urban mobility planning and growth machine politics more broadly.[12] By

Figure 20. Indego bikeshare station in a "tactical urbanist" pedestrian plaza on Grays Ferry Avenue in Philadelphia, June 2017.

January 2017, more than two hundred bikeshare systems were planned or in operation across the country.[13] While many of these systems are managed by local nonprofits, corporate interest in these systems grew rapidly over the course of the 2010s. The lead firm in the industry is Motivate, a for-profit firm that from 2015 to 2018 was owned by ReqX Ventures, a partnership between a luxury real estate developer and a high-end fitness center chain.[14] ReqX's CEO Jeff Blau explained his investment in bikeshare: "As cities do well, we do well."[15]

The three systems discussed below vary substantially. Philadelphia's system, Indego, was purchased with city funds, less common among American bikeshare systems, and its robust, municipally led planning process and subsidized low-income memberships have made it a model for equitable bikeshare planning. Detroit's MoGo, which launched in May 2017, is one of the country's newest major station-based bikeshare systems. Though consciously modeled on Indego, MoGo was spearheaded by downtown corporations and philanthropic institutions with significantly less public involvement. Finally, Ford GoBike, a privately owned and operated regional system serving San Francisco, San Jose, Berkeley, Emeryville, and Oakland, expanded the Bay Area's publicly funded pilot, launched in 2013, from seven hundred to seven thousand bikes in July 2017. Planners and city leaders celebrated it as "the most equitable bikeshare system in the country," but its launch was marred by vandalism, controversy over gentrification, and criticism of its accountability to the public.[16] In short, the incorporation of "equity" does not quell the fractious spatial politics of bikeshare but expands them.

Bikeshare as Splintering Urbanism

A basic tension in transportation is the trade-off between system efficiency and accessibility.[17] In other words, a transportation system that maximizes the number of passengers per vehicle will necessarily be temporally and spatially limited, but efficient, while one that maximizes the number of passengers reached will be temporally and spatially accessible, but potentially inefficient. This is at its core a sociotechnical question concerning the "affordances" and constraints of the system and how they distribute motility in urban space.[18] "Motility" refers here to how infrastructure articulates with differences in social power to shape the capacity to move.[19] For example, suburban areas have abundant automobile infrastructure, but only those with access to a vehicle can take advantage of these facilities. For others, the mobility landscape is actually worsened.[20]

The Neoliberalization of Mobility Infrastructure

Bikeshare is emblematic of already "splintered" infrastructure provision, in an era where public-private partnerships have dramatically expanded the control of nominally public goods by private actors and eroded the capital base of the public sector.[21] One of the salient features of this enlarged private role is the breakdown of urban "spatial Keynesianism" in favor of a more "entrepreneurial" orientation toward public services like mobility.[22] Municipal and regional leaders subject to fiscal austerity approach infrastructure investment as a mechanism for increasing urban competitiveness. At the same time, they are reluctant to expend public funds on these investments. In this way, the requirements of the private sector, particularly efficiency and financial sustainability, directly affect the spatial coverage of infrastructure.

This does not mean that all public-private partnerships in mobility infrastructure display the same spatial effects. Instead, the partnership itself is a field of power, and the resulting infrastructure is shaped by the balance of forces between actors involved, including the city and other government bodies, the provider firm, and institutions and other groups mobilized by the planning process.[23] In the case of bikeshare, spatial coverage is directly influenced by cost structure, equipment ownership, title sponsorship, grants and subsidies, and operational targets. In other words, the neoliberal framework for action—flexibility, revenue neutrality, and entrepreneurialism—

does not necessarily prevent broader considerations of accessibility and spatial justice so much as subject them to the same logic, such as by funding equity initiatives through competitive grants. While bikeshare planning has adapted to these constraints and delivered tangible benefits to marginalized residents of some cities, the scope of such action remains limited. Even with many working-class residents enjoying subsidized access, bikeshare remains tied primarily to central business districts and their immediate surroundings.

As infrastructure, however, bikeshare systems occupy an interstitial role. They are large enough investments to affect motility in key locations in the urban fabric but not large enough to *shape* patterns of construction and investment on their own—thus affecting accessibility—as highway and rail networks do. Thus they build on existing patterns of uneven development. Planners assess bikeshare demand based on residential density, destinations (employment centers, commercial districts, and major institutions), and existing transportation infrastructure, including bicycle facilities. Furthermore, because they depend overwhelmingly on "walk-up" rides, typically by tourists and other casual users who cross-subsidize the rest of the system, extending to areas without numerous destinations exacts a penalty. Bikeshare therefore privileges the central business district and its immediate surroundings, tending to bypass both elite enclaves—which are low in density by design—and poor neighborhoods that are not gentrifying— which are low in density due to disinvestment. But due to the uneven geography of gentrification, zones of feasibility may "stretch" to include outlying poles of growth, while "valleys" of insufficient density form within the ostensible radius of the service area. These valleys may be offset by additional grant funding, but according to strict efficiency considerations, they are likely to underperform. Thus, while bikeshare is hailed as a "last mile" solution to improve transit access, it remains concentrated in the areas that are already poles of accumulation and relative transit density, rather than more broadly increasing accessibility to regional mass transit facilities beyond these nodes.[24]

The geography of bikeshare has roots in a longer history of racialized investment in the built environment as well. The prime residential areas for bikeshare, which are proximal to the central business district and major infrastructure, tend to have been those neighborhoods previously graded "C" ("yellow-lined") or "D" ("redlined") under the federal mortgage insurance guidelines that shaped the postwar housing industry.[25] These areas, starved of investment from the 1930s through the late 1970s, now form the gentrification "frontier." Ironically, this underinvestment also justifies the placement of bikeshare stations in these historically "underserved" neighborhoods, regardless of current development trajectories.[26] In other words, bikeshare service areas track the current intensive "seesaw" path of uneven development, while the extensive, car-dependent postwar suburbs, which are becoming more racially diverse, have limited access to this infrastructure.[27]

Experiments with Bikeshare Equity in the Neoliberal Sandbox

As noted in previous chapters, the restructuring of the urban policymaking landscape in the era of neoliberalization has created both unprecedented latitude for experimentation and a narrowed terrain of possibility. The "denationalization" of urban policy has led to increasingly rapid circulation of policy models, often upsetting presumed hierarchies of core and periphery. Due to a combination of pragmatic experimentation and deference to global "best practices," what Jamie Peck and Nik Theodore call "fast policy" tends toward "experimental churning within narrow (financial, institutional, ideological) parameters."[28] We might refer to bikeshare in this vein as "fast infrastructure." But its material properties as infrastructure make it both more uniform across systems and more flexible in context.[29]

At the same time, because bikeshare is physical infrastructure embedded in the built environment, with a wide potential user base and a spectacular quality, often it must enroll larger infrastructural publics into its translation in place than the social programs Peck and Theodore describe.[30] For example, bikeshare implementation mobilizes municipal staff, business communities, philanthropic institutions, and bicycle advocacy networks, as well as potential users, creating points of leverage over the shape of the resulting system. For the most part, however, substantive contestation is fleeting and occurs within established constraints. In instances where contestation does alter the geography of the system—expanding it to serve "unfeasible" areas for political reasons, for example—the costs must be funded in some way, often through philanthropic grants or in-kind contributions by developers and employers. This "social shaping" places essentially undemocratic funding sources, even when more or less benevolent, into leadership roles in developing public infrastructure.[31]

Equity and Spatial Justice

A key feature of contemporary neoliberal American urbanism, to which bikeshare is perfectly adapted, is the hegemony of the extraordinarily malleable "equity" frame amid broadly inequitable development trajectories.[32] In this context, bikeshare is a governmental practice that manages the challenges of adapting the built environment—particularly the geographically inequitable distribution of resources—to changed political-economic conditions.[33] The urban "postpolitical" consensus that Erik Swyngedouw and others have identified, in which technocratic governance is articulated through "participation" with an array of "stakeholders" that are known in advance, both adequately describes and falls short of fully capturing the governmental function of bikeshare.[34]

"Roll-back" neoliberalization, leading to a focus on gentrifying neighborhoods and downtown redevelopment, has partially ruptured the links between poor neighborhoods and the municipal state that were forged by midcentury federal programs like the Great Society.[35] "Roll-out" neoliberalization, in which elements of the planning process are subcontracted to private firms, amplifies the "knowledge gap" between these neighborhoods and the infrastructural public mobilized by bikeshare planning. In short, bikeshare planners often do not know who to talk to when organizing the "participation" process. In some cases, this means that well-organized groups of new residents in gentrifying neighborhoods fulfill these elements. In others, the failure to connect to the "right" neighborhood brokers leads to opposition to and even rejection of infrastructure. Planners are forced to delicately balance their pro-business mandate with a recognition of the material history of infrastructural harm. As one bicycle advocate told me in an email on her experiences with bikeshare planning, "We are trying to be trusted by people who don't trust the city and simultaneously to have a seat at the city's decision-making table."

Equity initiatives in bikeshare planning have two main components. The first involves *social equity*: reducing the barriers to poor and marginalized people who wish to use the system, through outreach and education, discounted memberships, and cash payment systems for the unbanked. Philadelphia and Boston were early pioneers in this realm.[36] The second involves *geographic equity*: extending the bikeshare service area to places that have been historically underserved. With dock-based systems like those considered here, this involves placing stations in areas where they may not perform optimally. In some cases, this is cross-subsidized by revenue from other stations; in others, dedicated funding provides additional stations that stretch the service area.

Neither of these equity modes is immune to rhetorical sleight of hand. Many beneficiaries of subsidized memberships are casual users whose marginal costs to the system are low and deliver intangible benefits like advertising and what might be called "credibility." On the other hand, serving marginalized *places* as a way of serving marginalized *people* has its pitfalls. Many underserved areas are in fact undergoing gentrification, meaning that bikeshare providers are able to meet "equity" goals by placing stations in areas of high potential demand, where they likely would have already been feasible in the near future. Thus the denuded principle of "equity" in practice, separated from its roots in building capacities among the marginalized, exacts very little in terms of spatial justice—conceived as a recognition and overcoming of the mutual embedding of unjust social and spatial relations.[37]

Bikeshare Facilities and the Uneven Development of Motility

All bikeshare planners (particularly in the United States) must work with a constrained and uneven built environment, with a correspondingly uneven capacity to support a functioning system, even in the densest areas near the central business district (CBD). Key factors like population, employment, and commercial density, transit service, and existing patterns of bicycle use are cumulatively self-reinforcing. This is not simply a technical issue, however, because the willingness and ability of operators to absorb the costs of expanding beyond high-demand service areas is a political question that affects where infrastructure is located and who it serves. This raises the issue of not only existing patterns of growth but also the inclination of state, private, and nongovernmental actors to counteract the efficiency requirements embedded in the public–private partnership model. While bikeshare systems are relatively expensive compared to bike lanes, they are a bargain compared to almost any other transit investment.[38] The limitations facing more comprehensive coverage are thus political and institutional, not abstractly fiscal.

Public Ownership and Locational Flexibility in Philadelphia

In Philadelphia, initial support for bikeshare came from highly vocal and well connected advocates, most notably Russell Meddin, who began pushing for bikeshare in Philadelphia after a visit to Lyon in 2005. As early as 2008 the municipal government took an active role in planning and development, with a great deal of behind-the-scenes cajoling from Meddin.[39] Nevertheless, staff treated the system they were planning like a public utility. Planning was done in public as well, with an outspoken commitment from city leaders like Mayor Michael Nutter, and especially Deputy Mayor of Transportation and Utilities Rina Cutler, to serve all Philadelphians.[40] This included open debate and the commissioning of a study of potential business models by the city council and ultimately the appropriation of city funds to support capital investment.[41] This is not to say Philadelphia's approach is not neoliberal, but it does give the system and its institutional framework a different character.

150 BICYCLE SHARING AS SPLINTERED INFRASTRUCTURE

The council-commissioned study called bikeshare a "critical component of both an efficient circulation system and a healthy development environment," and key to Philadelphia's "evolution into a vibrant 24-hour city."[42] Based on GIS analysis of population and job density and proximity to tourist attractions, parks and recreation, and transit, the study recommended "core" (high demand) and "expanded" (lower or intermittent demand) market areas (Figure 21). The core consisted of the main central business district, the museum and cultural district to its northwest, historic residential neighborhoods adjacent to the CBD, and higher education clusters at Temple University to the north and the University City District of West Philadelphia. The expanded market area included the more residential areas of University City, rapidly developing parts of the city's inner northeast, and virtually all of South Philadelphia. Notably, the study found very low feasibility measures in poor, largely African American inner North Philadelphia neighborhoods to the east and west of Temple, including the

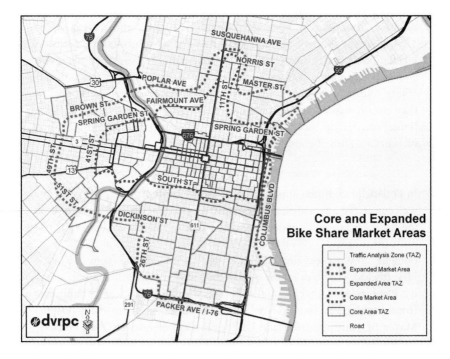

Figure 21. Initial recommendation for the bikeshare market area of Central Philadelphia, 2010. Source: JzTI et al., 2010, *Philadelphia Bikeshare Concept Study*. http://bikesharephiladelphia.org/PhilaStudy/PhiladelphiaBikeshareConceptStudy feb2010.pdf (accessed August 8, 2017).

Strawberry Mansion area, where substantial elements of the Indego system's equity efforts would ultimately focus.[43] While the study recommended phasing outward from the central business district into surrounding residential neighborhoods, the authors expected lower demand in these areas until their development justified station densities comparable to those of the CBD.[44] The authors concluded that public ownership and a nonprofit operator would maximize the "flexibility" to achieve program goals of equitable distribution.[45] A 2013 study by the Toole Design Group reiterated these conclusions, noting the spatial unevenness of bikeshare implementation in other cities, such as Washington, D.C., and how this disadvantaged low-income neighborhoods.[46]

This raised a central tension in any public-private partnership: the degree of up-front capital investment the city would have to undertake. Philadelphia lacked funding for a fully public system like D.C.'s, nor would a fully private system like New York's meet the city's goals of serving residents beyond the usual users of bikeshare: white, middle-class professionals.[47] The City Council and the Mayor's Office of Transportation and Utilities settled on a hybrid solution in which public and philanthropic money would cover capital costs and user fees and sponsorships would support operations.[48] The City Council allocated $3 million to the bikeshare program in anticipation of an additional $4.5 million in state and federal funds and $2.5 million in private and foundation sources.[49] The rest of the roughly $16 million to launch the system and operate it for five years came from the title sponsor, Independence Blue Cross, as did the name: Indego.[50] Local firm Bicycle Transit Systems (BTS), a relative newcomer that had spun off from Motivate, won the contract to manage the system.

Indego launched in April 2015 with seventy stations in the "core" service area, twenty of them in low-income neighborhoods, defined as having median incomes below 150 percent of the federal poverty line. It was also the first bikeshare system in the country to have a fully automated low-income membership program—the $5 a month Access Pass—that did not require an office visit, as well as a cash payment option through 7-Eleven and Family Dollar for members without bank accounts. A $3 million grant as part of the Better Bike Share Partnership facilitated these initiatives, which allowed planners to "sacrifice network efficiency and optimize for equity," as planner Cara Ferrentino put it.[51] The second phase, in 2016, was even more aggressive in pursuing inclusion. With another $1.5 million in grant funding from the William Penn Foundation earmarked to provide access to green space for low-income people, Indego staff placed twenty-four stations in low-income neighborhoods, including the Strawberry Mansion area of North Philadelphia, a deeply disinvested, majority-Black neighborhood well beyond the direct path of gentrification. In 2017 Indego added another fourteen stations, a combination of "infill" and coverage area expansion. A well-funded and "culturally sensitive" outreach and education effort by the Bicycle Coalition of Greater Philadelphia built neighborhood support.[52] While the city plays a major role in system planning, BTS must manage the resulting infrastructure and remain profitable. In order to do so, BTS assesses station performance according to separate categories of what each station is intended to achieve: revenue, ride volume, or "equity." In other words, they evaluate equity-oriented stations differently, creating a finer grain for judging performance rather than applying efficiency criteria across a heterogeneous network.[53] According to Data and Evaluation Manager Claudia Setubal, Indego had committed to the goal of serving existing residents with a flexible and low-cost mobility option, despite the fact that some parts of the service area were less optimal from the standpoint of profitability."[54] As a result of the 2016 expansion, Indego's second year saw a significant increase in ridership, especially among Black users, but not revenue.[55] While planners with the city regarded this as a sign of success, BTS CEO Alison Cohen's enthusiasm, when we spoke, was tempered by concern for Indego's financial sustainability.[56] The 2017 expansion was designed to fill in the network in higher-performing areas to make up for the less efficient "equity" phase.

Old Divisions in the "New Detroit"

The planning of Detroit's bikeshare system, MoGo, which was consciously modeled on Indego, faced even deeper spatial obstacles and fiscal constraints. Bikeshare planning efforts, which began the same year that Detroit became the largest city ever to declare bankruptcy, inherited a landscape of deep racial and economic inequality and a built environment plagued by disinvestment. In this context, and despite the efforts of planners and advocates, bikeshare in Detroit follows an established theme in planning the "shrinking city," exemplified by the "right-sizing" paradigm of the Detroit Future City plan, which focuses resources only on places where growth can be fostered (see chapter 2). In other words, some areas of the city must eventually disappear. Bikeshare also reinforces the centrality of downtown in Detroit's political economy, while selectively expanding into "the neighborhoods" without long-term, dedicated funding sources to support underperforming areas.

Bikeshare in Detroit was spearheaded by the Downtown Detroit Partnership (DDP), a classic growth coalition comprised of downtown firms like Quicken and General Motors, major philanthropic institutions like the Kresge Foundation, and state and local policymakers.[57] The DDP and its affiliates have increasingly oriented their work toward "placemaking" in the 7.2 square miles of greater downtown as a way to attract and retain new residents.[58] Bikeshare contributes directly to this mission, which has knock-on effects for the attractiveness of downtown as an investment environment, a key goal of Quicken CEO Dan Gilbert, the downtown area's largest property owner and promoter.[59] It also serves as a critical "last mile" solution for another project of the downtown growth machine, the $180 million QLine streetcar that opened in May 2017 (see chapter 2).[60]

Planning efforts began in 2013 with Lisa Nuszkowski of Wayne State University's Office of Economic Development, another key growth coalition partner.[61] With philanthropic support, Nuszkowski contracted Portland's Alta Planning + Design for a feasibility study.[62] While bankruptcy slowed implementation, by 2015 bikeshare was moving forward, with federal, state, and regional government funding, as well as local foundation support, and Nuszkowski had moved from Wayne State to DDP, where the bikeshare program would remain.[63] In 2016 Nuszkowski selected Shift Transit as the provider and Henry Ford Health System and Health Alliance Plan as the title sponsors, and renamed the system MoGo. In the spring and summer of 2017, MoGo launched with 43 stations and 430 bikes.[64] The first week of operations, which coincided with an internationally renowned electronic music festival, saw 4,000 trips made using MoGo bikes.

The 2013 feasibility study emphasized the deep spatial divisions in the city, which directly affected projected demand. Based on population and job density, the study identified a service area that joined the booming Woodward corridor and waterfront in an inverted "T," where bikeshare would enable lateral travel to neighborhoods into which development was starting to seep, filling the "T" out into a triangle. The study authors summarized these areas, including New Center, Midtown, and downtown, as "where people 'live, work, shop, play, and take transit.'"[65] Based on an equity analysis, which assessed the percentage of households below the poverty line, the location of low-income housing, and the percentage of non-English–speaking households, the study also highlighted Midtown and New Center as areas where goals of serving marginalized Detroiters could be met simultaneously.[66] On the whole, though, very low densities in most poor neighborhoods, many of them far from the city center, limit the viability of bikeshare as a motility improvement in these places. Recommendations from an online station suggestion map launched in 2013 were quite widely distributed across the city but were concentrated in the primary service area and reinforced places already identified as "high demand."[67]

Density was the issue to which everyone connected to bikeshare planning consistently returned, reflecting wider concerns in Detroit over how to manage abandonment while encouraging growth where it is occurring. By the same token, few wanted to confirm that there were places that would never see a bikeshare station. They argued that finding local community support would prove a "market" for bikeshare that they could take to foundations and other sources of funding.[68] Omari Colen, Shift Transit's MoGo manager, envisioned an ideal Detroit of "10,000 stations and 100,000 bikes" and said that if certain areas could show interest, his perspective was, "How can we get a station here?" Nevertheless, he confirmed that "spots that don't have people buying houses, going out to eat, working, shopping" could not support bikeshare.[69] Rebecca Quinn, Shift's general manager, said that their contract gave MoGo free rein but noted that "if they wanted to put a station out in Timbuktu we might push back against that."[70] On the DDP side, Adriel Thornton, MoGo's Marketing and Access Manager, noted the obstacles that faced places where there was a desire for access but no contiguity with the rest of the system: "What's the radius? You need destinations that bikeshare is useful to get to." He noted the same challenges in reference to Detroit Future City: "There are places where it literally doesn't make sense to keep providing services."[71]

At the same time, MoGo staff saw good reasons to stretch the boundaries of "feasibility" in some cases. When planning, Lisa Nuszkowski envisioned locations that lacked a "dollars and cents justification" but made sense from an access and economic development perspective—seen here more in terms of access to opportunity than real estate development.[72] Two areas in particular "stretched" the service area based on local support and available funding, revealing the selective application of austerity within bikeshare system planning. One was the North End, a low-income, mainly residential district that the 2013 study had profiled but did not recommend for inclusion. Located northeast of New Center, the North End has been hailed as the city's newest exciting neighborhood, with a potent brew of small entrepreneurs, artists, community groups, and neighborhood gardens that would be connected to the northern terminus of the QLine.[73] For Nuszkowski, locating a MoGo station in the North End would improve connections to employment for this underserved area, as well as showing residents a commitment to "keeping [them] in the conversation."[74]

In this respect, MoGo's goals for the neighborhood were similar to those of Philadelphia's Indego in Strawberry Mansion, though the North End is closer to the path of development. Local bikeshare champions reflected the neighborhood's changing composition, however. One of the loudest voices in support of bikeshare belonged to the Michigan Urban Farming Initiative, a community garden founded in 2011 by two University of Michigan graduates with the goal of founding "America's first sustainable urban agrihood." Since its founding, MUFI had attracted large amounts of philanthropic funding and become one of the neighborhood's most ardent boosters. As one founder put it to me, putting MoGo in proximity to the farm was a natural choice because it had the "right demographic": "People who come to urban farms ride bikes and use bikeshare. It's just a fact." However, a rivalry between MUFI and more established organizations in the area, due in part to its connections to real estate interests,[75] led Nuszkowski to opt for more "neutral" territory.[76] More broadly, the concentration of "activity" in the North End, combined with its proximity to the QLine, acted as a clear signal to override a strict efficiency calculus in station location.

The second "stretch" was West Village, a gentrifying neighborhood on the east side far beyond the service area. The study had identified West Village as a potential candidate for future expansion, despite poor bicycle facilities and a gap with the rest of the system, but had not recommended it for the first phase.[77] West Village, an archetypal gentrified commercial strip in miniature, surrounded by renovated row houses and apartments, is precisely the type of place where bikeshare thrives in other cities. It is also the target of a concerted effort by foundations and the city to prime the pump of growth. The implementation of bikeshare here provides a clearer example of this negotiation of efficiency standards—in this case, as part of a neighborhood reinvestment plan building on molecular processes of gentrification.

West Village is located adjacent to Indian Village, an elite enclave of mansions in an otherwise deeply disinvested area roughly three miles east of downtown. It has a significantly higher population density than surrounding neighborhoods and is among the few districts outside of the downtown core and waterfront that are seeing market-rate multifamily housing development. The central hub of the neighborhood consists of a one-block commercial strip with a beer garden, a vinyl record store, a coffee shop, a vegan cafe, a "modern American" restaurant, and an exercise studio. Unusual for most Detroit neighborhoods where single-family homes predominate, the area is anchored by two large, recently restored 1920s apartment buildings.[78] During the planning phase, residents there showed strong support for bikeshare, using the online station suggestion map and citing the neighborhood's "up and coming," "bustling" character; its "young professional" demographic; its accessibility to downtown and the waterfront; and its status as a destination in its own right.[79] Amina Daniels, a

Black native Detroiter, founder of the Live Cycle Delight exercise studio, and MoGo ambassador, echoed these sentiments: "We are already buying into the new Detroit. This is part of the new Detroit."[80]

But what appears to be a more "authentic," neighborhood-based development trajectory is also in part the extension of the reach of growth-machine actors into key nodes in the broader urban fabric, as well as a continuation of the logic of strategic service withdrawal advanced by Detroit Future City.[81] In 2016, the Detroit Strategic Neighborhoods Fund (SNF) included West Village in its plans for several "micro-districts" across the city, a strategy that borrows the planning paradigm of "20-minute neighborhoods" from Portland, Oregon, envisioning neighborhoods where daily necessities are within a twenty-minute walk or bike ride.[82] In target areas, "20-minute neighborhood" plans include greenways, protected bike lanes, streetscaping, retail investment, home and apartment renovations, and demolitions.[83] The SNF's activities in West Village include partial funding of a twelve-unit condominium, the area's first new market-rate apartment building in recent memory, while most of the small businesses that give the neighborhood its "bottom-up" character received some form of seed funding from affiliated grantmaking institutions.[84] In support of these efforts, the community development financial institution Invest Detroit funded an extra MoGo station for West Village.[85] This location is over a mile from the nearest station, which Nuszkowski described as "not ideal" from a strict operations perspective. Nevertheless, she was enthusiastic about the support from residents and funders.[86]

In short, in both the North End and the West Village, planners stretched the "feasible" service area in the interest of increasing motility and fostering neighborhood-based development. This microscale reshaping of system priorities would not be conceivable in a larger transportation system with more capital-intensive fixed investments and firmly established engineering principles. Bikeshare, however, is both nodal and flexible, with a limited degree of "scientific" orthodoxy regarding station placement and network design. This creates a platform that is open to modification based on localized priorities—be they fostering gentrification, "community-based" development, or some combination of the two. More broadly, though, each of these sites represents a location that is prioritized by Detroit's development paradigm. The expansion of bikeshare system coverage in these areas represents a selective—and precarious—modulation of infrastructural austerity.

Uneven Regional Development and Bay Area Bike Share

If bikeshare systems in Philadelphia and Detroit reinforce the centrality of downtown, in the San Francisco Bay Area bikeshare reinforces uneven development at both the intracity and regional scales. Within the cities that are included in the regional bikeshare system, particularly San Francisco and Oakland, stations are organized according to a logic similar to Philadelphia, Detroit, and others: residential and employment density are the primary factors, with agglomeration driving expected demand. But at the scale of the region, nodes in the system are arranged according to preexisting transportation connections, density of destinations, and political will. Thus, bikeshare planning, like smart growth initiatives, reinforces patterns of existing density, rather than increasing accessibility in less well-connected places. Most important, what began as a public funding commitment eroded with the adoption of a privatized model that gives cities and public agencies less control over system design.

The Bay Area arrived somewhat late to the bikeshare game, launching a publicly owned pilot system, Bay Area Bike Share, in the summer of 2013.[87] Using Alta Bicycle Share (now Motivate) equipment, the pilot was owned and operated by the Bay Area Air Quality Management District and supported by $11.2 million in federal, regional, and local funds.[88] It began with seven hundred bikes and seventy stations along the Caltrain regional rail corridor from San Francisco to San Jose. In this respect, while it was a "regional" system spread across three counties and some fifty miles, it remained limited to core neighborhoods of San Francisco and San Jose, with a handful of stations in the Peninsula and Silicon Valley cities of Redwood City, Palo Alto, and Mountain View.[89] After a year of operation, the Metropolitan Transportation Commission regarded the pilot as a qualified success, with a "modest" effect on vehicle miles traveled and carbon emissions, and approved an additional $16.5 million in federal funds to support expansion.[90] In the long term, MTC staff recommended shifting toward a public-private partnership model with corporate sponsorship to support expansion.[91]

In May 2015, without outside bidding, the MTC renewed its partnership with Motivate for a tenfold expansion of the pilot system, bringing the total number of bikes to 7,000 across 700 stations. This time, based on the success of its fully private Citi Bike system, Motivate proposed a revenue-neutral model supported by a title sponsorship, touting the provision of the service "at no cost to taxpayers."[92] This included a commitment, required by MTC, to locate at least 20 percent of stations in "Communities of Concern," a designation referring to the concentration of nonwhite and low-income households used for regional planning (see chapter 2).[93] It also planned to offer a 60 percent discount for qualified low-income members.[94] With a $50 million contribution from Ford as the title sponsor, and support from Alaska Airlines and City National Bank, Motivate launched Ford GoBike over the second half of 2017, enlarging its footprint in San Francisco and San Jose and expanding into Berkeley, Oakland, and Emeryville. Meanwhile, in partially divesting from bikeshare, the MTC reallocated public funds that could have served to offset the geographic inequalities of bikeshare. The $4.5 million (40 percent) that remained were reserved for capital grants to municipalities left out of the expansion, and could not be used for operations or outreach, though cities are free to spend their own money to "buy" stations.[95] If such programs were to be a source of funding for regional motility redistribution, they would need to expand.

Within cities already in the service area, feasibility analyses adopted essentially the same metrics as other studies and yielded similar patterns (Figure 22). Studies of San Francisco in preparation for the pilot used standard measures of housing, retail, employment, and tourism density, as well as transit access, commercial zoning, terrain, bicycle commute rates and infrastructure, and, notably, per capita income. The pilot service area

Figure 22. Proposed market area for Bay Area Bike Share expansion into Oakland and the East Bay. From U. Vogler and S. Co, Memorandum: RE: Bay Area Bike Share Update (2014). https://s3.amazonaws.com/media.legistar.com/mtc/meeting_packet_documents/agenda_2307/6_Bay_Area_Bike_Share_Memo_with_attachment.pdf (accessed October 10, 2017).

was largely as expected, covering the city's main economic and institutional clusters: the South of Market Area (SOMA) and southern waterfront high-tech clusters, the Financial District, the Union Square shopping district, Mid-Market, and Civic Center along Market, and the northern waterfront tourism zone. This zone was also "stretched" during implementation to include a station in western SOMA, an area with a low suitability score but directly accessible to a cluster of tech firms, including Adobe, Airbnb, and Zynga.[96] Meanwhile, the Tenderloin, an extremely low-income neighborhood, was not part of the pilot, despite its high density, proximity to the rest of the service area, and relatively high suitability score. The clear privileging of tech sector workers over poor people in this extension of the suitability area was done by a public agency, not in the service of private profit but was doubtlessly constrained by the need for the system to perform well as a pilot.

The Ford GoBike expansion in 2017 put stations in largely residential neighborhoods for the first time. Motivate and city staff celebrated the fact that the system's design had far exceeded MTC's mandate of equitable coverage, with fully 35 percent of stations located in Communities of Concern.[97] However, a large number of these were sited in Census tracts defined by UC Berkeley's Center for Community Innovation as either undergoing "advanced gentrification" or "at risk of gentrification or displacement" (Maps 10 and 11).[98] At the same time, in Oakland Motivate did not plan to place stations east of High Street, the boundary of East Oakland proper, where just over a quarter of the city's population, and roughly half of its Black and Latino population, resides.[99] Here, fulfilling a static definition of underserved *places*, like Communities of Concern, stands in for addressing the needs of underserved *people*. This omission, on the grounds of system performance, would become a quite public critique of the expansion.

Making New Infrastructural Publics

Bikeshare did not come to Philadelphia, Detroit, and the San Francisco Bay Area in a vacuum but was relayed through networks of learning, competitive adaptation, and selective emulation. Bikeshare became "fast infrastructure" in two somewhat conflicting ways. On one hand, a consensus that bicycle sharing systems were a mandatory element of a competitive city in the global scramble for "talent" was well established by the mid-2010s. In this regard, bikeshare symbolizes a city in step with the dominant trends in sustainable mobility and "world class" urban planning. On the other hand, by this time there was a growing recognition that bikeshare was largely the province of the white, male, professional classes

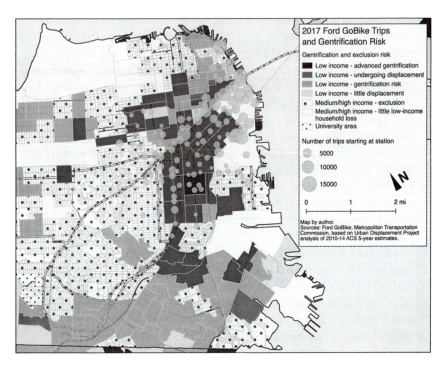

Map 10. Ford GoBike stations and gentrification risk in San Francisco. Map by the author.

and that existing models were inadequate from the perspective of racial and economic equity. Thus, the bikeshare model that became mobile after 2015 was an internally contradictory hybrid: a form of infrastructure that was both a valuable amenity and a means of including "underserved" people and places. Philadelphia, and the Better Bike Share Partnership anchored by the Indego planning process, became a fulcrum of this new paradigm. But the "Philadelphia model" mutated as it traveled, often losing key elements that made Indego a relative success. In particular, subsequent systems celebrated inclusive outreach and subsidized memberships rather than the expensive redistributive work of spatial justice.

At a deeper level, the uneven rollout of the "Philadelphia model" reveals the extent to which new infrastructures require the construction of new infrastructural publics.[100] The pre-existing infrastructural public for bikeshare, which has developed over the course of the past decade, is rooted in largely middle-class bicycle advocacy groups and the new wave of "livability" organizations that gentrification has fed. What is often described as a "cultural" barrier to using bikeshare in poor neighborhoods of color is

BICYCLE SHARING AS SPLINTERED INFRASTRUCTURE   161

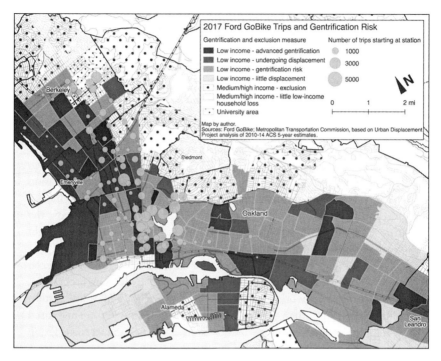

Map 11. Ford GoBike stations and gentrification risk in the East Bay. Map by the author.

fundamentally a matter of the social infrastructure of practices linking everyday life to an infrastructural base.

The "Philadelphia Model"

Philadelphia's early start in bikeshare planning came to a halt with the financial crisis. With schools and libraries shuttering, planners took the opportunity to learn from the rapidly evolving landscape of new bikeshare systems.[101] "Every city wants to be the first at something," said Aaron Ritz, who managed the Bicycle and Pedestrian Program of the Mayor's Office of Transportation and Utilities at the time and took over as Indego's manager in 2016. "We were not going to be the first to bikeshare . . . so the question became, 'What can we be the first at?'"[102] The answer was "equity." Despite a rapid wave of post-Recession gentrification, Philadelphia had the ironic "advantage" of having high-poverty neighborhoods relatively close to the CBD, which the system could serve for equity reasons without stranding stations and users in far-flung parts of the city.[103] The Strawberry Mansion neighborhood, noted above, was one such neighborhood.

External funding for stations in Strawberry Mansion enabled planners to disregard efficiency in the interest of spatially defined accessibility. Capital ownership and—more important—the will to invest in equity made city staff the "final decisionmaker[s]" and "the face and voice of the system" vis-à-vis BTS, who for their part also firmly supported the equity agenda.[104] A critical element of this agenda was a stream of additional funding for outreach. The JPB Foundation, one of the initial funders of Indego, had committed $6 million to the Better Bike Share Partnership (BBSP) with the explicit goal of developing transferable models for more equitable bikeshare systems. This was divided between national-level research by PeopleForBikes and the National Association of City Transportation Officials (NACTO) and on-the-ground work in Philadelphia by Indego and the Bicycle Coalition of Greater Philadelphia. In other words, the purpose of the work was to turn Philadelphia into a model that could inform planning efforts in other cities.

The BBSP grant provided support for an unusually robust outreach process. While most bikeshare systems have a public planning process, including community workshops, stakeholder meetings, and online station location suggestion maps, Indego planners took extra steps. They hired the Temple University Institute for Survey Research to conduct focus group interviews with low-income Philadelphians about how they might use a bikeshare system. Because of the racialization of poverty in the city, this research in practice meant focusing on African American residents, particularly Black women. Researchers learned that Black women did not see themselves using bikeshare for transportation but were more likely to use it for recreation. Many of them had children with bicycles, but they lived in small houses and did not have a bicycle themselves. They also had a difficult time envisioning themselves as typical bikeshare users, because existing imagery of bikeshare showed largely white, middle-class professionals. As focus group respondents put it: "Enough with the yuppies!"[105]

The findings altered the business model of the system itself, as well as its public engagement approach. The industry standard checkout period of thirty minutes would not be sufficient for recreational use, so planners increased the time to an hour. Indego also changed its marketing approach, keeping the standard images of thin white millennial models on bikeshare for tourist brochures and instead showing ordinary Philadelphians using Indego for most of its materials.[106] In addition to the standard online station siting tool, bicycle coalition staff, supported by the JPB grant, organized social events in neighborhoods like Strawberry Mansion, placing large vinyl decals in prospective locations with a text number for comments.[107] Finally, the grant allowed the bicycle coalition to hire teams of neighborhood ambassadors in order to build relationships with "local champions" in the neighborhoods beyond the CBD and immediate surroundings.[108]

In short, Indego had begun to chip away at a durable consensus on the function of bikeshare, which was to extend the "last mile" of transit access to downtown, divert car trips, and support tourism, which often does not reflect mobility needs in working-class neighborhoods. Ritz, who had come from the bike world, said this pushed him to rethink the purpose of bikeshare: "I'm a convert. [Before] I had thought of bikeshare as solving a logistical or transportation problem." Sometimes, during outreach, this meant deemphasizing bikes themselves in favor of job placement and health.[109] These efforts also shifted the bikeshare program's mandate to serve Philadelphians of all incomes, with which city staff had begun, to an explicit focus on racial equity and rectifying historical wrongs.[110] As Ritz put it, they were "doing penance" for how planning was done in the past, an outlook he credited BBSP Grant Manager Carniesha Kwashie with fostering.[111] Furthermore, during community meetings where residents raised needs only tangentially related to bikeshare, Indego staff could speak to these broader issues because of their position within the city bureaucracy. Outreach Coordinator Waffiyah Murray said this was what drew her to the role: that Indego could serve as a model for not just bikeshare but equity planning more broadly.[112] As Alison Cohen put it, stations in low-income areas without a large market need support within the community to succeed—a human infrastructure, in Adonia Lugo's words.[113] In short, these efforts were all focused on building new infrastructural publics among residents who were not often consulted on major infrastructure projects.

Among the most widely celebrated and imitated aspects of the "Philadelphia model," however, was its Access Pass, which was also made possible by BBSP funding and which had enrolled roughly a thousand members by the end of 2016.[114] The Access Pass and cash payments are key to Indego's reputation for equity and the lead details in countless articles in the mobility blogosphere about the system.[115] They have also become key discussion points for equity initiatives in other cities, whether or not they reference Philadelphia's influence. But these widely acclaimed achievements on equity also point to the limits of revenue neutrality. Were it not for the substantial control over the geography of infrastructure investment and the ability to fund operating losses in the name of accessibility, Indego would likely have not seen the success it did, particularly the leap in Black memberships. At the same time, it was likely not enough to simply accept losses on underperforming stations in poor neighborhoods without also placing the cost of membership within reach and doing the hard work of making the system relevant to residents in these areas. Both of these efforts were enabled by large public and nonprofit funding sources as well as public control over priorities. As we get farther from conditions on the ground in Philadelphia, these threads disentangle, and subsidized memberships and "underserved areas" appear more as an equity menu from which planners can choose.

MoGo Detroit and the Limits of Formal Imitation

Lisa Nuszkowski looked toward Philadelphia as her main inspiration when planning Detroit's system, and she proudly proclaimed that "imitation is the sincerest form of flattery."[116] Nevertheless, the translation of the Philadelphia model to Detroit was shaped by the city's *lack* of involvement and bikeshare's origination from within the growth machine as part of a laundry list of "placemaking" investments that would support economic recovery, particularly downtown development.[117]

The most widely noted feature of MoGo when it launched was a five-dollar-a-*year* Access Pass membership for participants in Michigan Food Assistance, Medicaid, and other programs, payable in cash at Family Dollar and 7-Eleven and funded by the Knight Foundation. This in particular was part of MoGo's debt to the Philadelphia model, and after six months of operation Nuszkowski could celebrate that a significant number of users had purchased the Access Pass and that all ZIP codes of the city were represented in the membership rolls.[118]

MoGo also borrowed from Indego's neighborhood ambassadors program. These programs are ostensibly about building "buy-in" in neighborhoods where residents might be unfamiliar with or suspicious of bikeshare, and even new investments in general, because of the perception that it is "not for them."[119] But they also enable bikeshare providers to learn about neighborhoods with which they had few ties. In Philadelphia, ambassadors obtained fine-grained input because they were "trusted faces" to ask, and were able to identify "the right people" for Indego staff to consult. Carniesha Kwashie, whose background was in workforce development, considered the matter in reverse: the goal was to learn from the people, not get buy-in for the system.[120] Under MoGo's system, fourteen ambassadors from the ten neighborhoods in the service area received a stipend for six months of service beginning just prior to system launch to organize MoGo-funded outreach events and report on outreach efforts at monthly ambassador meetings.[121] MoGo staff did not officially approach the ambassador program as a social justice initiative, but Lisa Nuszkowski and ambassador program coordinator Rory Lincoln were proud that the majority of ambassadors were people of color, and that their priority was a "community-centric" orientation rather than a background in bicycling. As a Midtown ambassador and mobility intern with the city, Jeffrey Nolish was emphatic in his commitment to "making a dent in . . . transport poverty."[122]

Notwithstanding, ambassadors are not foolproof insurance against conflict, nor is the landscape of local organizations always transparent. This is because bikeshare is ultimately the priority of downtown interests, where systems typically roll out first. As MoGo's Adriel Thornton put it, "We're not dumb, we know we launched in the 7.2," referencing how downtown-led planning efforts typically fail to address the neighborhoods.[123] This downtown-neighborhoods divide "unmaps" residential areas, particularly those that are not making a name for themselves through gentrification. In one Philadelphia neighborhood, talking to the "wrong" local brokers led to the removal of a station. From a bike-centric perspective, this was a loss, but Murray was not concerned: "Otherwise, how will they feel it's for them?"[124] In Detroit's North End, the vandalism of a station with house paint prompted the local ambassador, Black artist and poet Jamii Tata, to organize an event to bridge the fragmented organizations in the area, between whom bikeshare had become a point of contention.[125] In the West Village, on the other hand, the challenge was reaching beyond the small bourgeois enclave where bikeshare already fits neatly. Amina Daniels, the West Village ambassador, said she would personally benefit from its narrow function of serving the "new Detroiters" moving in, but she envisioned more: "You can ride five blocks east and nobody knows what MoGo will ever be."[126] In effect, this situation recreates the downtown–neighborhood divide in miniature.

But what is possible in outreach relates directly back to the institutional political economy of the system itself. Part of what Indego staff saw as effective in their work was the fact that they represented the city—"a public system for the public," as Ritz called it—and this connected their efforts to the broader provision of services that have nothing to do with mobility. In Detroit, the opposite is true. The city in fact lacks a permanent staff position charged with managing its relationship with MoGo, apart from issuing permits.[127] Discussions surrounding bikeshare in Detroit tap into a deep current of suspicion regarding city government and its services, which becomes depoliticized by institutional fragmentation. For example, in a Facebook post shortly after the launch, activist and political candidate David Sanchez asked, "Who is making these decisions? So we can't keep Vernor [Street, in Southwest] from being flooded for days and days but we can afford bike lanes and bike kiosks. . . ." Adriel Thornton replied, "While the city has been a necessary part of this, it is not their initiative. Again, we reached out to every community we put stations in and it was, in fact, the community members that helped us decided to place stations where they are. . . . Neither the city nor the state are funding this in any way, meaning no tax dollars were used from the community."[128] This positive affirmation of revenue-neutrality stands in sharp contrast to the spirit and institutional architecture of the Philadelphia "model." Most systems, though, lack this function as a public interface, and their planners effectively declare their independence from the city, despite the fact that it is, for better or worse, the most tangible object of political claims based on inhabitation and citizenship. Instead, the terrain on which most public–private bikeshare systems operate is instrumental, based on the city's delegation of responsibility to deliver a specific service.[129]

Ford GoBike and the Limits of Outreach

By the time that Ford GoBike launched in the Bay Area, "equity" had become a hegemonic frame, but one increasingly unmoored from its spatial and institutional aspects. At the same time, "equity" created an opening around which critics of extant planning practices could mobilize with demands for spatial justice that exceeded the narrow frame through which bikeshare implementation proceeded.

In June 2017, Ford GoBike launched with speeches from elected leaders, mobility advocates, and Motivate CEO Jay Walder, who declared Ford GoBike to be the "most equitable bikeshare system in the country." He touted Bike Share for All, a $5 membership program for the first year (and $5 a month thereafter) offered to qualified low-income users, the "robust" planning process, and the fact that Motivate superseded the mandate for locating stations in Communities of Concern. All of this was, as he said, "at no cost to the taxpayer." At the Oakland launch event, Mayor Libby Schaaf claimed that social equity was "baked in" to what would "becom[e] the most inclusive program" in the United States.[130] To underscore this point with Oakland flavor, Champ and R.B. of the Scraper Bike Team brought a Ford GoBike decorated in the Scraper aesthetic, which Schaaf rode to start the celebration.

But almost immediately it became clear that GoBike was regarded in many quarters as neither equitable nor well planned. While many celebrated, a dominant thread was surprise at the sudden appearance of stations in residential areas.[131] Images of vandalized bikes, one hanging from a tree and another floating in Lake Merritt in Oakland circulated via social media, often with a measure of glee at the rejection of a corporate invasion.[132] Local hip-hop artist Mistah F.A.B. had a station removed from in front of his clothing store in the Longfellow neighborhood of North Oakland, citing parking issues and lack of outreach.[133] More visibly, the merchants association of the Calle 24 Latino Cultural District roundly rejected the placement of stations in its territory, asserting that the bikes were meant primarily for wealthier Anglos moving to the neighborhood and that Latino residents already had their own bikes.[134] Regional news outlets pounced on this fresh controversy in San Francisco's gentrification wars, and comments sections raged with debate, no shortage of which impugned Calle 24 for NIMBYism, the ultimate insult in the Bay Area's new gilded age.[135] There was a clear consensus, though, that the rollout could have gone more smoothly.

Despite some hyperbolic criticism that the system had rolled out with no outreach at all, Motivate did conduct the stakeholder meetings and public outreach, at its own expense, as required by its contract with MTC.[136] This began with an online station suggestion tool, like other systems, and continued with in-person outreach work at the start of 2016.[137] Initial site plans were introduced in May 2016 after eight public meetings, and by September another round of stations had been planned after a total of seventeen public events.[138] By this point, however, no events had been held in East or West Oakland, and neither neighborhood had been included in the first two phases. Carlos Hernandez, bikeshare manager for the City of Oakland at the time, explained to me that, "as bad as that looks," this was intentional: saving East and West Oakland for the end gave planners the opportunity to build support in those neighborhoods, efforts that would be handled by a different strategy.[139]

This parallel strategy was organized by local mobility justice organization TransForm with a $260,000 grant from MTC (roughly half of which was contributed by Motivate) to support regional equity outreach activities.[140] TransForm partnered with community bike organization Cycles of Change, the Original Scraper Bike Team, and Bike East Bay, as well as San Francisco's Yellow Bike Project, the San Francisco Bicycle Coalition, and the Silicon Valley Bicycle Coalition on outreach activities in "underserved" areas—the equivalent of ambassadors on the Indego or MoGo model.[141] Through this partnership, TransForm sponsored a pair of Oakland Mobility 101 (OakMob 101) events in East and West Oakland in October 2016 that explicitly addressed lack of input from these communities in the planning process as a whole. The events also presented a more general opportunity to raise community awareness of the changing mobility landscape, including the launch of bikeshare and car-sharing services, with booths hosted by TransForm, Cycles of Change, Ford GoBike, AC Transit, and ZipCar, as well as a barbecue and live music performances. Speaking at OakMob 101 in West Oakland, Brytanee Brown of Trans-Form, a Black Berkeley native, framed bikeshare as inevitable and urged those in attendance to organize to make it serve their needs: "We need to be involved in planning if [bikeshare] is a resource we want. . . . It is coming here but we need to realize that it might not come to our community."[142] OakMob 101 was the only bikeshare outreach event held in West Oakland, and one of only two held in East Oakland.

In June 2017, Motivate issued a report on the previous eighteen months of outreach efforts, entitled "Ford GoBike: Bike Share Designed by Bay Area Residents." The report documented a total of over three hundred stakeholder meetings with community groups, business leaders, and elected officials, with "civic and business associations" predominating, as well as roughly thirty community events and open houses, and over three thousand unique suggestions made to the online tool.[143] The following month, TransForm struck a different tone with its own report on the OakMob 101 advocacy campaign. The report outlined the history of infrastructural injury in Oakland's flatlands, arguing that these neighborhoods have always been on the losing end of mobility change. It held out the potential of bike- and carshare to reduce car dependency and facilitate more equitable and sustainable mobility but expressed skepticism about their current form: "Bike share expansion plans do not include significant portions of East Oakland. These neighborhoods have been literally wiped off the map." It also noted that during the Bay Area Bike Share pilot, bikeshare users were disproportionately male, college educated, and high income.[144]

The OakMob report struck a mixed tone. On one hand, in response to the OakMob events and the implicit pressure placed on its public image, Ford GoBike had extended the checkout period for low-income members to one hour, added cash payment options and expanded the qualifying programs for low-income access, and pledged to pilot access technology for people with disabilities. On the other hand, the report concluded that the window of opportunity to modify Oakland's rollout, such as by "including communities from the earliest stages of a planning process," had passed.[145] Also, with the exception of the pilot of adaptive technology, the modifications that Motivate made under pressure were all essential features of the "Philadelphia model," now two years old and widely celebrated throughout the bikeshare world. Since Oakland is itself a partner city in the BBSP, it is not clear why these elements would not have been included from the start, if the purpose of the partnership is to develop and deploy best practices.

Seemingly in response to bad publicity, Motivate gave TransForm, the Scraper Bike Team, and Bike East Bay greater latitude to sign up Bike Share for All members in Communities of Concern in Oakland, though these efforts remained gravely underfunded.[146] TransForm and its allies began organizing members through their own Bike Share For All platform—in effect, a more autonomous ambassador program—and even building support for a distinct, community-based bikeshare system not controlled or managed by Motivate. The website, www.bikeshareforall.org, offered a less-than-subtle critique of Ford GoBike: "While bike share is available in many locations throughout the Bay, it doesn't serve all neighborhoods. We believe a true bike share for all is one that puts often-forgotten neighborhoods—ones where the majority of neighbors are working class families and people of color—first."[147] On a Bike Share For All ride in October 2017 organized by the Scraper Bike Team, a Bike East Bay activist gave a speech to the mostly youthful crowd about "making sure we [people of color] have access to this mobility option no matter where we are, even in the East . . . whether it's Ford GoBike or some other community-based bikeshare." In a minor but not insignificant way, the ambassador program had become a site of counter-organizing. More broadly, Motivate, which due to permitting delays was substantially behind schedule with the system launch, retooled the phasing plan and instead installed as many stations as possible, particularly in areas like East Oakland where they were receiving criticism.[148]

The pressure of alternate bikeshare models may have played into this truncated timeline as well. As of October 2017, several smartphone-based "dockless" bikeshare systems had launched in the Bay Area: a JUMP Bikes pilot collaboration with UC Berkeley in the Mission, the Bayview, and UC Berkeley's family housing in Albany; Lime, a San Mateo–based dockless bike startup operating in Alameda (which was not included in the GoBike system); and San Francisco–based Spin and Portland-based Social Bicycles (which owns JUMP), who operate small fleets on the Peninsula and in Silicon Valley.[149] While such outfits were initially prevented from operating in Ford GoBike's five core cities due to Motivate's exclusive contract with MTC, by late 2018 the explosion of the dockless industry, in both bikes and scooters, forced compromises.[150] For Ford GoBike, the stakes of demonstrating equitable access in the face of agile, disruptive, and venture capital–subsidized startup competition are greater now than ever before. In June 2018 Ford GoBike reported resounding success in its Bike Share For All program, claiming the highest percentage of low-income annual passholders of any system in the country, with the proportion in San Jose particularly high (but with low overall membership).[151] At the same time, outreach coordinators I spoke to expressed strong doubts that the low-income members they signed up would renew once that year expired in 2019 and felt their efforts had been largely cosmetic.

The goal of this chapter has been to examine how efforts to expand the bikeshare user base beyond the largely white, male, professional stratum of the central city reveal the contradictions of uneven and racialized urban and regional development. In particular, the conflicting mandates to provide access to "territorially stigmatized" places and maintain revenue neutrality become embedded in bikeshare systems themselves.[152] The geography of "feasibility" is stretched according to political priorities, available funding streams, and local neighborhood trajectories. While many of the results are admirable, particularly in the Philadelphia case, where substantial public investments and a public spirit enabled expanded coverage beyond the gentrification "frontier," the broader structure of austerity constrains these experiments. These constraints are both ideological (there is little appetite for more mobility infrastructures that require subsidies) and material (public funding sources for investment in bikeshare are spotty, leaving the bulk of the task to the private and nonprofit sector). Thus, while Indego has shown great promise, its maximum likely service area contains less than a third of the population of the city and less than a tenth of that of the metro area.

This raises the second major theme of the chapter: the mobility and mutation of policy, in this case "fast infrastructure." If policies and infrastructures are heterogeneous ensembles, as many argue, then the question of their mobility must focus on what is learned and how it is translated across places. No policies are imported in toto, because no two places are the same. What features are selected and why are crucial aspects of understanding the paths of influence that link places where policymakers pursue similar initiatives and learn from one another. A number of cities have adopted the "faster" elements of Philadelphia's success: subsidized memberships, cash payment, and community-based ambassador programs. Comparatively fewer have replicated the combination of public investment and democratic accountability, because the political organization required is a greater challenge.

In short, the contradictions of bikeshare are essentially the contradictions of contemporary urban capitalism. In conditions of fiscal austerity, bikeshare planning must focus on areas where it will be viable according to profit calculations, or at least financial sustainability. Beyond these areas, expansion incurs a cost that must be borne somewhere. "Underserved" areas that are contiguous to the most viable service area and do not incur additional costs tend to be located along the gentrification "frontier." Residents of these areas may desire improvements, but increasing amenities brings the threat of deepening unaffordability. Hence the risk of defining equity *spatially*. Defining equity *socially* implies that if costs are reduced low-income customers will materialize, regardless of whether the geography of the system is relevant or useful in everyday life. If the goal is infrastructural change in order to improve motility for the least advantaged, then the occasional bikeshare ride may generate a photo op but will not reweave the spatial fabric of motility. Finally, bikeshare is ultimately too small an investment to steer urbanization but is significant enough to be marketed as an amenity, or a "hygiene factor," in places already undergoing gentrification. Because of this, it is unlikely to go where accessibility improvements are most needed as people of color and the working class are displaced from the center city. Instead, it is put in place where "motility capital" is already high, enabling further growth without additional congestion (see chapter 2). As infrastructure, it reveals the interregnum currently facing mobility in the American metropolis.

CONCLUSION

Notes on a Passive Revolution in Mobility

I am on a bicycle in Austin, Texas, in April 2018, waiting at an intersection to cross Airport Road, a busy, six-lane arterial lined with discount retailers, gas stations, and convenience stores. Facing me in the intersection, another man on a bicycle doesn't wait: he crosses the southbound lanes, waits as northbound traffic passes, then crosses those as well. He then crosses in front of me using the crosswalk, and sets off northward on Airport Road, which has a very narrow shoulder and no bike lane. I can see that he is a Latino man in his thirties, riding a bike that is a little too big, and the bike is functional but in slight disrepair. He seems to fit the often-used description advocates often use of "invisible cyclists," who cycle out of need rather than choice, and are frequently ignored by bicycle planning. As he rides out of view on Airport Road, he reaches out to brush the leaves of an overhanging bush with his hand. This minor gesture changes the inflection of the moment. To my view, it shows that despite his marginalization as a working-class Latino man riding a bicycle on an unsafe road in a segregated city, he seemingly *enjoyed* what he was doing. At the same time, cyclists like him find few places in today's bicycling city.

In a piece for Salon titled "It's Time to Love the Bus," Will Doig writes: "The bus suffers from an image problem. But not long ago, so did bicycles. Now bikes are the cool kid's transport, and all it took was a little investment and some reputation rehab."[1] In this book, I have outlined key elements of this "reputation rehab," as bicycle advocates in cities throughout the United States strive to prove the benefits of bicycle infrastructure investment, just at a moment when the flow of capital back into urban cores has transformed the cities in which they work.

Bicycle infrastructure is now seen as an inexpensive way to redeem unhealthy bodies, disinvested places, carbon-intensive cities, and car-choked regions. It is part of a suite of investments in livability that proves a city's capacity to attract labor "talent"—a favored position within the racialized and gendered global division of labor today.[2] Bicycle infrastructure also allows cities to take visible action on climate change—though the results are difficult to measure—without going to capital markets or wary voters in order to build new transportation systems. The political communities that have formed around bicycling have been part of a broader shift in the valence of the word "urban" itself, from signifying crime and decay to excitement and possibility. This shift in tacit meaning has involved a shift in the populations who are targets of urban development policy, from the racialized poor to the equally racialized (as white) "new middle class." The former come under the gaze of the carceral state, while the latter claim their place as the rightful heirs of the city and make moral claims on its governance.[3]

What of those people who signify the old, pre-renaissance city? When I began this research project in 2011, the notion that bicycling, which was not only cheap but also ecologically positive, could contribute to gentrification seemed counterintuitive. As with so many debates on gentrification, my attempts to understand the bicycle's role in the process frequently met with a zero-sum implication: make urban spaces more livable and risk their gentrification, or keep them run-down to keep them affordable. I recall an argument at a friend's dinner party that ended with, "Well, would you rather there be liquor stores on every corner?" This perfectly illustrates the perverse bargain of the neoliberal city outlined by Winifred Curran and Trina Hamilton: when any improvement to the lived experience of place can be capitalized as exchange-value, it seems that only territorial stigmatization can preserve economic diversity.[4]

These antagonisms are symptomatic of the fundamentally contradictory process within which bicycle infrastructure planning and implementation unfolds. Planners of bicycle facilities have a broad mandate to create an equitable distribution of infrastructure across the city, and plans are voted on and adopted by ostensibly democratic city governments. Overt and organized support for bicycle infrastructure is often more easily found in gentrifying neighborhoods, however, where the need for access to the central business district evinces clear demand for specific bicycle routes. This is compounded by the efforts of bicycle advocates, who have made remarkable gains on the strength of a growing body of research showing the economic contributions of cyclists. These arguments are ultimately tactical, rather than essential to bicycle advocacy, but they have captured the attention of mayors and elected officials. Meanwhile, bicycle planners still contend with entrenched engineering practices and a built environment designed to facilitate automobility above all else. Pushing through a piece of bicycle infrastructure can be politically costly if it is not well utilized, and elected officials are loath to be on record adding to traffic congestion for a "special interest."[5] These contradictions are scaled up with bikeshare systems, which are more expensive and must function efficiently in order to remain financially sustainable, and thus concentrate where they will be successful. Bikeshare by default adds large numbers of less experienced cyclists to city streets, increasing the pressure to improve infrastructure in these areas, potentially exacerbating its centralization. Within these constraints, is it at all surprising that bicycle infrastructure tracks gentrification—and often reinforces it?

A challenge with any history of the present is that the present keeps changing. New lines of flight appear, upsetting what appear to be settled patterns and reshaping the terrain of the possible. Below I sketch three emergent dynamics that complicate the stories told in this book.

Rideouts and Wheelie Kids: Contesting Spatial Confinement

In chapter 3 I examined the history of cyclists appropriating urban space en masse, the most recent iterations of which have been, broadly speaking, mutations of Critical Mass. To put it in oversimplified terms, despite its consciously anti-capitalist politics, Critical Mass—composed largely of déclassé white office and creative industries workers—was in effect the first roar of a new generation of gentrifiers laying claim to the city. Bike Party, Slow Roll, and other contemporary group rides are to varying extents mutations—not merely derivative—of the ensemble of practices that made up Critical Mass.

In April 2017, commuters on Philadelphia's Vine Street Expressway had front-row seats to a quintessentially Philadelphia moment: hundreds of mostly Black and Brown teenagers on bikes doing wheelies had taken over the westbound side of the highway (Figure 23).[6] It was the first introduction many Philadelphians had to a youth subculture that had been brewing for the better part of a decade: "wheelie kid" crews of kids on bikes who amass in groups of twenty or more for "rideouts" that take over city streets. Philadelphia's most well-known crew is One Way.[7] Not completely spontaneous gatherings, spur-of-the-moment rideouts are typically organized by crew members via social media like Instagram. Much like scraper bikes are a rearticulation of East Oakland car culture, "pedal bike" tricks are rooted in Black working-class motorcycle and quad-cycle stunt riding traditions in Philadelphia. Most youth ride models by SE Bikes, a 1980s BMX brand that rebooted and captured the urban youth

CONCLUSION

Figure 23. "Wheelie bike" crew on I-676 in downtown Philadelphia, April 23, 2017. Still captured from Instagram video posted by jinxedstore. https://www.instagram.com/p/BTPy9Q9Aw-a (accessed May 13, 2019).

market. In the summer of 2017, "wheelie kid" culture exploded on both coasts, and in May SE Bikes organized a rideout in Oakland to celebrate the launch of a Beast Mode edition designed by Oakland Raiders football star Marshawn Lynch. Joined by Lynch, whose fame enabled the unplanned and illegal ride to proceed smoothly, hundreds of youths took over Oakland's streets and even the MacArthur Freeway before finishing at the Beast Mode storefront in downtown Oakland.

The wheelie bike phenomenon, or "#bikelife" movement as it's known more broadly, can be read at one level as something kids have always done on bikes—having reckless fun—that spread through social media and on which bike manufacturers have cleverly capitalized.[8] Certainly, the youth involved make no secret of their brand loyalty, or their debt to motorized stunt cultures—at odds with the notional anti-capitalist and anti-motor ethos of Critical Mass. 2017 also saw the emergence of a classic "moral panic," ranging from Staten Island to the United Kingdom, over the practice of "swerving," in which kids ride wheelies against traffic and dart away from oncoming cars at the last second.[9] To the issue of dangerous riding, however, the education coordinator for the Bicycle Coalition of Greater Philadelphia noted, "No one was too upset when white hipsters were doing Critical Mass across the city. . . . There are other bike rides . . . that attract a young, hip white person, and they're not following the rules either."[10] Furthermore, while rideouts might be seen as a kind of "prepolitical" social formation à la Eric Hobsbawm, in March 2017 some three hundred wheelie kids suddenly appeared in downtown Philadelphia and shut down a pro-Trump rally.[11]

The wheelie bike phenomenon is in fact all of these things simultaneously: a complex brew of youthful recklessness, ludic play, subcultural consumerism, and immanently political practices.[12] But, as many have noted, it also challenges the silences of mainstream bicycle advocacy regarding the practices of people of color on bicycles, who are by turns invisible and hyper-visible, the constitutive outside to the normative professional commuter for whom infrastructure is being planned.[13] In particular, wheelie kids practice a politics of space in which they implicitly contest their confinement to territorially stigmatized zones of North and South Philadelphia. It is not by coincidence that they seize main streets and grand boulevards in the central business district; it is a political practice. It remains to be seen how wheelie culture will shape the politics of the bicycle, particularly as these youths become adults eligible to drive cars, but it speaks to how the "lively" body-bicycle cyborg seems to irresistibly call forth certain kinds of ungovernable practices.[14]

Race, Traffic Enforcement, and Vision Zero

A second emergent issue is the role of the state apparatus not just in building infrastructure but policing it. The efforts to build in-street bicycle infrastructure discussed in chapters 4 and 5 did not focus as directly on enforcing its proper use. Of course, advocates have long pointed to an "enforcement gap" (evinced by rampant double-parking in bike lanes, for example), but in response to driver behavior they have tended to support self-regulating infrastructure: protected bike lanes, bike-only traffic signals, turn boxes, and right-turn diversions for cars. Paradoxically, some of these infrastructures designed to rationalize the street also make it more complex, possibly raising enforcement requirements. At the same time, many cycling practices rely on tacit acceptance of law breaking (which in many cases improves the flow of traffic), and advocates fear increased exposure to enforcement—traffic citations and licensing requirements, for instance—resulting from greater scrutiny.[15]

Many police department cultures continue to show a deeply ingrained bias against bicyclists and pedestrians. The San Francisco Bicycle Coalition charged the SFPD with taking a "blame the victim" approach in a number of high-profile traffic deaths.[16] The risk is greater for cyclists of color, who are disproportionately stopped and cited by police (see chapter 3), and even when on the job are subject to increased regulation and punitive force.[17] Meanwhile, an economic boom coupled with the rise of ride-hailing apps like Uber and Lyft has dramatically increased traffic congestion, particularly curbside stops, playing havoc with existing complete-streets infrastructure. On Valencia Street (see chapter 4), bicycle advocates have called for a protected cycle track due to passenger pickups and drop-offs in the bike lane, and SF Transformation (SFMTrA), a protest group playing on the MTA's name and unaffiliated with the city, was formed after the deaths of two cyclists in the same day in 2016, has also mobilized to physically protect key bike lanes across the city, including installing unauthorized flexible posts on Valencia and Folsom Streets (see chapter 4).[18] Complaining of planning delays and absent enforcement, SFMTrA employs a "tactical urbanist" approach to the urgency of bicycle and pedestrian safety.[19]

In response to a number of high-profile deaths in collisions between cyclists and delivery trucks in the South of Market neighborhood, San Francisco adopted a plan, Vision Zero, in 2014 to eliminate traffic deaths within ten years. Since the mid-2010s, cities across the United States have competed to adopt the Vision Zero framework to reflect a commitment to safer, less car-dominated streets; San Francisco's plan was modeled on New York City's Vision Zero, which itself was borrowed from Sweden. By the mid-2010s, Vision Zero had become the emerging new hegemonic frame for infrastructural interventions previously understood as "livability," "complete streets," and so on.[20] This in part reflects the centrality of mayors and city administrations in setting urban mobility policy, and Vision Zero in this regard is an uncontestable goal: who could oppose efforts to eliminate traffic deaths in cities? It can also rightly be seen as a sort of "anti-politics machine," as James Ferguson puts it: the *politics* of automobility, and the way that individualized, private transport in deadly vehicles are central to American life, often become lost in the details of ever more precise metrics, key corridors, and study tours.[21]

Of the three "pillars" of Vision Zero—engineering, education, and enforcement—the last has become a choke point. Vision Zero rose to prominence in urban policy just as Black Lives Matter protests had politicized the application of carceral control to Black life. As Adonia Lugo, who was at the time chair of the League of American Bicyclists' Equity Advisory Council, put it: "I was alarmed that a pillar of Vision Zero was increased police enforcement of traffic violations, in the same year that multiracial groups were filling streets across the United States to call attention to the deadly effects of racial profiling in policing."[22] By 2015, some advocates were noting that Vision Zero was backfiring for vulnerable road users even apart from racism: San Francisco's "Focus on the Five" (the five most dangerous traffic violations) policy increased ticketing of cyclists and pedestrians far more than drivers.[23] Many advocates instead support more "neutral" technological measures that automatically sanction drivers who speed or use transit-only lanes.[24] While there is a growing debate on Streetsblog, CityLab, and related online media over issues of racism and traffic enforcement, the obduracy of the car-based built environment poses a fiscal challenge for infrastructural solutions, while enforcement poses a political and moral one.[25]

Has the issue of safety displaced the economic arguments supporting bicycle infrastructure outlined in chapters 4 and 5? I do not think so. While safety is rarely framed economically (e.g., dangerous streets threaten economic growth), safety is a malleable term that is experienced differently, and always has an economic dimension. It usually falls to advocates of color to explain why safety does not mean the same thing in gentrifying neighborhoods—where new residents might welcome increased police presence enforcing traffic laws and personal safety—as in low-income ones—where residents are as likely to see the police themselves as a threat.[26] In practice, safety from traffic risk, a priority for bicyclists and pedestrians, might conflict with safety from law enforcement for Black motorists, and it might look different still from safety from residential displacement. In this respect, seemingly neutral efforts to improve urban life by transforming the built environment breathe new life into durable antagonisms along lines of race and class, rather than abolishing them. Moreover, safety is the new organizing frame for the Global Designing Cities Initiative, an emerging program to remake urban streets across the globe, undertaken by Bloomberg Philanthropies in partnership with NACTO, which has built its authority over—and knowledge base about—

street planning precisely through the lens of economic benefits.[27] Thus, the safety and political economy frames work in tandem.

Bikeshare, Big Data, and Platform Urbanism

As noted in chapter 6, bicycle sharing systems, which allow members to borrow a bike for short trips in the same way one might use a taxi, intensify some of the key contradictions of bicycle infrastructure planning more generally. They more straightforwardly court high-income residents and tourists, while their operating costs create added obstacles to equitable coverage. And they more directly contribute to growth-oriented competitiveness, particularly "talent" attraction and firm growth, by offering a "livable" urban realm as a commodified amenity. In some cases, bikeshare stations are part of placemaking strategy contributing to gentrification dynamics rather than just reflecting them. As suggested in the previous chapter, however, the fact that they are ongoing operations that use a centrally managed fleet, rather than one-time installations, allows them to do something that even the most sophisticated protected bike lanes do not: produce user-linked *data*, the coin of the realm in contemporary capitalism. Indeed, the generation of data is one of the central functions of bikeshare, rather than just an ancillary benefit, and it is growing in importance.

A number of scholars have commented on the start of a shift away from a society of ownership to one of "sharing." This "sharing economy" has empowered platforms: digital infrastructures like Amazon Web Services or Google that intermediate multisided markets and interactions, generating value through "network effects" and capturing rents in the process.[28] Bikeshare systems have not been deployed directly based on this logic, but emerging patterns in the bikeshare industry are increasing its contribution to what Sarah Barns and others have called "platform urbanism," or the mutual constitution of urban and digital life through platform services.[29] One example is Ford GoBike. In late 2016, reports began circulating that Ford's real interest in sponsoring bikeshare lay in access to user data.[30] A new Ford subsidiary, Ford Smart Mobility, had acquired Chariot, a "dynamic shuttle" startup, and launched the FordPass app, a mobility platform that integrates real-time bikeshare, shuttle, carshare, transit, and parking garage data.[31] Ford GoBike data would be a key input to this platform.[32] As Ford Smart Mobility chairman Jim Hackett explained to investors at the time: "We want you to hear 'data' when we're talking about bikes."[33]

While Ford cannot sell this data to third parties, its sponsorship of San Francisco's system gives it access to one of the most valuable and technologically savvy customer pools in the world for testing digital products.

CONCLUSION 181

Moreover, while the data will also be publicly available in aggregated form for planning and analysis purposes, it can only provide information about bikeshare usage—not private bicycles. The idea that the richness of this data could crowd out other ways of understanding bicycle usage—particularly those of poor people beyond the service area—is a reasonable concern.

Almost as soon as MoGo and Ford GoBike were on the ground, however, many in the industry were foreseeing their supersession by "dockless" systems, both bikes and small electric scooters, which use a smartphone interface and GPS to locate and check out the bicycle and can be parked anywhere, all for as little as a dollar a ride (Figure 24). Proponents argue that this makes them less expensive, allowing greater coverage at a lower cost, and eliminates disruption related to station siting and parking. The bikes themselves are lighter and cheaper, and because they are GPS enabled, the work of rebalancing—a major cost for a dock-based system—can be "gamified": users can earn credits for riding a bike from low-demand to high-demand areas. Some anticipate crediting users based on the carbon use that they offset, or fitting bicycles with carbon-scrubbing filters.[34] Dockless

Figure 24. Chinese firm Mobike's "dockless" bikeshare fleet in Manchester, United Kingdom, September 2017, which closed in 2018. Photograph by the author.

firms tout their potential for more equitable coverage, taking advantage of the inequalities built into station-based systems, and based on initial anecdotal reports, youth of color have taken up dockless bikes in greater numbers than they have traditional bikeshare.[35]

In 2017 the number of dockless bikeshare firms, and investment in their operations, exploded. The two largest firms at the time, Ofo and Mobike, came from China, where bikeshare was growing rapidly at the same time that rates of traditional working-class bicycle usage were falling. These firms in fact acted as proxies in a battle between two titans of Chinese venture capital: social media and gaming firm Tencent and retailer Alibaba. By 2018, they were joined in the United States by Bay Area startups Lime and JUMP, a dockless electric assist bike produced by Social Bicycles, which provides equipment for "hybrid" bikeshare systems in Portland and New Orleans. The sector is extraordinarily dynamic. In April 2018 alone, Uber bought JUMP for $200 million and Chinese on-demand service provider Meituan Dianping bought Mobike for $2.7 billion.[36] The feeding frenzy reached even dock-based providers. In June 2018 Lyft bought Motivate for a reported $250 million, giving it control of a company with exclusive operating rights in the country's top markets.[37] 2018 also saw the launch of electric scooter–sharing startups Bird, Spin, Wind, and many others, as well as scooters from Lime, which had received investment from Uber, and from Lyft. The "micro-mobility" revolution had finally attracted the investors who work the levers of the digital economy and hope to create the "Amazon of transportation."[38]

While the launch of Mobike and Ofo, among others, in Global North cities like Manchester in the United Kingdom and Dallas has raised specters of what one writer has called "mobility spam," abetted by images of vast piles of discarded bikeshare bikes in Shanghai, a more interesting set of questions revolves around what kinds of platforms these companies are.[39] Are they "first and last mile" solutions or data collection devices? Are they part of a fluid mobility "ecosystem" or in the process of being incorporated into larger monopolistic platforms seeking to become the "obligatory passage points" for urban mobility practices? Regardless, what they do not do yet is earn a profit. With vast pools of venture capital and teaser prices designed to capture market share, Ofo and Mobike are hemorrhaging revenue just like Uber and Lyft.[40] Like Uber and Lyft, they rely on casual, piece-rate labor, outsourcing or underinvestment in maintenance, and regulatory evasion to cut costs and expand rapidly. In October 2017 a smaller Chinese bikeshare startup, Bluegogo, which had tried to operate in San Francisco but was barred by Motivate's exclusive agreement, went under.[41] In July 2018 Ofo announced a drastic reduction in its services in North

America, Europe, and South Asia, and a 70 percent reduction in its workforce, in order to "prioritize growth in viable markets."[42] Mobike also pulled out of Washington, D.C., shortly thereafter, citing excessive regulations, and Manchester, England, citing rampant vandalism.[43] Such wild fluctuations in service due to dependence on venture capital raises questions about the long-term viability of these systems, especially as ways to address climate change.

The transformation of bicycling as a tool for the urban environment to the bicycle as a platform to generate monopolizable data may represent the subsumption of bicycling as a practice into the global circuits of capital accumulation in the "intangible economy."[44] In effect, in the political economy of data and the construction of platforms to aggregate it, the bicycle is a waste product.[45] But this subsumption is far from complete. Just as ride-sharing and self-driving vehicles proliferate alongside old cars and trucks, the practice of bicycling will remain heterogeneous for the foreseeable future. If the center of gravity of cycling as a mode of urban transport continues to shift toward privately owned platforms, possibly distorting bicycle planning in order to facilitate this function, then it may have dire consequences for the equitable distribution of a less carbon intensive and more survivable form of life.

The Obdurate City

Antonio Gramsci's concept of a "passive revolution" outlines the way in which faltering hegemony can be stabilized through quite substantial changes that nonetheless do not challenge the overall structure of social power.[46] In many ways, this neatly captures the "passive revolution" in mobility in American cities, which has quite profoundly transformed a relatively small number of places within certain metropolitan areas. Moreover, this transformation has primarily been one of spatial form, rather than social process.[47]

The American city is an obdurate beast, and the models that inspire American urbanists, which come largely from northern Europe and the occasional Bogotá, often mistake the political-economic basis on which processes of urbanization are founded.[48] Conservative commentators are partially correct in arguing that these progressive urbanists want to make American cities into Scandinavian ones, and that in this they are fighting a losing battle. As reasons they generally point to differences in national culture, or more grimly, greater social homogeneity.[49] But the fundamental reality that separates American cities from Scandinavian ones is not culture in the abstract but the political economy of land. American urbanism, predicated on the ability to expand onward and outward, is fundamentally settler colonial.[50]

The uphill battle that faces American urbanists who are inspired by Scandinavian cities is not just that most Americans seem to prefer automobiles and detached single-family homes but that building these landscapes remains extraordinarily profitable. It is profitable because of the "free gifts" of "empty" land and the extraordinary subsidies to home and car ownership. In response, advocates have drifted ever more toward an argument that denser, more lively places are not just more environmentally sustainable but economically valuable. Soaring demand in these places is the proof. As the CEO of a major Finnish "mobility as a service" platform Maas Global put it, summarizing today's common sense: "When they compete for a cutting edge workforce, creativity and investment, which one do you think has the upper hand, the web of beautiful hubs ["human-scale" places with hubs of seamless mobility] or the sewer city [places designed only for traffic flow]? Why do you think people are moving to Vancouver, not to Detroit?"[51]

But the trouble is that in conditions of austerity, bicycle infrastructure cannot be placed everywhere systematically and comprehensively. Thus planners are limited both to spectacular interventions as proof of their viability and to ad hoc measures like competitive grants and voter-approved bonds or tax initiatives to fund them.[52] Meanwhile, without large public investments in housing and mass transit, the rising costs of urban life, proof of their "success," provide a built-in justification for expansion on the urban fringe, necessitating car usage. The problem is not even necessarily that cities are too expensive, although international speculative flows seeking dollar-denominated assets exert tremendous inflationary pressure. It is that the suburbs are too cheap. Suburbanization is a way of capturing and capitalizing "cheap nature," and in the long run underproducing it.[53]

The contradictions of bicycle planning, from the Bay Area to Philadelphia to Detroit, reflect the absence of a territorial agency able to impose a "structured coherence" on regional urbanization.[54] In other words, the widespread recognition that accumulation on the extensive suburbanization model has stalled has not automatically led to an organizational form that can regionally coordinate planning along redistributive lines. Instead, in true neoliberal fashion, planning operates through inducements to entrepreneurial approaches by neighborhoods and municipalities, and offering better mobility choices in order to reshape individual behavior—implicitly that of the carbon-intensive middle classes. In practice, these inducements feed the creation of place-based accumulation patterns around existing corridors, through a model that rewards market-rate development on devalued urban land but avoids disturbing existing pockets of low-density residential wealth or the power of the landowning class as a whole.

My argument in this book is that the both the successes and limitations of bicycle infrastructure as a solution to carbon-intensive urban capitalism are fundamentally geographical in nature. Bicycle infrastructure planning confronts the obduracy of the built environment through largely tactical interventions at the corridor level, while regional restructuring generates pressure on governments to transform these corridors in the interest of sustaining growth. Neither the scale of the corridor nor the region preexists the processes that produce it.[55] Bicycle advocates have made corridors key sites for claiming the value—both ideologically and materially—of transforming mobility practices, rescaling their roles within the metropolis. The violent "see-saw" dialectic of capital, and the racialized population shifts it has provoked, remake the shape of the region and the functional relationships that constitute it. In other words, the relocalization that bicycling performs is intimately linked to the economic resurgence of urban cores and the ideological denigration of exurban sprawl, with very material consequences for both climate futures and spatial justice.[56]

The contribution of bicycle advocates to remaking the street has reshaped the municipal state and its planning practices, if not its ultimate priorities of fostering capital accumulation. Advocates have broadened the scope of street planning and the scope of who counts as an expert, articulating new social formations into the networks of expertise that physically make the city. They have worked hard to lengthen these networks and leverage their own relative marginality, forming large, well-funded organizations like NACTO as an alternative repository of expert knowledge. These moves have been critical to changing the common sense of urbanization. By building bicycle infrastructure into a narrative of urban livability, sustainability, and competitiveness, they make the reshaping of mobility a key part of urban restructuring. The bicycle is a unique window into these processes because bicycle infrastructure renders gentrification intelligible—rightly or wrongly—in a new way.

Returning to the political conjunctures I outlined above, how might we salvage the critical power of thinking through the lens of the bicycle by decentering it? What kinds of claims would this permit bicycle advocates to make regarding gentrification, displacement, affordable housing, and access to jobs? How might bicycle infrastructure be rethought not as an amenity and an improvement to quality of life but as a survival strategy and a necessity for a just metropolis? Fortunately, bicycle advocates of color have been at the forefront of exactly these questions. Thanks to their efforts, by 2018 "equity" had shifted from an ancillary concern to a constant topic of debate within bicycle advocacy. Much of this push came from bicycle advocates of color. As noted in chapter 1, the formation of the League of American Bicyclists' Equity Advisory Council in 2013 was a key inflection point that revealed how far the bike movement would have to come on questions of race. Nevertheless, support from the Robert Wood Johnson Foundation led to a pair of reports—*The New Movement* and *Pedaling Towards Equity*—profiling local initiatives and rising voices that were challenging the whiteness and class position of the traditional bicycle advocacy world. This momentum continued to build, particularly with support from NACTO and its Better Bike Share Partnership, because while the whiteness of cycling on the whole was debatable, the whiteness of bikeshare users was unignorable.

Meanwhile, a number of local advocates "jumped scales" and became national leaders. Tamika Butler, a queer Black woman from Nebraska, was hired by Los Angeles County Bicycle Coalition—itself something of an incubator of strong advocates of color—as executive director with a "fresh perspective" around this time, and which quickly became known within growing equity circles.[57] In an electrifying speech at the 2016 NACTO Designing Cities conference, she described "Planning While Black" as a condition of being unable to ignore the quotidian violence of white supremacy, and she called out white planners for their fragility. "This is me giving you permission to go about your work in a different way," she told a room full of national leaders in mobility planning.[58] Adonia Lugo and other advocates (a number of them from Los Angeles) formed Untokening Collective, which emerged out of "The Untokening: A Convening for Just Streets and Communities," which in turn had brought together mobility justice planners, researchers, and activists in Atlanta in 2016. "Prioritize people over profit, property or placemaking," "Reject policing as a street safety solution," and "Discard best practices" form part of the collective's "Ten Principles of Mobility Justice."[59] Finally, in 2017 Olatunji Oboi Reed, who was a leader in Red, Bike and Green and later Slow Roll in Chicago (see chapter 3) and received a White House Transportation Champion of Change award in 2015, became a key voice pushing back against the Chicago Police Department's role in Vision Zero, given its grave record of racially profiling both drivers and cyclists.[60] Drawing on this momentum he launched Equiticity, an organization based on his vision of a "city where racial equity is fully integrated at the policy and legislative levels into every function, department, resource and budget associated with city operations, services and programs."[61] In short, in the context of broad shifts surrounding the Black Lives Matter movement and national discussions of inequality and gentrification, advocates of color have responded to mainstream complicity with planning as usual by forming their own organizations. These shifts are felt locally as well. A coalition to stop gang injunctions in the Fruitvale neighborhood in 2014 that included tenants' rights group Causa Justa/Just Cause and prison abolitionists' Critical Resistance, as well as Bikes 4 Life (discussed in chapter 3) and Cycles of Change, was an early glimpse.[62] Oakland-based transit justice advocacy group TransForm played a key role in expanding access to the Ford GoBike system.[63] It has made affordable housing a main plank of its work for improving mobility and simultaneously improving mobility as a way of reducing housing costs by reducing parking demand.[64] Even official planning efforts have partially accepted the decentering of bicycles. In the spring of 2018, Cycles of Change and the Scraper Bike Team led meetings in East Oakland on the new bicycle plan where residents wanted safer conditions but remained skeptical of the photogenic "world class" infrastructure that city leaders and mainstream advocates were now demanding (see chapter 5). They also questioned the frame of safety itself, since they did not consider cars the primary danger on the streets in some of their neighborhoods.[65] These notes show some of the ways that the bike movement must go beyond the bicycle. They have gone halfway, engaging questions of how urban space is produced. Now the journey involves the question of *for whom* it is produced.

Ultimately, the bicycle is dwarfed by the scale of the processes with which it is entangled. Yet cycling is crucial to how the urban future is imagined, fought for, and enacted in the present. This book has explored what the burst in interest in cycling has to tell us about the changing dynamics of the production of urban space. I have tried to show how attempts to transform cities into more livable and sustainable places have become entangled with efforts to remake them as more effective generators of private profit. The varied social formations brought together through cycling necessarily exceed their usefulness to capital, however. They generate new antagonisms and potentialities, even in times of austerity. Nonetheless, I am convinced that the deep transformations the political economy and ecology of urbanization that our current situation requires are not yet considered politically possible. My hope in writing this is that, through political struggle, they become so.

ACKNOWLEDGMENTS

Any project this long in the making tends to incur a large ledger of debts, intellectual and otherwise. First, I acknowledge the immense influence of Jason Weidemann at the University of Minnesota Press, who contacted me in 2012, long before I could even envision the end of my dissertation, and convinced me of my project's potential. Two reviewers offered supportive comments on early drafts and helped to push the project forward. My writing partners Naomi Adiv and Jennifer Tucker provided accountability, guidance, and support, without which I could not have finished. Joshua Akers, Hannah Birnbaum, Erin Collins, Jennifer Devine, Kimberley Kinder, Sarah Knuth, Kathe Newman, and Alexander Tarr all contributed in some way, from big questions of framing to detailed line edits. Finally, at the University of Minnesota Press, the hard work of Gabriel Levin, Rachel Moeller, and Margery Tippie caught details that had long since become invisible to me.

The research that made this book possible received generous support at various stages from the University of California, Berkeley, including the Regent's Fellowship, the Dean's Normative Time Fellowship, the Center for Teaching and Learning Lecturers Teaching Fellowship, and the Academic Personnel Office Professional Development Award. An award from the National Science Foundation's Science, Technology, and Society funding program (Award ID 1734665) supported a new project that helped deepen my thinking as I completed the manuscript. In the fall of 2017, Nathan Sayre invited me to teach an open-ended class to work through the ideas in this book, and my brilliant students were kind enough to oblige me. After leaving Berkeley, I joined the Sustainable Consumption Institute at the University of Manchester, another vibrant scholarly community that gave me an invaluable comparative perspective.

One exciting thing about this book is how quickly the world changed while I was writing it. Raising critical questions regarding bicycling and the city no longer seems rude at best and counterrevolutionary at worst, and this is because of the pioneering work of a growing group of scholars that I am proud to call my colleagues. Manisha Anantharaman, Jesus Barajas, Jason Henderson, Melody Hoffman, David Horton, Adonia Lugo, Sarah McCullough, Sergio Montero, Lusi Morhayim, Emily Reid-Musson, Oscar Sosa López, and Justin Spinney have all been major sources of inspiration and encouragement. They demonstrate their commitment to a more just version of the cycling city in deeds as well as words.

I owe this book to the critical engagement, unfailing comradeship, and generous support of colleagues and mentors at the University of California, where I completed my PhD and then taught as a lecturer for several years. Iain Boal, Wendy Brown, Paul Groth, Gillian Hart, Jake Kosek, David O'Sullivan, Ananya Roy, Nathan Sayre, and Richard Walker all played crucial roles in my intellectual formation. Jake Kosek threw me into the deep end of theory my first semester of grad school, and I found it to my liking. Ananya Roy's insistence on contextualizing the bicycle within the broader history of planning led me toward some of the most exciting findings of the entire project. Richard Walker demanded crisp, direct writing even on early dissertation drafts; I chafed at this but now must admit he was right. Michael Watts offhandedly mentioned the political economy of the bicycle as a possible topic, planting the seed in my mind that something like this book was possible in critical geography. They were consummate mentors, always pushing my work in new directions and confident in my abilities even when I wasn't. Alison Post and Joan Walker led the Global Metropolitan Studies seminars in which I workshopped early versions of several chapters; these helped expand my thinking beyond the critical geography bubble. Erin Collins, Alicia Cowart, Shannon Cram, John Elrick, Meleiza Figueroa, Anthony Fontes, Ilaria Giglioli, Katy Guimond, Julie Klinger, Zachary Levenson, Nicki List, Seth Lunine, Jeff Martin, Shaina Potts, Annie Shattuck, Alberto Velazquez, and Max Woodworth shared the joys and trials of graduate student life with me and became an extended intellectual family that has spread across the globe. Graduate student union comrades Amanda Armstrong, Shane Boyle, Mandy Cohen, Katy Fox-Hodess, Nick Kardahji, Sara Smith, and Jessica Taal deepened my political education. Department staff Delores Dillard, Marjorie Ensor, Darin Jensen, Josh Mandel, Carol Page, Dan Plumlee, and Nat Vonnegut supported me as a student, researcher, and teacher with their mastery of the details of the university bureaucracy. Geography at Berkeley became my home in more ways than I knew.

I must also acknowledge the interlocutors—bicycle advocates, planners, and activists—who shaped this project. Cynthia Armour, Brytanee Brown, Reggie Burnett, Jenna Burton, Clarrissa Cabansagan, Paolo Cosulich-Schwartz, Brian Drayton, LisaRuth Elliott, Sarah Fine, Chema Hernandez Gil, Jason Hall, Carlos Hernandez, Morgan Kanninen, Chris Kidd, Jeffrey Nolish, Jason Patton, Robert Prinz, René Rivera, Najari Smith, and Dave Snyder all invited me into their social circles, taught me new things, and encouraged me to share my insights as they shared theirs. They are the "organic intellectuals" of the bicycle world. Dave Campbell, Chris Carlsson, Clarrissa Cabansagan, Katie Monroe, and Lisa Nuzskowski were particularly generous with their time, energy, and social networks. Though at times I'm sure they felt they were under a microscope, I can only promise that I worked hard to place myself under the same microscope.

I owe special thanks to Box Dog Bikes, a worker cooperative in San Francisco where I worked part-time from 2009 to 2015 while doing the bulk of the research for this book. It was a pleasure to turn wrenches alongside Geoffrey Coburn, E. Conner, Gabe Ehlert, Ian Lautze, Eric Lonowski, Jackie Musick, Gabe Peterson, Anderson Reed, Sarah Roberts, Jon Stynes, and Kenn Sutto, and the combination of intellectual and manual labor helped to keep me sane. E. Conner became one of my closest friends in the process. I also thank Curtis Anthony, Jeff Cuellar, Joel Flood, David Rodan, and Matthew Woods at Via Bicycle in Philadelphia for their mentorship when I was just a fledgling mechanic fresh out of college. My lifelong friend Joey Parent deserves both credit and blame for getting me into bikes in the first place.

I must note that I wrote large parts of this book at that essential "third space," the café (and occasionally the bar). I owe special thanks to the workers and proprietors at Arbor Café, Black Spring Coffee, Commonwealth Café and Public House, and Rooz Café for their indulgence and caffeination.

Mary Casper accompanied me at the start of this intellectual journey and remained a friend even after we parted ways. Steven Ellis, a Philadelphia friend and my Oakland roommate for a number of years, tolerated my habit of leaving books and chapter drafts strewn about our cramped apartment. Josh Berkow, Ryan Ellis, Emily Kovach, Lauren Kovach, and Sarah Pappas generously put me up during research trips to Detroit and Philadelphia. Many of these friends were around for the moments that ultimately formed the ideas in this book.

I have been especially lucky to have the constant support of my family. In particular, my mom, Cathy Caldwell, has always been my biggest fan, and while she prefers a different style of writing, her sharp editorial eye is an inspiration. I might never have taken a wrench to a bike if not for my father, Bill Stehlin, whose inveterate tinkering clearly rubbed off on me. My sister Kate reminds me in her own way that empathy is a loftier goal than critique, a point easily lost in the academic world. Finally, in the course of working on this book, I gained new family members; the Rockefeller Harris family welcomed me into their lives and shared their wisdom and encouragement.

Logan Rockefeller Harris has supported me emotionally and intellectually with more grace than I could have imagined possible. There is little that is more thankless than steadfastly accompanying someone from the final throes of a doctoral degree through the insecurity of the academic job market and the final push to complete a book manuscript. With her wit, clarity of thought, and insistence on rigor, she has pushed me harder than I could have pushed myself, and with more kindness. She is smart, funny, and cool. The magnitude of my love and gratitude defies description.

NOTES

Introduction

1. Personal interview, June 13, 2012.
2. Melody Hoffmann, *Bike Lanes Are White Lanes: Bicycle Advocacy and Urban Planning* (Lincoln: University of Nebraska Press, 2016). "Rolling signifier" here references the concept of race as a "floating signifier," popularized by Stuart Hall. See Stuart Hall and Sut Jhally, "Race, the Floating Signifier," videorecording (Northampton, Mass.: Media Education Foundation, 1997), http://www.mediaed.org/transcripts/Stuart-Hall-Race-the-Floating-Signifier-Transcript.pdf.
3. Robert D. Bullard, "Overcoming Racism in Environmental Decisionmaking." *Environment: Science and Policy for Sustainable Development* 36, no. 4 (1994): 10–44.
4. Ernesto Laclau and Chantal Mouffe, *Hegemony and Socialist Strategy: Towards a Radical Democratic Politics* (London: Verso, 1985).
5. Neil Smith, *The New Urban Frontier: Gentrification and the Revanchist City* (New York: Routledge, 1996).
6. Stuart Hall, "Race, Articulation, and Societies Structured in Dominance," in *Race Critical Theories: Text and Context*, ed. Philomena Essed and David Theo Goldberg (Malden, Mass.: Wiley-Blackwell, 2001), 38–68; Emma Jackson and Tim Butler, "Revisiting 'Social Tectonics': The Middle Classes and Social Mix in Gentrifying Neighbourhoods," *Urban Studies* 52, no. 13 (2015): 2349–65.
7. Ivan Illich, *Tools for Conviviality*. New York: Harper and Row, 1973.
8. Richard Florida, *Cities and the Creative Class* (New York: Routledge, 2005).
9. Michael Storper and Anthony J. Venables, "Buzz: Face-to-Face Contact and the Urban Economy," *Journal of Economic Geography* 4, no. 4 (August 1, 2004): 351–70.
10. Stephen Graham and Simon Marvin, *Splintering Urbanism: Networked Infrastructures, Technological Mobilities and the Urban Condition* (New York:

Routledge, 2001); Mark Fisher, *Capitalist Realism: Is There No Alternative?* (Alresford, UK: Zero Books, 2009).

11. Mike Lydon and Anthony Garcia, *Tactical Urbanism: Short-Term Action for Long-Term Change* (Washington, D.C.: Island Press, 2015); Oli Mould, "Tactical Urbanism: The New Vernacular of the Creative City," *Geography Compass* 8, no. 8 (2014): 529–39; John G. Stehlin and Alexander R. Tarr, "Think Regionally, Act Locally? Gardening, Cycling, and the Horizon of Urban Spatial Politics," *Urban Geography* 38, no. 9 (2017): 1329–51.

12. Chris Carlsson, *Critical Mass: Bicycling's Defiant Celebration* (Oakland, Calif.: AK Press, 2002); Chris Carlsson, *Nowtopia: How Pirate Programmers, Outlaw Bicyclists, and Vacant-Lot Gardeners Are Inventing the Future Today* (Oakland, Calif.: AK Press, 2008).

13. Marcia D. Lowe, *The Bicycle: Vehicle for a Small Planet* (Washington, D.C.: Worldwatch Institute, 1989); Gillian Hart, "D/developments after the Meltdown," *Antipode* 41, no. S1 (2012): 117–41.

14. During the oil crisis of the 1970s, bicycle commuting was briefly but seriously considered as a possible solution, but without sufficient funding for the infrastructure required, the proposals did not last. See "The Environment: L.A. River Channel Use by Cyclists Proposed," *Los Angeles Times*, April 28, 1972, http://search.proquest.com/docview/156923027; "The Environment: Use of City Streets for Bicycle Paths Urged," *Los Angeles Times*, November 13, 1973, http://search.proquest.com/docview/157445777. The state of Oregon passed the most aggressive funding measure of the era in 1971, mandating that one percent of state transportation funding be set aside for bicycle projects; today, Oregon still has the highest rates of bicycle commuting in the country. Davis, California, also saw a massive investment in bicycle infrastructure in this period. See Carlton Reid, *Bike Boom: The Unexpected Resurgence of Cycling* (Washington, D.C.: Island Press, 2017).

15. Immanuel Wallerstein, "New Revolts against the System," *New Left Review* 18, November–December (2002): 29–39.

16. John Pucher, Ralph Buehler, and Mark Seinen, "Bicycling Renaissance in North America? An Update and Re-Appraisal of Cycling Trends and Policies," *Transportation Research Part A: Policy and Practice* 45, no. 6 (2011): 451–75. The Federal-Aid Highway Act of 1973 provided $120 million (over $700 million in 2019 dollars) for bicycle projects over the following three years, but this spending was not sustained. See Reid, *Bike Boom*, 111.

17. Data from the Federal Highway Administration's Federal-Aid Highway Program Funding for Pedestrian and Bicycle Facilities and Programs website, available at http://www.fhwa.dot.gov/environment/bicycle_pedestrian/funding/bipedfund.cfm (accessed January 3, 2017); and the FHWA Highway Statistics Series, availableathttp://www.fhwa.dot.gov/policyinformation/statistics/2010/2010disbchrt.cfm (accessed July 13, 2016).

18. Susan L. Handy, Barbara McCann, Linda Bailey, Michelle Ernst, Lanier McRee, Emily Mehareg, Reid Ewing, and Kate Wright, *The Regional Response to*

Federal Funding for Bicycle and Pedestrian Projects, research report UCD-ITS-RR-09-15 (Davis, Calif: Institute of Transportation Studies, University of California, Davis, 2009), http://pubs.its.ucdavis.edu/publication_detail.php?id=1304.

19. John Pucher, Jennifer Dill, and Susan Handy, "Infrastructure, Programs, and Policies to Increase Bicycling: An International Review," *Preventive Medicine* 50 (January 2010): S106–25, http://www.ncbi.nlm.nih.gov/pubmed/19765610; Jennifer Dill and Kim Voros, "Factors Affecting Bicycling Demand: Initial Survey Findings from the Portland, Oregon, Region," *Transportation Research Record.*, no. 2031 (2007): 9–17.

20. League of American Bicyclists, "70 Largest Cities Ranked by Bike Commuting" (Washington, D.C., 2012), http://bikeleague.org/sites/default/files/70 largest cities.xls; U.S. Census Bureau, "5-Year American Community Survey, 2010–2014" (Washington, D.C., 2015), www.factfinder2.census.gov. Author calculations.

21. Carolyn Szczepanski, "Cities and Businesses Discover That Cycling Pays," *Urbanful*, March 2015, https://urbanful.org/2015/03/02/cities-and-businesses-discover-that-cycling-pays.

22. Joni Balter, "Amazon's HQ2 Search Is about Politics, Too," *Bloomberg*, April 2, 2018, https://www.bloomberg.com/view/articles/2018-04-02/amazon-s-hq2-search-is-about-politics-too.

23. Smith, *The New Urban Frontier*; Neil Smith, "New Globalism, New Urbanism: Gentrification as Global Urban Strategy," *Antipode* 34, no. 3 (2002): 427–50.

24. Elly Blue, "A Field Guide to 'Bikewashing,'" *Taking the Lane*, July 31, 2012, available at http://takingthelane.com/2012/07/31/a-field-guide-to-bikewashing.

25. On the concepts of "scapes," see Arjun Appadurai, *Modernity at Large: Cultural Dimensions of Globalization* (Minneapolis: University of Minnesota Press, 1996).

26. Doreen Massey, *Space, Place, and Gender* (Minneapolis: University of Minnesota Press, 1994), 154.

27. Henri Lefebvre, *The Production of Space*, trans. Donald Nicholson-Smith (Malden, Mass.: Blackwell, 2004), 288.

28. Henri Lefebvre, *The Survival of Capitalism: Reproduction of Relations of Production* (London: Allison and Busby, 1976).

29. Michel Foucault, *The History of Sexuality* (New York: Pantheon Books, 1978), 110.

30. Aidan While, Andrew E. G. Jonas, and David Gibbs, "The Environment and the Entrepreneurial City: Searching for the 'Urban Sustainability Fix' in Manchester and Leeds," *International Journal of Urban and Regional Research* 28, no. 3 (2004): 549–69; Andrew E. G. Jonas, David Gibbs, and Aidan While, "The New Urban Politics as a Politics of Carbon Control," *Urban Studies* 48, no. 12 (2011): 2537–54.

31. See Justin Spinney, "Fixing Mobility in the Neoliberal City: Cycling Policy and Practice in London as a Mode of Political-Economic and Biopolitical

Governance," *Annals of the American Association of Geographers* 106, no. 2 (2016): 450–58. This strength may now be in the process of eroding due to the growth of Uber on one hand and shared electric scooters like Lime on the other.

32. Graham and Marvin, *Splintering Urbanism*.

33. See National Bicycle Dealers Association, "Industry Overview," 2013, http://nbda.com/articles/industry-overview-2013-pg34.htm.

34. Neil Smith, "Toward a Theory of Gentrification: A Back to the City Movement by Capital, Not People." *Journal of the American Planning Association* 45, no. 4 (1979): 538–48.

35. Smith, *The New Urban Frontier*.

36. I use the term "hipster" here as a relational category that is key to how my movements through gentrifying space, *especially* by bike, are likely to be interpreted by others within the same social space. See Mark Greif, Kathleen Ross, and Dayna Tortorici, eds., *What Was the Hipster? A Sociological Investigation* (New York: n+1 Foundation, 2010), 2.

37. This perception is supported by serious policy research as well, which confirms the overlap between gentrification and high rates of cycling to work. See John Pucher and Ralph Buehler, "Analysis of Bicycling Trends and Policies in Large North American Cities: Lessons for New York," *Transportation Research Part A* 45 (2011): 451–75.

38. John Joe Schlichtman and Jason Patch, "Gentrifier? Who, Me? Interrogating the Gentrifier in the Mirror," *International Journal of Urban and Regional Research* 38, no. 4 (July 30, 2014): 1491–1508.

39. Alastair Bonnett, "'White Studies': The Problems and Projects of a New Research Agenda," *Theory, Culture & Society* 13, no. 2 (May 1, 1996): 145–55.

40. Eric de Place, "Race, Class, and the Demographics of Cycling," *Grist*, April 7, 2011, available at http://grist.org/biking/2011-04-06-race-class-and-the-demographics-of-cycling.

41. Cyclists of color are often framed as using bicycles for need rather than by choice, and thus less "real" as cyclists. They are consistently positioned as subjects of care, concern, and outreach, "invisible cyclists" rather than political actors, though this narrative is beginning to erode thanks largely to the initiatives of cyclists of color themselves. See Tanya Snyder, "Cyclists of Color: Invisible No More," *Streetsblog USA*, blog, May 29, 2013, http://usa.streetsblog.org/index.php/2013/05/29/cyclists-of-color-invisible-no-more; League of American Bicyclists, "The New Majority: Pedaling towards Equity," 2013, https://www.bikeleague.org/content/pedaling-toward-equity; Eric Arnold, "Oakland 'Bike Black' Group Goes National," *Oakland Local*, 2012, http://newamericamedia.org/2012/05/oakland-bike-black-group-goes-national.php.

42. Iain Boal, "Toward a World History of the Bicycle," in *Cycle History 11: Proceedings of the 11th International Cycling History Conference*, ed. Iain Boal and Andrew Ritchie (Osaka, Japan: Cycle Publishing, 2000).

43. Matthew Paterson, "Governing Mobilities, Mobilising Carbon," *Mobilities* 9, no. 4 (2014): 570–84.

44. Dani Simons, "NACTO Wrap-Up: Cities Are Doing It for Themselves," *Streetsblog USA*, blog, October 26, 2012, http://www.streetsblog.org/2012/10/26/nacto-wrap-up-cities-are-doing-it-for-themselves.

45. Bruce Katz and Julie Wagner, "The Rise of Innovation Districts: A New Geography of Innovation in America," Brookings Institution, 2014, http://www.brookings.edu/~/media/Programs/metro/Images/Innovation/InnovationDistricts1.pdf; Storper and Venables, "Buzz"; Florida, *Cities and the Creative Class*; Gregory M. Spencer, "Knowledge Neighbourhoods: Urban Form and Evolutionary Economic Geography," *Regional Studies* 49, no. 5 (2015): 883–98.

46. Alex Schafran, "Origins of an Urban Crisis: The Restructuring of the San Francisco Bay Area and the Geography of Foreclosure," *International Journal of Urban and Regional Research* 37, no. 2 (March 5, 2013): 663–88; Susan Fainstein, Norman Fainstein, and P. Jefferson Armistead, "Restructuring the City: The Political Economy of Urban Redevelopment," in *Restructuring the City: The Political Economy of Urban Redevelopment*, ed. Susan Fainstein et al. (New York: Longman, 1983), 202–44.

47. Giovanni Pesce, "An Aesthetic Rebellion (Milan, Italy)," in *Critical Mass: Bicycling's Defiant Celebration* (Oakland, Calif.: AK Press, 2002), 52–54; Susan Blickstein and Susan Hanson, "Critical Mass: Forging a Politics of Sustainable Mobility in the Information Age," *Transportation* 28 (2001): 347–62; Steven T. Jones, "Critical Mass at 20: The Movement Changed the Rules in Cities All over the World—and Almost, Almost Took the Bay Bridge," *San Francisco Bay Guardian* 46, no. 52 (2012): 10–14.

48. Stephen J. Collier, James Christopher Mizes, and Antina von Schnitzler, "Preface: Public Infrastructures / Infrastructural Publics," *Limn* 7, November (2016): 1–12, https://limn.it/preface-public-infrastructures-infrastructural-publics.

49. Jamie Peck and Nik Theodore, *Fast Policy* (Minneapolis: University of Minnesota Press, 2015).

50. Suzanne Hoadley, "Mobility As a Service: Implications for Urban and Regional Transport," POLIS Position Paper, September 2017, available at https://www.polisnetwork.eu/uploads/Modules/PublicDocuments/polis-maas-discussion-paper-2017---final_.pdf; Nick Srnicek, *Platform Capitalism* (London: Polity, 2016); Paul Langley and Andrew Leyshon, "Platform Capitalism: The Intermediation and Capitalization of Digital Economic Circulation," *Finance and Society* 3, no. 1 (2017): 11–31.

1. The City and the Cyclescape

1. Janette Sadik-Khan, "The Bike Wars Are Over, and the Bikes Won," *New York Magazine*, March 8, 2016, http://nymag.com/daily/intelligencer/2016/03/bike-wars-are-over-and-the-bikes-won.html.

2. One bicycle advocate I spoke to in Austin went so far as to say that seeing Sadik-Khan speak at the International Downtown Association conference in 2012 felt "exactly like a rock concert."

3. Julian Brash, *Bloomberg's New York: Class and Governance in the Luxury City* (Athens: University of Georgia Press, 2011).

4. PeopleForBikes is at its core a bicycle manufacturers' lobbying organization, but it supports a wide range of research and advocacy as well.

5. See http://nacto.org/program/bike-share-initiative (accessed May 9, 2018).

6. Data calculated from the Federal Highway Administration, 2009 National Household Travel Survey (NHTS), available at http://nhts.ornl.gov. The 2017 NHTS shows a plateau at roughly this level. The American Community Survey counts only the main form of transportation used for commuting to work by employed people. Meanwhile the NHTS, which counts all trips regardless of purpose, is conducted less frequently and can be unreliable below the state level.

7. "Interbike to Highlight Urban Cycling," *Bicycle Retailer and Industry News*, August 29, 2011, http://www.bicycleretailer.com/north-america/2011/08/29/inter bike-highlight-urban-cycling.

8. Carolyn Szczepanski, "How Bicycles Bring Business," *Momentum Magazine*, April 10, 2013, https://momentummag.com/how-bicycles-bring-business; PeopleForBikes, "Protected Bike Lanes Mean Business" (Washington, D.C., 2013), http://www.sfbike.org/wp-content/uploads/2014/04/Protected_Bike_Lanes_Mean_Business.pdf.

9. Mike Maciag, "Gentrification in America Report," *Governing*, February 2015, https://www.governing.com/gov-data/census/gentrification-in-cities-govern ing-report.html.

10. Based on S&P/Case-Shiller Home Price Index data available at https://fred .stlouisfed.org/series/SPCS20RSA.

11. Alan Berube and Elizabeth Kneebone, *Confronting Suburban Poverty in America* (Washington, D.C.: Brookings Institution, 2013); Christopher B. Leinberger, "The Death of the Fringe Suburb," *New York Times*, November 2011, http://www.nytimes.com/2011/11/26/opinion/the-death-of-the-fringe-suburb .html; Alex Schafran, "Origins of an Urban Crisis: The Restructuring of the San Francisco Bay Area and the Geography of Foreclosure," *International Journal of Urban and Regional Research* 37, no. 2 (March 5, 2013): 663–88. Exurban construction continues, but it no longer represents the frontier toward which builders are rushing. In California, for instance, units added in single-family homes no longer dramatically outpace multifamily construction as they did throughout the 1990s and 2000s. See the California Department of Finance at http://www.dof.ca.gov/ Forecasting/Economics/Indicators/Construction_Permits (accessed April 21, 2018).

12. Elvin Wyly et al., "Cartographies of Race and Class: Mapping the Class-Monopoly Rents of American Subprime Mortgage Capital," *International Journal of Urban and Regional Research* 33, no. 2 (June 2009): 332–54; Carolina Reid, "Sought or Sold? Social Embeddedness and Consumer Decisions in the Mortgage Market," Federal Reserve Bank of San Francisco, 2010, https://Econ Papers.repec.org/RePEc:fip:fedfcw:2010-09.

13. Alex Schafran, "Debating Urban Studies in 23 Steps," *City* 18, no. 3 (2014): 321–30.

14. The passage reads: "The old is dying and the new cannot be born; in this interregnum a great variety of morbid symptoms appear." Antonio Gramsci, *Selections from the Prison Notebooks*, ed. Quintin Hoare and Geoffrey Nowell Smith (New York: International, 1971), 276.

15. Chris Carlsson, *Critical Mass: Bicycling's Defiant Celebration* (Oakland, Calif.: AK Press, 2002); Chris Carlsson, LisaRuth Elliott, and Adriana Camarena, *Shift Happens!: Critical Mass at 20* (San Francisco: Full Enjoyment Books, 2012). See also Susan Blickstein and Susan Hanson, "Critical Mass: Forging a Politics of Sustainable Mobility in the Information Age" (2001): 347–62; John Arquilla and David Ronfeldt, eds., *Networks and Netwars: The Future of Terror, Crime, and Militancy* (Santa Monica, Calif.: RAND Corporation, 2001).

16. Jeff Ferrell, *Tearing Down the Streets: Adventures in Urban Anarchy* (New York: Palgrave, 2001); Zachary Furness, "'Put the Fun between Your Legs!': The Politics and Counterculture of the Bicycle" (PhD diss., University of Pittsburgh, 2006); Zachary Furness, *One Less Car: Bicycling and the Politics of Automobility* (Philadelphia: Temple University Press, 2010).

17. Chris Carlsson, *Nowtopia: How Pirate Programmers, Outlaw Bicyclists, and Vacant-Lot Gardeners Are Inventing the Future Today* (Oakland, Calif.: AK Press, 2008).

18. Dave Horton, "Environmentalism and the Bicycle," *Environmental Politics* 15, no. 1 (2006): 41–58. Of course, because bicycles are also commodities with a global supply chain stretching from Singapore, Taiwan, China, and Thailand to North America and Europe, their carbon footprint is hidden by the lack of direct, personal emissions.

19. See, for example, Jeff Mapes, *Pedaling Revolution: How Cyclists Are Changing American Cities* (Corvallis: Oregon State University Press, 2009); J. Harry Wray, *Pedal Power: The Quiet Rise of the Bicycle in American Public Life* (Boulder, Colo.: Paradigm, 2008); Peter Walker, *How Cycling Can Save the World* (New York: Penguin Random House, 2017).

20. Elly Blue's *Bikenomics* started as a series of posts on *Grist.com* on the personal economics of cycling and was published with the imprint Microcosm Press, whose logo is a bicycle gear with a heart in the center. *Bike Snob* emerged from popular blogger Eben Weiss's incisive and humorous critiques of bike culture. Influential musician and artist David Byrne's *Bicycle Diaries* celebrated meditative wandering by bicycle in the city. Elly Blue, *Bikenomics: How Bicycling Can Save the Economy* (Portland, Ore.: Microcosm, 2013); Eben Weiss, *Bike Snob: Systematically and Mercilessly Realigning the World of Cycling* (San Francisco: Chronicle Books, 2010); David Byrne, *Bicycle Diaries* (New York: Penguin Books, 2010).

21. Ralph Buehler and John Pucher, "Cycling to Work in 90 Large American Cities: New Evidence on the Role of Bike Paths and Lanes," *Transportation* 39, no.

2 (March 2012): 409–32; John Pucher, Ralph Buehler, and Mark Seinen, "Bicycling Renaissance in North America? An Update and Re-Appraisal of Cycling Trends and Policies," *Transportation Research Part A: Policy and Practice* 45, no. 6 (2011): 451–75; John Pucher and Ralph Buehler, *City Cycling* (Cambridge, Mass.: MIT Press, 2012); Jennifer Dill and Kim Voros, "Factors Affecting Bicycling Demand: Initial Survey Findings from the Portland, Oregon, Region," *Transportation Research Record*, no. 2031 (2007): 9–17; Jennifer Dill, "Categorizing Cyclists: What Do We Know? Insights from Portland, OR" in *Velo-City Global Conference* (Vancouver, BC, 2012).

22. Susan Shaheen, Stacey Guzman, and Hua Zhang, "Bikesharing in Europe, the Americas, and Asia," *Transportation Research Record: Journal of the Transportation Research Board* 2143 (December 1, 2010): 159–67; Susan Shaheen et al., "China's Hangzhou Public Bicycle," *Transportation Research Record: Journal of the Transportation Research Board* 2247 (December 1, 2011): 33–41; Elliot W. Martin and Susan Shaheen, "Evaluating Public Transit Modal Shift Dynamics in Response to Bikesharing: A Tale of Two U.S. Cities," *Journal of Transport Geography* 41 (2014): 315–24.

23. Sergio Montero, "San Francisco through Bogotá's Eyes: Leveraging Urban Policy Change through the Circulation of Media Objects," *International Journal of Urban and Regional Research*, 45, no. 5 (2018). Latin American sustainability urbanism is particularly influential in the current moment. Bogotá's pioneering *ciclovías*, or open streets events, initially conceived under Enrique Peñalosa's leadership, were direct antecedents to similar events in New York, Los Angeles, San Francisco, and Minneapolis today. See T. Angotti and C. Irazabal, "Planning Latin American Cities: Dependencies and 'Best Practices,'" *Latin American Perspectives* 44, no. 2 (2017): 4–17.

24. The "fetish" here refers to both Marx's idea of commodity fetishism, which hides the social relations of production (unequal cities and regions) and the traditional anthropological concept of objects endowed with supernatural power. See Maria Kaika and Erik Swyngedouw, "Fetishizing the Modern City: The Phantasmagoria of Urban Technological Networks," *International Journal of Urban and Regional Research* 24, no. 1 (2000): 120–38.

25. Jaime Lerner, *Urban Acupuncture: Celebrating Pinpricks of Change That Enrich City Life* (Washington, D.C.: Island Press, 2014).

26. This is distinct from the established literature in science and technology studies that focuses on the Victorian era, when the bicycle's basic form achieved "closure" and it became the industrial commodity par excellence. See Wiebe E. Bijker, *Of Bicycles, Bakelites, and Bulbs: Toward a Theory of Sociotechnical Change* (Cambridge, Mass.: MIT Press, 1997); Wiebe E. Bijker and Trevor Pinch, "The Social Construction of Facts and Artifacts: Or How the Sociology of Science and the Sociology of Technology Might Benefit Each Other," in *The Social Construction of Technological Systems: New Directions in the Sociology and History of Technology*, ed. Wiebe Bijker, Thomas Hughes, and Trevor Pinch (Cambridge,

Mass.: MIT Press, 2012), 11–44; Nicholas Oddy, "From Practicality to Femininity: Gender and the Dropped Frame Bicycle," in *The Gendered Object*, ed. Pat Kirkham (Manchester: Manchester University Press, 1996); Iain Boal, "Toward a World History of the Bicycle," in *Cycle History 11: Proceedings of the 11th International Cycling History Conference*, ed. Iain Boal and Andrew Ritchie (Osaka, Japan: Cycle, 2000).

27. Melody Hoffmann, *Bike Lanes Are White Lanes: Bicycle Advocacy and Urban Planning* (Lincoln: University of Nebraska Press, 2016). Other works engaging these questions include: Jeff Koehler, "Gentrification and Cultural Ownership in Denver, Colorado," *Praxis: Politics in Action* 1, no. 2 (2014): 18–35; Timothy A. Gibson, "The Rise and Fall of Adrian Fenty, Mayor-Triathlete: Cycling, Gentrification and Class Politics in Washington DC," *Leisure Studies* 34, no. 2 (2015): 230–49; K. T. Smiley, W. Rushing, and M. Scott, "Behind a Bicycling Boom: Governance, Cultural Change and Place Character in Memphis, Tennessee," *Urban Studies* 53, no. 1 (2016): 193–209; Amy Lubitow and Thaddeus R. Miller, "Contesting Sustainability: Bikes, Race, and Politics in Portlandia," *Environmental Justice* 6, no. 4 (2013): 121–26; Amy Lubitow, B. Zinschlag, and N. Rochester, "Plans for Pavement or for People? The Politics of Bike Lanes on the 'Paseo Boricua' in Chicago, Illinois," *Urban Studies* 53, no 12 (2016): 2637–53.

28. Adonia Lugo, "Body-City-Machine: Human Infrastructure for Bicycling in Los Angeles," (PhD diss., University of California, Irvine, 2013); Adonia Lugo and Allison Mannos, "Separate but Eco: Livable Communities for Whom?," *Streetsblog SF*, blog, May 21, 2012, http://la.streetsblog.org/2012/05/21/separate-but-eco-livable-communities-for-whom; Melody Lynn Hoffmann and Adonia Lugo, "Who Is 'World Class'? Transportation Justice and Bicycle Policy," *Urbanities* 4, no. 1 (2014): 45–61; Do Lee, "The Unbearable Weight of Irresponsibility and the Lightness of Tumbleweeds: Cumulative Irresponsibility in Neoliberal Streetscapes," in *Incomplete Streets: Processes, Practices, and Possibilities*, ed. Julian Agyeman and Stephen Zavestoski (New York: Routledge, 2015), 77–93; Sahra Sulaiman, "Equity 101: Bikes v. Bodies on Bikes," *Streetsblog LA*, blog, September 28, 2016, http://la.streetsblog.org/2016/09/28/equity-101-bikes-v-bodies-on-bikes; Emily Reid-Musson, "Shadow Mobilities: Regulating Migrant Bicyclists in Rural Ontario, Canada," *Mobilities* 13, no. 3 (2018), 308–24; Emily Reid-Musson, "Intersectional Rhythmanalysis: Power, Rhythm, and Everyday Life," *Progress in Human Geography* 42, no. 6 (2018), 881–97; Tamika Butler, "Planning While Black" (lecture, NACTO Designing Cities, Seattle, Wash., September 27, 2016), https://www.youtube.com/watch?v=T4R7MuNBMvk; Olatunji Oboi Reed, "Gone. Hope I Make It Home, . . ." *Slow Roll Chicago*, blog, December 18, 2017, http://slowrollchicago.org/blog/olatunji-oboi-reeed-gone-hope-i-make-it-home/2017/12/13.

29. Hoffmann, *Bike Lanes Are White Lanes*.

30. Koehler, "Gentrification and Cultural Ownership in Denver, Colorado"; Gibson, "The Rise and Fall of Adrian Fenty, Mayor-Triathlete"; Smiley, Rushing, and Scott, "Behind a Bicycling Boom"; Amy Lubitow, Thaddeus Miller, and Jeff

Shelton, "Contesting the North Williams Traffic Operations and Safety Project," 2013, https://archive.org/details/ContestingTheNorthWilliamsTrafficOperationsAnd SafetyProject; Lubitow, Zinschlag, and Rochester, "Plans for Pavement or for People?"; Sara Mirk, "It's Not About the Bikes," *Portland Mercury,* February 6, 2012, http://www.portlandmercury.com/portland/its-not-about-the-bikes/Content?oid =5619639.

31. Mimi Sheller, *Mobility Justice: The Politics of Movement in an Age of Extremes* (London: Verso, 2018); Stephen Zavestoski and Julian Agyeman, *Incomplete Streets: Processes, Practices, and Possibilities* (New York: Routledge, 2014).

32. Aaron Golub et al., *Bicycle Justice and Urban Transformation: Biking for All?* (London: Routledge Earthscan, 2016).

33. Matthew Paterson, *Automobile Politics: Ecology and Cultural Political Economy* (Cambridge: Cambridge University Press, 2007); Jason Henderson, *Street Fight: The Politics of Mobility in San Francisco* (Amherst: University of Massachusetts Press, 2013).

34. Al Letson, "Portland, OR: A Tale of Two Cities," *State of the Reunion,* radio program, (Portland, Ore.: National Public Radio, 2012), http://stateofthe reunion.com/portland-or-a-tale-of-two-cities; Lubitow, Miller, and Shelton, "Contesting the North Williams Traffic Operations and Safety Project"; Hoffmann, *Bike Lanes Are White Lanes.*

35. Paul Schwartzman and Chris L. Jenkins, "How D.C. Mayor Fenty Lost the Black Vote—and His Job," *Washington Post,* September 13, 2010; Gibson, "The Rise and Fall of Adrian Fenty, Mayor-Triathlete."

36. Jay Walljasper, "Bike Lanes in Black and White," *PeopleForBikes,* blog, October 21, 2013, http://www.peopleforbikes.org/blog/entry/bike-lanes-in-black -and-white.

37. Christian Lander, "#61: Bicycles," *Stuff White People Like,* blog, February 10, 2008, https://stuffwhitepeoplelike.com/2008/02/10/61-bicycles/; Eben Weiss, "No Getting around It: Cycling and Religion Clash Again," *BikeSnobNYC,* blog, October 27, 2008, http://bikesnobnyc.blogspot.com/2008/10/no-getting-around-it -cycling-and.html.

38. League of American Bicyclists, "The New Majority: Pedaling towards Equity," 2013, https://www.bikeleague.org/content/pedaling-toward-equity.

39. League of American Bicyclists, "The New Majority"; Hamzat Sani, "League Welcomes New Equity Advisory Council," Bike February 2013, *News from the League,* blog, http://blog.bikeleague.org/blog/2013/02/league-welcomes-new-equity -advisory-council; League of American Bicyclists, "The New Movement: Bike Equity Today," 2014. Adonia Lugo, who was hired as the league's equity initiative manager, left the post after a year with the sense that it was created out of tokenism rather than as a commitment to change the LAB's practices. See Adonia Lugo, "Unsolicited Advice for Vision Zero," *Urban Adonia,* blog, September 30, 2015, http://www.urbanadonia.com/2015/09/unsolicited-advice-for-vision-zero.html.

40. Michael Andersen, "Race on Wheels: 4 Lessons for Green Lanes amid Gentrification," *PeopleForBikes*, blog, April 9, 2013, http://www.peopleforbikes.org/blog/entry/race-on-wheels-4-lessons-for-green-lanes-amid-gentrification; PeopleForBikes and The Alliance for Biking and Walking, "Building Equity," 2015, http://sfgreatstreets.org/2009/11/the-sf-great-streets-project-talks-with-tim-tompkins.

41. Lerner, *Urban Acupuncture*.

42. John R. Logan and Harvey L. Molotch, *Urban Fortunes: The Political Economy of Place* (Berkeley: University of California Press, 2007 [1987]).

43. Ruth Glass, *London: Aspects of Change* (London: Centre for Urban Studies, MacGibbon and Kee, 1964), xviii–xix.

44. Jason Hackworth, "Gentrification as a Politico-Economic Window: Reflections on the Changing State of Gentrification." *Tijdschrift Voor Economische En Sociale Geografie* 110, no. 1 (2018): 47–53.

45. Jason Hackworth and Neil Smith, "The Changing State of Gentrification," *Tijdschrift Voor Economische En Sociale Geografie* 92 (2001): 464–77; Loretta Lees, Hyun Bang Shin, and Ernesto López-Morales, *Planetary Gentrification* (Cambridge: Polity, 2016).

46. Glass, *London*; Neil Smith, *The New Urban Frontier: Gentrification and the Revanchist City* (New York: Routledge, 1996); Neil Smith, "New Globalism, New Urbanism: Gentrification as Global Urban Strategy," *Antipode* 34, no. 3 (2002): 427–50; Melissa Checker, "Wiped Out by the 'Greenwave': Environmental Gentrification and the Paradoxical Politics of Urban Sustainability," *City and Society* 23, no. 2 (2011): 210–29; Mark Whitehead, "(Re)Analysing the Sustainable City: Nature, Urbanisation and the Regulation of Socio-Environmental Relations in the UK," *Urban Studies* 40, no. 7 (June 1, 2003): 1183–206.

47. Streets have played a relatively minor role in theories of gentrification and often appear in the context of the state excluding the poor from public spaces. See David Harvey, *Spaces of Hope* (Berkeley: University of California Press, 2000); Don Mitchell, *The Right to the City: Social Justice and the Fight for Public Space* (New York: Guilford Press, 2003). For a "green" mutation of this dynamic, see Susannah Bunce, "Developing Sustainability: Sustainability Policy and Gentrification on Toronto's Waterfront," *Local Environment* 14, no. 7 (2009): 651–67; Leslie Kern, "From Toxic Wreck to Crunchy Chic: Environmental Gentrification through the Body," *Environment and Planning D: Society and Space* 33 (2015): 67–83.

48. Smith, *The New Urban Frontier*, 39.

49. Neil Smith, "Toward a Theory of Gentrification: A Back to the City Movement by Capital, Not People," *Journal of the American Planning Association* 45, no. 4 (1979): 538–48. In essence, Smith theorized the reversal of the canonical "filtering" process in urban economics.

50. Daniel Hammel, "Re-Establishing the Rent Gap: An Alternative View of Capitalised Land Rent," *Urban Studies* 36, no. 8 (1999): 1290. This is obvious

with large, fixed transportation systems with controlled access points (freeways and rail transit, for example), which dramatically increase the accessibility of certain places over others. The creation of these infrastructures, usually by the state under the influence of local powerful capitalists, yields what Richard Walker calls "redistributive rents." See Richard A. Walker, "Urban Ground Rent: Building a New Conceptual Framework," *Antipode* 6, no. 1 (1974): 51–58.

51. Jane Jacobs, *The Death and Life of Great American Cities* (New York: Vintage, 1992); Michel de Certeau, *The Practice of Everyday Life* (Berkeley: University of California Press, 1984).

52. This is often considered the "consumption" explanation of gentrification. David Ley, "Gentrification and the Politics of the New Middle Class," *Environment and Planning D: Society and Space* 12 (1994): 53–74.

53. For Rose, these were white, middle-class, single mothers for whom a central location reduces the burden of social reproduction. See Damaris Rose, "Rethinking Gentrification: Beyond the Uneven Development of Marxist Urban Theory," *Environment and Planning D: Society and Space* 2, no. 1 (1984): 47–74.

54. Jacobs, *The Death and Life of Great American Cities*, 12, 50.

55. This current was especially strong in the Bay Area, where growth control had an early foothold. See Richard A. Walker, *The Country in the City: The Greening of the San Francisco Bay Area* (Seattle: University of Washington Press, 2008).

56. Writers like Ivan Illich, Theodore Roczak, and E. F. Schumacher added their appreciation of small-scale technologies to the cultural ferment as well. Appleyard's *Livable Streets* (1981) remains an influential handbook for making streets convivial spaces rather than high-speed car thoroughfares. See Donald Appleyard, M. Sue Gerson, and Mark Lintell, *Livable Streets, Protected Neighborhoods* (Berkeley: University of California Press, 1981); Allan Jacobs and Donald Appleyard, "Toward an Urban Design Manifesto," *Journal of the American Planning Association* 53, no. 1 (1987): 112–20.

57. Peter Hall, *Cities of Tomorrow* (Oxford: Blackwell, 1996), 283–84, 462–67.

58. Mark Gottdiener, *The Social Production of Urban Space* (Austin: University of Texas Press, 1985), 153; Logan and Molotch, *Urban Fortunes*.

59. Sharon Zukin, *Loft Living: Culture and Capital in Urban Change* (New Brunswick, N.J.: Rutgers University Press, 1989); David Ley, *The New Middle Class and the Remaking of the Central City* (New York: Oxford University Press, 1996); David Ley, "Artists, Aestheticisation and the Field of Gentrification," *Urban Studies* 40, no. 12 (November 2003): 2527–44.

60. Kenneth T. Jackson, *Crabgrass Frontier: The Suburbanization of the United States* (New York: Oxford University Press, 1985); David Freund, *Colored Property: State Policy and White Racial Politics in Suburban America* (Chicago: University of Chicago Press, 2010).

61. Sarah Dooling, "Ecological Gentrification: A Research Agenda Exploring Justice in the City," *International Journal of Urban and Regional Research* 33, no. 3 (2009): 621–39; Checker, "Wiped Out by the 'Greenwave'"; Isabelle Anguelovski, "From Toxic Sites to Parks as (Green) LULUs? New Challenges of Inequity, Privilege, Gentrification, and Exclusion for Urban Environmental Justice," *Journal of Planning Literature* 31, no. 1 (2016): 23–36; Kern, "From Toxic Wreck to Crunchy Chic"; Dan Immergluck and Tharunya Balan, "Sustainable for Whom? Green Urban Development, Environmental Gentrification, and the Atlanta Beltline," *Urban Geography* 39, no. 4 (2017): 546–62; Isabelle Anguelovski, James J. T. Connolly, Melissa Garcia-Lamarca, Helen Cole, and Hamil Pearsall, "New Scholarly Pathways on Green Gentrification," *Progress in Human Geography*, 2018, 1–23, doi:10.1177/0309132518803799.

62. Michael Hardt and Antonio Negri, *Commonwealth* (Cambridge, Mass.: Harvard University Press, 2011); Chris Carlsson, "Conundrums of the Commons," *The Nowtopian*, blog, June 2010, http://www.nowtopians.com/book-reviews/conundrums-of-the-commons.

63. Logan and Molotch, *Urban Fortunes*.

64. Hackworth and Smith, "The Changing State of Gentrification."

65. Eugene McCann, "Inequality and Politics in the Creative City-Region: Questions of Livability and State Strategy," *International Journal of Urban and Regional Research* 31, no. 1 (2007): 188–96.

66. Logan and Molotch, *Urban Fortunes*.

67. On the concept of articulation, see Stuart Hall, "Race, Articulation, and Societies Structured in Dominance," in *Race Critical Theories: Text and Context*, ed. Philomena Essed and David Theo Goldberg (Malden, Mass.: Wiley-Blackwell, 2001), 38–68. On mobility as a key site condensing these categories, see Tim Cresswell, "Towards a Politics of Mobility," *Environment and Planning D: Society and Space* 28, no. 1 (2010): 17–31.

68. Laura Pulido, *Black, Brown, Yellow and Left: Radical Activism in Los Angeles* (Berkeley: University of California Press, 2006).

69. Mark Garrett and Brian Taylor, "Reconsidering Social Equity in Public Transit," *Berkeley Planning Journal* 13, no. 1 (1999): 6–27; Timothy F. Welch, "Equity in Transport: The Distribution of Transit Access and Connectivity among Affordable Housing Units," *Transport Policy* 30 (2013): 283–93.

70. Where bus service is expanding, it is often as bus rapid transit (BRT), a system that combines elements of streetcars with the low cost of buses. While BRT was pioneered in Bogotá for reasons of social equity, in the United States it is used as a way to offer a "premium-type service" and *distinguish* it from the old racialized bus. See Federal Transit Administration and United States Department of Transportation, "Characteristics of Bus Rapid Transit for Decision-Making," 2004, sec. 2, http://www.nbrti.org/docs/pdf/Characteristics_BRT_Decision-Making.pdf.

71. Langdon Winner, *The Whale and the Reactor: A Search for Limits in an Age of High Technology* (Chicago: University of Chicago Press, 1989).

72. Jeffrey Kidder, *Urban Flow: Bike Messengers and the City* (Ithaca, N.Y.: Cornell University Press, 2011); Justin Spinney, "Cycling the City: Movement, Meaning and Method," *Geography Compass* 3, no. 2 (2009): 817–35; Ben Fincham, "Bicycle Messengers and the Road to Freedom," *Sociological Review* 54 (2006): 208–22; Rachel Aldred, "Incompetent or Too Competent? Negotiating Everyday Cycling Identities in a Motor Dominated Society," *Mobilities* 8, no. 2 (2013): 252–71.

73. Walter Benjamin, *Illuminations: Essays and Reflections* (New York: Schocken, 1968), 155–94. On the gendering of the *flâneur*, see Susan Buck-Morss, "The Flâneur, the Sandwichman, and the Whore: The Politics of Loitering," *New German Critique*, no. 39 (1986): 99–140.

74. de Certeau, *The Practice of Everyday Life*; Ferrell, *Tearing Down the Streets*; Lugo, "Body-City-Machine: Human Infrastructure."

75. John Urry, "The 'System' of Automobility," *Theory, Culture & Society* 21, no. 4/5 (2004): 25–39; Mimi Sheller and John Urry, "The City and the Car," *International Journal of Urban and Regional Research* 24, no. 4 (2000): 737–57. See also Alan Walks, *The Urban Political Economy and Ecology of Automobility: Driving Cities, Driving Inequality, Driving Politics* (London: Routledge, 2015); Paterson, *Automobile Politics;* Peter Merriman, "Automobility and the Geographies of the Car," *Geography Compass* 3, no. 2 (2009): 586–99.

76. Nik Heynen, Maria Kaika, and Erik Swyngedouw, *In the Nature of Cities* (New York: Routledge, 2006).

77. Walks, *The Urban Political Economy and Ecology of Automobility*; Paterson, *Automobile Politics*.

78. By "technical," here I mean in contrast to a social space governed more by rules and conventions, although even the most car-choked freeway is also this. The more "technical" the facilitation of movement, the more these conventions are embedded in the physical structure of the street. Many of the normal elements of streets in North America were laid down from 1910 to 1930 in battles over how the surge in cars should be incorporated into the city. See Peter D. Norton, *Fighting Traffic: The Dawn of the Motor Age in the American City* (Cambridge, Mass.: MIT Press, 2011).

79. David Harvey, *Paris, Capital of Modernity* (London: Routledge, 2005).

80. Anique Hommels, *Unbuilding Cities: Obduracy in Urban Socio-Technical Change* (Cambridge: MIT Press, 2005); Stephen J. Collier, *Post-Soviet Social: Neoliberalism, Social Modernity, Biopolitics* (Princeton, N.J.: Princeton University Press, 2011).

81. Urry, "The 'System' of Automobility"; Walks, *The Urban Political Economy and Ecology of Automobility*; Sheller and Urry, "The City and the Car."

82. Paterson, "Governing Mobilities, Mobilising Carbon."

83. One version of the classic space efficiency argument is available at http://www.austinchronicle.com/news/2014-06-27/getting-off-the-road/ (accessed May 12, 2018). For arguments about the inefficiencies of parking, see Donald C. Shoup, "The High Cost of Free Parking," *Journal of Planning Education and Research* 17, no. 10 (1997): 3–20; Jason Henderson, "The Spaces of Parking: Mapping the Politics of Mobility in San Francisco," *Antipode* 41, no. 1 (2009): 70–91. On bicyclists' propensity to shop more, see Szczepanski, "How Bicycles Bring Business."

84. In particular, level of service (LOS) guidelines evaluate street performance solely in terms of delay to cars. See Jason Henderson, "Level of Service: The Politics of Reconfiguring Urban Streets in San Francisco, CA," *Journal of Transport Geography* 19, no. 6 (2011): 1138–44. In recent years, advocates have sought to overhaul LOS, proposing an alternative multimodal level of service (MLOS) that would enable the construction of safer and more habitable pedestrian and cyclist environments.

85. Jason Patton, "A Pedestrian World: Competing Rationalities and the Calculation of Transportation Change," *Environment and Planning A* 39, no. 4 (2007): 928–44.

86. One point of contradiction between these dual functions of the street that is already embedded within automobility is parking. See Henderson, *Street Fight*.

87. David Owen, "Green Manhattan," *New Yorker*, October 18, 2004, https://www.newyorker.com/magazine/2004/10/18/green-manhattan; Richardson Dilworth and Robert Stokes, "Green Growth Machines, LEED Ratings and Value Free Development: The Case of the Philadelphia Property Tax Abatement," *Journal of Urbanism* 6, no. 1 (2013): 37–51.

88. The old guard has long promoted "vehicular cycling," an athletic approach that sees cyclists as safest when they behave like cars and opposes as dangerous any bicycle facility that "segregates" cyclists from the rest of traffic. See John Forester, *Effective Cycling*, 7th ed. (Cambridge, Mass.: MIT Press, 2012). The ranks of vehicular cyclists are dominated by white middle-class men, and until the 1990s bicycle coalitions reflected this ideology and social composition. See "Quick Releases," *Tube Times*, April 1999; Steven Bodzin, "SFBC Turns 30: A Look Back at Our Roots," *Tube Times*, August 2001.

89. Moreover, operating a bicycle on streets designed solely for car traffic is, for many white middle-class men, the first experience of something analogous to structural oppression. Susan King, personal interview, 2012.

90. Thomas Wald, personal interview, May 9, 2018.

91. Michael Maniates, "Individualization: Plant a Tree, Buy a Bike, Save the World?," in *Confronting Consumption*, ed. Thomas Princen, Michael Maniates, and Ken Conca (Cambridge, Mass.: MIT Press, 2002), 43–66; Bruce P. Braun, "A New Urban Dispositif? Governing Life in an Age of Climate Change," *Environment and Planning D: Society and Space* 32, no. 1 (2014): 49–64.

92. Jamie Peck and Nik Theodore, *Fast Policy* (Minneapolis: University of Minnesota Press, 2015).

93. Charles E. Lindblom, "The Science of 'Muddling Through,'" *Public Administration Review* 19, no. 2 (1959): 79.

94. Eric Avila, *The Folklore of the Freeway: Race and Revolt in the Modernist City* (Minneapolis: University of Minnesota Press, 2014).

95. Raymond A Mohl, "The Interstates and the Cities: Highways, Housing, and the Freeway Revolt," 2002, http://www.prrac.org/pdf/mohl.pdf; Robert Bullard, Glenn Johnson, and Angel Torres, *Highway Robbery: Transportation Racism and New Routes to Equity* (Cambridge, Mass.: South End Press, 2004); Robert Bullard, "MLK Day 2013: Why Transportation Is Still a Civil Rights Issue," Op Ed News, January 20, 2013, http://www.opednews.com/articles/MLK-Day-2013-Why-Transpor-by-Robert-Bullard-130119-639.html; Edward W. Soja, *Seeking Spatial Justice* (Minneapolis: University of Minnesota Press, 2010).

96. Richard A. Walker and Robert D. Lewis, "Beyond the Crabgrass Frontier: Industry and the Spread of North American Cities, 1850–1950," *Journal of Historical Geography* 27, no. 1 (2001): 3–19.

97. Jackson, *Crabgrass Frontier*; Freund, *Colored Property*.

98. David Roediger, *Working toward Whiteness: How America's Immigrants Became White* (New York: Basic Books, 2005).

99. David Harvey, *Limits to Capital* (London: Verso, 2007 [1982]); Neil Smith, *Uneven Development: Nature, Capital and the Production of Space* (Oxford: Blackwell, 1984).

100. Berube and Kneebone, *Confronting Suburban Poverty in America*; Fainstein, Fainstein, and Armistead, "Restructuring the City." For a qualification of the "suburbanization of poverty" thesis, focusing on inter- and intraregional differences, see Thomas J. Cooke and Curtis Denton, "The Suburbanization of Poverty? An Alternative Perspective," *Urban Geography* 36, no. 2 (2015): 300–313.

101. Manuel Castells, *The City and the Grassroots: A Cross-Cultural Theory of Urban Social Movements* (Berkeley: University of California Press, 1983); Avila, *The Folklore of the Freeway*; L. N. Dyble, "Revolt against Sprawl: Transportation and the Origins of the Marin County Growth-Control Regime," *Journal of Urban History* 34, no. 1 (2007): 38–66. On the racial politics of "urbicide," see Katherine McKittrick, "On Plantations, Prisons, and a Black Sense of Place," *Social & Cultural Geography* 12, no. 8 (2011): 947–63.

102. Andrew E. G. Jonas, David Gibbs, and Aidan While, "The New Urban Politics as a Politics of Carbon Control," *Urban Studies* 48, no. 12 (2011): 2537–54.

103. Harriet Bulkeley, "Cities and the Governing of Climate Change," *Annual Review of Environment and Resources* 35, no. 1 (2010): 229–53; David Wachsmuth and Hillary Angelo, "Green and Gray: New Ideologies of Nature in Urban Sustainability Policy," *Annals of the American Association of Geographers* 108, no. 4 (2018): 1038–56; Joshua Long and Jennifer L. Rice, "From Sustainable Urbanism to Climate Urbanism," *Urban Studies*, 2018; Owen, "Green Manhattan."

104. Harriet Bulkeley and Michele M. Betsill, "Rethinking Sustainable Cities: Multilevel Governance and the 'Urban' Politics of Climate Change," *Environmental Politics* 14, no. 1 (2005): 42–63.

105. Christopher Jones and Daniel M. Kammen, "Spatial Distribution of U.S. Household Carbon Footprints Reveals Suburbanization Undermines Greenhouse Gas Benefits of Urban Population Density," *Environmental Science and Technology* 48, no. 2 (2014): 895–902.

106. Erik Swyngedouw, "The Antinomies of the Postpolitical City: In Search of a Democratic Politics of Environmental Production," *International Journal of Urban and Regional Research* 33, no. 3 (2009): 601–20.

107. Florida, *Cities and the Creative Class*; Richard Florida, "America's Top Cities for Bike Commuting: Happier, Too," *Atlantic,* June 2011, http://www.the-atlantic.com/national/archive/2011/06/americas-top-cities-for-bike-commuting-happier-too/240265/; Bruce Katz and Julie Wagner, "What a City Needs to Foster Innovation," *Brookings Institution,* January 16, 2014, http://www.brookings.edu/research/opinions/2014/01/16-city-innovation-cafes-bike-lanes-3d-printers.

108. Michel Foucault, *The Birth of Biopolitics: Lectures at the Collège de France, 1978–1979* (Basingstoke, UK: Palgrave Macmillan, 2010).

109. Bob Jessop, *State Power* (Cambridge, Mass.: Polity, 2007).

110. Neil Brenner and Nik Theodore, "Cities and the Geographies of 'Actually Existing Neoliberalism,'" *Antipode* 34, no. 3 (2002): 349–79; Jamie Peck, Nik Theodore, and Neil Brenner, "Postneoliberalism and Its Malcontents," *Antipode* 41, no. 1 (2010): 94–116.

111. Peter North, "Eco-Localisation as a Progressive Response to Peak Oil and Climate Change: A Sympathetic Critique," *Geoforum* 41, no. 4 (2010): 585–94; Checker, "Wiped Out by the 'Greenwave'"; Mike Hodson and Simon Marvin, "Urbanism in the Anthropocene: Ecological Urbanism or Premium Ecological Enclaves?," *City* 14, no. 3 (2010): 298–313; Lugo and Mannos, "Separate but Eco."

112. John Hannigan, *Fantasy City: Pleasure and Profit in the Postmodern Metropolis* (New York: Routledge, 1998); Christopher Mele, *Selling the Lower East Side: Culture, Real Estate, and Resistance in New York City* (Minneapolis: University of Minnesota Press, 2000).

113. See Myron Orfield, "Metropolitics: A Regional Agenda for Community and Stability," *Forum for Social Economics* 28, no. 2 (1999): 33–49; Chris Benner and Manuel Pastor, *Equity, Growth, and Community: What the Nation Can Learn From America's Metro Areas* (Berkeley: University of California Press, 2016).

114. See Susan Fainstein, *The Just City* (Ithaca, N.Y.: Cornell University Press, 2010); Amartya Sen, "Capability and Well-Being," in *The Quality of Life*, ed. Martha Nussbaum and Amartya Sen (Oxford: Oxford University Press, 1993), 30–53.

115. Katz and Wagner, "What a City Needs to Foster Innovation."
116. Jamie Peck and Adam Tickell, "Neoliberalizing Space," *Antipode* 34, no. 3 (2002): 380–404.
117. Because I stress the role of grassroots advocates and critics in the creation of new technological forms, this is distinct from other uses of this term, such as Jason Chilvers and Jacquelin Burgess, "Power Relations: The Politics of Risk and Procedure in Nuclear Waste Governance," *Environment and Planning A* 40, no. 8 (2008): 1881–1900.

2. The Bicycle and the Region in Post-Crisis America

1. Richard Florida, *The Rise of the Creative Class: And How It's Transforming Work, Leisure, Community and Everyday Life* (New York: Basic Books, 2002).
2. Justin Spinney, "Fixing Mobility in the Neoliberal City: Cycling Policy and Practice in London as a Mode of Political-Economic and Biopolitical Governance," *Annals of the American Association of Geographers* 106, no. 2 (2016): 450–58; Anique Hommels, *Unbuilding Cities: Obduracy in Urban Socio-Technical Change* (Cambridge, Mass.: MIT Press, 2005).
3. David Harvey, *The Limits to Capital* (London: Verso, 2007); PeopleForBikes, "Protected Bike Lanes Mean Business" (Washington, D.C., 2013), http://www.sfbike.org/wp-content/uploads/2014/04/Protected_Bike_Lanes_Mean_Business.pdf.
4. See, for example, Christopher B. Leinberger, "The Death of the Fringe Suburb," *New York Times*, November 2011, http://www.nytimes.com/2011/11/26/opinion/the-death-of-the-fringe-suburb.html.
5. Karen Chapple, "Incomplete Streets, Complete Regions," in *Incomplete Streets: Processes, Practices, and Possibilities*, ed. Stephen Zavestoski and Julian Agyeman (Oxon, UK: Routledge Earthscan, 2015), 290–305; Brian S. Mckenzie, "Neighborhood Access to Transit by Race, Ethnicity, and Poverty in Portland, OR," *City and Community* 12, no. 2 (2013): 134–55.
6. Michael Storper et al., *The Rise and Fall of Regional Economies: Lessons from San Francisco and Los Angeles* (Stanford, Calif.: Stanford University Press, 2015); Richard A. Walker, *Pictures of a Gone City: Tech and the Dark Side of Prosperity in the San Francisco Bay Area*, Spectre (Oakland, Calif.: PM Press, 2018); Rob Krueger and David Gibbs, *The Sustainable Development Paradox: Urban Political Economy in the United States and Europe* (New York: Guilford Press, 2007).
7. Robert Cervero, "Transport and Land Use: Key Issues in Metropolitan Planning and Smart Growth," *Australian Planner* 38, no. 1 (2001): 29–37; Charles C. Bohl, "New Urbanism and the City: Potential Applications and Implications for Distressed Inner-City Neighbourhoods," *Housing Policy Debate* 11, no. 4

(2000): 761–801; Gerrit Knaap, "New Urbanism and Smart Growth: A Few Words from the Academy," *International Regional Science Review* 28, no. 2 (April 1, 2005): 107–18. In the 1990s, New Urbanism was more frequently applied to greenfield developments..

8. David Owen, "Green Manhattan," *New Yorker*, October 18, 2004, https://www.newyorker.com/magazine/2004/10/18/green-manhattan; David Wachsmuth and Hillary Angelo, "Green and Gray: New Ideologies of Nature in Urban Sustainability Policy," *Annals of the American Association of Geographers* 108, no. 4 (2018): 1038–56. In practice, bicycle plans cross between these categories.

9. Stephen Wheeler, "State and Municipal Climate Change Plans: The First Generation." *Journal of the American Planning Association* 74, no. 4 (2008): 481–96; Andrew E. G. Jonas, David Gibbs, and Aidan While, "The New Urban Politics as a Politics of Carbon Control," *Urban Studies* 48, no. 12 (2011): 2537–54; Harriet Bulkeley, *Cities and Climate Change* (New York: Routledge, 2013); Michael Hodson and Simon Marvin, "Intensifying or Transforming Sustainable Cities? Fragmented Logics of Urban Environmentalism," *Local Environment* 22, no. 1 (2017): 8–22.

10. Knaap, "New Urbanism and Smart Growth."

11. Karen Chapple, *Planning Sustainable Cities and Regions: Toward More Equitable Development* (New York: Routledge Earthscan, 2014).

12. Association of Bay Area Governments and Metropolitan Transportation Commission, "Plan Bay Area: Strategy for a Sustainable Region," 2013, http://files.mtc.ca.gov/pdf/Plan_Bay_Area_FINAL/Plan_Bay_Area.pdf. Even relatively powerful California MPOs have mainly carrots, rather than sticks, at their disposal. This promotes intransigence on the part of wealthy enclaves with a dose of Tea Party populism. Chapple, *Planning Sustainable Cities and Regions*, 47–48, 81–87; Karen Trapenberg Frick, "The Actions of Discontent: Tea Party and Property Rights Activists Pushing Back against Regional Planning," *Journal of the American Planning Association* 79, no. 3 (2013): 190–200. Such reactions have been voiced in both conservative and "liberal" vocabularies.

13. Smart Growth America, "Complete Streets Stimulate the Local Economy," http://www.smartgrowthamerica.org/documents/cs/factsheets/cs-economic.pdf (accessed April 19, 2013).

14. Dan Immergluck and Tharunya Balan, "Sustainable for Whom? Green Urban Development, Environmental Gentrification, and the Atlanta Beltline," *Urban Geography* 39, no. 4 (2018): 546–62; John Gallagher, "Once Fringe Greening Ideas Now Key Part of Detroit Rebirth," *Detroit Free Press*, September 3, 2016, http://www.freep.com/story/money/business/columnists/2016/09/03/detroit-traffic-architecture-planning-greening/89765208; Melody Hoffmann, *Bike Lanes Are White Lanes: Bicycle Advocacy and Urban Planning* (Lincoln: University of Nebraska Press, 2016); Melissa Checker, "Wiped Out by the 'Greenwave': Environmental Gentrification and the Paradoxical Politics of Urban Sustainability,"

City and Society 23, no. 2 (2011): 210–29; Leslie Kern, "From Toxic Wreck to Crunchy Chic: Environmental Gentrification through the Body," *Environment and Planning D: Society and Space* 33 (2015): 67–83.

15. Theresa Enright, "Contesting the Networked Metropolis: The Grand Paris Regime of Metromobility," in *Transport, Mobility, and the Production of Urban Space*, ed. Julie Cidell and David Prytherch (New York: Routledge, 2011), 172–86.

16. Michael Andersen, "Outer London Is about to Activate the 'Secret Weapon' of the Suburbs: The Bicycle," *PeopleForBikes*, blog, February 25, 2015, http://www.peopleforbikes.org/blog/entry/outer-london-is-about-to-embrace-the-secret-weapon-of-the-suburbs-the-bicyc.

17. Aaron Golub, "Moving beyond Fordism: 'Complete Streets' and the Changing Political Economy of Urban Transportation," in *Incomplete Streets: Processes, Practices, and Possibilities*, ed. Stephen Zavestoski and Julian Agyeman (New York: Routledge, 2014).

18. Golub, "Moving beyond Fordism."

19. Neil Smith, *Uneven Development: Nature, Capital and the Production of Space* (Oxford: Blackwell, 1984).

20. Christopher Jones and Daniel M. Kammen, "Spatial Distribution of U.S. Household Carbon Footprints Reveals Suburbanization Undermines Greenhouse Gas Benefits of Urban Population Density," *Environmental Science and Technology* 48, no. 2 (2014): 895–902.

21. Thomas Kemeny and Michael Storper, "The Sources of Urban Development: Wages, Housing, and Amenity Gaps across American Cities," *Journal of Regional Science* 52, no. 1 (2012): 85–108.

22. Kemeny and Storper, "The Sources of Urban Development"; Michael Storper and Anthony J. Venables, "Buzz: Face-to-Face Contact and the Urban Economy," *Journal of Economic Geography* 4, no. 4 (August 1, 2004): 351–70; Ashok Bardhan, Dwight Jaffee, and Cynthia Kroll, *Globalization and a High-Tech Economy: California, the United States and Beyond* (New York: Springer, 2004).

23. Chapple, "Incomplete Streets, Complete Regions."

24. John Urry, "The 'System' of Automobility," *Theory, Culture & Society* 21, no. 4/5 (2004): 25–39.

25. Mike Hodson and Simon Marvin, "Urbanism in the Anthropocene: Ecological Urbanism or Premium Ecological Enclaves?," *City* 14, no. 3 (2010): 298–313, doi:10.1080/13604813.2010.482277.

26. See http://peopleforbikes.org/our-work/political-work/for-policymakers (accessed December 7, 2017).

27. See https://bookstore.transportation.org/collection_detail.aspx?ID=110. For a detailed discussion of level of service (LOS), see Jason Henderson, "Level of Service: The Politics of Reconfiguring Urban Streets in San Francisco, CA," *Journal of Transport Geography* 19, no. 6 (2011): 1138–44.

28. See https://nacto.org (accessed December 8, 2017).

29. National Association of City Transportation Officials, "NACTO Cities for Cycling Affiliate Membership 2012," https://nacto.org/wp-content/uploads/2012/05/CitiesforCycling_AffiliateMembership_2012.pdf.

30. National Association of City Transportation Officials, *Urban Street Design Guide* (New York: Island Press, 2013).

31. Florida, *The Rise of the Creative Class*; Peter Hall, *Cities in Civilization* (New York: Pantheon Books, 1998); Edward L. Glaeser, *Triumph of the City: How Our Greatest Invention Makes Us Richer, Smarter, Greener, Healthier, and Happier* (New York: Penguin Press, 2011); Jane Jacobs, *The Economy of Cities* (New York: Random House, 1969).

32. Bruce Katz and Jennifer Bradley, *The Metropolitan Revolution: How Cities and Metros Are Fixing Our Broken Politics and Fragile Economy* (Washington, D.C.: Brookings Institution Press, 2013).

33. John R. Logan and Harvey L. Molotch, *Urban Fortunes: The Political Economy of Place* (Berkeley: University of California Press, 2007).

34. Steven Raphael and Michael A. Stoll, "Job Sprawl and the Suburbanization of Poverty," Brookings Institution (2010): 1–20, https://www.brookings.edu/wp-content/uploads/2016/06/0330_job_sprawl_stoll_raphael.pdf.

35. Alex Schafran, "Origins of an Urban Crisis: The Restructuring of the San Francisco Bay Area and the Geography of Foreclosure," *International Journal of Urban and Regional Research* 37, no. 2 (2013): 663–88.

36. Elizabeth Kneebone, "Job Sprawl Stalls: The Great Recession and Metropolitan Employment Location" (Washington, D.C.: Brookings Institution, 2013), http://www.brookings.edu/~/media/research/files/reports/2013/04/18-job-sprawl-kneebone/srvy_jobsprawl.pdf; Alan Berube and Elizabeth Kneebone, *Confronting Suburban Poverty in America* (Washington, D.C.: Brookings Institution, 2013). In many metropolitan areas, poverty grew in postwar inner-ring suburbs rather than exurbs. One exception was the San Francisco Bay Area. See Thomas J. Cooke and Curtis Denton, "The Suburbanization of Poverty? An Alternative Perspective," *Urban Geography* 36, no. 2 (2015): 300–313.

37. Walker, *Pictures of a Gone City*; on the prospects for suburban office clusters, see Adam Scavette and Ethan Haswell, "Research Brief: Is Urban Cool Cooling New Jersey's Job Market?," 2016, https://www.philadelphiafed.org/-/media/research-and-data/publications/research-brief/rb-20161201.pdf?la=en.

38. Kemeny and Storper, "The Sources of Urban Development"; Storper and Venables, "Buzz."

39. Richard Florida, *The New Urban Crisis: How Our Cities Are Increasing Inequality, Deepening Segregation, and Failing the Middle Class—and What We Can Do about It* (New York: Basic Books, 2017); for a critical assessment of Florida's about-face, see Danny Dorling, "The New Urban Crisis by Richard Florida Review—'Flawed and Elitist Ideas,'" *Guardian*, September 26, 2017, https://www.theguardian.com/books/2017/sep/26/richard-florida-new-urban-crisis-review-flawed-elitist-ideas.

40. For a trenchant critique of the overapplication of "services," see Richard A. Walker, "Is There a Service Economy? The Changing Capitalist Division of Labor," *Science and Society* 49, no. 1 (1985): 42–83.

41. This category includes early product stage prototyping and manufacturing of computers and peripherals, system design and management, software programming, research and development, and online media and website publishing.

42. Richard A. Walker, "The Boom and the Bombshell: The New Economy Bubble and the San Francisco Bay Area," in *The Changing Economic Geography of Globalization: Reinventing Space*, ed. Giovanna Vertova (London: Routledge, 2006), 112–38; Annalee Saxenian, "The Urban Contradictions of Silicon Valley: Regional Growth and the Restructuring of the Semiconductor Industry," in *Sunbelt/Snowbelt: Urban Development and Regional Restructuring*, ed. Larry Sawers and William Tabb (New York: Oxford University Press, 1984), 237–62.

43. Representation of Asians in both high- and middle-wage sectors reflects in part the substantial labor market differentiation along ethnic lines (e.g. Indian software engineers and Filipino health care support workers) within the extremely broad category of "Asian."

44. Steven Manson et al., "IPUMS National Historical Geographic Information System" (Minneapolis: University of Minnesota, 2017), http://doi.org/10.18128/D050.V12.0. The Bay Area also saw growth in specialized automotive and electronics production in the South Bay, amid an overall decline in manufacturing. See Bay Area Science and Innovation Consortium, "Reinventing Manufacturing: How the Transformation of Manufacturing Is Creating New Opportunity for California," 2016, http://www.bayareaeconomy.org/files/pdf/ReinventingMfgFullReport.pdf.

45. Unemployment rate extracted from the Local Area Unemployment Statistics data series, Bureau of Labor Statistics, series LAUCN060750000000003, LAUMT064186000000003, LAUMT064194000000003, available at https://data.bls.gov/pdq/SurveyOutputServlet, retrieved November 27, 2017.

46. City of Philadelphia Office of Manufacturing and Industry, "2016 Annual Report," 2016, https://www.phila.gov/commerce/Documents/2016 Manufacturing and Industry Annual Report.pdf.

47. These numbers should be approached with caution; the pace of abandonment in Detroit strongly reduces the reliability of the American Community Survey. See Seth E. Spielman, David Folch, and Nicholas Nagle, "Patterns and Causes of Uncertainty in the American Community Survey," *Applied Geography* 46 (2014): 147–57, doi:10.1016/j.apgeog.2013.11.002.

48. Joe Grengs, "Job Accessibility and the Modal Mismatch in Detroit," *Journal of Transport Geography* 18, no. 1 (2010): 42–54, http://linkinghub.elsevier.com/retrieve/pii/S0966692309000131; Michael Indergaard, "Detroit's Regional Question," *City and Community* 14, no. 2 (2015): 138–50, doi:10.1111/cico.12107; Detroit Regional Chamber of Commerce and Mich Auto, "Michigan Is Auto: Assets of the Motor State," 2013, http://www.detroitchamber.com/wp-content/uploads/2013/01/Michigan_Is_Auto_Report_1.0_Final.pdf.

49. Hudson-Webber Foundation et al., "7.2 SQ MI: A Report on Greater Downtown Detroit," 2015, http://detroitsevenpointtwo.com/resources/7.2SQ_MI_Book_FINAL_LoRes.pdf.

50. Stephen Hall and Andrew E. G. Jonas, "Urban Fiscal Austerity, Infrastructure Provision and the Struggle for Regional Transit in 'Motor City,'" *Cambridge Journal of Regions, Economy and Society* 7, no. 1 (2014): 189–206.

51. As executive VP Jim Farley put it, "It's such a conducive environment for sharing ideas, for collaboration and for accelerating our electric vehicle efforts." "Ford to Move 220 Workers to Former Factory in Detroit's Corktown," *Detroit Free Press*, December 4, 2017, https://www.freep.com/story/money/cars/ford/2017/12/14/ford-self-driving-team-move-old-hosiery-factory-corktown/953367001; Amy Crawford, "As Downtown Booms, Detroit's Suburbs Seek Reinvention," *CityLab*, April 25, 2018, https://www.citylab.com/design/2018/04/can-detroits-suburbs-survive-a-downtown-revival/558764.

52. Richard A. Walker and Suresh K. Lodha, *The Atlas of California: Mapping the Challenges of a New Era* (Berkeley: University of California Press, 2013), 61; Richard A. Walker and Alex Schafran, "The Strange Case of the Bay Area," *Environment and Planning A* 47 (2015): 10–29.

53. Alex Schafran and Jake Wegmann, "Restructuring, Race, and Real Estate: Changing Home Values and the New California Metropolis, 1989–2010," *Urban Geography* 33, no. 5 (2012): 630–54; Ashok Bardhan and Richard A. Walker, "California Shrugged: Fountainhead of the Great Recession," *Cambridge Journal of Regions Economy and Society* 4, no. 3 (November 2011): 303–22, doi:10.1093/cjres/rsr005; Carolina Reid, "Sought or Sold? Social Embeddedness and Consumer Decisions in the Mortgage Market," 2010, http://www.frbsf.org/community-development/files/wp2010-09.pdf; Elvin Wyly et al., "Cartographies of Race and Class: Mapping the Class-Monopoly Rents of American Subprime Mortgage Capital," *International Journal of Urban and Regional Research* 33, no. 2 (June 2009): 332–54; Carolyn Said, "Home Values Hold in Few Places in Bay Area," *San Francisco Chronicle*, August 12, 2008, http://www.sfgate.com/business/article/Home-values-hold-in-few-places-in-Bay-Area-3200347.php.

54. Kim-Mai Cutler, "How Burrowing Owls Lead to Vomiting Anarchists (Or SF's Housing Crisis Explained)," TechCrunch, April 14, 2014, http://techcrunch.com/2014/04/14/sf-housing; Richard A. Walker, "Why Is There a Housing Crisis?," East Bay Express, March 23, 2016, http://www.eastbayexpress.com/oakland/why-is-there-a-housing-crisis/Content?oid=4722242.

55. Mark Davidson, "Love Thy Neighbour? Social Mixing in London's Gentrification Frontiers," *Environment and Planning A* 42, no. 3 (2010): 524–44; Emma Jackson and Tim Butler, "Revisiting 'Social Tectonics': The Middle Classes and Social Mix in Gentrifying Neighbourhoods," *Urban Studies* 52, no. 13 (2015): 2349–65.

56. Kathleen Pender, "$1 Million City: S.F. Median Home Price Hits 7 Figures for 1st Time," *San Francisco Chronicle*, July 17, 2014, http://www.sfgate.com/

business/networth/article/1-million-city-S-F-median-home-price-hits-7-5626591. php; Carol Pogash, "Gentrification Spreads an Upheaval in San Francisco's Mission District," *New York Times*, May 22, 2015, http://www.nytimes.com/2015/05/23/us/high-rents-elbow-latinos-from-san-franciscos-mission-district.html?_r=0.

57. Jessica Pressler, "Philadelphia Story: The Next Borough," *New York Times*, August 14, 2005, http://www.nytimes.com/2005/08/14/fashion/sundaystyles/14PHILLY.html?pagewanted=all.

58. Kevin C. Gillen, "Philadelphia's 10-Year Property Tax Abatement," 2017, http://phillytaxabatement.com/pdf/BIA_Abatement_Full_Report_Final.pdf; Lei Ding, Jackelyn Hwang, and Eileen Divringi, "Gentrification and Residential Mobility in Philadelphia," *Regional Science and Urban Economics* 61, November (2016): 38–51.

59. Neil Smith, "Gentrification and Capital: Practice and Ideology in Society Hill," *Antipode* 11, no. 3 (1979): 24–35.

60. Sandy Smith, "Philly Gets Richer, Its Suburbs Get Poorer, and the Middle Class . . . Vanishes?," *Philadelphia Magazine*, November 5, 2013, http://www.phillymag.com/news/2013/11/05/philly-richer-suburbs-poorer-middle-class-vanishes; Alfred Lubrano, "An 'Uncomfortable' Life: Philly Still America's Poorest Big City," Philly.com, September 13, 2017, http://www.philly.com/philly/news/philadelphia-census-deep-poverty-poorest-big-city-income-survey-20170914.html; Vinnie Rotondaro, "Once-Aspirational Philadelphia Suburbs Struggle with Poverty," *National Catholic Reporter*, March 25, 2015, https://www.ncronline.org/news/parish/once-aspirational-philadelphia-suburbs-struggle-poverty.

61. Peter Marcuse, "Gentrification, Abandonment, and Displacement: Connections, Causes, and Policy Responses in New York City," *Journal of Urban and Contemporary Law* 28 (1985): 195–240.

62. Joshua M. Akers, "Making Markets: Think Tank Legislation and Private Property in Detroit," *Urban Geography* 34, no. 8 (2013): 1070–95. The Detroit Land Bank Authority remains the city's largest landowner.

63. Hudson-Webber Foundation et al., "7.2 SQ MI."

64. Rachel Aldred, James Woodcock, and Anna Goodman, "Does More Cycling Mean More Diversity in Cycling?," *Transport Reviews* 36, no. 1 (2016): 28–44.

65. Seth Schindler, "Detroit after Bankruptcy: A Case of Degrowth Machine Politics," *Urban Studies* 53, no. 4 (2016): 818–36; Peter Moskowitz, "The Two Detroits: A City Both Collapsing and Gentrifying at the Same Time," *Guardian*, February 5, 2015, https://www.theguardian.com/cities/2015/feb/05/detroit-city-collapsing-gentrifying.

66. Rebecca J. Kinney, *Beautiful Wasteland: The Rise of Detroit as America's Postindustrial Frontier* (Minneapolis: University of Minnesota Press, 2016).

67. Andrew Owen, Brendan Murphy, and David Levinson, "Access across America: Transit 2016," 2017, http://access.umn.edu/research/america/transit/2016; Matthew E. Kahn, "Gentrification Trends in New Transit-Oriented Communities:

Evidence from 14 Cities That Expanded and Built Rail Transit Systems," *Real Estate Economics* 35, no. 2 (2007): 155–82; Nick Revington, "Gentrification, Transit, and Land Use: Moving beyond Neoclassical Theory," *Geography Compass* 9, no. 3 (2015): 152–63.

68. "The City and the Car," *International Journal of Urban and Regional Research* 24, no. 4 (2000): 737–57. Because of poor labor market position, "low-skill" workers must compete across a wider spatial range for jobs. See J. S. Onésimo Sandoval, Robert Cervero, and John Landis, "The Transition from Welfare-to-Work: How Cars and Human Capital Facilitate Employment for Welfare Recipients," *Applied Geography* 31, no. 1 (2011): 352–62. This reality fuels the Left's general skepticism about congestion pricing.

69. Doreen Massey, *Space, Place, and Gender* (Minneapolis: University of Minnesota Press, 1994), 149.

70. Egon Terplan et al., "Job Sprawl in the Megaregion," September 2009, http://www.spur.org/publications/library/article/job_sprawl_megaregion; Robert Cervero and John Landis, "Suburbanization of Jobs and the Journey to Work: A Submarket Analysis of Commuting in the San Francisco Bay Area," *Journal of Advanced Transportation* 26, no. 3 (1992): 275–97, doi:10.1002/atr.5670260305; Joël Garreau, *Edge City: Life on the New Frontier* (New York: Anchor Books, 1991). Even long-planned extensions to the BART system now under construction do not adequately serve the new exurbs.

71. Bay Area Council Economic Institute, "The Bay Area: A Regional Economic Assessment," 2012, 34–35, http://www.bayareaeconomy.org/files/pdf/BAEconAssessment.pdf; Ted Egan, "Commute Equity: An Examination of Bay Area Trends," 2010, https://web.archive.org/web/20130730191805if_/http://www.bayareavision.org/initiatives/PDFs/Commute Equity.pdf.

72. One of the most famous human interest stories to come out of Detroit in the past few years told of James Robertson, the "Walking Man," whose daily round-trip commute to a suburban manufacturing plant combined multiple buses and twenty-one miles on foot. Bill Laitner, "Story of Detroit's Walking Man, James Robertson, to Be Documentary," *Detroit Free Press*, October 19, 2016, http://www.freep.com/story/news/local/michigan/wayne/2016/10/19/james-robertson-walking-man-detroit-mass-transit-election-rta-transit-tax-election-ddot-smart-buses/91968506.

73. Cycling in Detroit has been celebrated culturally more than it has as a commute mode, with the weekly Slow Roll bike ride regularly drawing thousands of participants from all over the region. See Tanya Moutzalias, "Slow Roll, Detroit's Massive Weekly Bike Ride, Kicks off Seventh Season," MLive.com, May 2, 2017, http://www.mlive.com/news/detroit/index.ssf/2017/05/slow_roll_detroit_kicks_off_it.html; Todd Scott, "Detroit's East Side Riders," *M-Bike.Org*, blog, 2011, http://www.m-bike.org/blog/2010/09/27/detroits-east-side-riders/.

74. Christine Ferretti, "DDOT Bumps Up Bus Routes with Expanded Services," *Detroit News*, January 30, 2017, http://www.detroitnews.com/story/news/local/

detroit-city/2017/01/30/ddot-launches-second-phase-service-expansion/97238514.

75. League of American Bicyclists, "The New Majority: Pedaling toward Equity," 2013, https://www.bikeleague.org/content/pedaling-toward-equity.

76. See, for example, Edwin M. Lee Mayor et al., "2012 San Francisco State of Cycling Report," 2012.

77. Jesus Miguel Barajas, "Making Invisible Riders Visible: Motivations for Bicycling and Public Transit Use among Latino Immigrants" (PhD diss., University of California, Berkeley, 2016).

78. Hamzat Sani, "League Welcomes New Equity Advisory Council," *Bikeleague.org*, blog, February 2013, http://blog.bikeleague.org/blog/2013/02/league-welcomes-new-equity-advisory-council.

79. Tanya Snyder, "Bike Summit: With a Seat at the Table, Cyclists Need to Master the Etiquette," *Streetsblog Capitol Hill*, blog, March 6, 2013, http://dc.streetsblog.org/2013/03/06/bike-summit-with-a-seat-at-the-table-cyclists-need-to-master-the-etiquette.

80. Spinney, "Fixing Mobility in the Neoliberal City."

81. Matthias Sweet, "Traffic Congestion's Economic Impacts: Evidence from US Metropolitan Regions," *Urban Studies* 51, no. 10 (2014): 2088–110. This includes both commuting and commercial traffic.

82. Aidan While, "Carbon Regulation and Low-Carbon Urban Restructuring," in *After Sustainable Cities?*, ed. Mike Hodson and Simon Marvin (New York: Routledge, 2014), 41–58.

83. Richard Florida and Charlotta Mellander, "Rise of the Startup City," *California Management Review* 59, no. 1 (2016): 14–38; Ramon Oldenburg and Dennis Brissett, "The Third Place," *Qualitative Sociology* 5, no. 4 (1982): 265–84; Gregory M. Spencer, "Knowledge Neighbourhoods: Urban Form and Evolutionary Economic Geography," *Regional Studies* 49, no. 5 (2015): 883–98; Henry W. Chesbrough, "The Era of Open Innovation," *MIT Sloan Management Review* 44, no. 3 (2003): 34–41. Many of these ideas derive from Jane Jacobs, *The Death and Life of Great American Cities* (New York: Vintage, 1992), 187–99.

84. Bruce Katz and Julie Wagner, "What a City Needs to Foster Innovation," *Brookings Institution*, January 16, 2014, http://www.brookings.edu/research/opinions/2014/01/16-city-innovation-cafes-bike-lanes-3d-printers.

85. Paul Groth, *Living Downtown: The History of Residential Hotels in the United States* (Berkeley: University of California Press, 1994); Susan Fainstein, Norman Fainstein, and P. Jefferson Armistead, "Restructuring the City: The Political Economy of Urban Redevelopment," in *Restructuring the City: The Political Economy of Urban Redevelopment*, ed. Susan Fainstein et al. (New York: Longman, 1983), 202–44; Chester Hartman, *City for Sale: The Transformation of San Francisco* (Berkeley: University of California Press, 2002).

86. C. W. Nevius, "Lamenting the Dead Zone in S.F.'s Core," *San Francisco Chronicle*, April 27, 2008, http://www.sfgate.com/bayarea/article/Lamenting-the-dead-zone-in-S-F-s-core-3216055.php.

87. Juan Carlos Cancino et al., "Central Market/Tenderloin Strategy," 2015, http://investsf.org/neighborhoods/cmtlstrategy; City and County of San Francisco, "About—Official Market Street Improvement Initiative," http://www.bettermarket streetsf.org/about.html (accessed April 27, 2013); Perkins and Will et al., "Better Market Street Project: Existing Conditions and Best Practices," 2011, http://better marketstreetsf.org/about-reports-existing-conditions.html.

88. Chris Carlsson, "Will We Ever Get Market Street Right?," *Streetsblog SF*, blog, March 23, 2009, https://sf.streetsblog.org/2009/03/23/will-we-ever-get-market-street-right.

89. Jason Henderson, *Street Fight: The Politics of Mobility in San Francisco* (Amherst: University of Massachusetts Press, 2013), 52. The policy was updated in 1999 to include pedestrians and bicyclists as "transit," but in practice few engineers were willing to reduce the level of service for cars in an already congested downtown. See Aaron Bialick, "At 40 Years, San Francisco's Transit-First Policy Still Struggles for Traction," *Streetsblog SF*, blog, March 23, 2013, http://sf.streets blog.org/2013/03/22/at-40-years-san-franciscos-transit-first-policy-still-struggles -for-traction.

90. SPUR Transportation Committee, "Transportation Principles for San Francisco," *SPUR Report*, 1999, http://www.spur.org/publications/spur-report/1999 –06–01/transportation-principles-san-francisco; SPUR, "Mid-Market Street Redevelopment District," 2002, http://www.spur.org/sites/default/files/migrated/anchors/ Mid-Market Street Redevelopment District.pdf; Tom Radulovich, "Multimodal Planning at MTA," 2004, http://www.spur.org/publications/spur-report/2004–09–01/ multimodal-planning-mta.

91. Tom Radulovich, personal interview, May 15, 2012.

92. See Henderson, *Street Fight*, 123–24; Phred Dvorak, "San Francisco Ponders: Could Bike Lanes Cause Pollution?," *Wall Street Journal*, August 20, 2008, http://www.wsj.com/articles/SB121919354756955249. The green lanes were permitted on Market despite the injunction because they were part of a pilot project subject to different regulations.

93. San Francisco Bicycle Coalition, "Real-Time Bike Counter to Be Installed on Market," April 16, 2013, http://www.sfbike.org/news/real-time-bike-counter -to-be-installed-on-market.

94. See http://www.sfbike.org/our-work/street-campaigns/market-street/ (accessed December 7, 2017).

95. Michael Cabanatuan, "SF's Market Street Plan Would Ban Private Cars, Add Bike Lanes," *San Francisco Chronicle*, August 2, 2017, http://www.sfgate.com/ bayarea/article/SF-s-Market-Street-plan-would-ban-private-cars-11725834.php.

96. Observations at a Better Market Street Project open house, July 17, 2012. On "eyes on the street," see Jacobs, *The Death and Life of Great American Cities*. Ironically, the racialized poor of the district are uniquely well protected, as are the social services they depend on, thanks to long and bitter struggles by housing activists. See Hartman, *City for Sale*.

97. Walker, "The Boom and the Bombshell."
98. Florida and Mellander, "Rise of the Startup City."
99. J. K. Dineen, "San Francisco Office Shift: Tenants Shed Space," *San Francisco Business Times*, September 14, 2012, http://www.bizjournals.com/sanfran cisco/print-edition/2012/09/14/san-francisco-office-shift-tenants.html?page=all; Colleen Taylor, "Boom Town: Tech Jobs Have Grown by a Third in San Francisco Since the Start of 2012," TechCrunch, August 27, 2012, http://techcrunch.com/2012/08/27/san-francisco-tech-job-data/; James Temple, "Tech's Space Appetite Eclipses Highs of Dot-Com Boom," *San Francisco Chronicle*, December 4, 2013, http://www.sfgate.com/technology/dotcommentary/article/Tech-s-space-appetite-eclipses-highs-of-dot-com-5033838.php; John Sailors, "San Francisco Beats Silicon Valley on Tech Job Growth," *San Francisco Business Times*, March 25, 2014, http://www.bizjournals.com/sanfrancisco/morning_call/2014/03/san-francisco-beats-out-silicon-valley-on-tech-job.html; Tim Bradshaw, "Google Hits Space Bar for Bay Area Start-Ups," *Financial Times*, February 16, 2014, https://www.ft.com/content/ab00362c-9739-11e3-a274-00144feab7de.

100. In effect, the plan revives a 2005 redevelopment plan that had foundered in committee, but this time with complete streets designs for the corridor. San Francisco Office of the Mayor, "Press Release: Mayor Newsom Announces Central Market Partnership to Revitalize Mid-Market Neighborhood As Part of His Local Economic Stimulus Plan," January 14, 2010, https://web.archive.org/web/2010011810 0056/http://www.sfmayor.org:80/press-room/press-releases/press-release -central-market-partnership.

101. Edwin Lee, "Mayor Ed Lee: What's Next for San Francisco," *The Commonwealth Club of California*, March 13, 2014, http://audio.commonwealthclub.org/audio/podcast/cc_20140313_lee.mp3.

102. The goals of the project also include stabilizing the existing community, "activating" the public realm, supporting the arts, combating vacancy, building the district's "identity," and improving safety. Central Market Partnership, "Central Market Strategy," 2011, http://commissions.sfplanning.org/cpcpackets/Central MarketEconomicStrategyCPC.pdf. Many of these properties were owned by large real estate interests awaiting just such an initiative.

103. David Chiu, *Ordinance No. 68–11: Payroll Expense Tax Exclusion in Central Market Street and Tenderloin Area* (San Francisco Board of Supervisors, 2011), http://www.sfbos.org/ftp/uploadedfiles/bdsupvrs/ordinances11/o0068-11 .pdf. The vote was not unanimous: John Avalos of the Excelsior and David Campos of the Mission opposed, calling it "the wrong precedent." Left-wing former supervisor Chris Daly called it a "land grab." Marcus Wohlsen, "San Francisco Lawmakers Approve Twitter Tax Break," *Huffington Post*, April 27, 2011, http://www.huffingtonpost.com/2011/04/06/twitter-tax-break-approved-san-francisco _n_845367.html; Chris Daly, "Mid-Market Payroll Tax Exemption: Downtown's Latest Land Grab," *Fog City Journal*, March 15, 2011, http://www.fogcityjournal .com/wordpress/2708/mid-market-payroll-tax-exemption-downtowns-latest-land

grab. The Twitter CBA notably included a nod to the San Francisco Bicycle Coalition and Sunday Streets (San Francisco's open streets event modeled on Bogotá's Ciclovía) under "Support Physical Neighborhood Improvements." City and County of San Francisco City Administrator, "Community Benefit Agreement 2014 Renewal Memorandum of Understanding Between City and County of San Francisco City Administrator and Twitter, Inc." (San Francisco, 2014), http://www.sfgsa.org/modules/showdocument.aspx?documentid=11484; Yoona Ha, "Twitter, Other Tech Companies Get S.F. Tax Breaks but Show Little Progress Hiring in Neighborhood," SF Public Press, 2013, http://sfpublicpress.org/news/2013–11/twitter-other-tech-companies-get-sf-tax-breaks-but-show-little-progress-hiring-in-neighborhood.

104. San Francisco Office of Economic and Workforce Development, "Central Market Turnaround 2011–2014" (San Francisco, 2014), http://wayback.archive-it.org/3051/20140423214611/http://www.oewd.org/media/docs/Central Market/CENTRAL MARKET TURNAROUND 04–14–14.pdf. An assessment conducted later in 2014 by the Office of the Controller listed the number of firms taking the exclusion at twenty-seven. Office of the Controller, "Review of the Impact of the Central Market Payroll Tax Exclusion," 2014, http://sfcontroller.org/Modules/ShowDocument.aspx?documentid=5914.

105. San Francisco Planning Department, "Downtown Plan Annual Monitoring Report 2016," 2017, http://sf-planning.org/citywide-policy-reports-and-publications.

106. Citybuild Academy, "San Francisco Construction Update: Presentation to Workforce Investment San Francisco (WISF)" (San Francisco, 2013), http://www.oewd.org/media/docs/WorkforceDevelopment/wisf/WISF Board/2013/12.11.2013/CityBuild WISF Presentation 12 11 13—Full Slides.pdf.

107. John Stehlin, "The Post-Industrial 'Shop Floor': Emerging Forms of Gentrification in San Francisco's Innovation Economy," *Antipode* 48, no. 2 (2016): 474–93; Andrea Bernstein and Kai Ryssdal, "Techies on the Cutting Edge . . . of Bike Commuting," Marketplace, February 22, 2012, http://www.marketplace.org/topics/tech/transportation-nation/techies-cutting-edge-bike-commuting.

108. James S. Russell, "With $2,000 Bikes, Tech Firms Flee Suburbs for City Homes," Bloomberg Technology, August 5, 2012, http://www.bloomberg.com/news/2012–08–06/with-2-000-bikes-tech-firms-flee-suburbs-for-city-homes.html; see also Bernstein and Ryssdal, "Techies on the Cutting Edge . . . of Bike Commuting." As a caller to a local NPR affiliate's radio program debating the tech boom argued, "[Tech] employees come here to choose this lifestyle. They want to bike to work, they want to go to cafes . . . they're inherently progressive . . . San Francisco is winning the global battle for talent." See Judy Campbell, "How Much Tech Can San Francisco Take?," *KQED Forum*, September 2012, http://www.kqed.org/a/forum/R201209250900.

109. See "Quick Releases," *Tube Times*, October 2001, http://web.archive.org/web/20060223125404/http://www.sfbike.org/download/tubetimes/html/issue082/

octquick2001.html; San Francisco Bicycle Coalition, "Golden Wheel Awards 2012," 2012, http://www.sfbike.org/?goldenwheel12. BOMA's public affairs manager insisted that they were responding to demand from its tenants, who were themselves "follow[ing] the market trend" of younger companies improving access for cyclists as a perk to attract a talented workforce. John Bozeman, personal interview, June 21, 2012.

110. City and County of San Francisco Mayor's Office, "Bay Area Bike Share Launch in San Francisco [Posted to YouTube]," YouTube, August 29, 2013, https://www.youtube.com/watch?v=YCorKYHOYN4.

111. See NEMA, "About," 2013, http://rentnema.com; NEMA, "Brochure," 2013, http://rentnema.com/pdf/Brochure_NEMA.pdf; Aaron Bialick, "Hey, Developers: NEMA Offers Free Bikes for Residents to Borrow," *Streetsblog SF*, blog, 2013, http://sf.streetsblog.org/2014/01/22/hey-developers-nema-offers-free-bikes-for-residents-to-borrow. Bicycle-friendly high-end developments are also increasingly common in the Mission. See Chapter 4.

112. For a thorough summary, see Walker, *Pictures of a Gone City*.

113. Campbell, "How Much Tech Can San Francisco Take?"; David Talbot, "How Much Tech Can One City Take?: Shaken by the Latest Digital Gold Rush, San Francisco Struggles for Its Soul," *San Francisco Magazine* (San Francisco, October 2012), http://www.modernluxury.com/san-francisco/story/how-much-tech-can-one-city-take. Talbot, echoing a common theme, warned that "everything that attracted these young digital workers to the city is in peril."

114. Rebecca Solnit, "Diary," *London Review of Books*, February 2013, http://www.lrb.co.uk/v35/n03/rebecca-solnit/diary; "Protesters Block Another Google Bus in San Francisco Ahead of March against Evictions," CBS San Francisco, April 11, 2014, http://sanfrancisco.cbslocal.com/2014/04/11/protesters-block-another-google-bus-in-san-francisco-ahead-of-march-against-evictions; Sean Hollister, "Welcome to Googletown: Here's How a City Becomes Company Property," The Verge, 2014, http://www.theverge.com/2014/2/26/5444030/company-town-how-google-is-taking-over-mountain-view; Kevin Montgomery, "Tech Founder Complains about the Shithole City He's Forced to Make His Millions In," *Uptown Almanac*, August 15, 2013, http://uptownalmanac.com/2013/08/tech-founder-complains-about-shithole-city-hes-forced-make-his-millions; Joe Fitzgerald Rodriguez, "Real Tech Worker Says SF Homeless 'Grotesque,' 'Degenerates,' 'Trash,'" *San Francisco Bay Guardian*, December 13, 2013, http://www.sfbg.com/politics/2013/12/11/real-tech-worker-says-sf-homeless-grotesque-degenerates-trash; Kim-Mai Cutler, "It Doesn't Have to Be This Way," TechCrunch, January 24, 2014, http://techcrunch.com/2014/01/24/it-doesnt-have-to-be-this-way/; Matt Smith, "As Mayor Edwin M. Lee Cultivates Business, Treatment of Backer Is Questioned," *New York Times*, March 31, 2012, http://www.nytimes.com/2012/04/01/us/as-mayor-edwin-m-lee-cultivates-business-treatment-of-backer-is-questioned.html?pagewanted=1&_r=3.

115. Gabriel Metcalf, "The San Francisco Exodus," The Atlantic Cities, October 14, 2013, http://www.theatlanticcities.com/housing/2013/10/san-francisco-exodus/7205; Gabriel Metcalf and Egon Terplan, "The Tech Boom," The Urbanist, no. 529 (December 2013), http://www.spur.org/publications/article/2013–12–17/tech-boom; SPUR, "Mid-Market Street Redevelopment District."

116. Steven Jones and Joel Chanoff, "Heading East: Artists in Flux," San Francisco Bay Guardian, April 10, 2012, http://www.sfbg.com/2012/04/10/san-franciscos-loss; Steven Jones and Yael Chanoff, "San Francisco's Loss," San Francisco Bay Guardian, April 10, 2012, https://48hills.org/sfbgarchive/2012/04/10/san-franciscos-loss.

117. Mike Davis, *City of Quartz: Excavating the Future in Los Angeles* (London: Verso, 1990); Neil Smith, *The New Urban Frontier: Gentrification and the Revanchist City* (New York: Routledge, 1996).

118. Thomas J. Vicino, "New Boundaries of Urban Governance: An Analysis of Philadelphia's University City Improvement District," *Drexel Law Review* 3 (2010): 339–56.

119. University City District, "The State of University City 2018," 2017, 12–13, https://www.universitycity.org/sites/default/files/documents/The State of University City 2018.pdf.

120. Fabiola Cineas, "CHOP's New $275M Research Tower Is Officially Complete," *Philadelphia Magazine*, May 12, 2017, http://www.phillymag.com/business/2017/05/12/chop-roberts-center-pediatric-research-philadelphia. See https://philly.curbed.com/maps/university-city-philadelphia-development-projects (accessed December 8, 2017).

121. Melissa Romero, "With Pennovation, Forgotten Bottom Looks to Its Future," *Curbed Philadelphia*, October 25, 2016, https://philly.curbed.com/2016/10/25/13241438/pennovation-forgotten-bottom-grays-ferry-history.

122. Melissa Romero, "Drexel University Unveils Massive $3.5B Schuylkill Yards Development Plans," *Curbed Philadelphia*, March 2, 2016, https://philly.curbed.com/2016/3/2/11147980/drexel-unveils-schuylkill-yards-renderings.

123. Melissa Romero, "South Street Is Getting a Protected Bike Lane in 2018," *Curbed Philadelphia*, December 13, 2017, https://philly.curbed.com/2017/12/13/16771808/south-street-bridge-protected-bike-lane.

124. University City District, "The State of University City 2018."

125. Scott Andes et al., "Connect to Compete: How the University City-Center City Innovation District Can Help Philadelphia Excel Globally and Serve Locally," 2017, https://www.brookings.edu/research/connect-to-compete-philadelphia.

126. See https://www.pps.org/projects/campusmartius (accessed December 9, 2017).

127. Opportunity Detroit, DHive Detroit, and Project for Public Spaces, "A Placemaking Vision for Downtown Detroit," 2013, http://opportunitydetroit.com/wp-content/themes/Opportunity_Detroit/assets/PlacemakingBook-PDFSm.pdf. Ironically, the configuration of the QLine (with center boarding in some locations

and curbside in others) prevented quality bicycle infrastructure on Woodward, souring advocates on the project.

128. New local firms like Shinola and Detroit Bikes have drawn on this image as well.

129. Midtown Detroit, Inc., "Midtown Housing & Infrastructure: Recently Completed (2010–2014), Underway and Pipeline (2014–Current)," 2015, http://midtowndetroitinc.org/sites/default/files/images/site-content/pdfs/3. Midtown_Housing_Infrastructure_List_11-12-15.pdf.

130. Detroit Future City, "139 Square Miles," 2017, 67, https://detroitfuturecity.com/wp-content/uploads/2017/11/DFC_139-SQ-Mile_Report.pdf.

131. DC3 was founded by the College for Creative Studies, which works to promote Detroit's "creative sectors" and helped to get Detroit added to UNESCO's Creative Cities Network and won its City of Design designation in 2015.

132. See http://midtowndetroitinc.org/what-we-do/community-development (accessed December 9, 2017).

133. Sasaki Associates, "Techtown District Plan Design Concepts," 2013, http://midtowndetroitinc.org/sites/default/files/images/site-content/pdfs/Sasaki.pdf.

134. Schindler, "Detroit after Bankruptcy."

135. Detroit Future City, "Year-End Report," 2014, https://detroitfuturecity.com/wp-content/uploads/2014/02/DFC_2014YearEndReport.pdf.

136. Akers, "Making Markets"; Kimberley Kinder, *DIY Detroit: Making Do in a City without Services* (Minneapolis: University of Minnesota Press, 2016).

137. Ryan Felton, "Face Time: Ken Cockrel Jr. Responds to Detroit Future City's Criticisms," *Detroit Metro Times*, December 24, 2014, https://www.metrotimes.com/detroit/face-time-ken-cockrel-jr-responds-to-detroit-future-citys-criticisms/Content?oid=2275328; Carlos Salazar, "The Assassination of Detroit," *Jacobin*, October 14, 2014, https://www.jacobinmag.com/2014/10/the-assassination-of-detroit.

138. Neil Smith, "New Globalism, New Urbanism: Gentrification as Global Urban Strategy," *Antipode* 34, no. 3 (2002): 427–50.

139. Stehlin, "The Post-Industrial 'Shop Floor': Emerging Forms of Gentrification in San Francisco's Innovation Economy." In practice, however, many such firms remain as cloistered as ever.

140. Stephen Graham and Simon Guy, "Digital Space Meets Urban Place: Sociotechnologies of Urban Restructuring in Downtown San Francisco," *City* 6, no. 3 (2002): 369–82.

141. David Harvey, "From Managerialism to Entrepreneurialism: The Transformation in Urban Governance," *Geografiska Annaler* 71, no. 1 (1989): 11; David Harvey, *Justice, Nature and the Geography of Difference* (Oxford: Blackwell, 1996), chap. 11; Logan and Molotch, *Urban Fortunes*.

142. Schafran and Wegmann, "Restructuring, Race, and Real Estate."

143. Robert Bullard, Glenn Johnson, and Angel Torres, *Highway Robbery: Transportation Racism and New Routes to Equity* (Cambridge, Mass.: South End

Press, 2004); Sarah Dooling, "Ecological Gentrification: A Research Agenda Exploring Justice in the City," *International Journal of Urban and Regional Research* 33, no. 3 (September 2009): 621–39; Checker, "Wiped Out by the 'Greenwave.'"

3. Everyday Practices and the Social Infrastructure of Urban Cycling

1. Richard Florida, "America's Top Cities for Bike Commuting: Happier, Too," *Atlantic*, June 2011, http://www.theatlantic.com/national/archive/2011/06/americas-top-cities-for-bike-commuting-happier-too/240265.

2. James Rojas, "The Enacted Environment: Examining the Streets and Yards of East Los Angeles," in *Everyday America: Cultural Landscape Studies After J.B. Jackson*, ed. Chris Wilson and Paul Groth (Berkeley: University of California Press, 2003).

3. James C. Scott, *Weapons of the Weak: Everyday Forms of Peasant Resistance* (New Haven, Conn.: Yale University Press, 1985). I do not claim that bicycling is in itself a form of subalternity, a claim often made by white, able-bodied men, but that it is a commonsense notion that the everyday practice of cycling interrupts the automobile-focused urban order.

4. In varying ways, Pierre Bourdieu, Bruno Latour, Jane Jacobs, and Doreen Massey point to how practices embedded in places shape social reality. See Pierre Bourdieu, *Outline of a Theory of Practice* (Cambridge: Cambridge University Press, 1977); Bruno Latour, *We Have Never Been Modern* (Cambridge, Mass.: Harvard University Press, 1993); Jane Jacobs, *The Death and Life of Great American Cities* (New York: Vintage, 1992); Doreen Massey, *Space, Place, and Gender* (Minneapolis: University of Minnesota Press, 1994).

5. AbdouMaliq Simone, "People as Infrastructure: Intersecting Fragments in Johannesburg," *Public Culture* 16, no. 3 (2004): 407–29; AbdouMaliq Simone, *City Life from Jakarta to Dakar: Movements at the Crossroads* (New York: Routledge, 2010); Adonia Lugo, "CicLAvia and Human Infrastructure in Los Angeles: Ethnographic Experiments in Equitable Bike Planning," *Journal of Transport Geography* 30 (June 2013): 202–7; Adonia Lugo, "Body-City-Machine: Human Infrastructure for Bicycling in Los Angeles" (PhD diss., University of California, Irvine, 2013). This is particularly true among urban bicycle users without the political power to shape infrastructure investments.

6. Michel de Certeau, *The Practice of Everyday Life* (Berkeley: University of California Press, 1984).

7. "DIY Urbanism," *Urbanist*, September 2010, http://www.spur.org/publications/urbanist-article/2010-09-01/diy-urbanism; Nitin Sawhney, Christo de Klerk, and Shriya Malhotra, "Civic Engagement through DIY Urbanism and Collective Networked Action," *Planning Practice & Research* 30, no. 3 (2015): 337–54; Jaime Lerner, *Urban Acupuncture* (Washington, D.C.: Island Press, 2014); Mike Lydon and Anthony Garcia, *Tactical Urbanism: Short-Term Action for Long-Term*

Change (Washington, D.C.: Island Press, 2015). The "acupuncture" frame revives organicist notions of the city as well.

8. Oli Mould, "Tactical Urbanism: The New Vernacular of the Creative City," *Geography Compass* 8, no. 8 (2014): 529–39; Carolina S. Sarmiento, J. Revel Sims, and Alfonso Morales, "Little Free Libraries: An Examination of Micro-Urbanist Interventions," *Journal of Urbanism: International Research on Placemaking and Urban Sustainability* 11, vol. 2 (2018): 233–53; Kimberley Kinder, *DIY Detroit: Making Do in a City without Services* (Minneapolis: University of Minnesota Press, 2016).

9. Peter D. Norton, *Fighting Traffic: The Dawn of the Motor Age in the American City* (Cambridge, Mass.: MIT Press, 2011).

10. Dave Horton, "Environmentalism and the Bicycle," *Environmental Politics* 15, no. 1 (2006): 48. For example, as Dan Kaufman, a Portland-based filmmaker, put it to me, "Bikes have changed the economic paradigm. Cyclists are more likely to shop at locally owned, mom and pop stores. . . . Bicyclists are going to go to the co-op, the small grocery store, and pump money back into local economy. . . . It's a small-scale economy, closer to bartering" (personal interview, May 21, 2012). There is a long history of positing bicycles and other "appropriate technology" as the keys to solving the problems of modern life. See Ivan Illich, *Tools for Conviviality* (New York: Harper and Row, 1973); Zachary Furness, *One Less Car: Bicycling and the Politics of Automobility* (Philadelphia: Temple University Press, 2010); Fred Turner, *From Counterculture to Cyberculture: Stewart Brand, the Whole Earth Network, and the Rise of Digital Utopianism* (Chicago: University of Chicago Press, 2008); Langdon Winner, *The Whale and the Reactor: A Search for Limits in an Age of High Technology* (Chicago: University of Chicago Press, 1989).

11. Luis Vivanco, *Reconsidering the Bicycle: An Anthropological Perspective on a New (Old) Thing* (New York: Routledge, 2013).

12. Alan Latham and Peter Wood, "Inhabiting Infrastructure: Exploring the Interactional Spaces of Urban Cycling," *Environment and Planning A* 47 (2015): 300–319; Jon Binnie et al., "Mundane Mobilities, Banal Travels," *Social & Cultural Geography* 8, no. 2 (2007): 165–74. On the concept of affordances in science and technology studies, see James J. Gibson, *The Ecological Approach to Visual Perception* (New York: Houghton Mifflin, 1979).

13. Justin Spinney, "Cycling the City: Movement, Meaning and Method." *Geography Compass* 3, no. 2 (March 2009): 817–35.

14. Bourdieu calls the bodily hexis "a political mythology realized, *em-bodied*, turned into a permanent disposition, a durable way of standing, speaking, walking, and thereby of feeling and thinking." See Pierre Bourdieu, *The Logic of Practice*, trans. Richard Nice (Stanford, Calif.: Stanford University Press, 1980), 69–70.

15. Walter Benjamin, *Illuminations: Essays and Reflections* (New York: Schocken, 1968).

16. Evan Friss, *The Cycling City: Bicycles and Urban America in the 1890s* (Chicago: University of Chicago Press, 2015), 82–99; Henry Kingman, "When Bicycles Ruled the City: The Golden Age of San Francisco Cycling," *Tube Times*, October 2001, http://web.archive.org/web/20040902212440/http://www.sfbike.org/download/tubetimes/html/issue082/10oct2001.html.

17. Phillip Gordon Mackintosh and Glen Norcliffe, "Men, Women, and the Bicycle: Gender and Social Geography of Cycling in the Late Nineteenth-Century," in *Cycling and Society*, ed. Paul Rosen, Peter Cox, and Dave Horton (London: Ashgate, 2012), 205; Wiebe E. Bijker and Trevor Pinch, "The Social Construction of Facts and Artifacts: Or How the Sociology of Science and the Sociology of Technology Might Benefit Each Other," in *The Social Construction of Technological Systems: New Directions in the Sociology and History of Technology*, ed. Wiebe Bijker, Thomas Hughes, and Trevor Pinch (Cambridge, Mass.: MIT Press, 2012), 11–44.

18. Zachary Furness, "Biketivism and Technology: Historical Reflections and Appropriations," *Social Epistemology* 19, no. 4 (2005): 401–17. The socialist influence was especially great in Europe.

19. James Longhurst, *Bike Battles: A History of Sharing the American Road* (Seattle: University of Washington Press, 2015); Winner, *The Whale and the Reactor*.

20. Horton, "Environmentalism and the Bicycle"; Chris Carlsson, *Nowtopia: How Pirate Programmers, Outlaw Bicyclists, and Vacant-Lot Gardeners Are Inventing the Future Today* (Oakland, Calif.: AK Press, 2008).

21. "The Environment: L.A. River Channel Use by Cyclists Proposed," *Los Angeles Times*, April 28, 1972, http://search.proquest.com/docview/156923027; Philip Hager, "30,000 Riders in S.F.: Bicycle Craze Catches-On, Tests Strength in Bay Area," *Los Angeles Times*, August 20, 1972, http://search.proquest.com/docview/157132183; "The Environment: Thousands Want Bike Paths, Cranston Says," *Los Angeles Times*, May 25, 1972, http://search.proquest.com/docview/156936700. An exception was Davis, California, a college town converted into a virtual laboratory for bicycle infrastructure experimentation, particularly off-street bicycle paths. See Longhurst, *Bike Battles*.

22. Dave Snyder, "Good for the Bicycling Cause," in *Critical Mass: Bicycling's Defiant Celebration*, ed. Chris Carlsson (Oakland, Calif.: AK Press, 2002), 112–15.

23. The most well-known of its techniques is the practice of "corking," wherein cyclists block intersections to prevent cars from attempting to cross while the ride passes.

24. Carlsson, *Nowtopia*, 140.

25. Carlsson, *Critical Mass*, 78.

26. Carlsson, *Critical Mass*, 70–71.

27. The *San Francisco Chronicle* reported, "Although festive, the ride was politicized by the war, which some cyclists say they believe is driven by a thirst for

oil and imperialism." See Steve Rubenstein and Wyatt Buchanan, "Prayers, Peace, Pedals: War Protesters, Troop Supporters, Bike Activists, Angry Drivers Fill the Streets," *San Francisco Chronicle*, March 29, 2003, http://www.sfgate.com/politics/article/Prayers-peace-pedals-War-protesters-troop-2659714.php#ixzz1tHS2exxQ. In New York, a Critical Mass ride of over five thousand against the Republican National Convention encountered a massive police response, resulting in hundreds of arrests and a class-action lawsuit. See Ben Shepard, "Community Building in the Era of the Patriot ACT; Arrested for Stickering, Biking, and Other Misadventures (with Creative Direct Action)," *Journal of Aesthetics and Protest*, March (2005), http://www.joaap.org/webonly/Shepard.htm; Susan G. Blickstein, "Automobility and the Politics of Bicycling in New York City," *International Journal of Urban and Regional Research* 34, no. 4 (2010): 886–905; *Still We Ride*, directed by Andrew Lynn, Elizabeth Press, and Chris Ryan, documentary, 37 min. (Plattsburgh, N.Y.: In Tandem Productions, 2005); Jim Dwyer, "Police Infiltrate Protests, Videotapes Show," *New York Times*, December 22, 2005, http://www.nytimes.com/2005/12/22/nyregion/22police.html.

28. Susan Blickstein and Susan Hanson, "Critical Mass: Forging a Politics of Sustainable Mobility in the Information Age," *Transportation* 28 (2001): 347–62; quote taken from Travis Culley, "The Power Is Here (Chicago)," in Carlsson, *Critical Mass*, 11–17. On Critical Mass's translation to local struggles, see Ben Shepard and Kelly Moore, "Reclaiming the Streets of New York," in Carlsson, *Critical Mass*, 195–203; Anonymous, "Critical Mass, London Style," in Carlsson, *Critical Mass*, 68–69. By the same token, localized conflicts involving Critical Mass travel rapidly through online networks and signify a shared, global cycling identity. Video of a Porto Alegre driver tearing through a Critical Mass ride in 2011 spread widely through social media. See Myrna Domit and J. David Goodman, "Brazil Driver Accused in Attack on Critical Mass Bike Ride," *New York Times*, March 2, 2011, http://www.nytimes.com/2011/03/03/world/americas/03brazil.html.

29. Paul Mason, *Why It's Still Kicking Off Everywhere: The New Global Revolutions* (London: Verso, 2013); John Arquilla and David Ronfeldt, eds., *Networks and Netwars: The Future of Terror, Crime, and Militancy* (Santa Monica, Calif.: RAND Corporation, 2001). Arquilla and Ronfeldt even draw on Critical Mass as a case study.

30. Gilles Deleuze and Félix Guattari, *A Thousand Plateaus: Capitalism and Schizophrenia*, trans. Brian Massumi (Minneapolis: University of Minnesota Press, 1987).

31. Snyder, "Good for the Bicycling Cause," 115. This aptly demonstrates what Furness refers to as the "radical flank effect." See Furness, *One Less Car*, 100.

32. Chris Carlsson, "An Anniversary to Remember," *The Nowtopian*, blog, 2012, http://www.nowtopians.com/my-writings-and-appearances/an-anniversary-to-remember; SF Critical Mass, "Many Voices on Critical Mass," *SFCriticalMass.Org*, 2012, http://www.sfcriticalmass.org/2012/09/27/many-voices-on-critical-mass. In Portland it is often said that Critical Mass is unnecessary because every day is

one, a claim that elides the fierce police repression Critical Mass experienced in Portland in the early 2000s, including the founding of a counterintelligence unit of the Portland Police Department devoted entirely to infiltrating the ride. See Furness, *One Less Car*, 98.

33. "Bike among the Ruins," *New York Times*, July 2009, http://www.nytimes.com/2009/07/05/opinion/05barlow.html.

34. Jack Van Dyke, personal interview, September 25, 2011.

35. Todd Scott, "Detroit's East Side Riders," *M-Bike.org*, blog, 2011, http://www.m-bike.org/blog/2010/09/27/detroits-east-side-riders.

36. Detroitblogger John, "Cycles of Change," *Metro Times*, blog, September 22, 2010, http://www2.metrotimes.com/culture/story.asp?id=15379; David Sands, "Detroit East Side Riders' Mind-Blowing Bikes Inspire Residents to Take Up Cycling," Huffington Post, April, 17, 2012, https://www.huffingtonpost.co.uk/2012/04/17/detroit-east-side-riders-bikes_n_1429684.html; Scott, "Detroit's East Side Riders."

37. There were a number of short-lived experiments in a "law abiding" Critical Mass at this time, such as San Francisco's "Courteous Mass" and Portland's "Critical Manners." See Jonathan Maus, "Would Critical Manners Catch on in Portland?," BikePortland.org, 2007, http://bikeportland.org/2007/08/14/would-critical-manners-catch-on-in-portland-4793.

38. SF Critical Mass, "Critical Mass Dos and Don'ts," *SFCriticalMass.Org*, 2009, http://www.sfcriticalmass.org/2009/10/27/critical-mass-dos-donts; Chris Carlsson, "A Brief History of San Francisco Critical Mass," *Streetsblog LA*, blog, 2009, http://la.streetsblog.org/2009/12/22/a-brief-history-of-san-francisco-critical-mass. As Carlsson notes elsewhere, "Mainstream bicycle advocates maintain that cyclists as a group must be extremely law-abiding, in order to reinforce the self-congratulatory fantasy that bikes are angels in the transit universe, compared to the (automobile) devil." See Carlsson, *Nowtopia*, 116. This "angelic" posture has been crucial to bicycling's subsequent successes, and even Critical Mass participants celebrated their ability to "self-police." See Adam Kessel, "Why They're Wrong about Critical Mass: The Fallacy of Bicycle Advocates' Critique," in Carlsson, *Critical Mass*, 106, 111.

39. Jay Johnson, Matthew Masucci, and Mary Anne Signer-Kroeker, "'Everything Looks Better from the Seat of a Bike': A Qualitative Exploration of the San José Bike Party," *Leisure/Loisir* 42, no. 2 (2018): 163–84.

40. While San Jose Bike Party began with little police connection, with growth it became necessary to formally partner with law enforcement and community institutions. Other Bike Parties have adopted this stance as well. The police involved are often also on bicycles, and far less on edge than the motorcycle cops that escort Critical Mass. At a Bike Party leaving from El Cerrito in the East Bay, I overheard one policeman say to another, "These things are pretty low-key." At the start of the April 2012 "Hella Big" Bike Party that brought together the three Bay Area Bike Parties with a contingent from LA's Midnight Ridazz, an organizer happily shared the turn-by-turn cue sheet with Oakland police, adding, "Thank you very

much for keeping us safe tonight," to which the officer cheerily responded, "We'll keep an eye on you." On the paradoxes of this, see Chris Carlsson, "Protest or Celebration? Or Something Deeper Still?," SFCriticalMass.org, 2011, http://www.sfcriticalmass.org/2011/01/29/protest-or-celebration-or-something-deeper-still.

41. Bike Party also claims Midnight Ridazz, a group that began in 2004 in Los Angeles as a counterpoint to Critical Mass, as an influence. As the group's blog put its mission: "What Midnight Ridazz is: Fun; Friendships; Non Confrontational; Family; Compassionate; Open-Minded; Multi-cultural. What Midnight Ridazz is NOT: Mean Spirited; Political; Commercialized; Non-inclusive; Abrasive; Protest." See https://web.archive.org/web/20120602162049/http://midnightridazz.com/about.php (accessed December 12, 2017). On these rides as appropriation of urban space for ludic play, see Lusi Morhayim, "Nightscapes of Play: Enjoyment of Architecture and Urban Space through Bicycling," *Antipode* 50, no. 5 (2018): 1311–29.

42. See https://web.archive.org/web/20140401224647/http://sfbikeparty.wordpress.com/about/how-we-ride-details (accessed December 12, 2017).

43. East Bay Bike Party received a "Best of the Bay" mention from the *East Bay Express* in the "Revolution" category in 2012, while San Francisco's edition won "Best Group Ride" from the *San Francisco Bay Guardian* in 2013. See Steven Jones and Caitlin Donohue, "Bike Party! San Francisco's Newest Group Ride Marks a Less Confrontational, More Booty-Shaking Phase in the City's Bike Movement," *San Francisco Bay Guardian*, May 11, 2011, http://www.sfbg.com/2011/05/10/bike-party.

44. Available at https://www.facebook.com/photo.php?fbid=10152464500370756 (accessed August 3, 2016).

45. Matthew Masucci, "You've Got to Fight for Your Right to Party! A Qualitative Exploration of the San José Bike Party," in *Association of American Geographers Annual Meeting* (New York, 2012).

46. Will Doig, "Are Urban Bicyclists Just Elite Snobs?," Salon, December 2011, http://www.salon.com/2011/12/04/are_urban_bicyclists_just_elite_snobs.

47. John Geluardi, "Bicycle Advocates Decry Arrest of Najari 'Naj' Smith," *East Bay Express,* August 15, 2018, https://www.eastbayexpress.com/SevenDays/archives/2018/08/15/bicycle-advocates-decry-arrest-of-najari-naj-smith.

48. Alysa Zavala-Offman, "Slow Roll Will Now Require a Membership to Participate," *Detroit Metro Times*, March 23, 2015, https://www.metrotimes.com/news-hits/archives/2015/03/23/slow-roll-will-now-require-a-membership-to-participate.

49. Apple, "Apple—iPad—Jason Hall—Slow Roll" (Vimeo, 2014), https://vimeo.com/112254143.

50. Katherine McKittrick, "On Plantations, Prisons, and a Black Sense of Place," *Social & Cultural Geography* 12, no. 8 (2011): 947–63.

51. Trunk Boiz, *Scraper Bike* (YouTube, 2007), https://www.youtube.com/watch?v=hQGLNPJ9VCE. As of December 2017, two versions of the video had

over 5 million views combined. A seven-minute documentary about the phenomenon entitled "Scrapertown" increased the team's visibility in 2010, with over 100,000 views in May alone. See Drea Cooper and Zackary Canepari, "Scrapertown" (California Is a Place Vimeo Channel, 2010), http://vimeo.com/9702393.

52. https://web.archive.org/web/20140815021606/http://originalscraperbikes.blogspot.com (accessed December 14, 2017). At the same time, one could view the Scraper Bike Team's focus on leadership cultivation as a sort of "vernacular neoliberalism," mobilizing masculinist narratives of personal responsibility in the service of viable Black futures. See Paul Gilroy, ". . . We Got to Get Over Before We Go Under . . . Fragments for a History of Black Vernacular Neoliberalism," *New Formations* 80–81 (2013): 23–38.

53. In 2014, with philanthropic support, the Scraper Bike Team and Colectivelo staff opened a new facility in a shipping container at a deep East Oakland branch of the Oakland Public Library. See "Scraper Bike Team Grand Opening of 'The Shed,'" Bike East Bay, 2015, https://bikeeastbay.org/events/scraper-bike-team-grand-opening-shed.

54. By April 2015 it had received over 70,000 hits, but as of December 2017, it no longer appeared on the Levi's YouTube channel, perhaps due to the marketing cycle.

55. Levi's Commuter, Levi's® Commuter: The Ride—Tyrone Stevenson, Jr. of Scraper Bike Movement (Vimeo 2014), https://vimeo.com/99682226.

56. Jonathan Maus, "Bikes Lend Support to Historic Protest at Occupy Portland," BikePortland.org, 2011, http://bikeportland.org/2011/11/13/bikes-lend-support-on-historic-night-of-protest-at-occupy-portland-photos-61947.

57. David Harvey, *Spaces of Hope* (Berkeley: University of California Press, 2000).

58. M. Danyluk and D. Ley, "Modalities of the New Middle Class: Ideology and Behaviour in the Journey to Work from Gentrified Neighbourhoods in Canada," *Urban Studies* 44, no. 11 (October 1, 2007): 2195–210; Judith DeSena, *The Gentrification and Inequality in Brooklyn: New Kids on the Block* (Lexington Books, 2009).

59. Hart Noecker, "Capitalism Getting You Down? Then Ride Your Fucking Bike," *Portland Radicle*, November 19, 2012, http://rebelmetropolis.org/capitalism-getting-you-down-then-ride-your-fucking-bike.

60. Susan King, personal interview, May 22, 2012.

61. LisaRuth Elliott, personal interview, August 9, 2012.

62. Adonia Lugo, *Bicycle/Race: Transportation, Culture, Resistance* (Portland, Ore: Microcosm, 2018); Horton, "Environmentalism and the Bicycle."

63. Marco te Brömmelstroet et al., "Travelling Together Alone and Alone Together: Mobility and Potential Exposure to Diversity," *Applied Mobilities* 2, no. 1 (2017): 1–15.

64. Carlsson, *Nowtopia*.

65. Laura McCamy, "Oakland's Creative Bicycle Culture," *Momentum Magazine*, August 2010, http://momentummag.com/oaklands-creative-bicycle-culture.

66. Sherry B. Ortner, *Anthropology and Social Theory: Culture, Power, and the Acting Subject*, vol. 2006 (Durham, N.C.: Duke University Press, 2006).

67. Adam Shapiro, personal interview, January 18, 2013. Shapiro was referencing, as a trained urban planner, the history of "redlining" in Black neighborhoods (see chapter 1). On the white spatial imaginary, see George Lipsitz, *How Racism Takes Place* (Philadelphia: Temple University Press, 2011).

68. Damaris Rose, "Rethinking Gentrification: Beyond the Uneven Development of Marxist Urban Theory," *Environment and Planning D: Society and Space* 2, no. 1 (1984): 47–74; Brian J. Godfrey, *Neighborhoods in Transition: The Making of San Francisco's Ethnic and Nonconformist Communities* (Berkeley: University of California Press, 1988).

69. Only when riding with female friends have I gotten a sense of the near-constant harassment female-gendered cyclists receive from men on the street.

70. Jenna Burton, personal interview, April 29, 2013. I had a complicated reaction to this statement. I recall being surprised that as a Black woman she felt fear riding through certain Oakland neighborhoods. My initial feeling was that fearing spaces coded as Black was something only white people did because of subconscious racism. Burton may be Black, but she also spoke as a college-educated inmigrant from the other side of the country, as new to Oakland as I was. The bicycle illustrates here the specificity of the articulation of race, place, and history that renders cyclists-out-of-place as strange.

71. Here, danger is also not "merely" ideological. Racialized spaces produce bodily insecurity for their residents. See Ruth Wilson Gilmore, *Golden Gulag: Prisons, Surplus, Crisis, and Opposition in Globalizing California* (Berkeley: University of California Press, 2007). These concerns appeared in the formal process for revising Oakland's bicycle plan, discussed in the Conclusion.

72. There is even a relatively new bicycle brand called "Virtue."

73. As the managing director for Interbike, an industry trade show, put it, "Urban cycling culture is here to stay and it's providing our industry with an incredibly dynamic landscape of products and lifestyle identities." See "Interbike to Highlight Urban Cycling," *Bicycle Retailer and Industry News*, August 29, 2011, http://www.bicycleretailer.com/north-america/2011/08/29/interbike-highlight-urban-cycling.

74. See http://publicbikes.com/c/RACKSPACE (accessed April 29, 2015).

75. Michael Maniates, "Individualization: Plant a Tree, Buy a Bike, Save the World?," in *Confronting Consumption*, ed. Thomas Princen, Michael Maniates, and Ken Conca (Cambridge, Mass.: MIT Press, 2002), 43–66.

76. See https://web.archive.org/web/20130808003801/http://publicbikes.com/c/VISION (accessed December 14, 2017).

77. Pierre Bourdieu, *Distinction: A Social Critique of the Judgement of Taste* (Cambridge, Mass.: Harvard University Press, 1984).

78. Laura McCamy, "How Green Is Your Bike?" *Momentum Magazine*, April 27, 2015, https://momentummag.com/how-green-is-your-bicycle-manufacturing.

79. Jan-Willem van Schaik, "Asian OEMs Open Bicycle Factories in Europe," *Bike Europe*, May 5, 2017, http://www.bike-eu.com/home/nieuws/2016/03/taiwanese-oems-open-bicycle-factories-in-europe-10125865; Keoni Everington, "Made-in-Taiwan Bicycles Lead the Pack in China, UK and Netherlands," *Taiwan News*, January 17, 2017, https://www.taiwannews.com.tw/en/news/3075857.

80. Shreya Dave, "Life Cycle Assessment of Transportation Options for Commuters," 2010, https://web.archive.org/web/20171104122433/http://files.meetup.com/1468133/LCAwhitepaper.pdf. There are some efforts to "reshore" bicycle production, particularly as part of bikeshare fleet procurement, but these are a minor part of the overall bicycle market.

81. Zed Bailey, "Tonight, Tomorrow: Occupy Your Bike!," *Crank My Chain! Cycle TV*, 2011, https://www.taiwannews.com.tw/en/news/307585.

82. Councilmember Desley Brooks, whose political base in these areas include solidly middle-class Black neighborhoods such as Havenscourt Avenue, where the city hopes to install bicycle infrastructure, put it bluntly to Oakland's Bicycle Facilities Coordinator: "There will never be bike lanes on Havenscourt." Jason Patton, personal interview, February 21, 2014.

83. Though little data exists on frequency of stops of cyclists by race, higher ticketing rates and pretextual stops of cyclists of color by police have become common. See Maria-Christina Fernández et al., "Pretextual Stops of Bicyclists: Report and Recommendations of the Police Complaints Board to Mayor Anthony A. Williams, the Council of the District of Columbia, and Chief of Police Charles H. Ramsey," vol. 20001 (Washington, D.C., 2005), http://policecomplaints.dc.gov/sites/default/files/dc/sites/police complaints/publication/attachments/policy_rec_bike.pdf; Alexandra Zayas and Kameel Stanley, "How Riding Your Bike Can Land You in Trouble with the Cops—If You're Black," *Tampa Bay Times*, April 17, 2015, http://www.tampabay.com/news/publicsafety/how-riding-your-bike-can-land-you-in-trouble-with-the-cops---if-youre-black/2225966.

84. Burton, personal interview.

85. Lugo and Mannos refer to "invisible cyclists" to highlight the erasure of cyclists of color in the dominant narrative of the growth of cycling in cities as increasing mobility *choices*. Implicitly, cycling out of need codes subaltern cyclists as "prepolitical," or not yet able to advocate for their own interests. See Adonia Lugo and Allison Mannos, "Separate but Eco: Livable Communities for Whom?," *Streetsblog SF*, blog, May 21, 2012, http://la.streetsblog.org/2012/05/21/separate-but-eco-livable-communities-for-whom. On the "prepolitical," see Eric J. Hobsbawm, *Primitive Rebels: Studies in Archaic Forms of Social Movement in the 19th and 20th Centuries* (Manchester, UK: Manchester University Press, 1971).

86. Lugo, *Bicycle/Race*.

87. Furness, *One Less Car*, 179.

88. Furness, *One Less Car*, 170.

89. J. Gibson-Graham, *The End of Capitalism (As We Knew It): A Feminist Critique of Political Economy* (Minneapolis: University of Minnesota Press, 2006).

90. Jacobs, *The Death and Life of Great American Cities*.

91. "It's all about teaching people to do things themselves and fostering a do-it-yourself mentality. . . . It's very powerful when someone comes in and realizes they don't need to be intimidated about fixing their own bike," co-founder Catherine Hartzell told Oberlin's alumni magazine. See Peter Meredith, "Pedal Pushers," *Oberlin Alumni Magazine*, 2005, http://www.oberlin.edu/alummag/summer 2005/feat_pedal_2.html.

92. Geoffrey Colburn, personal interview, January 23, 2013; Evangeline Lowrey, personal interview, January 23, 2013.

93. Evangeline Lowrey, personal interview.

94. They also "spin off" collective rides like those in the first section. LA's Bike Kitchen largely spawned Midnight Ridazzz. Lugo, *Bicycle/Race*.

95. On the concept of residualization, see Steven Graham and Simon Marvin, *Splintering Urbanism: Networked Infrastructures, Technological Mobilities and the Urban Condition* (New York: Routledge, 2001), chap. 3.

96. A number of other members of the Bike Kitchen diaspora had started bike shops in the Mission as well.

97. Anderson Reed, personal interview, July 9, 2012.

98. Justine Sharrock, "Evolution on 14th Street: If You Want to Create the Perfect Neighborhood, Do It Yourself," *San Francisco Bay Guardian*, February 23, 2005, https://web.archive.org/web/20120309010038/http://www.sfbg.com/39/21/x_biznews.html.

99. Reed, personal interview.

100. See http://wearemanifesto.com/ (accessed December 14, 2017).

101. See http://web.archive.org/web/20140131051816/http://www.wearemanifesto.com/whoweare.php (accessed December 14, 2017). As someone who is friendly with the shop owners, I was surprised when I first encountered this statement, and I am grateful to Erin Collins for pointing it out to me.

102. James Scott, *Domination and the Arts of Resistance: Hidden Transcripts* (New Haven, Conn.: Yale University Press, 1990); Bourdieu, *Distinction*. I introduce these examples to underscore that in my ten years of bike shop experience on two coasts, I have found the bike shop—and the bike world more generally—to be devoid of "official" practices surrounding race-class but overflowing with a "feel for the game," about which bodies may belong on which bikes in which spaces. I have even noticed myself precognitively making such determinations, to my dismay.

103. Brian Drayton, personal interview, 2013.

104. Drayton, personal interview.

105. Jacobs, *The Death and Life of Great American Cities*.

106. Bourdieu, *Distinction*.

107. Emma Jackson and Tim Butler, "Revisiting 'Social Tectonics': The Middle Classes and Social Mix in Gentrifying Neighbourhoods," *Urban Studies* 52, no. 13 (2015): 2349–65.

108. Mike Hodson and Simon Marvin, "Urbanism in the Anthropocene: Ecological Urbanism or Premium Ecological Enclaves?," *City* 14, no. 3 (2010): 298–313.

4. Gentrification and the Changing Publics of Bicycle Infrastructure

1. Chicago is a notable exception: the League of American Bicyclists awarded it a "Silver" rating in 2005, seven years before New York. City of Madison Department of Traffic Engineering, "All League of American Bicyclists Awarded Bicycle Friendly Communities as of 9/22/2006," https://www.cityofmadison.com/trafficEngineering/documents/bfclist2.pdf (accessed January 2, 2018).

2. As noted in chapter 3, vernacular bicycling is omnipresent in poor neighborhoods and among people of color as well, and there is some evidence that poor people use bicycles disproportionately to their numbers. However, they disappear in localized, fine-grained statistics. Eric de Place, "Race, Class, and the Demographics of Cycling," *Grist*, 2011, http://grist.org/biking/2011-04-06-race-class-and-the-demographics-of-cycling.

3. John Pucher and Ralph Buehler, "Analysis of Bicycling Trends and Policies in Large North American Cities: Lessons for New York," *Transportation Research Part A* 45 (2011): 451–75.

4. Al Letson, "Portland, OR: A Tale of Two Cities," *State of the Reunion*, radio program, (Portland, Ore.: National Public Radio, 2012), http://stateoftheunion.com/portland-or-a-tale-of-two-citie/; Amy Lubitow and Thaddeus R. Miller, "Contesting Sustainability: Bikes, Race, and Politics in Portlandia," *Environmental Justice* 6, no. 4 (2013): 121–26.

5. Paul Schwartzman and Chris L. Jenkins, "How D.C. Mayor Fenty Lost the Black Vote—and His Job," *Washington Post*, September 13, 2010, http://www.washingtonpost.com/wp-dyn/content/article/2010/09/18/AR2010091804286_pf.html; Timothy A. Gibson, "The Rise and Fall of Adrian Fenty, Mayor-Triathlete: Cycling, Gentrification and Class Politics in Washington DC," *Leisure Studies* 34, no. 2 (2015): 230–49.

6. Jay Walljasper, "Do Bike Lanes Fuel Gentrification?," *PeopleForBikes*, blog, 2013, http://www.utne.com/community/bike-lanes-gentrification.aspx.

7. John R. Logan and Harvey L. Molotch, *Urban Fortunes: The Political Economy of Place* (Berkeley: University of California Press, 2007).

8. Aaron Golub, "Moving beyond Fordism: 'Complete Streets' and the Changing Political Economy of Urban Transportation," in *Incomplete Streets: Processes, Practices, and Possibilities*, ed. Stephen Zavestoski and Julian Agyeman (New York: Routledge, 2014).

9. C. W. Nevius, "Gentrification No Longer a Dirty Word," *San Francisco Chronicle*, February 23, 2013, http://www.sfgate.com/bayarea/nevius/article/Gentrification-no-longer-a-dirty-word-4302093.php.

10. For an account of how Jacobs's critique of modernist planning became a guiding logic of urbanization today, see Scott Larson, *Building like Moses with Jacobs in Mind: Contemporary Planning in New York City* (Philadelphia: Temple University Press, 2013).

11. Mark Fisher, *Capitalist Realism: Is There No Alternative?* (Alresford, UK: Zero Books, 2009); see also Peter Marcuse, "Gentrification, Abandonment, and Displacement: Connections, Causes, and Policy Responses in New York City," *Journal of Urban and Contemporary Law* 28 (1985): 195–240.

12. Chris Benner and Manuel Pastor, "Collaboration, Conflict, and Community Building at the Regional Scale: Implications for Advocacy Planning," *Journal of Planning Education and Research* 35, no. 3 (2015): 307–22.

13. In 2011 Nevius abandoned his typical animosity toward cyclists, shocking readers by arguing, "Bikes are the future. We need to do a better job of dealing with it." His justification rested on portraying cycling as a mainstream activity of the urban middle class and an essential part of the cosmopolitan city of the future, while sparing no venom for Critical Mass. C. W. Nevius, "Bicycling the Wiggle in S.F. Points Way to Future," *San Francisco Chronicle*, July 28, 2011, http://www.sfgate.com/bayarea/nevius/article/Bicycling-the-Wiggle-in-S-F-points-way-to-future-2352956.php.

14. Another important aspect of this moment was the 1989 Loma Prieta earthquake, which damaged two widely reviled highway sections that were eventually removed. In Hayes Valley, the removal of the Central Freeway unleashed a massive gentrification boom, providing an object lesson in the economic benefits of reducing the space unnecessarily devoted to automobiles. See Jason Henderson, "Freeway Removed: The Politics of Automobility in San Francisco," in *The Political Economy and Ecology of Automobility*, ed. Alan Walks (New York: Routledge, 2014), 221–36.

15. David Ley, "Gentrification and the Politics of the New Middle Class," *Environment and Planning D: Society and Space* 12 (1994): 53–74.

16. Jason Henderson, *Street Fight: The Politics of Mobility in San Francisco* (Amherst: University of Massachusetts Press, 2013).

17. William Issel, "'Land Values, Human Values, and the Preservation of the City's Treasured Appearance': Environmentalism, Politics, and the San Francisco Freeway Revolt," *Pacific Historical Review* 68, no. 4 (1999): 611–46; Raymond A. Mohl, "The Interstates and the Cities: Highways, Housing, and the Freeway Revolt," 2002, http://www.prrac.org/pdf/mohl.pdf; Eric Avila, *The Folklore of the Freeway: Race and Revolt in the Modernist City* (Minneapolis: University of Minnesota Press, 2014); Manuel Castells, *The City and the Grassroots: A Cross-Cultural Theory of Urban Social Movements* (Berkeley: University of California Press, 1983).

18. Richard A. Walker, "An Appetite for the City," in *Reclaiming San Francisco*, ed. James Brook, Chris Carlsson, and Nancy J. Peters (San Francisco: City Lights Books, 1998), 1.

19. Manuel Castells, *City, Class, and Power* (New York: Macmillan, 1978); David Harvey, *The Limits to Capital* (London: Verso, 2007); Logan and Molotch, *Urban Fortunes*. Strictly speaking, for Harvey the consumption fund consists of both public and private assets involved in reproducing the labor force and relations of production more generally.

20. On considering the street through the lens of technology, see Peter D. Norton, *Fighting Traffic: The Dawn of the Motor Age in the American City* (Cambridge, Mass: MIT Press, 2011).

21. Oscar Sosa López and Sergio Montero, "Expert-Citizens: Producing and Contesting Sustainable Mobility Policy in Mexican Cities," *Journal of Transport Geography* 67, February (2018): 137–44.

22. Steven Graham and Simon Marvin, *Splintering Urbanism: Networked Infrastructures, Technological Mobilities and the Urban Condition* (New York: Routledge, 2001).

23. Stephen J. Collier, James Christopher Mizes, and Antina von Schnitzler, "Preface: Public Infrastructures / Infrastructural Publics," *Limn* 7, November (2016): 1–12, https://limn.it/preface-public-infrastructures-infrastructural-publics. I am grateful to Oscar Sosa López for introducing me to this concept.

24. Castells, *The City and the Grassroots*.

25. Mike Lydon and Anthony Garcia, *Tactical Urbanism: Short-Term Action for Long-Term Change* (Washington, D.C.: Island Press, 2015); Jaime Lerner, *Urban Acupuncture* (Washington, D.C.: Island Press, 2014).

26. Donald C. Shoup, "The High Cost of Free Parking," *Journal of Planning Education and Research* 17, no. 10 (1997): 3–20; Raymond A. Mohl, "The Expressway Teardown Movement in American Cities: Rethinking Postwar Highway Policy in the Post-Interstate Era," *Journal of Planning History* 11 (2012): 89–103.

27. Chris Carlsson, *The Political Edge* (San Francisco: City Lights Foundation Books, 2004); Richard A. Walker, "The Boom and the Bombshell: The New Economy Bubble and the San Francisco Bay Area," in *The Changing Economic Geography of Globalization: Reinventing Space*, ed. Giovanna Vertova (London: Routledge, 2006), 112–38. High-tech industry had previously been more concentrated in the South Bay, and in advanced manufacturing.

28. Chester Hartman, *City for Sale: The Transformation of San Francisco* (Berkeley: University of California Press, 2002), 331–36; Anti-Eviction Mapping Project, "Ellis Act Evictions," Anti-Eviction Mapping Project, 2014, https://antievictionmap.squarespace.com/#/ellis (accessed May 2, 2018).

29. Dave Snyder, "Making Real Change in SF," *Tube Times*, April 2001; John Fall, "Outreach Project to Broaden SFBC," *Tube Times*, July 2001; "Quick Releases," *Tube Times*, April 1999; "Quick Releases," *Tube Times*, October 2002.

30. San Francisco Department of Parking and Traffic, "San Francisco Bicycle Plan Draft Report" (San Francisco, 1995).

31. Some representative comments: "There are numerous bicyclists in the Mission District who may have comments but are unaware of the proposal. They are non-English speaking and you should keep this community in mind because they may have special needs"; "Removing median [this had already occurred prior to 1996] on Valencia is not enough. Remove a parking lane"; "Remove one or two motor vehicle lanes on Valencia"; and, "Why not mark a bike lane on Valencia?" San Francisco Department of Parking and Traffic, "San Francisco Bicycle Plan," 1996, https://ia600403.us.archive.org/31/items/sanfranciscobicy1719sanf/sanfranciscobicy1719sanf.pdf.

32. James A. Throgmorton and Barbara Eckstein, "Desire Lines: The Chicago Area Transportation Study and the Paradox of Self in Post-War America," *Chicago Essays*, A Project Website of the Three Cities Project (Nottingham, UK, 2000).

33. Mary Brown, personal interview, 2013.

34. Dave Snyder, personal interview, 2012.

35. Jason Henderson, "Level of Service: The Politics of Reconfiguring Urban Streets in San Francisco, CA," *Journal of Transport Geography* 19, no. 6 (2011): 1142. Tom Radulovich, an interview subject of both Henderson and myself, affirmed this interpretation.

36. Henderson, *Street Fight*, 121. A member of the BART board of directors reportedly made a similar remark to East Bay Bicycle Coalition representatives when the system opened in 1972. Bicycle access on BART in 1975 was the EBBC's first victory.

37. Brown, personal interview. At the time, the DPT's Bicycle Program had just three staff members (up from one a few years prior), all of them young recent graduates of Berkeley and San Francisco State, along with two summer interns. Adam Gubser, Manito Velasco, and Virginia Summerell, "Implementing San Francisco's Bicycle Route and Sign System," 1998, http://archives.sfmta.com/cms/rbikes/documents/route_network.pdf.

38. Brown recounted with humor needing to borrow a suit for a meeting with a supervisor—a far cry from the professionalized SFBC of today. Brown, personal interview. As Dave Snyder told the *Christian Science Monitor*, "I could rent a place for $285 per month and so was able to devote my time to starting up the San Francisco Bicycle Coalition." Paul Van Slambrouck, "San Francisco: Now, More Like Everyplace Else," *Christian Science Monitor*, October 17, 2000, https://search.proquest.com/docview/405655314. While activists may have been endowed with cultural capital, no credible observer would have claimed that cycling was being encouraged by the city as a proxy for gentrification.

39. By the same token, feelings of membership in such a community rely on race-classed notions of identity. It is unlikely that literally all bicycle users in the space of the Mission at the time knew one another or recognized each other as part of the same social world.

40. Brown, personal interview.

41. Steven Bodzin, "Nearly Seven Years Old, Critical Mass Still Going Strong," *Tube Times*, August 1999.

42. Image available at http://www.brasscheck.com/cm (accessed May 2, 2018).

Still We Ride, directed by Andrew Lynn, Elizabeth Press, and Chris Ryan, documentary, 37 min. (Plattsburgh, N.Y.: In Tandem Productions, 2005).

43. Michael Krasny, "KQED Forum: Critical Mass, 20 Years Later," 2012, http://www.kqed.org/a/forum/R201209241000.

44. Dave Snyder, "Grassroots Movements in Hard Times: Occupying the Public Sphere," in *22nd Annual California Studies Association Conference* (Oakland, Calif., 2012). Adam Gubser, head of the DPT's bicycle program, publicly shared this explanation for the anger over cycling issues that Critical Mass represented. Other bicycle advocates were less charitable: in the same *Los Angeles Times* article, former director of the SFBC Darryl Skrabak called Critical Mass "mob rule." See Mary Curtius, "Bike Rallies Fray Nerves in San Francisco," *Los Angeles Times*, August 18, 1997.

45. Glen Martin, "Sunday Interview: Two-Wheeled Revolutionary," *San Francisco Chronicle*, August 10, 1997.

46. Brown, personal interview.

47. San Francisco Board of Supervisors, *Resolution Establishing Bicycle Lanes on Valencia Street* (San Francisco: San Francisco Board of Supervisors, 1998).

48. San Francisco Board of Supervisors, *Resolution*.

49. Leah Shahum, "Bicycling on Valencia Street Doubles," *Tube Times*, July 1999.

50. Tom Radulovich, personal interview, May 15, 2012.

51. Cycling was measured only on Valencia, not on higher-volume parallel streets Guerrero, Mission, and Van Ness, where car traffic increased slightly. According to Dave Snyder, the net result of the Valencia road diet was that parallel routes Guerrero and Mission became "sacrifice streets" for cars and transit, respectively. Guerrero residents won a lower speed limit (to 25 mph), while Mission Street, with a high concentration of Latino-owned businesses and low-income housing, saw an 8 percent increase in car traffic. Michael Sallaberry, "Valencia Street Bicycle Lanes: A One-Year Evaluation" (San Francisco, 2000), http://industrializedcyclist.com/Valencia_bikelanes.pdf.

52. Sallaberry, "Valencia Street Bicycle Lanes."

53. Dave Snyder, "Bike Network Coming Soon," *Tube Times*, May 2001.

54. Leah Shahum, "Victory on Valencia Street . . . Finally!," *Tube Times*, December 1998. Of course, the nature of this "stake" hinges on the distinction between use-values and exchange-values.

55. San Francisco Bicycle Advisory Committee, "SF Bicycle Advisory Committee Annual Report," 2001, http://sfgov.org/bac/sf-bicycle-advisory-committee-annual-report-2001.

56. Dave Snyder, "Award Winners Honored for Outstanding Contributions," *Tube Times*, August 1999. The success of Valencia also helped the SFBC to reframe

the rationale for a road diet on Polk Street, another commercial corridor near the Tenderloin where merchants were wary of losing parking to add a bike lane: "If Polk St. follows the success of Valencia St., we should see an increase in bike use, a decrease in injury accidents among all types of road users, and improvements to the overall neighborhood and shopping environment." The piece quoted a cyclist supportive of the new commercial environment: "I would never think about stopping and shopping on Polk St. if I weren't on a bike. I can actually look because I'm on a bike and I go slow enough. I can see a blouse in the window and stop and buy it." Leah Shahum, "Finally! Polk Street Bike Lanes," *Tube Times*, June 2000.

57. Emily Drennen, "Economic Effects of Traffic Calming on Urban Small Businesses" (San Francisco State University, 2003), http://www.sfbike.org/down load/bikeplan/bikelanes.pdf.

58. Drennen, "Economic Effects of Traffic Calming," 31–34. The study references a methodology utilized for large-scale transportation projects, discussed in David J. Forkenbrock, Shauna Benshoff, and Glen Weisbrod, "Assessing the Social and Economic Effects of Transportation Projects," *Transportation Research Board, National Cooperative Highway Research Program*, vol. 31, 2001, http://online pubs.trb.org/onlinepubs/nchrp/nchrp_w31.pdf.

59. Drennen, "Economic Effects of Traffic Calming," 46.

60. Drennen, "Economic Effects of Traffic Calming," 7.

61. Because the prevailing view in transportation engineering held that slowing down cars constituted an economic harm, it was not enough to prove a neutral effect or slight positive benefit. See Henderson, "Level of Service."

62. Emily Drennen, personal interview, 2014.

63. Drennen, "Economic Effects of Traffic Calming," 7.

64. Smart Growth America claims, "The total savings from biking, walking, or taking transit instead of driving can really add up across a city, ranging from $2.3 billion in Chicago to an astounding $19 billion a year in New York City. This 'green dividend' means that residents can spend that money in other ways, such as housing, restaurants, and entertainment, that keep money circulating in the local economy." Smart Growth America, "Complete Streets Stimulate the Local Economy," http://www.smartgrowthamerica.org/documents/cs/factsheets/cs-economic .pdf (accessed April 19, 2013). Of course, with the financialization of real estate, there is no reason to believe that this "green dividend" stays local.

65. Brown, personal interview." In one of many similar pieces in *Tube Times* urging support for the Valencia road diet, Leah Shahum wrote, "Help ensure that the new bike lanes (which are a one-year trial) keep working. Let Valencia merchants know that you're a bicyclist and a customer and that you support the lanes." Leah Shahum, "Bike Lane Enforcement V.I.A.B.L.E. on Valencia," *Tube Times*, April 1999.

66. Michel Callon, "What Does It Mean to Say That Economics Is Performative?" in *Do Economists Make Markets? On the Performativity of Economics*, ed. Donald MacKenzie, Fabian Muniesa, and Lucia Siu (Princeton, N.J.: Princeton

University Press, 2007), 311–57. Although the extent of this performance's influence is unclear, Drennen found that 30 percent of survey respondents had heard about the road diet from the SFBC, while 56 percent had heard about it from customers and neighbors. Drennen, "Economic Effects of Traffic Calming," 43–44.

67. Brown, personal interview. This kind of "policy tourism" is increasingly prevalent in the context of entrepreneurial urbanism, and it has become a local industry in its own right in Amsterdam. See Kevin Ward, "Entrepreneurial Urbanism, Policy Tourism, and the Making Mobile of Policies," in *The New Blackwell Companion to the City*, ed. Gary Bridge and Sophie Watson (Malden, Mass.: Wiley, 2011); Eugene McCann and Kevin Ward, "Policy Assemblages, Mobilities and Mutations: Toward a Multidisciplinary Conversation," *Political Studies Review* 10, no. 3 (2012): 325–32; Astrid Wood, "Moving Policy: Global and Local Characters Circulating Bus Rapid Transit through South African Cities," *Environment and Planning A* 46, October (2014): 2654–69.

68. Evelyn Nieves, "Mission Fights Case of Dot-Com Fever: San Francisco Enclave Resists Changes," *New York Times*, November 5, 2000, https://search.proquest.com/docview/91358405.

69. Brown recalled considering the possibility that the changes to the street could spur gentrification, but she didn't think bicycles could affect the process, especially because of the scale of the forces involved: "The changes snowballed in the late '90s. It felt like a train." Brown, personal interview.

70. Bill Hayes, "Artists vs. Dot-Coms: Fighting San Francisco's Gold Rush," *New York Times*, December 14, 2000, https://search.proquest.com/docview/91370623. An infamous flyer from the Mission Yuppie Eradication Project encouraged direct action against vehicles in particular: "MAKE THE MISSION A SPORT-UTILITY VEHICLE FREE ZONE. NOT ONE YUPPIE VEHICLE SHOULD BE SAFE ON THE STREETS OF THE MISSION!" Kevin Keating, "Mission Yuppie Eradication Project," 1999, http://www.infoshop.org/myep/cw_posters4.html.

71. Damaris Rose, "Rethinking Gentrification: Beyond the Uneven Development of Marxist Urban Theory," *Environment and Planning D: Society and Space* 2, no. 1 (1984): 47–74.

72. Anna Marie, "The Mission District: Everybody Wants In," *Curbed San Francisco*, February 4, 2013, http://sf.curbed.com/archives/2013/02/04/the_mission_district_everybody_wants_in.php.

73. Sally Kuchar, "Are You Sitting Down? SF's Median Rent Rate Is $3,200/Month," *Curbed San Francisco*, April 14, 2014, http://sf.curbed.com/archives/2014/04/14/are_you_sitting_down_sfs_median_rent_rate_is_3200month.php; Tracy Elsen, "Mapping Rent Prices by Neighborhood all over San Francisco," *Curbed San Francisco*, September 18, 2015, http://sf.curbed.com/2015/9/18/9919888/mapping-rent-prices-by-neighborhood-all-over-san-francisco. See www.trulia.com.

74. Nancy Keats and Geoffrey Fowler, "San Francisco's Hot Real-Estate Spot for the Rising Tech Generation," *Wall Street Journal*, March 16, 2012; Gabriel

NOTES TO CHAPTER 4

Metcalf, "The San Francisco Exodus," *The Atlantic Cities*, October 14, 2013, http://www.theatlanticcities.com/housing/2013/10/san-francisco-exodus/7205; Gabriel Metcalf, "It's Not Too Late to Make San Francisco Affordable Again. Here's How," *The Atlantic Cities*, January 20, 2014, http://www.theatlanticcities.com/housing/2014/01/its-not-too-late-make-san-francisco-affordable-again/8106.

75. Carol Pogash, "Gentrification Spreads an Upheaval in San Francisco's Mission District," *New York Times*, May 22, 2015, http://www.nytimes.com/2015/05/23/us/high-rents-elbow-latinos-from-san-franciscos-mission-district.html?_r=0.

76. In 2011 manual counts, Valencia Street had seen a disproportionately large increase of 95 percent since 2006, versus 71 percent for the city as a whole. By 2015, Valencia was roughly even with the city, seeing an increase of 275 percent. San Francisco Municipal Transportation Agency, "2011 Bicycle Count Report," 2011, http://128.121.89.101/cms/rbikes/documents/City_of_San_Francisco_2010_Bicycle_Count_Report_edit12082010.pdf; San Francisco Municipal Transportation Agency, "San Francisco Bicycle Count Report 2015," 2016, https://www.sfmta.com/sites/default/files/reports/2016/Annual Bicycle Count Report 2015_04152016.pdf.

77. Author calculations from data available at https://data.sfgov.org/Transportation/Bicycle-Parking-Public-/2e7e-i7me (accessed July 28, 2016).

78. Data retrieved from http://data.sf.gov.

79. SFBC staff do not release data on membership by neighborhood, but one booklet published in 2012 placed 40 percent of members in the heated zone of gentrification encompassing Noe Valley, the Mission, Potrero Hill, the Dogpatch, and the Castro.

80. Some emerging shifts toward the frame of "safety"—informed by ongoing traffic deaths—and "equity"—pressed by bicycle activists of color—are discussed in the conclusion.

81. Eugene McCann, "Urban Policy Mobilities and Global Circuits of Knowledge: Toward a Research Agenda," *Annals of the Association of American Geographers* 101, no. 1 (January 21, 2011): 107–30; J. Peck and N. Theodore, "Mobilizing Policy: Models, Methods, and Mutations," *Geoforum* 41, no. 2 (2010): 169–74.

82. PeopleForBikes, "Protected Bike Lanes Mean Business" (Washington, D.C., 2013), 30, http://www.sfbike.org/wp-content/uploads/2014/04/Protected_Bike_Lanes_Mean_Business.pdf. In this report, a sidebar claimed that 66 percent of merchants saw increased sales, despite the fact that Drennen's study selected a small sample and asked whether merchants *perceived* changes in business.

83. See Smart Growth America, "Complete Streets Stimulate the Local Economy."

84. Tanya Snyder, "Bike Summit: With a Seat at the Table, Cyclists Need to Master the Etiquette," *Streetsblog Capitol Hill,* March 6, 2013, http://dc.streetsblog.org/2013/03/06/bike-summit-with-a-seat-at-the-table-cyclists-need-to-master-the-etiquette.

85. Tanya Snyder, "Bicycling Means Business: How Cycling Enriches People and Cities," *Streetsblog Capitol Hill*, March 8, 2013, http://usa.streetsblog.org/2013/03/08/bicycling-means-business-how-cycling-enriches-people-and-cities. For the hyperlinked version, see Angie Schmitt, "More Evidence That Bike Facilities Are Good for Local Businesses," *Streetsblog*, November 15, 2011, http://streetsblog.net/2011/11/15/more-evidence-that-bike-lanes-are-good-for-local-businesses.

86. Drennen, personal interview.

87. These included Leslie Katz, Mark Leno, Sophie Maxwell, and José Medina.

88. Leno in particular, representing the Fifth District, including the Castro, Noe Valley, and the wealthier western edge of the Mission, was an early ally. Evincing their growing alliance, in 2001 Leno invited an SFBC representative to the San Francisco Small Business Summit to provide a counterpoint to merchant narratives of the need for parking. See Dave Snyder, "Reflecting on the SFBC's Political and Grassroots Future," *Tube Times*, November 1999; Leah Shahum, "The Bike Vote Makes a Difference," *Tube Times*, December 2000; "Letters to the Editor," *Tube Times*, December 2000; "SFBC Shorts," *Tube Times*, April 2001.

89. City and County of San Francisco, "Election Results 1999," http://sfgov2.org/index.aspx?page=1681 (accessed May 2, 2015); Tom Radulovich, "Multimodal Planning at MTA," 2004, http://www.spur.org/publications/spur-report/2004-09-01/multimodal-planning-mta.

90. "City Leaders Take to Two Wheels: Record Numbers Ride to City Hall," *Tube Times*, June 2001.

91. John Wildermuth, "Fall of the Machine: Political Shift in S.F., Democratic Establishment Keeps Losing Ground," *San Francisco Chronicle*, December 16, 2003, https://www.sfgate.com/politics/article/Fall-of-the-machine-Political-shift-in-S-F-2545930.php.

92. Daniel B. Wood, "Bicyclists Winning a War of Lanes in San Francisco," *Christian Science Monitor*, September 12, 2006, https://www.csmonitor.com/2006/0912/p01s01-ussc.html.

93. Rachel Gordon, "Cycling Supporters on a Roll in S.F.," *San Francisco Chronicle*, August 21, 2006, http://www.sfgate.com/news/article/Cycling-supporters-on-a-roll-in-S-F-Bicycle-2513550.php.

94. Dave Snyder, "City's Bike Policy Shifts from 'What If?' to 'How Soon?,'" *Tube Times*, August 2001.

95. On the formation of SPUR, which originally stood for "San Francisco Planning and Urban *Renewal*," see Hartman, *City for Sale*, 10–11.

96. Snyder, "Bike Network Coming Soon."

97. TLC received funding from the Evelyn and Walter Haas, Jr. Fund, the Hellman Foundation, the Lane Family Charitable Trust, the Rose Foundation, and the San Francisco Foundation, as well as $226,000 from the California Department of Transportation for the SFBC to conduct outreach for the bike plan. "Quick Releases," *Tube Times*, June 2002; Dave Snyder, "Unprecedented Opportunities Ahead," *Tube Times*, August 2002.

98. "The SFBC Goes to Amsterdam," *Tube Times*, September 2000; Leah Shahum, "Bicycling Bliss Is Possible in a Big City," *Tube Times*, September 2000; Dave Snyder, "Losing Patience, Gaining Determination," *Tube Times*, September 2000. This would be repeated with then-Executive Director Leah Shahum's seven-month sabbatical in Amsterdam in 2010, after which she wrote, "It's not often that you get to take your idea of utopia out for a test ride." See Leah Shahum, "Lessons from Amsterdam: How SF Can Bicycle toward Greatness," *Streetsblog SF*, September 19, 2011, http://sf.streetsblog.org/2011/09/19/lessons-from-amsterdam-how-sf-can-bicycle-toward-greatness;"Quick Releases," *Tube Times*, May 2001, http://web.archive.org/web/20040926152045/http://www.sfbike.org/download/tubetimes/html/issue079/mayquick2001.html.

99. San Francisco Bicycle Advisory Committee, "SF Bicycle Advisory Committee Annual Report."

100. Under the California Environmental Quality Act, any local projects deemed to have potentially "significant impact" trigger a costly and lengthy environmental impact review. Under planning conventions not written into law, level of service downgrading was sufficient to trigger an EIR, even if the modifications facilitated an *increase* in persons passing a given point in the roadway via other modes and could lead to fewer net auto trips. See San Francisco County Transportation Authority, "Strategic Analysis Report on Transportation System Level of Service (LOS) Methodologies," 2003, http://www.sfcta.org/sites/default/files/content/legacy/documents/FinalSAR02-3LOS_Methods_000.pdf. Anderson, a prolific blogger, explained that his motivations in opposing the plan were not about air quality, but about showing the "small, arrogant, politically aggressive minority" of "bike zealots" that they had "badly overreached" and punishing them for it. See Rob Anderson, "District 5 Diary to Supes: Don't Do It!," *District 5 Diary*, blog, April 18, 2005, http://district5diary.blogspot.com/2005/04/district-5-diary-to-supes-dont-do-it.html. See Henderson, *Street Fight*, for a thorough analysis of this period. Anderson's opposition was emblematic of largely conservative attacks on bicycle infrastructure in this period, including proto-Trumpian Toronto mayor Rob Ford's removal of a number of bike lanes. See Max Applebaum et al., "Beyond the Backlash: Equity and Participation in Bicycle Planning" (New York: Hunter College, 2011), http://www.hunter.cuny.edu/ccpd/repository/files/es_beyond-the-backlash-2011.pdf; Janette Sadik-Khan, "The Bike Wars Are Over, and the Bikes Won," *New York Magazine*, March 8, 2016, http://nymag.com/daily/intelligencer/2016/03/bike-wars-are-over-and-the-bikes-won.html; Alan Walks, "Stopping the 'War on the Car': Neoliberalism, Fordism, and the Politics of Automobility in Toronto," *Mobilities* 10, no. 3 (2015): 402–22.

101. Rachel Gordon and Jill Tucker, "Ruling Paves Way for San Francisco Bike Lanes," *San Francisco Chronicle*, 2010, http://www.sfgate.com/bayarea/article/Ruling-paves-way-for-San-Francisco-bike-lanes-3256815.php.

102. Matthew Roth, "SF Responds to Bike Injunction with 1,353 Page Enviro Review," *Streetsblog NY*, blog, November 28, 2008, http://www.streetsblog.org/

2008/11/28/sf-responds-to-bike-injunction-with-1m-1353-page-enviro-review. In November 2014, pro-automobile forces regrouped to sponsor Proposition L, a ballot initiative to "restore balance" to San Francisco's nominally transit-first transportation policy. This was soundly defeated at the polls. See https://ballotpedia.org/City_of_San_Francisco_%22Restore_Transportation_Balance%22_Parking_Meter_and_Traffic_Laws_Initiative,_Proposition_L_(November_2014) (accessed May 7, 2019).

103. Josh Switzky and Leah Shahum, "Bicycle-Friendly Future for Market Street," *Tube Times*, June 2002.

104. San Francisco Department of Public Works, "San Francisco Great Streets Program: The Livable City Initiative," 2007, http://sfdpw.org/ftp/uploadedfiles/sfdpw/projects/Divisadero_Wkshp2_PowerPoint.pdf.

105. The SFBC's "Connecting the City" campaign subsequently adopted the "8 to 80" age-based measure of infrastructure effectiveness, the namesake of the 8–80 Cities organization, of which Peñalosa is the executive director.

106. See preceding note.

107. San Francisco Department of Public Works, "Valencia Street Streetscape Factsheet," 2010, http://www.sfdpw.org/Modules/ShowDocument.aspx?documentid=142. This lane reduction appears to have been technically permitted under the injunction because it removed a center turn lane rather than a travel lane.

108. San Francisco Great Streets Project, "Great Streets Project Thanks You!," *Great Streets Project*, May 31, 2012, http://sfgreatstreets.org/2012/05/great-streets-project-thanks-you.

109. Radulovich, personal interview.

110. Radulovuch personal interview.

111. Realism, of course, implies working within the epistemic boundaries of the neoliberal city. See Fisher, *Capitalist Realism*.

112. Sergio Montero, "San Francisco through Bogotá's Eyes: Leveraging Urban Policy Change through the Circulation of Media Objects," *International Journal of Urban and Regional Research* 42, no. 5 (2018): 751–68.

113. Lydon and Garcia, *Tactical Urbanism*; Radulovich, personal interview.

114. Pierre Bourdieu, *Distinction: A Social Critique of the Judgement of Taste* (Cambridge, Mass.: Harvard University Press, 1984); Oli Mould, "Tactical Urbanism: The New Vernacular of the Creative City," *Geography Compass* 8, no. 8 (2014): 529–39.

115. Roger Rudick, "Safety Guerrillas Hit Valencia Street," *Streetsblog SF*, blog, October 24, 2016, https://sf.streetsblog.org/2016/10/24/safety-guerrillas-hit-valencia-street; Joe Fitzgerald Rodriguez, "After Uber, Lyft Swarm Valencia Bike Lanes, Supervisors Demand Barriers," *San Francisco Examiner*, August 7, 2017, http://www.sfexaminer.com/uber-lyft-swarm-valencia-bike-lanes-supervisors-demand-barriers.

116. Matt Brezina (@brezina), "The long fought beginnings of protected bike lanes on Valencia were installed this morning! Much more to do (as evidenced by

4 cars parked in the bike lane on the next block), but a huge accomplishment for @SFMTrA and @PeopleProtected Way to go members!" Twitter, March 15, 2018, https://web.archive.org/web/20180523155311/https:/twitter.com/brezina/status/974369496516386816 (accessed May 23, 2018).

117. London Breed (@London Breed), "Had a great time with @PeoplePro tected. Check out my plan to make transportation safe for all of us!" Twitter, May 9, 2018, https://web.archive.org/web/20180523160327/https:/twitter.com/LondonBreed/status/994387242759196672 (accessed May 23, 2018). It is worth noting that Breed, a Black woman raised in San Francisco's public housing projects, was a favored mayoral candidate of the young, largely white tech-worker-led YIMBY (Yes in My Back Yard) coalition in the city's increasingly acrimonious housing politics. This further demonstrates the growing gap between complete streets advocacy and the rest of the city's progressive and socialist Left, who opposed Breed.

118. See https://web.archive.org/web/20180523171150/https://www.crunchbase.com/organization/skinny-labs-inc (accessed May 23, 2018).

119. Snyder, personal interview.

120. Aaron Bialick, "Cesar Chavez: A Traffic Sewer Transformed Into a Safer Street," *Streetsblog SF*, blog, January 29, 2014, http://sf.streetsblog.org/2014/01/29/cesar-chavez-a-traffic-sewer-transformed-into-a-safer-street.

121. In 2016 Hernandez Gil left the SFBC for San Francisco Rising, an electoral coalition focused on racial and economic justice.

122. Jeff Maskovsky, "Governing the 'New Hometowns': Race, Power, and Neighborhood Participation in the New Inner City," *Identities* 13, no. 1 (2006): 73–99; Loretta Lees, "Gentrification and Social Mixing: Towards an Inclusive Urban Renaissance?," *Urban Studies* 45, no. 12 (2008): 2449–70.

123. Beatriz Herrera, personal interview, 2014.

124. Roger Rudick, "City Prepares to Remove Paul Avenue Bike Lane," *Streetsblog SF*, blog, October 20, 2017, https://sf.streetsblog.org/2017/10/20/city-prepares-to-remove-paul-avenue-bike-lane.

125. Henderson, *Street Fight*.

126. By "overdetermined," I mean that no one factor can be isolated as decisive apart from the contingent influence of all the others. See Louis Althusser, *For Marx* (New York: Pantheon Books, 1969).

127. Hartman, *City for Sale*.

128. Richard Florida, "America's Top Cities for Bike Commuting: Happier, Too," *Atlantic*, June 2011, http://www.theatlantic.com/national/archive/2011/06/americas-top-cities-for-bike-commuting-happier-too/240265.

129. Peck and Theodore, "Mobilizing Policy."

130. Ananya Roy, Stuart Schrader, and Emma Shaw Crane, "'The Anti-Poverty Hoax': Development, Pacification, and the Making of Community in the Global 1960s," *Cities* 44 (2014): 139–45.

131. Robert Self outlines a similar dynamic in Oakland, for instance. See Robert Self, *American Babylon: Race and the Struggle for Postwar Oakland* (Princeton, N.J.: Princeton University Press, 2003).

132. The Calle 24 Merchants Association, still a key force in maintaining the Latino character of Twenty-fourth Street businesses, was formed in this period. There was some measure of room for small-scale "sweat equity" gentrification by white in-migrants as well. As Castells notes, "The settlement of young middle class couples or even of lesbian households did not meet with open hostility, as long as they fitted into the neighbourhood, collaborated on its upgrading and got along well with the predominant Latino culture." See Castells, *The City and the Grassroots*, 109–37.

133. Kevin Roderick, "Typically Atypical San Francisco Census," *Los Angeles Times*, May 20, 1991.

134. Jane Jacobs, *The Death and Life of Great American Cities* (New York: Vintage, 1992). There is no extant evidence that the Mission Anti-Displacement Coalition, for instance, formed in the late 1990s to counter the dot-com onslaught, regarded bicycle advocates with any suspicion. To the contrary, some anti-displacement activists, including Latinos, used bicycles themselves. See Christine Elizabeth Selig, "The Role of Education in Strengthening Social Movements: A Case Study of the Mission Anti-Displacement Coalition in San Francisco" (PhD diss., University of California, Berkeley, 2005), https://search-proquest-com.manchester.idm.oclc.org/docview/60010412; June Lee Gin, "'We're Here and We're Not Leaving': Framing, Political History, and Community Response to Gentrification in the San Francisco Bay Area" (PhD diss., University of Michigan, 2007), https://search-proquest-com.manchester.idm.oclc.org/docview/61747462.

135. As noted above, comments on early drafts of the 1997 Bicycle Plan indicated that while many working-class Latinos used bicycles, their interests as cyclists were not represented on the advisory committee or in the planning process.

136. Miranda Joseph, *Against the Romance of Community* (Minneapolis: University of Minnesota Press, 2002).

137. Kelvin Mason and Mark Whitehead, "Transition Urbanism and the Contested Politics of Ethical Place Making," *Antipode* 44, no. 2 (March 14, 2012): 493–516.

138. As noted above, between Valencia and Polk (see note 56), Polk was always more politically controversial than Valencia, and more vulnerable to merchant counteroffensives over the loss of parking, despite the SFBC's hopes that it would follow Valencia's success.

139. Michel Foucault, *The History of Sexuality* (New York: Pantheon Books, 1978), 100.

5. Institutional Power and Intraclass Conflict over Complete Streets

1. Tanya Snyder, "Bike Summit: With a Seat at the Table, Cyclists Need to Master the Etiquette," *Streetsblog Capitol Hill*, blog, March 6, 2013, http://dc

.streetsblog.org/2013/03/06/bike-summit-with-a-seat-at-the-table-cyclists-need-to-master-the-etiquette.

2. Mary Lauren Hall, "San Francisco Architect: Better Bike Lanes = Higher Land Value," *PeopleForBikes*, blog, 2013, http://www.peopleforbikes.org/blog/entry/san-francisco-architect-protected-bike-lanes-will-boost-property-value.

3. Jonathan Maus, "To Boost Business, Beaverton Will Build Separated Bikeways on Western Ave," BikePortland.org, October 17, 2017, https://bikeportland.org/2017/10/17/to-boost-business-city-of-beaverton-will-build-separated-bikeways-on-western-ave-247398; City of Beaverton, "West Five Employment District Strategy," 2017, https://www.beavertonoregon.gov/1828/West-Five-Employment-District.

4. J. Peck and N. Theodore, "Mobilizing Policy: Models, Methods, and Mutations," *Geoforum* 41, no. 2 (2010): 169–74.

5. Jason Neil Zimmerman, "The First Cycle of Gentrification in West Oakland, California: 1998–2008" (master's thesis, San Francisco State University, 2009), https://degentrification.wordpress.com/2010/02/14/thesis.

6. Steven Jones and Yael Chanoff, "San Francisco's Loss," *San Francisco Bay Guardian*, April 10, 2012, https://48hills.org/sfbgarchive/2012/04/10/san-franciscos-loss/.

7. Barbara Grady, "Why Oakland's a Tech Start-up Game Changer," Oakland Local, December 24, 2014, http://oaklandlocal.com/2014/12/why-oaklands-a-tech-start-up-game-changer; Carolyn Said, "Rents Rise in S.F., Oakland, San Jose," SFGate, October 2012, http://www.sfgate.com/realestate/article/Rents-rise-in-S-F-Oakland-San-Jose-3961019.php.

8. U.S. Census Bureau, Means of Transportation for Workers 16 Years and Over, ACS 2010 1-Year Estimates, prepared by Social Explorer. https://www.socialexplorer.com/tables/ACS2010/R11547782 (accessed December 15, 2017); U.S. Census Bureau, Means of Transportation for Workers 16 Years and Over, ACS 2010 1-Year Estimates, prepared by Social Explorer. https://www.socialexplorer.com/tables/ACS2015/R11547783 (accessed December 15, 2017). These figures are derived from the American Community Survey 1-year estimates, and at small geographies they are less reliable than the full decennial Census, which no longer asks about commuting patterns.

9. League of American Bicyclists, "70 Largest Cities Ranked by Bike Commuting" (Washington, D.C., 2012), http://bikeleague.org/sites/default/files/70largest cities.xls.

10. Calculated from time-lapse maps of Oakland bicycle facilities available at http://www2.oaklandnet.com/Government/o/PWA/s/BicycleandPedestrianProgram/Map1/index.htm (accessed December 15, 2017). As of May 2019, the final draft of an update to the plan awaited Council approval.

11. Will Kane, "Oakland Racing to Meet Demand for Bike Lanes," *San Francisco Chronicle*, April 27, 2014, http://www.sfgate.com/bayarea/article/Oakland-racing-to-meet-demand-for-bike-lanes-5433977.php.

12. Jen Kinney, "Oakland Gets New DOT for a New Kind of Transportation Planning," *Next City*, July 1, 2016, https://nextcity.org/daily/entry/oakland-first-dot-transportation-planning; Oakland Office of the Mayor, "Mayor Libby Schaaf Launches Oakland's First Department of Transportation," June 8, 2016, http://www2.oaklandnet.com/oakca1/groups/mayor/documents/pressrelease/oak059117.pdf.

13. Kenneth T. Jackson, *Crabgrass Frontier: The Suburbanization of the United States* (New York: Oxford University Press, 1985); Martin Anderson, *The Federal Bulldozer: A Critical Analysis of Urban Renewal, 1949–1962* (Cambridge, Mass.: MIT Press, 1964).

14. Doreen Massey, *Space, Place, and Gender* (Minneapolis: University of Minnesota Press, 1994).

15. Marilynn Johnson, *The Second Gold Rush: Oakland and the East Bay in World War II* (Berkeley: University of California Press, 1993).

16. Robert Self, *American Babylon: Race and the Struggle for Postwar Oakland* (Princeton, N.J.: Princeton University Press, 2003).

17. Self, *American Babylon*, 135–76.

18. David Freund, *Colored Property: State Policy and White Racial Politics in Suburban America* (Chicago: University of Chicago Press, 2010). The effect was strongest in North Oakland. See Robert K. Nelson et al., "Mapping Inequality: Redlining in New Deal America," in *American Panorama*, ed. Robert K. Nelson and Edward L. Ayers, 2016, https://dsl.richmond.edu/panorama/redlining/#loc=4/36.71/-96.93&opacity=0.8.

19. Mary Ellen Perry, "Council Adopts Sweeping Plan of Civic Betterment," *Oakland Post*, November 18, 1971, http://search.proquest.com/docview/371665062; "Black Caucus Wants Action on Grove-Shafter Freeway," *Sun Reporter*, May 10, 1979, http://search.proquest.com/docview/370683068; Joseph A. Rodriguez, "Rapid Transit and Community Power: West Oakland Residents Confront BART," *Antipode* 31, no. 2 (April 1999): 212–28.

20. Jim DuPont, Elissa Dennis, and Tom Csekey, "Oakland for the Elite Only? As City Officials Urge Housing Downtown, Don't Forget the Others," *San Francisco Chronicle*, November 23, 1999, http://www.sfgate.com/opinion/openforum/article/Oakland-for-the-Elite-Only-As-city-officials-2893875.php.

21. Chris Rhomberg, *No There There: Race, Class, and Political Community in Oakland* (Berkeley: University of California Press, 2004), 183–86.

22. Zusha Elison, "As Oakland Mayor, Jerry Brown Remade Himself and Downtown," *New York Times*, September 2, 2010, http://www.nytimes.com/2010/09/03/us/politics/03bcbrown.html.

23. Alex Salazar, "Designing a Socially Just Downtown in Oakland, CA with Grassroots Housing Advocacy," *Shelterforce*, no. 145 (2006).

24. Sylvie Tissot, *Good Neighbors: Gentrifying Diversity in Boston's South End*, trans. David Broder and Catherine Romatowski (London: Verso, 2015).

25. Eric Avila, *The Folklore of the Freeway: Race and Revolt in the Modernist City* (Minneapolis: University of Minnesota Press, 2014); Self, *American Babylon*.

26. Daniel Hammel, "Re-Establishing the Rent Gap: An Alternative View of Capitalised Land Rent," *Urban Studies* 36, no. 8 (1999): 1283–93; Manuel B. Aalbers, "Colored Maps," in *Place, Exclusion and Mortgage Markets* (Oxford: Blackwell, 2011), 124–64.

27. Steve King, "Who Owns Your Neighborhood: The Role of Investors in Post-Foreclosure Oakland," Urban Strategies Council, June 2012, https://community-wealth.org/content/who-owns-your-neighborhood-role-investors-post-foreclosure-oakland.

28. Data retrieved from https://web.archive.org/web/20171216204745https://www.trulia.com/real_estate/Temescal-Oakland/7971/market-trends (accessed December 16, 2017).

29. Despite relatively greater social power, the Italian American residents of Temescal west of Grove Street were unsuccessful in their struggle to prevent the freeway. However, because it largely followed a decommissioned railroad grade, the freeway destroyed fewer houses in its pass east through the district. For detailed oral histories of this period, see Jeff Norman, *Temescal Legacies: Narratives of Change from a North Oakland Neighborhood* (Oakland, Calif.: Shared Ground Press, 2006).

30. Data extracted from Trulia and archived at https://web.archive.org/web/20171216213925/https://www.trulia.com/real_estate/Longfellow-Oakland/7918/market-trends (accessed December 16, 2017). During the housing market collapse from 2007 to 2011, gales of foreclosure in these areas revealed the extent of racialized predation that swept through these areas. Here, where many long-term residents owned their homes outright, homeowners of color were targeted for home equity lines of credit; others still with mortgages often refinanced. See Carolina Reid, "Sought or Sold? Social Embeddedness and Consumer Decisions in the Mortgage Market," Federal Reserve Bank of San Francisco, 2010, http://www.frbsf.org/community-development/files/wp2010-09.pdf.

31. Moreover, the freeway network, combined with the branching lattice pattern of Oakland's historical development as a streetcar city, creates no simple solution for installing relatively direct bikeways parallel to busy arterials. Bicycle infrastructure planners have been forced to take on some of the busiest, most well-traveled streets, chief among them Telegraph Avenue.

32. League of American Bicyclists, "70 Largest Cities Ranked by Bike Commuting."

33. By city estimates, dooring caused 25 percent of bicycle accidents on the corridor. Community Design + Architecture and Fehr & Peers, "Telegraph Avenue Complete Streets Project Materials," 2014, http://www2.oaklandnet.com/Government/o/PWA/o/EC/s/TelegraphAvenue/index.htm#materials. Because of the historic streetcar pattern noted above, Telegraph is also the widest street in the vicinity, which accommodates buses, bicycling, and parking as well as encouraging high speeds.

34. BART Marketing and Research Department, "2008 BART Station Profile Study," 2008, www.bart.gov/about/reports/profile; BART Marketing and Research Department, "2015 BART Station Profile Study," 2016, https://www.bart.gov/sites/default/files/docs/StationProfile2015_HomeOriginOnePagers_rev0629.pdf; East Bay Bicycle Coalition, "Telegraph Avenue Survey," 2013. Membership density calculated based on anonymized membership counts shared privately by Advocacy Director Dave Campbell.

35. Colin Burgett, a strategic planner with the city's Community and Economic Development Agency, wrote: "I have a concern about the existing priority routes selected by the [advisory commission]. While the committee has done a good job of selecting priority routes in North Oakland, our job is to create a *citywide* plan. This is a fact that will not be lost on City Council representatives that have little in the way of existing or proposed high-priority (top 8) bicycle routes in our plan [emphasis original]." Colin Burgett, "Memo to Bicycle & Pedestrian Advisory Committee, Re: Bicycle Master Plan," February 10, 1999, City of Oakland Department of Public Works, Bicycle and Pedestrian Advisory Commission archive.

36. Just twenty-four (7.4 percent) both identified as people of color and reported living within a few blocks of Telegraph. East Bay Bicycle Coalition, "Telegraph Avenue Survey."

37. Oscar Sosa López and Sergio Montero, "Expert-Citizens: Producing and Contesting Sustainable Mobility Policy in Mexican Cities," *Journal of Transport Geography* 67 (2017): 137–44.

38. This does not mean that advocacy organizations were smoothly integrated into the planning apparatus without conflict. Jason Patton, head of Oakland's Bicycle Facilities Program, recalled strong tensions between the city and the EBBC in the early 2000s. Jason Patton, personal interview, January 17, 2013.

39. Jason Patton, personal interview, February 21, 2014; Aaron Shapiro, "The Tactics That Be: Contesting Tactical Urbanism in New Orleans," *The Urban Fringe*, May 14, 2013, http://ced.berkeley.edu/bpj/2013/05/the-tactics-that-be-contesting-tactical-urbanism-in-new-orleans. Fittingly, in early 2014 the EBBC "rebranded," becoming Bike East Bay.

40. WOBO emerged from efforts of a group of neighbors in the light-industrial area just northeast of downtown Oakland to shape a planned Whole Foods into a more walkable development. See Laura McCamy, "Cycling in the City: Walk Oakland, Bike Oakland Steps It Up for Spring," Oakland Local, March 2, 2010, http://archive.oaklandlocal.com/article/cycling-city-walk-oakland-bike-oakland-steps-it-spring.html. When we spoke, WOBO board member Jonathan Bair cheered the city's development trajectory, calling himself "the last capitalist in Oakland." Jonathan Bair, personal interview, 2014.

41. Cory Weinberg, "SPUR to Open Oakland Office to Push 'Inclusive Growth' Policies," *San Francisco Business Times*, October 6, 2014, https://www.bizjournals.com/sanfrancisco/blog/real-estate/2014/10/spur-to-open-oakland-office-development.html.

NOTES TO CHAPTER 5

42. Jamie Parks, head of the Telegraph project in the Public Works Department, speculated that Telegraph had the highest ridership of any comparable corridor lacking adequate bicycle infrastructure: "We've made the street really bad for cyclists, and they still use it." Jamie Parks, personal interview, July 31, 2014.

43. Jason Patton, "A Pedestrian World: Competing Rationalities and the Calculation of Transportation Change," *Environment and Planning A* 39, no. 4 (2007): 928–44.

44. In the heart of Temescal, the owner of upscale Italian restaurant Pizzaiolo, a minor restaurant impresario in the area, underwent a "conversion experience" upon visiting Copenhagen in 2013 and approached Bike East Bay about being their partisan on the corridor. To the south, Arbor Café, where mostly white twenty- and thirty-somethings tap away all day at laptops and the bike racks inside and out are always full, was honored with a "Bicycle-Friendly Business" award by Bike East Bay in 2012 and hosted several Oakland Bikeways Campaign planning meetings. When accepting the award, the Arbor co-owner said: "About a 3rd of our staff bike to work to the Cafe and I would estimate that at least half of our customers get here by bike. . . . The only thing I can think of that the City could help with is striping a bike lane on Telegraph Avenue." See https://bikeeastbay.org/2012awards (accessed December 17, 2017). In fact, large portions of this book were written at Arbor Café.

45. Dave Campbell, "Active Shoppers Are Majority of Buying Power in Temescal District," Bike East Bay, December 18, 2014, https://bikeeastbay.org/news/active-shoppers-are-majority-buying-power-temescal-district.

46. In fact, much of the "grassroots" feel of Temescal's culture on the whole is shaped by the actions of the BID. For example, Sarita Waite, who owns Temescal Alley, a collection of artisanal boutiques, a traditional barber shop, an ice cream parlor, and a café, has been aggressive in resisting chain stores and curating a local character for the area. Rachel Swan, "New Growth in Temescal Alley Means Death for Polymorph Recording," *East Bay Express*, October 3, 2012, http://www.eastbayexpress.com/oakland/new-growth-in-temescal-alley-means-death-for-polymorph-recording/Content?oid=3353216. See also Carolyn Said, "Oakland's Temescal District a Hip Haven," *San Francisco Chronicle*, June 28, 2009, http://www.sfgate.com/realestate/article/Oakland-s-Temescal-district-a-hip-haven-3227476.php. For an introductory discussion of business improvement districts, see Richardson Dilworth, "Business Improvement Districts and the Evolution of Urban Governance," *Drexel Law Review* 3 (2010): 1–10.

47. The group's minutes show an obsessive concern with its distinctiveness. The word "iconic" is used in every mention of the proposed branding symbol: an "I [bicycle symbol] OAKLAND" marker signifying the district's character as a "green BID." Temescal Telegraph Business Improvement District, "Meeting Minutes," March 2012, http://temescaldistrict.org/Leadership-Minutes; Temescal Telegraph Business Improvement District, "Meeting Minutes," April 2012, http://temescaldistrict.org/Leadership-Minutes.

48. This lawsuit, the first use of the California Environmental Quality Act to block bicycle infrastructure on the basis of the lack of an environmental impact review, was the model for the infamous injunction filed against San Francisco's bicycle plan in 2006 (see chapter 4). Rob Anderson, "Hands across the Water," *District 5 Diary*, blog, July 25, 2006, http://district5diary.blogspot.com/2006/07/hands-across-water.html. Jason Patton had a charitable reading of the merchants' position at the time, which he described as, "Hey, we're trying to turn this district around that Highway 24 killed, we're not going to let you kill it with this poorly thought-out roadway reconfiguration." Patton, personal interview, February 21, 2014.

49. In fact, efforts by bicycle advocates to counter the lawsuit at the time mobilized the economic value of livability as well. In 1999 Kathryn Hughes, who was then Bicycle and Pedestrian Facilities Coordinator, argued, "The bottom line is that Telegraph Avenue is 'way too wide' to be a viable street commercially. . . . The entire strip from Berkeley to Oakland simply needs to slow down. And the slowing of traffic will ultimately be good for business. The area needs to experience what I called a road diet. . . . Curbing the flow of traffic will allow commuters to smell the variety of foods in the area and actually see what's available in the wonderful shops along the street." Clifford L. Williams, "Bicycle Lanes vs. Traffic Gridlock," *Oakland Post*, November 14, 1999, http://search.proquest.com/docview/367359585/FFA74E670D2D4489PQ/28.

50. Patton, personal interview, February 21, 2014.

51. Sara Mirk, "Bicycle Race," *Portland Mercury*, November 19, 2009, http://www.portlandmercury.com/portland/bicycle-race/Content?oid=1854486; Al Letson, "Portland, OR: A Tale of Two Cities," *State of the Reunion*, radio program, (Portland, Ore.: National Public Radio, 2012), http://stateofthereunion.com/portland-or-a-tale-of-two-cities; Amy Lubitow, B. Zinschlag, and N. Rochester, "Plans for Pavement or for People? The Politics of Bike Lanes on the 'Paseo Boricua' in Chicago, Illinois," *Urban Studies* 53, no 12 (2016): 2637–53. I also shared insights from my own brief fieldwork trips to Portland.

52. When we spoke later, he told me he felt he should be doing volunteer work on affordable housing to offset his work as a bicycle advocate.

53. At the same time, Chinatown merchants were adamantly opposed to the bike lanes planned for the redevelopment surrounding the Lake Merritt BART station on the grounds that cyclists were poor and undesirable.

54. Matthew Ridgway, personal interview, 2014.

55. Bruno Latour, *We Have Never Been Modern* (Cambridge, Mass.: Harvard University Press, 1993).

56. National Association of City Transportation Officials, "Oakland: Cities for Cycling Roadshow Program," 2014, http://nacto.org/wp-content/uploads/2014/03/Oakland_RoadShow_Program.pdf.

57. See https://bikeeastbay.org/cities4cycling (accessed December 17, 2017).

58. Patton, personal interview, January 17, 2013.

59. Max Hunter, personal interview, 2013.

60. Community Design + Architecture and Fehr & Peers, "Telegraph Avenue Complete Streets Project Materials."

61. In a grim underscore to the stakes of the street's transformation, a pedestrian was struck and killed in the corridor's busiest intersection just before the meeting began.

62. Another questioner brought up Latham Square, a downtown pedestrian plaza that was abruptly cut short after a debate in which both sides had cited merchant support for their positions. "Any chance the city will axe this project as well?" he asked. See Laura McCamy, "Oakland Planning Director Cuts Off Latham Square Pilot, Lets Cars Back In," *Streetsblog SF*, November 1, 2013, http://sf.streetsblog.org/2013/11/01/oakland-planning-director-cuts-off-latham-square-pilot-lets-cars-back-in.

63. He went on, regarding the consensus: "The hard-core vehicular cyclists were significant before, they're totally marginalized now. The things they were saying didn't resonate. . . . And Sarita Waite isn't interested in leading the opposition again." Parks, personal interview.

64. As late as December 2013, even after meeting with NACTO representatives at the Road Show, they claimed to be "blindsided" by Jamie Parks's statement about "how best to accommodate bikes on Telegraph Avenue in Temescal, recognizing that Telegraph will remain a major bike route in the future." Temescal Telegraph Business Improvement District, "Meeting Minutes," December 2013, temescaldistrict.org/Leadership-Minutes. On the other side, the promoter of the annual Temescal Street Fair lampooned the BID's proposal in the lingua franca of modern bicycle advocacy: "Wouldn't it be wonderful to have Temescal slide back to the way it was in 2004, before the BID started, when there weren't so many darn people (especially those latte-sipping, Oaklandish style hipsters/bicyclists) that now are almost everywhere you look?" Karen Hester, "Temescal Streets-Cars Get a Throw-A-Way and Bikes a Snuggle," *Loakal.com*, blog, April 25, 2014, http://www.loakal.com/temescal-streets-cars-get-a-throw-a-way-and-bikes-a-snuggle.

65. Robert Pratt, personal interview, 2014.

66. Robin Urevich, "The Accidental Developer: The Transformation of Temescal," News21 Berkeley, http://berkeley.news21.com/intersections/51–2/the-accidental-developer (accessed July 15, 2014); Rachel Swan, "New Growth in Temescal Alley Means Death for Polymorph Recording," East Bay Express, October 3, 2012, https://www.eastbayexpress.com/oakland/new-growth-in-temescal-alley-means-death-for-polymorph-recording/Content?oid=3353216.

67. To include bike lanes in the heart of Temescal would have required "a political decision to accept congestion" and discard the LOS guidelines, according to Jamie Parks, or a decision to remove parking and anger vocal business interests.

68. A reference to the influential typology of cyclists from Jennifer Dill and Kim Voros, "Factors Affecting Bicycling Demand: Initial Survey Findings from the Portland, Oregon, Region," *Transportation Research Record*, no. 2031 (2007): 9–17.

69. Ernesto Laclau and Chantal Mouffe, *Hegemony and Socialist Strategy: Towards a Radical Democratic Politics* (London: Verso, 1985).

70. See Melanie Curry, "Oakland Unnecessarily Pits Safe Bicycling vs. Transit on Telegraph Avenue," *Streetsblog SF*, blog, September 9, 2014, https://sf.streetsblog.org/2014/09/19/oakland-unnecessarily-pits-safe-bicycling-vs-transit-on-telegraph-avenue/; Melanie Curry, "Tomorrow: Oakland Drops Protected Bike Lanes on Telegraph Avenue," *Streetsblog SF*, blog, September 10, 2014, https://sf.streetsblog.org/2014/09/10/tomorrow-oakland-drops-protected-bike-lanes-on-telegraph-avenue/; Melanie Curry, "Parking-Protected Bike Lanes Partially Back in Oakland's Telegraph Ave Plan," *Streetsblog SF*, blog, November 26, 2014, https://sf.streetsblog.org/2014/11/26/parking-protected-bike-lanes-partially-back-in-oaklands-telegraph-ave-plan.

71. Oakland City Council, "Resolution Authorizing the Removal of Travel Lanes and the Installation of Bicycle Lanes on Telegraph Avenue from 19th Street to 41st Street . . ." December 9, 2014, https://oakland.legistar.com/View.ashx?M=F&ID=3418080&GUID=21240434-BBB3-468C-B530-DCEEF0B2633A. In particular, advocates were heartened by language in the resolution that raised the minimum standard for bicycle facilities through Temescal, where the draft plan had included only sharrows.

72. Koreatown-Northgate Community Benefits District, "Annual Report to City Council," 2015, https://diy5b2kdeokq1.cloudfront.net/upload-8044747797311979369.pdf.

73. Melanie Curry, "Oakland Council Approves Protected Bike Lanes on Telegraph Ave," *Streetsblog SF*, blog, December 10, 2014, http://sf.streetsblog.org/2014/12/10/oakland-council-approves-protected-bike-lanes-on-telegraph-ave.

74. Dave Campbell, "Oakland Celebrates a New Telegraph," Bike East Bay, May 10, 2016, https://bikeeastbay.org/news/oakland-celebrates-new-telegraph.

75. John R. Logan and Harvey L. Molotch, *Urban Fortunes: The Political Economy of Place* (Berkeley: University of California Press, 2007).

76. Data retrieved from https://data.acgov.org.

77. U.S. Census Bureau, Means of Transportation for Workers 16 Years and Over, ACS 2011–15 5-Year Estimates, prepared by Social Explorer. https://www.socialexplorer.com/tables/ACS2015_5yr/R11548417 (accessed December 15, 2017). Totals aggregated for Census tracts 4073–8, 4082–98, and 4101–4. Bike count data retrieved from the City of Oakland Bicycle and Pedestrian Facilities Program website, www2.oaklandnet.com/Government/o/PWA/o/EC/s/BicycleandPedestrianProgram/OAK024559 (accessed May 12, 2018).

78. BART Marketing and Research Department, "2008 BART Station Profile Study," https://www.bart.gov/about/reports/profile-2008; BART Marketing and Research Department, "2015 BART Station Profile Study," https://www.bart.gov/about/reports/profile.

79. This is not entirely new. In 2001, Councilmembers Ignacio de la Fuente and Larry Reid of East Oakland opposed a bike lane on Bancroft Avenue connecting

the Lake Merritt area to San Leandro. Ultimately, advocates prevailed through an alliance with the Oakland Police Department, who wanted to reduce "sideshows" (stunt driving by local young men of color) by reducing the street width. "Short Reports," *RideOn: The Newsletter of the East Bay Bicycle Coalition*, 2001, 3.

80. Federal Transit Administration and United States Department of Transportation, "Characteristics of Bus Rapid Transit for Decision-Making," 2004, http://www.nbrti.org/docs/pdf/Characteristics_BRT_Decision-Making.pdf; Stephen Smith, "The U.S. Can't Afford Nice Transit, So Everyone's Fawning Over BRT," Next City, September 24, 2013, http://nextcity.org/infrastructure/entry/the-u.s.-cant-afford-nice-transit-so-everyones-fawning-over-brt#.UkIZu77ltkc.twitter; Astrid Wood, "Moving Policy: Global and Local Characters Circulating Bus Rapid Transit through South African Cities," *Environment and Planning A* 46, October (2014): 2654–69.

81. Aaron Bialick, "Advocates Rebuff Merchant's Absurd Argument against East Bay BRT," *Streetsblog SF*, blog, July 10, 2012, http://sf.streetsblog.org/2012/07/10/advocates-rebuff-merchants-absurd-argument-against-east-bay-brt; Nathanael Johnson, "Bus Rapid Transit Watch: East Bay Update," *KALW Crosscurrents*, blog, April 28, 2010, http://kalwnews.org/blogs/nathanaeljohnson/2010/04/28/bus-rapid-transit-watch-east-bay-update_332344.html; Randy Reed, "My Word: Planned Bus Rapid Transit Will Hurt Businesses Badly," *Oakland Tribune*, July 9, 2012, http://www.insidebayarea.com/ci_21037548.

82. J. Douglas Allen-Taylor, "What's Left of BRT?," *East Bay Express*, February 2, 2011, http://www.eastbayexpress.com/oakland/whats-left-of-brt/Content?oid=2414177; Aaron Bialick, "Oakland City Council Gives Final Approval to East Bay BRT," *Streetsblog SF*, blog, July 18, 2012, http://sf.streetsblog.org/2012/07/18/oakland-city-council-gives-final-approval-to-east-bay-brt.

83. Robert Prinz of Bike East Bay put it in almost exactly these terms on Streetsblog: "What is really going to happen is the reduced[-]scope San Leandro-Oakland BRT is going to be built, it will be a huge boon for the communities along that corridor, and then the Telegraph merchants with a collective case of selective memory loss will start lining up to ask for an expensive extension into their business districts." Later, in sharply worded comment on his story, Prinz added, "I'm certainly not rich, but by not driving a car I have a lot more discretionary income burning a hole in my pocket than I would otherwise. . . . Local business owners who appreciate this dynamic and learn to adapt are the ones who are going to stay afloat despite a changing economy and transportation network." Bialick, "Advocates Rebuff Merchant's Absurd Argument."

84. For more details on the partnership, see https://web.archive.org/web/20171218060605/http://www.greatcommunities.org/oakland-intl-blvd-tod-implementation (accessed December 17, 2017).

85. Other points of contention included the added distance between stops and a proposal to hire a private security service to police the stations.

86. Logan and Molotch, *Urban Fortunes*.

NOTES TO CHAPTER 6   257

87. Jenna Burton, "Using a Cultural Approach to Address Social Injustice," Bicicultures Roadshow Symposium, Davis, Calif., April 17, 2013.

88. Anonymous, personal communication, May 8, 2018.

89. Winifred Curran and Trina Hamilton, "Just Green Enough: Contesting Environmental Gentrification in Greenpoint, Brooklyn," *Local Environment* 17, no. 9 (2012): 1027–42.

90. Amy Lubitow, Thaddeus Miller, and Jeff Shelton, "Contesting the North Williams Traffic Operations and Safety Project," 2013; Lubitow, Zinschlag, and Rochester, "Plans for Pavement or for People?"

91. Manuel Castells, *The City and the Grassroots: A Cross-Cultural Theory of Urban Social Movements* (Berkeley: University of California Press, 1983); Rhomberg, *No There There*.

92. "Coalition Suit Charges Grove-Shafter Freeway Violates Federal Laws," *Oakland Post*, July 27, 1972, http://search.proquest.com/docview/371637901; "Black Caucus Wants Action on Grove-Shafter Freeway."

93. Julian Agyeman and Tom Evans, "Toward Just Sustainability in Urban Communities: Building Equity Rights with Sustainable Solutions," *Annals of the American Academy of Political and Social Science* 590, no. 1 (November 1, 2003): 35–53.

94. Fred Turner, *From Counterculture to Cyberculture: Stewart Brand, the Whole Earth Network, and the Rise of Digital Utopianism* (Chicago: University of Chicago Press, 2008).

95. Alex Schmidt, "The Invisible Cyclists: Immigrants and the Bike Community," *Good Magazine*, January 14, 2011, http://www.good.is/posts/80; Damien Newton, "The Invisible Cyclists: Immigrants and the Bike Community," *Streetsblog LA*, blog, January 2011, http://la.streetsblog.org/2011/01/18/the-invisible-cyclists-immigrants-and-the-bike-community/.

96. The most extreme version of the latter can be found at the (frankly appalling) blog *A Better Alliance*, http://abetteralliance.blogspot.com (accessed March 7, 2019).

97. The complete plan is available at http://www2.oaklandnet.com/Government/o/PBN/OurOrganization/PlanningZoning/OAK028334 (accessed March 7, 2019).

98. City of Oakland, "West Oakland Specific Plan Public Review Draft" (Oakland, Calif., 2014), http://ec2-54-235-79-104.compute-1.amazonaws.com/Government/o/PBN/OurOrganization/PlanningZoning/OAK028334.htm.

6. Bicycle Sharing Systems as Already-Splintered Infrastructure

1. Melody Hoffmann, *Bike Lanes Are White Lanes: Bicycle Advocacy and Urban Planning* (Lincoln: University of Nebraska Press, 2016).

2. Edward W. Soja, *Seeking Spatial Justice* (Minneapolis: University of Minnesota Press, 2010); Mimi Sheller, *Mobility Justice: The Politics of Movement in an Age of Extremes* (London: Verso, 2018).

3. Because it is not officially categorized as transit, bikeshare is ineligible for federal subsidies for operations, only capital. The Bikeshare Transit Act (Blumenauer, D-Oregon) failed in the House of Representatives in 2016, while the Bike to Work Act (Crowley, D-New York; Paulsen, R-Minnesota) introduced in 2017 faces significant challenges in the political climate of the Trump administration. On the debates that have influenced these efforts, see Josh Cohen, "These U.S. Reps Want to Redefine Bike-Share," Next City, January 25, 2016, https://nextcity.org/daily/entry/federal-bill-redefine-bike-share-us.

4. Eric Jaffe, "Bike-Share Is (Still) Struggling to Reach Poor People across North America," CityLab, October 12, 2014, http://www.citylab.com/commute/2014/10/bike-share-is-still-struggling-to-reach-poor-people-across-north-america/381822.

5. Joe Grengs, "The Abandoned Social Goals of Public Transit in the Neoliberal City of the USA," *City* 9, no. 1 (April 2005): 51–66. The penalty for ignoring efficiency is municipalization, closure, or both. For example, Seattle's nonprofit-owned, privately operated bikeshare system folded in early 2017 after the city refused to commit public money to salvaging it. See T. R. Goldman, "The Disruption That's Putting Bikeshare into a Higher Gear," Politico, November 16, 2017. https://www.politico.com/magazine/story/2017/11/16/bike-share-dockless-washington-dc-what-works-seattle-birmingham-215833.

6. Jamie Peck and Nik Theodore, *Fast Policy* (Minneapolis: University of Minnesota Press, 2015), xx.

7. Most of the fifty initial bikes were confiscated by the police, after which the group advocated theft as "a means of collectivization." See Clyde Farnsworth, "Beatnik Provos: The New Anarchists: Lazy and Hairy, but They Cause Much Trouble," *Chicago Tribune*, March 19, 1967, https://search.proquest.com/docview/179169094. Similar programs sprang up in Austin, Texas, and Madison, Wisconsin. In the case of Madison's, users paid a small deposit for the use of "library" of bikes, improving retention. See https://web.archive.org/web/20180106124612/http://redbikes.org/history-of-red-bike-project (accessed January 6, 2017).

8. Susan Shaheen, Stacey Guzman, and Hua Zhang, "Bikesharing in Europe, the Americas, and Asia," *Transportation Research Record: Journal of the Transportation Research Board* 2143 (2010): 159–67.

9. Susan Shaheen, Elliot W. Martin, and Nelson D. Chan, "Public Bikesharing in North America: Early Operator and User Understanding, MTI Report 11-19," *Mineta Transportation Institute Publications*, 2012, http://scholarworks.sjsu.edu/mti_publications/73.

10. Elisabeth Rosenthal, "Bicycle-Sharing Mania Takes Hold in Europe," *New York Times*, November 9, 2008, http://www.nytimes.com/2008/11/09/world/europe/09iht-pedal.4.17664280.html.

11. Toole Design Group and Foursquare Integrated Transportation Planning, "Philadelphia Bike Share Strategic Business Plan," 2013, http://www.bikesharephiladelphia.org/philastudy/completebusinessplan.pdf.

12. With nearly $50 million in investments from Citibank and MasterCard, Citi Bike was uniquely free of public or philanthropic spending. Zak Stone, "The Business of Bike-Share," Next City, May 5, 2014, https://nextcity.org/features/view/bike-share-make-money-start-up-citi-bike-business-sharing-economy.

13. "Two kinds of mayors" is also now repeated often at policy gatherings and press conferences.

14. Motivate was formed in 2014 when ReqX purchased Alta Bicycle Share, an offshoot of Portland bicycle planning and consulting firm Alta Planning + Design, following its bankruptcy. Motivate shored up the losses of Citi Bike in New York by raising monthly membership prices over 50 percent, an increase permitted without city approval under the terms of the sale. See Claire Moses, "Related Affiliate to Buy Citi Bike Operator," *The Real Deal*, blog, July 2, 2014, http://therealdeal.com/blog/2014/10/27/affiliate-of-related-to-buy-alta-bicycle-share; Alta Bicycle Share, "Press Release: Bikeshare Holdings LLC Signs Agreement to Acquire Alta Bicycle Share," October 28, 2014, https://www.motivateco.com/bikeshare-holdings-llc-signs-agreement-to-acquire-alta-bicycle-share; Sarah Kessler, "Love Citi Bike? You Have a Real Estate Developer to Thank," Fast Company, January 12, 2016, http://www.fastcompany.com/3055168/love-citi-bike-you-have-a-real-estate-developer-to-thank.

15. Dana Rubinstein, "Deal Takes Shape to Bolster Citi Bike," Politico New York, July 2, 2014, http://www.politico.com/states/new-york/city-hall/story/2014/07/deal-takes-shape-to-bolster-citi-bike-014094; Dana Rubinstein, "Private Report Suggests Citi Bike Could Be a Going Concern," Politico New York, April 21, 2014, http://www.politico.com/states/new-york/city-hall/story/2014/04/private-report-suggests-citi-bike-could-be-a-going-concern-012372.

16. Andrew Small, "Ford GoBike Expands in San Francisco (But Not All Of It)," City Lab, August 4, 2017, https://www.citylab.com/transportation/2017/08/san-francisco-gobike-launch/532083; "Mission Advocates Call for New 'Moratorium' on Bikesharing," *San Francisco Examiner*, August 8, 2017, http://www.sfexaminer.com/mission-advocates-call-new-moratorium-bikesharing; Sam Levin, "'It's Not for Me': How San Francisco's Bike-Share Scheme Became a Symbol of Gentrification," *Guardian*, August 21, 2017, https://www.theguardian.com/us-news/2017/aug/21/bike-sharing-scheme-san-francisco-gentrification-vandalism.

17. Grengs, "The Abandoned Social Goals of Public Transit in the Neoliberal City of the USA"; Alan T. Murray and Xiaolan Wu, "Accessibility Tradeoffs in Public Transit Planning," *Journal of Geographical Systems* 5, no. 1 (2003): 93–107.

18. James J. Gibson, *The Ecological Approach to Visual Perception* (New York: Houghton Mifflin, 1979); Paul M. Leonardi, "When Flexible Routines Meet Flexible Technologies," *MIS Quarterly* 35, no. 1 (2011): 147–67.

19. Vincent Kaufmann, Manfred Max Bergman, and Dominique Joye, "Motility: Mobility as Capital," *International Journal of Urban and Regional Research* 28, no. 4 (2004): 745–56.

20. A growing issue facing pedestrians in suburban areas. See Mike Owen Benediktsson, "Beyond the Sidewalk: Pedestrian Risk and Material Mismatch in the American Suburbs," *Mobilities* 12, no. 1 (2017): 76–96.

21. Jamie Peck and Adam Tickell, "Neoliberalizing Space," *Antipode* 34, no. 3 (2002): 380–404; David Harvey, *A Brief History of Neoliberalism* (New York: Oxford University Press, 2007); Steven Graham and Simon Marvin, *Splintering Urbanism: Networked Infrastructures, Technological Mobilities and the Urban Condition* (New York: Routledge, 2001).

22. Neil Brenner and Nik Theodore, "Cities and the Geographies of 'Actually Existing Neoliberalism,'" *Antipode* 34, no. 3 (2002): 349–79; David Harvey, "From Managerialism to Entrepreneurialism: The Transformation in Urban Governance," *Geografiska Annaler* 71, no. 1 (1989): 3–17.

23. Alfons van Marrewijk et al., "Managing Public-Private Megaprojects: Paradoxes, Complexity, and Project Design," *International Journal of Project Management* 26, no. 6 (2008): 591–600.

24. Susan Shaheen, Elliot W. Martin, and Nelson D. Chan, "Public Bikesharing in North America: Early Operator and User Understanding, MTI Report 11-19," *Mineta Transportation Institute Publications* (San Jose, Calif.: San Jose State University, 2012), https://scholarworks.sjsu.edu/mti_publications/73.

25. See Robert K. Nelson et al., "Mapping Inequality: Redlining in New Deal America," in *American Panorama*, ed. Robert K. Nelson and Edward L. Ayers, 2016, https://dsl.richmond.edu/panorama/redlining/#loc=4/36.71/-96.93&opacity=0.8; David Freund, *Colored Property: State Policy and White Racial Politics in Suburban America* (Chicago: University of Chicago Press, 2010); Richard Rothstein, "The Making of Ferguson: Public Policies at the Root of Its Troubles," 2014, http://s3.epi.org/files/2014/making-of-ferguson-final.pdf.

26. Metropolitan Transportation Commission, "News Release: Motivate and MTC Announce Expanded Bike Share Equity Program," October 18, 2016, http://mtc.ca.gov/whats-happening/news/motivate-and-mtc-announce-expanded-bike-share-equity-program.

27. Neil Smith, *Uneven Development: Nature, Capital and the Production of Space* (Oxford: Blackwell, 1984); Alan Berube and Elizabeth Kneebone, *Confronting Suburban Poverty in America* (Washington, D.C.: Brookings Institution, 2013).

28. Peck and Theodore, *Fast Policy*, 225.

29. Uniformity is reinforced by the fact that three manufacturers supply most of the equipment in use in North America, creating a degree of path dependency in policy circulation. Similarly, a small number of consulting firms conduct the majority of feasibility studies, an equally small number of operators plan and manage bikeshare systems, and real-time bikeshare usage data is now harmonized across different systems through the General Bikeshare Feed Specification. See North American Bikeshare Assocation, "Press Release: North American Bikeshare Systems Adopt Open Data Standard," November 23, 2015, http://us11.campaign-archive1.com/?u=8327d4c9221c755645cd5334f&id=bfc8d7b6f0&e=ec9a6946e8.

30. Stephen J. Collier, James Christopher Mizes, and Antina von Schnitzler, "Preface: Public Infrastructures / Infrastructural Publics," *Limn* 7, November (2016): 1–12, https://limn.it/preface-public-infrastructures-infrastructural-publics.

31. Robin Williams and David Edge, "The Social Shaping of Technology," *Research Policy* 25, no. 6 (1996): 865–99.

32. Lisa K. Bates and Marisa A. Zapata, "Revisiting Equity: The HUD Sustainable Communities Initiative," *Progressive Planning* 194, Winter (2013): 14–17; Marisa A. Zapata and Lisa K. Bates, "Equity Planning Revisited," *Progressive Planning 35*, no. 3 (2015), 245–48; Anna Livia Brand, "The Politics of Defining and Building Equity in the Twenty-First Century," *Journal of Planning Education and Research* 35, no. 3 (2015): 249–64.

33. Robert D. Bullard, "Overcoming Racism in Environmental Decisionmaking," *Environment: Science and Policy for Sustainable Development* 36, no. 4 (1994): 10–44.

34. Erik Swyngedouw, "The Antinomies of the Postpolitical City: In Search of a Democratic Politics of Environmental Production," *International Journal of Urban and Regional Research* 33, no. 3 (September 2009): 601–20.

35. Peck and Tickell, "Neoliberalizing Space."

36. Anita Hamilton, "Has Philadelphia Made a Bike Share That Can Get the Entire City Biking?," Fast Company, March 30, 2015, https://www.fastcompany.com/3044431/has-philadelphia-made-a-bike-share-that-can-get-the-entire-city-biking.

37. Soja, *Seeking Spatial Justice*.

38. For example, the Detroit Regional Transportation Authority estimated BRT to cost between $4 million and $9 million per mile to build and roughly $20 million per year to operate for a twenty-five-mile line. By comparison, MoGo cost roughly $2 million to launch and $1 million a year to operate, or just over 10 percent of Detroit's police overtime budget in 2016. Eric Lawrence, "Commuter Rail, Bus Rapid Transit Keys to RTA Plan," *Detroit Free Press*, April 16, 2016, https://www.freep.com/story/news/local/michigan/detroit/2016/04/16/rta-plans-brt-commuter-rail-detroit/82760008; Eric Lawrence, "MoGo Is a Go: You Can Now Try Detroit's Bike Share System," *Detroit Free Press*, May 23, 2017, https://www.freep.com/story/news/local/michigan/detroit/2017/05/23/mogo-detroit-bike-share-launches/339458001; George Hunter, "Detroit Police Overtime Hours, Costs Soar," *Detroit News*, June 13, 2017, http://www.detroitnews.com/story/news/local/detroit-city/2017/06/13/police-overtime/102798536.

39. Russell Meddin, personal interview, June 21, 2018.

40. "Bike Sharing at the Philadelphia Urban Sustainability Forum," YouTube, January 20, 2008, https://www.youtube.com/watch?v=7CqIpnfuZmE.

41. Council of the City of Philadelphia, "Stated Meeting," January 24, 2008, http://legislation.phila.gov/transcripts/Stated Meetings/2008/sm012408.pdf; Council of the City of Philadelphia, "Joint Committees on the Environment and Transportation and Public Utilities," April 30, 2008, http://legislation.phila.gov/transcripts/

Public Hearings/transpor/2008/tr043008.pdf; Council of the City of Philadelphia, *Resolution: Requesting the Administration and the Deputy Mayor of Transportation and Utilities to Commission a Study to Provide Recommendations on Location, Demand, and Usage for Public Use Bicycle Stations* . . . , 2008, http://www.bikesharephiladelphia.org/pdf/public use bicycle report 61208.pdf.

42. JzTI et al., "Philadelphia Bikeshare Concept Study," 2010, 85, http://bikesharephiladelphia.org/PhilaStudy/PhiladelphiaBikeshareConceptStudyfeb2010.pdf.

43. JzTI et al., "Philadelphia Bikeshare Concept Study"; Gregory R. Krykewycz et al., "Defining a Primary Market and Estimating Demand for Major Bicycle-Sharing Program in Philadelphia, Pennsylvania," *Transportation Research Record: Journal of the Transportation Research Board* 2143 (2010): 117–24.

44. JzTI et al., "Philadelphia Bikeshare Concept Study," 73.

45. JzTI et al., "Philadelphia Bikeshare Concept Study," 67.

46. Toole Design Group and Foursquare Integrated Transportation Planning, "Philadelphia Bike Share Strategic Business Plan," 19.

47. The mandate to "serv[e] users in minority and low-income communities" included in the city's request for proposals came directly from Mayor Nutter and Deputy Mayor for Transportation and Utilities Rina Cutler. Andrew Stober, personal interview, June 21, 2017; City of Philadelphia Procurement Department, "Request for Proposals to Design, Install, Operate and Maintain a Bike Sharing System for the City of Philadelphia," http://bikesharephiladelphia.org/PDF DOC/Final Bike Share Procurment Dept RFP.pdf (accessed August 14, 2017).

48. Stober, personal interview.

49. City of Philadelphia Planning Commission, "The Recommended FY2014–2019 Capital Program City of Philadelphia," 2013, 65, http://www.phila.gov/finance/pdfs/FINALFY14_19RecCapitalProgram3 15 13.pdf.

50. Hamilton, "Has Philadelphia Made a Bike Share?"

51. Carniesha Kwashie and Cara Ferrentino, personal interview, 2017.

52. Alison Cohen, personal interview, June 13, 2017.

53. Claudia Setubal, personal interview, June 16, 2017.

54. Setubal, personal interview.

55. Between 2015 and 2016, the percentage of Black members rose from 8 percent to 19 percent. Because Indego tracks race/ethnicity and income for users through an optional survey (with a roughly 70 percent response rate), staff are able to assess with some confidence whether geographic attempts at equity have the desired effect. Indego, "2nd Birthday Snapshot, April 2015–April 2017," 2017, https://u626n26h74f16ig1p3pt0f2g-wpengine.netdna-ssl.com/wp-content/uploads/2017/05/INDEGO_SNAPSHOT.pdf.

56. Cohen, personal interview.

57. See https://web.archive.org/web/20171227225726/http://downtowndetroit.org/about-ddp/ddp-board (accessed December 27, 2017).

58. For instance, Hudson-Webber's $100,000 grant supporting bikeshare was part of a wider effort, the "15x15 Initiative," launched in 2008 to bring 15,000 "young, talented households" to downtown by 2015. See http://www.hudson-web ber.org/missionvision/15x15-initiative (accessed October 20, 2017). Hudson-Webber also funds the DDP and Invest Detroit. See "Hudson-Webber Foundation," *Detroit Ledger*, https://www.detroitledger.org/#!/organizations/274 (accessed August 29, 2017).

59. David Segal, "Dan Gilbert's Quest to Remake Downtown Detroit," *New York Times*, April 13, 2013, http://www.nytimes.com/2013/04/14/business/dan-gilberts-quest-to-remake-downtown-detroit.html; http://content-static.detroitnews.com/projects/dan-gilbert-detroit-properties/interactive-map.htm. Rock Ventures joined the cause of downtown "placemaking" in 2013 with its Opportunity Detroit "community" investment arm, and it sponsored the Project for Public Spaces's "Placemaking Vision for Downtown Detroit" (chapter 2).

60. As DDP president Eric Larson put it in a Kresge Foundation–funded report on the M-1 project, "What the QLine has done is take the entire length of Woodward from the river to Grand Boulevard and provide an attractive reason to develop and redevelop. . . . So a lot more of the infill opportunities that were not quite ready are now sitting in a very good position." See Stephen Hall and Andrew E. G. Jonas, "Urban Fiscal Austerity, Infrastructure Provision and the Struggle for Regional Transit in 'Motor City,'" *Cambridge Journal of Regions, Economy and Society* 7, no. 1 (2014): 189–206; Bill Shea, "Complex Funding Puts M-1 Rail on Right Track," *Crain's Detroit Business*, October 26, 2014, http://www.crainsdetroit.com/article/20141026/NEWS/310269949/complex-funding-puts-m-1-rail-on-right-track; Darren A. Nichols and Tom Walsh, "M-1 Rail Development and Construction Inclusion Report 2013–2017," 2017, https://m-1rail.com/wp-content/uploads/2017/05/M-1-RAIL-Development-and-Construction-Inclusion-Report-2013-2017.pdf. While the QLine's land development purpose would be easily achieved without bikeshare, planners envisioned bikeshare as a way to enhance its effectiveness by extending the "last mile" of what was ultimately a limited rail line. See Alta Planning + Design and LivingLAB, "Bike Share Feasibility Study for Greater Downtown Detroit," 2013, http://economicdevelopment.wayne.edu/documents/detroit_bike_sharing_report_final.pdf.

61. David Sands, "Detroit Bike Share Service Is Studied by Wayne State and Detroit Businesses, Organizations," Huffington Post, September 21, 2012, http://www.huffingtonpost.com/2012/09/20/detroit-bike-sharing-service-share-program_n_1900951.html.

62. The complete list of study sponsors included Blue Cross Blue Shield of Michigan, Downtown Detroit Partnership, DTE Energy, Henry Ford Health System, the Hudson-Webber Foundation, NextEnergy, Midtown Detroit Inc., Quicken Loans, and Wayne State University. See Sands, "Detroit Bike Share Service Is Studied"; Alta Planning + Design and LivingLAB, "Bike Share Feasibility Study."

63. Southeastern Michigan Council of Governments Transportation Coordinating Council, "Transportation Coordinating Council Agenda," July 22, 2015, https://www.semcog.org/desktopmodules/SEMCOG.Publications/GetFile.ashx?file name=TransportationCoordinatingCouncilAgendaSeptember2015.pdf; Marti Benedetti, "Detroit Bike Share Program Moves Forward with Naming of Vendor," Crain's Detroit Business, August 4, 2016, http://www.crainsdetroit.com/article/20160804/NEWS/160809927/detroit-bike-share-program-moves-forward-with-naming-of-vendor.

64. Most stations opened on May 23, but permitting delayed a few of them until July.

65. Alta Planning + Design and LivingLAB, "Bike Share Feasibility Study," 60.

66. Alta Planning + Design and LivingLAB, "Bike Share Feasibility Study," 63.

67. Alta Planning + Design and LivingLAB, "Bike Share Feasibility Study," 71.

68. Rebecca Quinn, personal interview, June 5, 2017.

69. Omari Colen, personal interview, June 5, 2017.

70. Quinn, personal interview.

71. Adriel Thornton, personal interview, May 31, 2017.

72. Lisa Nuszkowski, personal interview, August 16, 2016.

73. Dennis Archambeault, "North End Neighborhood Rising," Model D Media, February 26, 2013, http://www.modeldmedia.com/features/northend213.aspx.

74. Lisa Nuszkowski, personal interview, May 26, 2017. Like much of Detroit, the North End was redlined, with some nearby areas graded yellow. See Robert K. Nelson et al., "Mapping Inequality: Redlining in New Deal America," *American Panorama*, ed. Robert K. Nelson and Edward L. Ayers, 2016, https://dsl.richmond.edu/panorama/redlining.

75. In a well-publicized 2013 spat, the executive director of longtime neighborhood CDC Vanguard asserted in an open letter that MUFI was acting as cover for speculators, which MUFI disputed, although by 2015 co-founder Darin McLeskey was reported to own eighty properties across the city as a whole. See Khalilah Burt Gaston, "Letter to Michigan Urban Farming Initiative," November 11, 2013, http://challengedetroit.org/darinmcleskey/files/2014/04/MUFI-Letter.pdf; Darin McLeskey, "Response Letter," *Fellows Blog*, Challenge Detroit, blog, April 6, 2014, http://www.challengedetroit.org/blog/response-letter; Gus Burns, "One-of-a-Kind Airbnb to Offer Travelers Authentic Detroit Experience," MLive.com, October 26, 2015, http://www.mlive.com/news/detroit/index.ssf/2015/10/one-of-a-kind_airbnb_to_offer.html.

76. Nuszkowski, personal interview, August 16, 2016.

77. Alta Planning + Design and LivingLAB, "Bike Share Feasibility Study," 59, 65.

78. Paul Beshouri, "Parkstone and Parkhurst Apartment Buildings Ask over $18M," Curbed Detroit, January 4, 2013, https://detroit.curbed.com/2013/1/4/10289354/parkstoneparkhurst.

79. See https://mogodetroit.org/suggest-a-station (accessed October 11, 2016).

80. Amina Daniels, personal interview, June 3, 2017.

81. Lisa Nuszkowski chose to move bikeshare under the roof of the Downtown Detroit Partnership because "even though the core function of DDP is focused on the central business district, they also provide services to other parts of the city. . . . We knew bike share needed to exist beyond downtown, so we were thinking of an entity that could support programs in a variety of areas of the city." Nuszkowski, personal interview, May 26, 2017.

82. E. B. Allen, "Partners for Progress: Teamwork Guides Multi-Million-Dollar Neighborhood Fund," The Hub Detroit, August 10, 2017, http://www.thehubdetroit.com/partners-progress-teamwork-guides-multi-million-dollar-neighborhood-fund.

83. JPMorgan Chase & Co., "Corporate Responsibility Report," 2017, 29, https://www.jpmorganchase.com/corporate/Corporate-Responsibility/document/2016-JPMorgan-Chase-CR-Report.pdf.

84. Annalise Frank, "First Look inside The Coe at West Village," Crain's Detroit Business, January 20, 2017, http://www.crainsdetroit.com/article/20170120/NEWS/170129987/take-a-look-inside-the-coe-at-west-village; Louis Aguilar, "Small Developers Target Detroit's Near East Side," Detroit News, March 2, 2017, http://www.detroitnews.com/story/news/local/detroit-city/2017/03/02/small-developers-target-detroits-near-east-side/98669732. Many of the small business development seed funds are interwoven with larger downtown interests like Rock Ventures, JP Morgan Chase, and the Detroit Economic Growth Corporation.

85. As above, this reflects the selective extension of growth interests into neighborhood nodes. Invest Detroit began as the Detroit Investment Fund, which was founded by Business Leaders for Michigan, a regional business roundtable. See https://businessleadersformichigan.com/about/who-we-are; https://investdetroit.com/about-us. The president and CEO of Invest Detroit, David Blaszkiewicz, has also served concurrently as president and CEO of the DDP, and sits on the board of M-1 Rail (i.e., QLine). See https://investdetroit.com/about-us/management/david.html; https://www.linkedin.com/in/dave-blaszkiewicz-0b09127 (accessed January 2, 2018).

86. Nuszkowski, personal interview, May 26, 2017.

87. Michael Cabanatuan, "Bay Area Bike Share Program about to Begin," San Francisco Chronicle, August 28, 2013, http://www.sfgate.com/bayarea/article/Bay-Area-Bike-Share-program-about-to-begin-4769703.php.

88. A total of $7 million had been expended on the program as of December 2014. See Metropolitan Transportation Commission, "Climate Initiatives Program: Evaluation Summary Report," 2015, https://mtc.ca.gov/sites/default/files/CIP Evaluation Summary Report_7–13–15_FINAL.pdf; "San Francisco Bay Area Gears Up for Bike Sharing," Environment News Service, August 13, 2013, http://ens-newswire.com/2013/08/13/san-francisco-bay-area-gears-up-for-bike-sharing.

89. See https://web.archive.org/web/20161011103337/http://www.bayareabikeshare.com:80/stations (accessed October 11, 2016).

90. Ursula Vogler and Sean Co, "Memorandum: RE: Bay Area Bike Share Update," November 5, 2014, https://s3.amazonaws.com/media.legistar.com/mtc/meeting_packet_documents/agenda_2307/6_Bay_Area_Bike_Share_Memo_with_attachment.pdf. MTC estimated that bikeshare annually reduced VMT by 314,000 miles and carbon emissions by 79 tons (compared to a *daily* VMT of 172 million for the Bay Area as a whole). See Metropolitan Transportation Commission, "Climate Initiatives Program: Evaluation Summary Report," 24–25; https://web.archive.org/web/20171228191831/http://www.vitalsigns.mtc.ca.gov/daily-miles-traveled (accessed December 28, 2017), (accessed October 11, 2016).

91. Metropolitan Transportation Commission Programming and Allocations Committee, "MTC Resolution No. 3925, Revised and Resolution 4035, Revised," April 9, 2014, https://s3.amazonaws.com/media.legistar.com/mtc/meeting_packet_documents/agenda_2207/5a_Climate_Initiatives_Program.pdf.

92. "Major Expansion Approved for Bay Area Bike Share," *San Francisco Examiner*, May 27, 2015, https://archives.sfexaminer.com/sanfrancisco/major-expansion-approved-for-bay-area-bike-share/Content?oid=2931458; Metropolitan Transportation Commission, "Meeting Minutes," May 27, 2015, https://mtc.legistar.com/View.ashx?M=M&ID=400671&GUID=034516A6-7A6F-48D8-AEA3-CAB0BA3179ED. Motivate CEO Jay Walder frequently uses the phrase "at no cost to the taxpayer" in speeches to the New York City Council and at launch ceremonies for the bikeshare expansion in San Francisco and Oakland. See New York City Council Committee on Transportation, "Oversight—The Present and Future of Citibike in NYC," November 28, 2016, http://legistar.council.nyc.gov/View.ashx?M=F&ID=4881932&GUID=E3CD9329-AA96-41DF-9986-3F14679EAFD7.

93. Communities of Concern are defined as Census tracts where at least 70 percent of households are "minority-headed" and at least 30 percent are below 200 percent of the federal poverty line, or cross a specific threshold in at least four of the following variables: households with limited English proficiency (20 percent), lack of vehicle access (10 percent), senior citizens seventy-five and over (10 percent), members with disabilities (25 percent), single parent status (25 percent), or cost-burdened renters (15 percent). See Alix Bockelman and Metropolitan Transportation Commission, "Memorandum: RE: MTC Resolution No. 4217: Equity Framework for Plan Bay Area 2040," December 31, 2015, https://mtc.legistar.com/LegislationDetail.aspx?ID=2542165&GUID=D89FCABA-8814-4F0C-990D-B6803291A4D5&Options=&Search=.

94. Kevin Mulder, "Bikeshare Expansion Proposal," May 21, 2015, https://s3.amazonaws.com/media.legistar.com/mtc/meeting_packet_documents/agenda_2415/ATWG_5-21-15_KM_REV_052015.pdf.

95. These funds are restricted to capital expenditures, and cannot be used to support operations. See Metropolitan Transportation Commission, Bike Share Capital Program Call for Projects, https://mtc.ca.gov/sites/default/files/Bike_Share_Capital_Program_Application_Draft-Final.pdf. In the end, despite efforts by local

bicycle advocates, the funds were reallocated away from active transportation projects (email communication with Clarrisa Cabansagan, October 17, 2017). Steve Heminger, "Memorandum RE: Bike Share Expansion Proposal: Motivate International, Inc." (May 6, 2015), https://s3.amazonaws.com/media.legistar.com/mtc/meeting_packet_documents/agenda_2415/02_0_Bike_Share_Expansion_Proposal.pdf. In late 2017 MTC awarded funding for expansions in Richmond, Fremont, and the Sonoma/Marin Area Rapid Transit corridor. Notably, the capital award to these three cities used over half of the available funding, adding just five hundred bicycles and forty-two stations. Steve Heminger, "Memorandum Re: MTC Resolution No. 3925, Revised—Bike Share Capital Program Phase I," November 8, 2017, https://mtc.legistar.com/LegislationDetail.aspx?ID=3202994&GUID=185CC970-90FB-483E-8C7D-D380511EC887.

96. Matt Lasky, "San Francisco Bicycle Sharing Pilot," in New Partners for Smart Growth Annual Conference, February 3, 2012, https://newpartners.org/2012/docs/presentations/Friday/10—11.30am/Friday 3rd   10—11.30pm Learning to Share/NP12_Lasky.pdf. As of early 2014, the route from this area to Caltrain was among the most traveled in the system, based on a February 2014 analysis of Bay Area Bike Share Data Challenge data by Tyler Field, available at: http://thfield.github.io/babs (accessed December 28, 2017).

97. Jay Walder, comments at Ford GoBike Oakland launch ceremony, July 11, 2017.

98. Indeed, virtually all of the Oakland and Berkeley flatlands are Communities of Concern, while the Mission District's protracted state of advanced gentrification has displaced enough low-income and households of color that most of its Census tracts no longer qualify. Those that do are the next horizon of gentrification in the area. Based on MTC Communities of Concern analysis data, available at http://opendata.mtc.ca.gov/datasets/communities-of-concern-2017 (accessed October 20, 2017). The methodology for these categories comes from the UC Berkeley Center for Community Innovation's Urban Displacement Project, available at http://www.urbandisplacement.org (accessed December 30, 2017).

99. U.S. Census Bureau, "Hispanic or Latino by Race, 2011–15 American Community Survey 5-year Estimates." Prepared by Social Explorer. https://www.socialexplorer.com/tables/ACS2015_5yr/R11552441 (accessed December 28, 2017).

100. Collier, Mizes, and von Schnitzler, "Preface."

101. Stober, personal interview.

102. Waffiyah Murray and Aaron Ritz, personal interview, June 15, 2017. This was repeated to me almost verbatim by Andrew Stober.

103. Stober, personal interview. When I relayed Stober's observation about ungentrified but accessible neighborhoods like Strawberry Mansion to Carniesha Kwashie, his old coworker at Indego, she added with a wry grin, "Yet." Kwashie and Ferrentino, personal interview.

104. Cohen, personal interview.

NOTES TO CHAPTER 6

105. April Corbin, "Philadelphia Focus Group: Market Bike Share to 'Team Chunk,' Not Hipsters," *PeopleForBikes*, blog, January 26, 2015, http://www.peopleforbikes.org/blog/entry/philadelphia-focus-group-market-bike-share-to-team-chunk-not-hipsters.
106. Murray and Ritz, personal interview.
107. The BCGP had access to $400,000 for outreach activities, a substantial portion of which focused on Strawberry Mansion, beyond what was set aside from the JPB grant for Indego's marketing. Cohen, personal interview.
108. In 2017, Indego altered the structure of the ambassadors program to partner with local community organizations. Stefani Cox, "Philly Bike Share Ambassador Program Rolls Forward with a New Structure," *Better Bike Share Partnership*, blog, September 21, 2017, http://betterbikeshare.org/2017/09/21/philly-bike-share-ambassador-program-rolls-forward-new-structure.
109. Murray and Ritz, personal interview.
110. Kwashie and Ferrentino, personal interview.
111. Murray and Ritz, personal interview.
112. Murray and Ritz, personal interview.
113. Cohen, personal interview; Adonia Lugo, "CicLAvia and Human Infrastructure in Los Angeles: Ethnographic Experiments in Equitable Bike Planning," *Journal of Transport Geography* 30 (June 2013): 202–7.
114. Setubal, personal interview. The Access Pass makes membership more attractive to users from low-income neighborhoods who might only ride on weekends, and thus pay effectively more per ride.
115. Cohen, personal interview; Rebecca Sheir, Dianna Douglas, and Matthew Schwartz, "How Philly Is Getting Poor People to Use Bike Share," *Slate Placemakers*, podcast, 2016, http://www.slate.com/podcasts/placemakers/how_philly_is_getting_poor_people_to_use_bike_share.html; Cassie Owens, "Even at $5 a Month, Philly's Underserved Still Say Indego 'Isn't for Us,'" *Billy Penn*, blog, July 1, 2016, https://billypenn.com/2016/07/01/even-at-5-a-month-phillys-underserved-still-say-indego-isnt-for-us; Hamilton, "Has Philadelphia Made a Bike Share That Can Get the Entire City Biking?"; Cassie Owens, "Philly Bike Share Is Growing, but Will It Attract the City's Poor?," *Spoke Magazine*, January 5, 2016, http://www.spokemag.co/philly-bike-share-is-growing-but-will-its-ridership-diversify.
116. Nuszkowski, personal interview, August 16, 2016. Support from the BBSP included expert visits from Indego, NACTO, and People for Bikes, as well as a community bikeshare advocate representing Brooklyn's historically Black Bedford-Stuyvesant neighborhood. Setubal, personal interview.
117. For instance, the Alta feasibility study argued that "American cities are increasingly aware of bicycling as an economic development tool to attract creative class businesses and workers, and to help retain local talent . . . Bike share systems can become high-profile additions to a city that in themselves become an attraction for visitors and tourists and generate positive national and international media

exposure that would otherwise be difficult or costly to generate." Alta Planning + Design and LivingLAB, "Bike Share Feasibility Study," 12.

118. Annalise Frank, "MoGo Reaches Bike Ridership Goal More Than 6 Months Early," Crain's Detroit Business, October 17, 2017, http://www.crains detroit.com/article/20171017/news/642301/mogo-reaches-bike-ridership-goal-more-than-6-months-early.

119. Owens, "Even at $5 a Month, Philly's Underserved Still Say Indego 'Isn't for Us.'"

120. Kwashie and Ferrentino, personal interview.

121. Rory Lincoln, personal interview, May 30, 2017. One additional ambassador was recruited from deeper in Southwest Detroit, in the hope of building support for expansion into that area.

122. Jeffrey Nolish, personal interview, May 26, 2017.

123. Thornton, personal interview.

124. Murray and Ritz, personal interview.

125. Rory Lincoln, personal interview, August 29, 2017.

126. Daniels, personal interview.

127. Until mid-2017, the strongest link between MoGo and the city was Jeffrey Nolish, a 2015–17 Detroit Revitalization Fellow serving as a mobility specialist with the city's Planning and Development Department and a MoGo ambassador. See https://detroitfellows.wayne.edu/about.

128. See https://web.archive.org/web/20171006064130/https://www.facebook.com;davidsanchezdetroit/posts/10154459179062019. For a common statement about Detroit's prioritization of bicycling, see also Nancy Derringer, "Detroit Is a City with Many Needs. So Why Are Bikes Such a Priority?" Crain's Detroit Business, August 25, 2017, https://www.crainsdetroit.com/article/20170825/news/637256/detroit-is-a-city-with-many-needs-so-why-are-bikes-such-a-priority.

129. This is particularly acute in Detroit due to the rationing of governmental capacity; see Joshua Akers, "Emerging Market City," *Environment and Planning A* 47, no. 9 (2015): 1842–58.

130. "Ford GoBike Brings Bike Share to the East Bay for the First Time," MTC News, July 11, 2017, https://mtc.ca.gov/whats-happening/news/ford-gobike-brings-bike-share-east-bay-first-time.

131. The suddenness of implementation even took many in the "target demographic" of bikeshare by surprise; for a few weeks, various middle-class, well-educated friends of mine, aware of my research on the topic, pressed me for answers about what the bikes were and where they had suddenly come from.

132. Roger Rudick, "Bike Share Takes a Beating," *Streetsblog SF*, blog, August 8, 2017, https://sf.streetsblog.org/2017/08/08/bike-share-takes-a-beating.

133. "Mistah FAB Fights Gentrification, RJMrLA Does Oakland, New Mozzy and Philthy Rich Albums?—The Latest Bay Area Rap and Hip-Hop Music—Thizzler on the Roof," *TZLR News*, blog, 2017, http://www.thizzler.com/blog/2017/7/14/tzlr-news-mistah-fab-fights-gentrification-rjmrla-does-oakla.html.

134. Rachel Dovey, "Why a Neighborhood Group Said 'No' to Bike-Share," *Next City*.org, July 19, 2017, https://nextcity.org/daily/entry/san-fran-latino-cultural-district-said-no-to-bike-share. Whether Calle 24 acted in good faith as a neighborhood broker or not, it is true that Motivate never held a public event in that part of the Mission and that Calle 24's opposition was staunch quite early in the process. Personal communication with Carlos Hernandez, May 17, 2016.

135. Brock Keeling, "Gentrification Fears Push Bikeshare out of Mission," *Curbed SF*, July 18, 2017, https://sf.curbed.com/2017/7/18/15986716/ford-gobike-mission-gentrification; Small, "Ford GoBike Expands"; Dovey, "Why a Neighborhood Group Said 'No' to Bike-Share"; Levin, "'It's Not for Me': How San Francisco's Bike-Share Scheme Became a Symbol of Gentrification."

136. San Francisco Board of Supervisors, *Coordination Agreement between the Metropolitan Transportation Commission, Bay Area Motivate, LLC, as Operator of the Bay Area Bike Share Program; the City of Berkeley, the City of Emeryville, the City of Oakland, the City and County of San Francisco by and through the San Francisco Municipal Transportation Agency, and the City of San Jose for the Bay Area Bike Share Program* (San Francisco Board of Supervisors, 2015), sec. 20.2, https://sfgov.legistar.com/View.ashx?M=F&ID=4127926&GUID=6937C0F9–0A1D-4EAF-9C47–3A05E29948BC.

137. See https://web.archive.org/web/20160706124710/http://www.bayareabikeshare.com/expansion (accessed October 20, 2017).

138. See https://web.archive.org/web/20160604175754/http://www.bayareabikeshare.com:80/expansion#ProposedExpansionSites (accessed October 20, 2017). The timing of their release was determined using the Internet Archive's Wayback Machine; first instances for each area are available here: https://web.archive.org/web/20160324035108/http://www.bayareabikeshare.com/expansion; https://web.archive.org/web/20160502074744/http://www.bayareabikeshare.com:80/expansion (accessed October 20, 2017).

139. Carlos Hernandez, personal interview, May 12, 2017.

140. See https://mtc.ca.gov/whats-happening/news/motivate-and-mtc-announce-expanded-bike-share-equity-program (accessed December 28, 2017).

141. It took until after the launch to formalize some of these partnerships, as some groups were suspicious of it. Carlos Hernandez told me that, as a board member of Cycles of Change, he saw this suspicion firsthand.

142. Public comments at OakMob 101, October 22, 2016.

143. Motivate and Ford GoBike, "Ford GoBike: Bike Share Designed by Bay Area Residents," 2017, https://d21xlh2maitm24.cloudfront.net/fgb/Ford-GoBike-Outreach-Report-June-2017-Final.pdf. Back-of-the-envelope arithmetic suggests that thirty open meetings for over five hundred stations entails much thinner coverage than the ten MoGo held for its forty-three.

144. Brytanee Brown and TransForm, "OakMob 101: A Case Study in Expanding Access to Shared Mobility," 2017, 5–6, http://www.transformca.org/sites/default/files/OakMob_FINAL.pdf.

145. Brown and Transform, "OakMob 101," 22.
146. Clarrissa Cabansagan, personal interview, August 18, 2017.
147. See https://web.archive.org/web/20171230052448/https://www.bikeshareforall.org (accessed December 30, 2017). This approach is, of course, impossible with the current model of bikeshare planning.
148. Paolo Cosulich-Schwartz, personal interview, January 30, 2018.
149. Marisa Kendall, "Bike Sharing Startups Battle over Hot Silicon Valley Market," *San Jose Mercury News*, August 8, 2017, http://www.mercurynews.com/2017/08/08/bike-sharing-battles-startups-pioneering-a-new-breed-of-bike-borrowing-fight-for-market-share.
150. Joe Fitzgerald Rodriguez, "Bluegogo to Pull Its Bikes Off SF Streets," *San Francisco Examiner*, March 30, 2017, http://www.sfexaminer.com/bluegogo-pull-bikes-off-sf-streets.
151. Ford GoBike, "Ford GoBike Bike Share System Passes Growth Milestones," *FordgoBike*, blog, January 11, 2018, https://www.fordgobike.com/blog/ford-gobike-passes-growth-milestones. This claim is difficult to assess, since until recently Philadelphia's low-income passes were only monthly, while Ford GoBike's are annual.
152. Loic Wacquant, "Revisiting Territories of Relegation: Class, Ethnicity and State in the Making of Advanced Marginality," *Urban Studies* 53, no. 6 (2016): 1077–88; Tom Slater, "Planetary Rent Gaps," *Antipode* 49, no. 51 (2015): 1–24.

Conclusion

1. "It's Time to Love the Bus," Salon, March 3, 2012, http://www.salon.com/2012/03/03/its_time_to_love_the_bus.
2. Richard Florida, *The Rise of the Creative Class, Revisited: 10th Anniversary Edition* (New York: Basic Books, 2012); Brenda Parker, "Beyond the Class Act: Gender and Race in the 'Creative City' Discourse," in *Gender in an Urban World*, ed. Judith DeSena (Bingley, UK: Emerald Group, 2008), 201–32.
3. Puck Lo, "In Gentrifying Neighborhoods, Residents Say Private Patrols Keep Them Safe," Al-Jazeera America, May 30, 2014, http://america.aljazeera.com/articles/2014/5/30/oakland-private-securitypatrols.html; Eric K. Arnold, "Oakland Gang Injunctions: Gentrification or Public Safety?," *Race, Poverty and the Environment* 18, no. 2 (2011), http://reimaginerpe.org/18-2/arnold. An example of the moral claims levied on the city by these new residents is the YIMBY (Yes In My Back Yard) movement, dominated by young professionals confronted with the failure of the housing market to provide for them.
4. Winifred Curran and Trina Hamilton, "Just Green Enough: Contesting Environmental Gentrification in Greenpoint, Brooklyn," *Local Environment* 17, no. 9 (2012): 1027–42; John R. Logan and Harvey L. Molotch, *Urban Fortunes: The Political Economy of Place* (Berkeley: University of California Press, 2007).

5. While many elected officials are happy to sign on to a citywide "complete streets" policy like Oakland's, accepting a lower level of service is a political liability. See chapter 5, note 67.

6. Claire Sasko, "Watch: Hundreds of Kids on Bikes Flood I-676," *Philadelphia Magazine*, April 24, 2017, http://www.phillymag.com/news/2017/04/24/wheelie-kids-on-bikes-i-676.

7. Claire Sasko, "OneWay to Glory: They're Young. They're Reckless. And They're Redefining the Way Philly Kids Bike," *Spoke Magazine*, no. 005 (2017), http://www.spokemag.co/one-way-philadelphia-pedal-bikers.

8. Kimberly Kinchen, "A Bike Brand Goes Viral," *PeopleForBikes*, blog, October 5, 2017, https://peopleforbikes.org/blog/bike-brand-goes-viral.

9. David Meyer, "NYPD Files Criminal Charges against Kids for Biking on Hylan Boulevard," *Streetsblog NYC*, blog, February 22, 2017, https://nyc.streetsblog.org/2017/02/22/nypd-files-criminal-charges-against-kids-for-biking-on-hylan-boulevard; Samar Maguire and Toby Meyjes, "'I Had No Idea My Child Was This Stupid': Mum Criticises Son, 14, for Playing Dangerous 'Swerve the Car' Game on Bike," *Mirror*, November 1, 2017, http://www.mirror.co.uk/news/uk-news/i-no-idea-child-stupid-11446067. On moral panics, see Stuart Hall et al., *Policing the Crisis: Mugging, the State, and Law and Order* (London: MacMillan, 1978); George Lipsitz, *How Racism Takes Place* (Philadelphia: Temple University Press, 2011).

10. Sasko, "OneWay to Glory."

11. Eric J. Hobsbawm, *Primitive Rebels: Studies in Archaic Forms of Social Movement in the 19th and 20th Centuries* (Manchester, UK: Manchester University Press, 1971); Joey Sweeney, "Unlikely Heroes of the Moment: Wheelie Kids," *Philebrity*, blog, March 27, 2017, https://www.philebrity.com/blog/2017/3/27/unlikely-heroes-of-the-moment-wheelie-kids.

12. In this regard, it is largely in keeping with classic studies of subculture. See John Clarke et al., "Subcultures, Cultures and Class: A Theoretical Overview," in *Resistance through Rituals: Youth Subcultures in Postwar Britain*, ed. Stuart Hall and Tony Jefferson (London: Unwin Hyman, 1976), 9–74; Dick Hebdige, *Subculture: The Meaning of Style* (London: Routledge, 1979).

13. On the constitutive outside, see Ernesto Laclau and Chantal Mouffe, *Hegemony and Socialist Strategy: Towards a Radical Democratic Politics* (London: Verso, 1985).

14. Michel de Certeau, *The Practice of Everyday Life* (Berkeley: University of California Press, 1984).

15. Michael Cabanatuan and Kale Williams, "S.F. Bike Riders' Wiggle Protest Slows Traffic," *San Francisco Chronicle*, July 29, 2015, http://www.sfgate.com/bayarea/article/S-F-bike-riders-Wiggle-protest-could-stop-6413072.php.

16. SFBC News, "Supervisors, Advocates and Public Call on SFPD for Fair and Equal Investigations," San Francisco Bicycle Coalition News, October 3, 2013,

http://www.sfbike.org/news/supervisors-advocates-and-public-call-on-sfpd-for-fair-and-equal-investigations.

17. Alexandra Zayas and Kameel Stanley, "How Riding Your Bike Can Land You in Trouble with the Cops—If You're Black," *Tampa Bay Times*, April 17, 2015, http://www.tampabay.com/news/publicsafety/how-riding-your-bike-can-land-you-in-trouble-with-the-cops—-if-youre-black/2225966; Do Lee, "The Unbearable Weight of Irresponsibility and the Lightness of Tumbleweeds: Cumulative Irresponsibility in Neoliberal Streetscapes," in *Incomplete Streets: Processes, Practices, and Possibilities*, ed. Stephen Zavestoski and Julian Agyeman (New York: Routledge, 2015), 77–93.

18. Roger Rudick, "Safety Guerrillas Hit Valencia Street," *Streetsblog SF*, blog, October 24, 2016, https://sf.streetsblog.org/2016/10/24/safety-guerrillas-hit-valencia-street.

19. SFMTrA, "Making Protected Bike Lanes Work in Golden Gate Park," *SFMTrA.org*, blog, May 4, 2017, http://www.sfmtra.org/blog/2017/4/21/making-protected-bike-lanes-work-in-golden-gate-park; Mike Lydon and Anthony Garcia, *Tactical Urbanism: Short-Term Action for Long-Term Change* (Washington, D.C.: Island Press, 2015).

20. Adonia Lugo, "Unsolicited Advice for Vision Zero," *Urban Adonia*, blog, September 30, 2015, http://www.urbanadonia.com/2015/09/unsolicited-advice-for-vision-zero.html.

21. James Ferguson, *Anti-Politics Machine: Development, Depoliticization, and Bureaucratic Power in Lesotho* (Minneapolis: University of Minnesota Press, 1994).

22. Lugo, "Unsolicited Advice for Vision Zero."

23. Aaron Bialick, "SFPD Tickets to Peds, Cyclists, Grow 7X Faster Than 'Focus on the Five,'" *Streetsblog SF*, blog, May 9, 2014, http://sf.streetsblog.org/2014/05/09/sfpd-tickets-to-peds-cyclists-grow-7x-faster-than-focus-on-the-five.

24. Roger Rudick, "Punishment Pass on Valencia Highlights Enforcement Chasm," *Streetsblog SF*, blog, July 5, 2017, https://sf.streetsblog.org/2017/07/05/punishment-pass-on-valencia-highlights-enforcement-chasm; Aaron Bialick, "All Muni Buses Now Have Transit Lane Enforcement Cameras," *Streetsblog SF*, blog, March 24, 2015, https://sf.streetsblog.org/2015/03/24/all-muni-buses-now-have-transit-lane-enforcement-cameras.

25. Angie Schmitt, "The Threat of Racial Profiling in Traffic Enforcement," *Streetsblog USA*, blog, September 22, 2016, https://usa.streetsblog.org/2016/09/22/the-threat-of-racial-profiling-in-traffic-enforcement.

26. Tamika Butler, "Planning While Black" (lecture, NACTO Designing Cities, Seattle, Wash., September 27, 2016), https://www.youtube.com/watch?v=T4R7MuNBMvk.

27. See https://globaldesigningcities.org/network (accessed March 8, 2019).

28. Nick Srnicek, *Platform Capitalism* (London: Polity, 2016), chap. 2; Paul Langley and Andrew Leyshon, "Platform Capitalism: The Intermediation and Capitalization of Digital Economic Circulation," *Finance and Society* 3, no. 1 (2017):

11–31; Frank Pasquale, "Two Narratives of Platform Capitalism," *Yale Law and Policy Review* 35 (2016): 309–20.

29. Sarah Barns, "Mine Your Data: Open Data, Digital Strategies and Entrepreneurial Governance by Code," *Urban Geography* 37, no. 4 (2016): 554–71; Shenja van der Graaf and Pieter Ballon, "Navigating Platform Urbanism," *Technological Forecasting and Social Change* 142 (May 2019): 364–72. Not surprisingly, mobility platforms like Uber have led this trend.

30. Joe Fitzgerald Rodriguez, "Mission Advocates Call for New 'Moratorium' on Bikesharing," *San Francisco Examiner*, August 8, 2017, http://sfexaminer.com/mission-advocates-call-new-moratorium-bikesharing; Chema Hernandez Gil (@elsanfranciscan), "To thrice slay the slain, I present the privacy policy 'Information We Share' sections of three bike share systems run by @motivate," Twitter, July 19, 2017, https://twitter.com/elsanfranciscan/status/887782570389196801 (accessed October 20, 2017). Ford's somewhat ominous privacy policy did not help matters: "[W]e share your personal information with Ford Motor Company ('Ford') and its service providers to enable the integration between Ford GoBike and FordPass, including shared login and shared account functionality, and to enable Motivate and Ford to provide and improve their respective services." The authorization of data sharing with the sponsor is unusual among bikeshare systems, although other user agreements do not explicitly prevent it. Ford GoBike's complete privacy policy is available at https://web.archive.org/web/20171020062750/https://assets.fordgobike.com/privacy-policy.html (accessed October 20, 2017).

31. Johana Bhuiyan, "Ford Is Buying Shuttle Service Chariot to Dominate San Francisco's Transport System," Recode, September 9, 2016, https://www.recode.net/2016/9/9/12860834/ford-chariot-motivate-gobike-san-francisco-mobility.

32. Ford Motor Company Media Center, "Press Release: Ford Partnering with Global Cities on New Transportation; Chariot Shuttle to Be Acquired, Ford GoBike to Launch in San Francisco," September 9, 2016, https://media.ford.com/content/fordmedia/fna/us/en/news/2016/09/09/ford-partnering-with-global-cities-on-new-transportation—chario.html. Chariot folded in early 2019.

33. He boasted to shareholders: "Listen, here is the deal—the opportunity is not bikes. That is not why Ford is in it. The opportunity is data. And the data is super valuable because it tells us these invisible paths that people are taking in this complex city in terms of how they want to get around." Ford Motor Company Investor Relations and Thomson-Reuters Streetevents, "Ford Motor Company Investor Day Edited Transcript," September 14, 2016, http://shareholder.ford.com/~/media/Files/F/Ford-IR-V2/events-and-presentations/2016/09-14-2016/f-transcript-2016-09-14t14-00.pdf.

34. Amy Westervelt, "Bike-Sharing Grows Up: New Revenue Models Turn a Nice Idea into Good Business," Forbes, August 22, 2011, http://www.forbes.com/sites/amywestervelt/2011/08/22/bike-sharing-grows-up-new-revenue-models-turn-a-nice-idea-into-good-business/#23615c7e3943; Anne Quito, "Studio Roosegaarde and Ofo: The First Smog-Filtering Bicycles Will Roll Out in China by the End of

the Year," *Quartz*, August 8, 2017, https://qz.com/1049213/studio-roosegaarde-and-ofo-the-first-smog-filtering-bicycles-will-roll-out-in-china-by-the-end-of-the-year.

35. Henry Grabar, "Dock-Less Bike Share Is Ready to Take Over U.S. Cities.," *Slate*, December 18, 2017, https://slate.com/business/2017/12/dock-less-bike-share-is-ready-to-take-over-u-s-cities.html; Kristin Jeffers, "It's Ok to Critique Dockless Bikeshare. It's Not Ok to Be Bigoted," *Greater Greater Washington*, January 23, 2018, https://ggwash.org/view/66280/its-ok-to-critique-dockless-bikesare-its-not-ok-to-be-bigoted; LimeBike, "Marshawn Lynch Partners with LimeBike to Bring Dock-Less Bike Sharing to Urban Communities and College Campuses," Cision PR Newswire, November 20, 2017, https://www.prnewswire.com/news-releases/marshawn-lynch-partners-with-limebike-to-bring-dock-less-bike-sharing-to-urban-communities-and-college-campuses-300559079.html.

36. "Meituan Dianping Acquires Bike-Sharing Firm Mobike," *CNBC*, April 4, 2018, https://www.cnbc.com/2018/04/04/meituan-dianping-acquires-bike-sharing-firm-mobike.html.

37. Eillie Anzilotti, "With Its Acquisition of Motivate, Lyft Gets in on Bike Share," *Fast Company*, July 2, 2018, https://www.fastcompany.com/90179311/with-its-acquisition-of-motivate-lyft-gets-in-on-bikeshare.

38. Johana Bhuiyan, "Lyft Is Also Building an 'Amazon of Transportation,' Just like Uber," *Recode*, June 7, 2018, https://www.recode.net/2018/6/7/17435634/lyft-shared-rides-transit-uber-google-maps.

39. Scott Smith, "New Transport Horizons or Mobility Spam?," *Medium*, August 16, 2016, https://medium.com/@changeist/new-transport-horizons-or-mobility-spam-b1d16807b128; Benjamin Haas, "Chinese Bike Share Graveyard a Monument to Industry's 'Arrogance,'" *Guardian*, November 25, 2017, https://www.theguardian.com/uk-news/2017/nov/25/chinas-bike-share-graveyard-a-monument-to-industrys-arrogance.

40. Adrian Lim, "Is Bike Sharing Worth the Bumps?," *Straits Times*, June 6, 2017, http://www.straitstimes.com/opinion/is-bike-sharing-worth-the-bumps.

41. "China's Bicycle-Sharing Giants Are Still Trying to Make Money," *Economist*, November 25, 2017, https://www.economist.com/news/business/21731675-one-answer-would-be-ofo-and-mobike-merge-chinas-bicycle-sharing-giants-are-still-trying.

42. Biz Carson, "Chinese Bike-Share Startup Ofo Lays Off Majority of U.S. Staff As It Scales Back Global Ambitions," *Forbes*, July 18, 2018, https://www.forbes.com/sites/bizcarson/2018/07/18/ofo-bikes-us/#41759b6b2785.

43. Luz Lazo, "Mobike Becomes Second Dockless Bike Operator to Pull Out of D.C.," *Washington Post*, July 25, 2018, https://www.washingtonpost.com/news/dr-gridlock/wp/2018/07/25/mobike-becomes-second-dockless-bike-operator-to-pull-out-of-d-c/.

44. Sheila Yu, "Mobike Announces 'Magic Cube,' an AI Made from Its Mountains of User Data," *TechNode*, April 13, 2017, http://technode.com/2017/04/13/

mobike-magic-cube-ai; Jonathan Haskel and Stian Westlake, *Capitalism without Capital: The Rise of the Intangible Economy* (Princeton, N.J.: Princeton University Press, 2018).

45. Lim, "Is Bike Sharing Worth the Bumps?"

46. For Gramsci, a passive revolution is composed of "molecular changes which in fact progressively modify the pre-existing composition of forces, and hence become the matrix of new changes." Antonio Gramsci, *Selections from the Prison Notebooks*, ed. Quintin Hoare and Geoffrey Nowell Smith (New York: International, 1971), 109.

47. David Harvey, *Spaces of Hope* (Berkeley: University of California Press, 2000).

48. Anique Hommels, *Unbuilding Cities: Obduracy in Urban Socio-Technical Change* (Cambridge, Mass.: MIT Press, 2005).

49. Doug Gordon, "This Isn't Amsterdam," Brooklyn Spoke, October 14, 2011, https://brooklynspoke.com/2011/10/14/this-isnt-amsterdam.

50. Lorenzo Veracini, "Suburbia, Settler Colonialism and the World Turned Inside Out," *Housing, Theory and Society* 29, no. 4 (2012): 339–57; David Hugill, "What Is a Settler-Colonial City?" *Geography Compass* 11, no. 5 (2017): 1–11.

51. Sampo Hietanen, "Sampo's blog: Sewer City or a Web of Beautiful Hubs—City Planning In the Age of MaaS," *Maas Global*, blog, September 21, 2018, https://maas.global/blog-sewer-city-or-a-web-of-beautiful-hubs-city-planning-in-the-age-of-maas.

52. For instance, by means of a ballot measure, in 2014 Alameda County voters approved Measure BB, the extension of a half-percent sales tax increase (previously approved in 2000) to fund mass transit, pedestrian, and bicycle improvements. Measure BB's passage nearly doubled the size of Oakland's bicycle and pedestrian facilities program overnight.

53. Jason W. Moore, "The End of Cheap Nature, or, How I Learned to Stop Worrying about 'the' Environment and Love the Crisis of Capitalism," in *Structures of the World Political Economy and the Future of Global Conflict and Cooperation*, ed. Christian Suter and Christopher Chase-Dunn (Münster: Lit Verlag, 2014).

54. David Harvey, *The New Imperialism* (Oxford: Oxford University Press, 2003).

55. Neil Smith, "Contours of a Spatialized Politics: Homeless Vehicles and the Production of Geographical Scale," *Social Text* 33 (1992): 54–81.

56. Alex Schafran, "Origins of an Urban Crisis: The Restructuring of the San Francisco Bay Area and the Geography of Foreclosure," *International Journal of Urban and Regional Research* 37, no. 2 (March 5, 2013): 663–88.

57. "Introducing, the New Executive Director of the Los Angeles County Bicycle Coalition," Santa Monica Spoke, December 18, 2014, http://smspoke.org/2014/12/18/introducing-the-new-executive-director-of-the-los-angeles-county-bicycle-coalition.

58. Tamika Butler, "Planning While Black" (lecture, NACTO Designing Cities, Seattle, Wash., September 27, 2016).

59. Untokening Collective, "10 Principles of Mobility Justice," 2017, http://www.untokening.org/updates/2017/11/11/untokening-10-principles-of-mobility-justice. The last of these in particular goes directly against the core tendency of mainstream bicycle advocacy to develop and circulate repeatable best practices.

60. John Greenfield, "Oboi Reed Blasts the City's Failure to Address Its Biased Bike Ticketing Problem," *Streetsblog Chicago*, blog, February 19, 2018, https://chi.streetsblog.org/2018/02/19/oboi-reed-blasts-the-citys-failure-to-address-its-biased-bike-ticketing-problem.

61. See https://www.equiticity.org/about (accessed May 17, 2018). Carniesha Kwashie, who was instrumental in Indego's equity vision, sits on the board of directors.

62. A list of organizations opposing the injunctions can be found here: https://stoptheinjunction.wordpress.com/endorsements (accessed May 10, 2015).

63. Dan Brekke, "Bike Share for All? Activists Want to See Expansion of Network in Oakland," KQED News, July 17, 2017, https://ww2.kqed.org/news/2017/07/17/ford-gobike-bike-share-east-oakland.

64. TransForm, "2020 Priorities," 2018, http://www.transformca.org/sites/default/files/TransForm_2020_Priorities.pdf.

65. Anonymous, personal communication, May 8, 2018.

INDEX

accessibility (transportation), 9, 12, 21, 22, 34, 51, 111, 145, 146, 155, 157, 162, 163, 171, 204
Access Pass, 151, 163, 164, 268
affordances, 56, 89, 145
agglomeration, 24, 47, 157
Airbnb, 159
Alioto, Joseph, 108
Alliance for Biking and Walking, 6
Alta Planning + Design, 153, 259, 268
American Community Survey (ACS), 25, 248
Amsden, Mike, 124
Amsterdam, 5, 6, 15, 17, 102, 143, 244
Anderson, Rob, 41, 102, 244
Anne T. and Robert M. Bass Initiative on Innovation and Placemaking, 24, 47
anti-globalization movement, xvii, 58
Appleyard, Donald, 9, 204
Austin, Texas, 7, 45, 78, 86, 173, 197, 258
automobility, xi, 5, 12, 14, 17, 22, 35, 71, 75, 88, 89, 175, 178, 207

Back Alley Bikes, 78, 80
Bay Area. *See* San Francisco Bay Area
Bay Area Air Quality Management District, 157
Bay Area Bike Share, 42, 44, 131, 156–58, 168, 270. *See also* Ford GoBike
Bay Area Rapid Transit (BART), 26, 35, 73, 111, 114, 115, 116, 118, 134, 138, 217, 238, 253
Benjamin, Walter, 12, 56
Berkeley, California, 35, 36, 82, 115, 116, 133, 135, 144, 158, 168, 169, 238, 253, 267. *See also* San Francisco Bay Area
Better Bike Share Partnership (BBSP), 162, 163, 168, 268
Better Market Street Project, 41, 107
BiciCocina, 78. *See also* bike kitchens
Bicing, 143
Bicycle Advisory Committee, 95
Bicycle and Pedestrian Advisory Commission, 251
Bicycle Coalition of Greater Philadelphia, 152, 162, 177
Bicycle-Friendly Business District, 120
Bicycles for Humanity, xiv
Bicycle Transit Systems (BTS), 151–52, 162
bike boom (1970s), xiii, 78
Bike Church, 80

INDEX

bike clubs, 59, 65; East Side Riders, 59; Grown Ladies on Wheels (GLOW), 65; Grown Men on Bikes (G-MOB), 59; Midnight Ridazz, 229, 230, 234; One Way "wheelie crew," 175; Peace Riderz, 65; Scraper Bike Team, 66–67, 69, 77, 78, 125, 137, 166, 167, 169, 175, 187, 231
Bike East Bay, 69, 76, 77, 112, 118–20, 122, 123, 125, 126, 130, 131, 132, 136, 167, 169, 231, 251, 252, 256. *See also* East Bay Bicycle Coalition
bike kitchens, xiv, 80
bike lanes, xii, xiv, xix, xx, xxii, 1, 7, 35, 40, 42, 48, 71, 86, 91, 93, 85, 96, 97, 100–103, 105, 107, 109, 111, 112, 116, 120, 122, 123, 127, 128–30, 132, 133, 135, 136, 137, 139, 142, 149, 156, 165, 173, 177, 178, 180, 233, 238, 240, 244, 246, 252–55. *See also* cycle tracks
bike messengers, xix, 74
Bike Party, 59, 60, 61, 62, 63, 64, 65, 175, 229, 230
Bikes 4 Life, 82, 187
bike share, xi, xvi, xxi, xxii, 1, 5, 7, 42, 44, 48, 69, 75, 105, 125, 131, 141–49, 151, 156, 157, 159, 160, 162, 166–71, 175, 180, 181, 182, 186, 233, 258, 259, 260, 263, 265, 266, 268, 269, 274. *See also* dockless scooters and bicycles
Bike Share For All, 169
bike shops, xiv, xviii, 71, 76, 78–82, 97, 100, 137, 234
BikeSnobNYC, 7
Bikes Not Bombs, 58
Bike Summit, 100, 218
Bike Swarm, 69
Bike to Work Day, xiv, 75– 77, 101, 105, 123, 124, 132

"bikewashing," xv, 86
BIXI Montréal, 143
Black Lives Matter, 69, 179, 186
Black Women Bike, 7
Blickstein, Susan, 58
Bloomberg, Michael, 1, 44, 179
Bluegogo, 182
BMX bikes, 74, 175
bodies, 11, 12, 55, 56, 72, 113, 173, 177, 232, 234; "bodily hexis," 56, 69, 81, 226
Bogotá, Colombia, 6, 103, 183, 200, 205, 221
Boston, xviii, 4, 124, 125, 148
Box Dog Bikes, 80, 191
Breed, London, 105, 246
Bridge Housing, 102
Brookings Institution, 24
Brown, Brytanee, 168
Brown, Jerry, 115
Brown, Mary, 92–93, 96
Brown, Willie, 88, 92, 101
Brundtland Report, 16
Burnett, Reggie (R.B.), 66, 77
Burton, Jenna, 73, 232
bus rapid transit (BRT), 19, 205, 261
Butler, Tamika, 6, 186
Bycyken, 143

California, xx, 16, 21, 31, 60, 66, 103, 124, 194, 198, 211, 227, 243, 244, 253
Calle 24 Latino Cultural District, 167
CalTrain, 35, 42
Campbell, Dave, 120, 123, 129, 131
Carlsson, Chris, 57, 60, 229, 230
Castells, Manuel, 88, 247
Causa Justa/Just Cause, 115, 187
central business district (CBD), 10, 25, 34, 35, 38, 41, 45, 47, 114, 116, 133, 142, 143, 146, 149, 150, 151, 161, 163, 174, 177, 265
Central Market Strategy, 43

Chicago, xiv, 7, 58, 124, 125, 137, 186, 235, 240
China, 1, 57, 75, 182, 199
Citi Bike, 143, 157, 259
Cities for Cycling Roadshow, 123
CityLab, 6, 179
class (socioeconomic), ix–xii, xv, xviii, xix–xxii, 8, 11, 14, 15, 16, 18, 55, 60, 64, 65, 72, 73, 78, 82, 83, 105, 110, 112–14, 119, 123, 125, 131, 134, 137–41, 159, 179, 186, 238; business owners and merchants, 92, 94–96, 100, 101, 109, 118, 119–20, 126, 130, 131, 133, 135–36, 140, 167, 240, 242, 243, 247, 253, 254, 256; creative, xiii, 25, 268; homeowners and property owners, 8, 9, 14, 44, 119, 122, 126, 129, 131, 136, 144, 153, 185, 216, 250; low income and poor, x, xiii, xxi, 6, 7, 10, 12, 16, 27, 33, 38, 41, 42, 78, 82, 85, 100, 125, 132, 143, 136, 139, 146, 148, 150, 153, 155, 159, 160, 163, 174, 181, 203, 219, 235, 253; middle, xviii, xix, 6, 8, 11, 12, 34, 70, 73, 75, 114, 115, 128, 139, 151, 160, 162, 204, 207, 233, 269; "new middle class," xx, 12, 88, 174; petit bourgeoisie, xviii, 12, 17, 22, 69; upper, ix, xii, xix, 1, 33, 34, 86, 95, 112, 125, 136, 167, 185, 211, 243; working, xix–xxi, 8, 10, 15–20, 22, 24, 25, 27, 29, 33, 51, 56, 70, 78, 79, 85, 86, 91, 97, 100, 108, 109, 114, 146, 163, 169, 171, 173, 175, 182, 247
Cleveland, 20
climate change, 16, 20, 22, 174, 183
Coalition for Adequate Review (CAR), 102. *See also* Anderson, Rob
Coalition to Save Telegraph Avenue, 122
Cohen, Alison, 152, 163, 262
Colectivelo, El, 66, 67
Communities of Concern, 159, 166, 169, 266, 267
Congress for New Urbanism, 102
Connect to Compete report, 47
Copenhagen, 5, 6, 15, 42, 143, 252
creative destruction, 136
Critical Mass, xiii, xx, xxii, 5, 53, 57–66, 69–71, 76, 80–82, 86, 90, 92, 93, 101, 107, 122, 130, 133, 175, 177, 228–30, 236, 239
Cyclescape, 1, 197
Cycles of Change, 78, 137, 167, 168, 187, 270
cycle tracks, 123, 130, 131
Czech Republic, 75

Daly, Chris, 101, 220
Daniels, Amina, 155, 165
decarbonization, 12, 16
de Certeau, Michel, 12, 55, 90
"degrowth machine," 47, 50. *See also* growth machine
Deleuze, Gilles, 58
Department of Transportation, 1, 23, 103, 112, 124, 127, 243
Designing Cities conference, 186
Detroit, xvii, xx, xxi, 6, 19, 20, 25, 27–38, 47–50, 59, 64, 65, 78, 80, 141, 142, 144, 152, 154–59, 164, 165, 184, 214, 215, 217, 224, 261, 263–65, 269; Techtown, 47–49; West Village, 155, 156, 165; Woodward Avenue, 28, 34, 38
Detroit Creative Corridor Center (DC3), 48, 224
Detroit Future City, 50, 152, 154, 156
Detroit Greenways Coalition, 6
Detroit Strategic Neighborhoods Fund (SNF), 156
disinvestment, xvii, 41, 50, 72, 107, 113, 115, 116, 146, 152

INDEX

division of labor, xii, xx, 18, 22, 25, 35, 42, 50, 51, 174
dockless scooters and bicycles, 1, 22, 75, 105, 169, 181, 182, 196
do it yourself (DIY), xvii, 5, 55, 78, 80, 234
Downtown Detroit Partnership (DDP), 47, 152–54, 263, 265
Drennen, Emily, 76, 95, 96, 100, 101, 108, 240–42
Drexel University, 45, 46

East Bay Bicycle Coalition, 118, 238, 251, 256. *See also* Bike East Bay
East Bay Bus Rapid Transit (BRT), 134–36, 205, 256, 261
Enright, Theresa, 21
environmentalism, xii–xix, 2, 5, 8–10, 15, 20–22, 40, 51, 53, 71, 75, 85, 87, 92, 93, 102, 103, 105, 107, 109, 130, 140, 184, 226, 244, 253
Environmental Protection Agency (EPA), 21
Equiticity, 186
equity, xiv, 7, 17, 80, 87, 142, 145–49, 151–53, 160–64, 166, 167, 171, 179, 186, 202, 205, 242, 247, 250, 262
Equity Advisory Council, 7, 179, 186, 202
exurbs, 4, 20, 24, 29, 33, 185, 198, 213, 217

Federal Highway Administration, 15, 194, 198
Fenty, Adrian, 7, 86
Ferndale, 36, 38
Ferrentino, Cara, 151
fetish, 6, 75, 200; commodity fetishism, 74
Fisher, Mark, 87
fixed gear bicycles (fixies), 16, 61, 74
flâneur, 12, 56, 74

Florida, Richard, 24, 25, 108
Folks for Polk, 109
Forbes, Rob, 74
Ford, 28, 48, 144, 157–61, 166, 168, 169, 180, 181, 187
Ford GoBike, 144, 158–61, 166, 168, 169, 180, 181, 187, 271, 274. *See also* Bay Area Bike Share
Fordism/Fordist, 16, 22, 57, 87; post-, 16, 20, 57, 87
FordPass, 180, 274
Ford Smart Mobility, 180
Foucault, Michel, xvi, 110, 185
Freedman, Nicole, 124, 125

gender, ix, xii, 11, 53, 55, 73, 78, 174, 206, 232; men, xi, 12, 38, 56, 58, 78, 159, 168, 170; women, 7, 12, 11, 53–56, 64, 65, 73, 78, 81, 92, 152, 186, 232
General Motors, 48, 152
gentrification, ix, xii, xvii–xxii, 4, 6–11, 17, 20–22, 25, 28, 29, 34, 35, 39, 44, 64, 80, 82, 85, 96, 97, 100, 106, 107, 141, 142, 146, 148, 155, 174, 196, 203, 204, 231, 236, 238, 241, 242, 247, 267
Gibson-McElhaney, Lynnette, 132, 133
Gilbert, Dan, 28, 153, 263
Gilmore, Ruth Wilson, 78, 232
Global Designing Cities Initiative, 179
Godinez, Shari, 132
Golden Wheel Awards, 95, 222
Good Roads Movement, 56
Graham, Stephen, xiii, xvii, 75, 89
Gramsci, Antonio, 5, 183, 199, 276
grassroots, xiv, xxi, 11, 88–90, 107, 109, 126, 134, 210, 252
Great Recession, 1, 4, 24, 27, 38, 116, 120
Great Streets Project, 102–4
Green Party, 101, 103

INDEX

greenways, xiv, xix, 6, 21, 156
growth machine, xxi, 8, 11, 28, 41, 47, 51, 86, 88, 90, 102, 137, 143, 153, 156, 164. *See also* "degrowth machine"
Guattari, Félix, 58

Hall, Jason, 65
Hall, Stuart, xii, 193
Hanson, Susan, 58, 197, 199, 228
Harvey, David, 51, 88, 237
Health Alliance Plan, 153
Henderson, Jason, 41, 88, 107, 219, 236
Hernandez Gil, Chema, 106, 246, 274
hipsters, ix–xi, xviii, 7, 28, 34, 67, 69, 82, 134, 141, 177, 196, 254
Hobsbawm, Eric, 177
Hoffman, Melody, x, 6, 193
Housing Action Coalition, 102
Houston, Texas, xviii, 2, 4, 85
How Cycling Can Save the World, 5
Hubway Bikeshare, 125
Hughes, Kathryn, 253

Illich, Ivan, 204, 226
Indego, 144, 151, 152, 154, 160–65, 167, 170, 262, 267, 268, 277
infrastructure, xii, xv, xvii, xix, xx, 6, 9, 11, 14, 15, 17, 20, 21, 35, 38, 39, 42, 46, 48, 55, 56, 59, 83, 86, 89, 96, 103, 106, 112, 114, 118–20, 124, 132, 133, 136, 137, 139–43, 145–49, 152, 158–61, 163, 170, 171, 174, 175, 177, 178, 180, 187, 194, 204, 223–25, 227, 233; bicycle, x, xii–xiv, xvi, xx, xxi, 1, 2, 6, 7, 10, 11, 17, 19, 21, 23, 39, 40, 41, 47, 50, 51, 76, 77, 85–90, 92, 95–97, 101–2, 106–9, 111–13, 118–20, 122, 123, 125, 126, 131–40, 142, 173–75, 177, 179, 180, 184, 185, 194, 224, 227, 244, 250, 252, 253; social or human, 6, 55, 161, 163
"innovation districts," xx, xxi, 15, 24, 40, 44, 46, 47, 48, 49, 51, 66, 101, 103, 159, 267
Interbike, 232
Intermodal Surface Transportation Efficiency Act, xiv, 91
Invest Detroit, 156, 263, 265

Jacobs, Allan, 9
Jacobs, Jane, 9, 17, 79, 109, 129, 225, 247
"Jerryfication," 115
job sprawl, 24, 35, 213, 217

Katz, Bruce, 40
Katz, Leslie, 243
Kidd, Chris, 132
Knight Foundation, 164
Kresge Foundation, 153, 263
Kwashie, Carniesha, 164, 267, 277

labor and labor markets, 24, 69, 82, 108, 142, 174, 182, 214, 217, 237
Latino Unity Council, 138
Latour, Bruno, 124, 225
Leadership in Environmental Design, 22
League of American Bicyclists, 6, 7, 23, 76, 120, 179, 186, 235
League of American Wheelmen, 56
Leal, Susan, 93
Lee, Ed, 43
Lefebvre, Henri, xv
Leno, Mark, 94, 101, 243
level of service (LOS), 23, 102, 212, 219, 240, 244, 272
light rail, xix, 11, 48
Lime, 169, 182, 196
Lincoln, Rory, 164, 269
Lipscombe, Adrian, 7, 86

livability, xxii, xxiii, 8, 11, 14, 15, 18, 23, 41, 44, 46, 51, 85, 86, 88, 103–5, 107–9, 118, 119, 126, 129–131, 133, 174, 185, 253
Livable City, 41, 70, 93, 102–4
Live Cycle Delight, 156
López, Oscar Sosa, 89, 118, 237
Los Angeles, 2, 7, 20, 44, 56, 78, 85, 141, 186, 230
Los Angeles County Bicycle Coalition, 186
Love to Ride, 76
Lugo, Adonia, 6, 163, 179, 186, 202, 233
Lyft, 105, 178, 182
Lynch, Kevin, 9
Lynch, Marshawn, 176

MaaS Global, 184
Manifest Destiny, xii
Manifesto Bicycles, 81
Market Street Association, 103
Market Street Committee, 103
Marvin, Simon, xiii, xvii, 75, 89
Massey, Doreen, xv, 35, 112, 225
Mayor's Office of Transportation and Utilities, 151, 161
Measure BB (ballot measure), 276
Meituan Dianping, 182
metropolitan planning organizations (MPOs), 16, 21
metropolitan statistical areas (MSAs), 25, 33
Metropolitan Transportation Commission, 102, 157, 211, 265, 266, 270
Miami, 15
Midtown Detroit, Inc. (MDI), 49
millennials, xvii, 162
Mission Coalition Organization, 108
"Mission Makeover" mural, ix, x
Mission Merchants Association, 92, 95
Mobike, 181, 182

mobility, ix–xiii, xvi, xix–xxi, 5, 6, 8, 11, 12, 16, 18–20, 24, 39–42, 44, 47, 48, 51, 55, 56, 71, 74, 75, 79, 82, 87, 89, 107, 113, 118, 119, 124, 135, 138, 139, 142, 143, 145, 152, 159, 163, 165–71, 178, 180, 182–87, 205, 233, 269; justice, 6, 167, 186; policy, 111, 160, 241; as a service, xxii, 184. *See also* automobility
Model Cities Program, 108
MoGo, 48, 141, 144, 152–56, 164, 165, 167, 181, 261, 269, 270
Momentum Magazine, 54
Montero, Sergio, 89, 104, 118, 200
motility, 145, 146, 149, 153, 156, 158, 171
Motivate, 144, 151, 157, 159, 166–69, 182, 259, 266, 270, 274
Mountain View, California, 42, 157
Murray, Waffiyah, 163, 165

National Association of City Transportation Officials (NACTO), 1, 23, 111, 118, 123–25, 131, 137, 162, 179, 185, 186, 254, 268; NACTO Urban Street Design Guide, 23
National Bike Month, 76
National Bike Summit, 100, 102
National Household Travel Survey, 2, 39, 198
Natural Resources Defense Council (NRDC), 21
Neighborhood Bike Works, 78, 80
neoliberalism, xix, 17, 88, 90, 105, 142, 143, 145, 147, 149, 174, 184, 231, 245
neoliberalization, 17, 18, 145, 147, 148
network effect, 143, 180
Nevius, C. W., 41, 87, 236
New Center, 34, 48, 49, 153, 154
New Movement, The, 186

INDEX

Newsom, Gavin, 101, 105, 220
New Urbanism, 20, 102, 138
New York City, xii, xviii, xix, 1, 2, 17, 20, 23, 33, 56, 74, 103, 111, 124, 125, 127, 143, 151, 178, 200, 228, 235, 240, 259, 266; Bronx, 15; Brooklyn, 1, 7, 268
Next City, 6
Not In My Back Yard (NIMBYism), 167
Nuszkowski, Lisa, 153–56, 164, 264, 265
Nutter, Michael, 149, 262

OakDOT, 112, 119
Oakland, xviii, xx–xxii, 6, 7, 26, 29, 33, 35, 36, 38, 42, 44, 45, 60, 63, 64, 66, 67, 69, 72, 73, 76–78, 80–82, 111–20, 122–26, 128–40, 142, 144, 157–59, 166–69, 175, 176, 187, 229–33, 247, 249, 250–56, 266, 267, 272, 276; Grove Shafter Freeway, 115, 116, 120, 138, 139; Telegraph Avenue, 113–16, 118–20, 122–39, 251–54, 256; Temescal District, 116, 121; West Oakland, 15, 73, 82, 112, 114, 140, 167, 168. *See also* San Francisco Bay Area
Oakland Bikeways Campaign, 118, 119, 123, 252
Oakland City Council, 112, 255
Oakland Redevelopment Agency, 114
Oakland Sustainable Neighborhoods Initiative (OSNI), 136
obduracy, 5, 12, 19, 21, 85, 105, 179, 183, 185
Occupy Movement, 58, 69
Office of Transportation and Infrastructure Systems. *See* Mayor's Office of Transportation and Utilities
Oregon, 4, 21, 56, 111, 156

Ortner, Sherry, 72
Ovarian Cycos, 7

Palo Alto, 35, 36, 42, 157
Parks, Jamie, 130, 252, 254
Patton, Jason, 112, 122, 126, 233, 251, 253
Peck, Jamie, 15, 108, 142, 147
Pennovation Works, 45, 47
People for Bikes, 268
People Mover, 38
People Organized to Win Employment Rights (POWER), 106
People Organizing to Demand Environmental and Economic Justice (PODER), 106
Peskin, Aaron, 101
Philadelphia, xvii, xviii, xx–xxii, 6, 19, 20, 25, 27, 29, 30, 32–36, 38, 45, 79, 142, 144, 149–51, 154, 156, 157, 159, 160–66, 168, 170, 175–77, 262, 271; Center City, 45, 46; Schuylkill Yards, 46, 47; Strawberry Mansion, 151, 154, 161, 162, 267, 268; University City District, 25, 45–47, 150; Vine Street Expressway, 175; West Philadelphia, xvii, 10, 27, 33, 38, 45, 46, 80, 150
placemaking, xiii, xxii, 23, 24, 42, 47, 103, 153, 164, 263
Placemaking Vision for Downtown Detroit, 47, 263
platforms, 50, 156; digital, xxii, 76, 180, 183, 184, 274; policing, 22, 61, 63–65, 69, 77, 78, 92, 106, 107, 139, 177–79, 186, 228, 229, 233, 256, 258, 261, 273; political, 7, 53, 169
policy entrepreneurship, 15
Portland, Oregon, xvii, 4, 7, 21, 69, 78, 86, 137, 153, 156, 169, 182, 228, 229

Pratt, Robert, 129–30
Project for Public Spaces, 24, 47, 103, 223, 263
Protected Bike Lanes Mean Business report, 100, 127
Public Bikes, 13, 74

QLine, 38, 48, 153–55, 223, 263, 265
quality of life, 9, 11, 23, 44, 47, 50, 88, 109, 126, 185
Quicken Loans, 27, 28, 48, 152, 153, 263

race and racism, ix–xii, xv, xvii, xix, xx, 6, 7, 10, 11, 15, 16, 18, 20, 22, 29, 38, 41, 53, 55, 58, 59, 63–65, 72, 73, 77, 78, 81–83, 86, 100, 106, 108, 110, 112–15, 118, 123, 125, 133, 137–41, 146, 147, 152, 160–63, 165, 169, 170, 174, 177–79, 182, 185, 186, 193, 196, 205, 219, 232, 233, 235, 242, 246, 250, 251, 256, 262, 267
Rackspace, 74
Radulovich, Tom, 104, 105
Red, Bike and Green (RBG), 7, 73, 137, 185
redlining, 73, 112, 114, 116, 146, 232, 264
Reed, Olatunji Oboi, 6, 186
Reiskin, Ed, 104, 125
rent, 8–9, 14, 33, 34, 70, 79, 80–82, 89, 97, 117, 238; economic, 180; "redistributive," 89, 204; "rent gap," 8, 10, 43, 46, 79, 115
Rich City Rides, 82
Richmond, Virginia, xvii
rideouts, 175–77
Ritz, Aaron, 161, 163, 165
Rivera, René, 119, 132
Roberts Center for Pediatric Research, 45
Robert Wood Johnson Foundation, 186
Rock Ventures, 47, 263, 265
Roczak, Theodore, 204
Rojas, James, 53

Sadik-Khan, Janette, 1, 23, 103, 124, 197, 244
safety, xxii, 18, 64, 71, 73, 76, 78, 93, 95, 100, 105, 128, 130, 178–80, 186, 187, 220, 242
Sanchez, David, 165
Sander, Elliot, 23
San Francisco, ix, xii, xx, xxi, 4, 13, 14, 17, 19–21, 24, 25, 28–30, 32, 33, 35, 36, 38, 40–48, 56–58, 60, 62, 63, 70, 72, 78–80, 86, 88, 90–95, 97, 100–107, 111, 112, 114, 116, 118, 126, 138, 144, 156–60, 167, 169, 178–80, 182, 200, 213, 221, 230, 238, 243–46, 253, 266, 267, 274; César Chavez Street, 105–6; Divisadero Street, 103; Dogpatch, 106, 242; Market Street, 40–43, 103, 107, 219, 220; Mission District, ix, xvi, xxi, 33, 79, 80, 86, 87, 90, 91, 106, 238, 267; Polk Street, 96, 103, 109–10, 240, 247; South of Market (SOMA), 42, 44, 111, 159, 178; Tenderloin, 43, 96, 159, 220, 240; Valencia Street, 72, 76, 86, 87–101, 103, 105, 107, 109, 111, 122, 126–28, 131, 138, 178, 238–40, 242, 246, 247
San Francisco Bay Area, xvii, xx, xxi, 4, 19, 20, 24, 25, 28–30, 32, 35, 36, 42, 44, 69, 97, 107, 111, 114, 128, 131, 144, 156–59, 166–69, 182, 184, 213; Fruitvale, 138, 187; Hayward, 25, 29; Richmond, 25, 82, 267
San Francisco Bicycle Coalition (SFBC), 6, 41, 57, 59, 78, 86,

INDEX

88–96, 100–104, 106, 107, 109, 110, 112, 118, 119, 167, 178, 221, 238
San Francisco Bike Kitchen, 78–80, 234. *See also* bike kitchens
San Francisco Department of Parking and Traffic (DPT), 91, 93–95, 101, 238, 239. *See also* San Francisco Municipal Transportation Agency (SFMTA)
San Francisco Municipal Railway (Muni), 41, 93, 101, 273
San Francisco Municipal Transportation Agency (SFMTA), 101–3, 105
San Francisco Planning and Urban Research (SPUR), 41, 102, 107–19, 137
San Jose, 4, 25, 29, 32, 33, 36, 38, 60, 144, 157, 158, 169, 229
scale, xii, xiii, xvii, xix, xxi, 12, 22, 45, 47, 50, 55, 58, 81, 90, 103, 104, 112, 124, 131, 133, 138, 157, 184, 186, 187, 204, 226, 240, 241, 247; neighborhood, 6, 8–10, 15, 16, 22, 39, 75, 87, 89, 122, 131, 156, 185; regional, 5, 16, 21, 22, 89, 157, 185
Schaaf, Libby, 132, 133, 166
Schindler, Seth, 50
Schumacher, E. F., 204
Seattle, Washington, 20, 258
SE Bikes, 175–76
Setubal, Claudia, 152
SF Transformation (SFMTrA), 105, 178, 246
Shahum, Leah, 94, 101–2, 240, 244
sharrows, 42, 102, 130, 135, 255
Sheller, Mimi, 6, 12
Shift Transit, 153–54
Silicon Valley, 1, 29, 42, 44, 87, 157, 167, 169
Silicon Valley Bicycle Coalition, 167

Slow Roll Detroit, 64–66, 67, 175, 186, 217
smart growth, 10, 20–22, 100, 157, 240, 267
Smith, Najari, 64, 82
Smith, Neil, xii, 22, 50, 203
Snyder, Dave, 59, 91–93, 96, 102, 106, 238, 239
Social Bicycles, 169, 182
social media, 5–7, 58, 63, 96, 120, 163, 165, 166, 175, 179, 182, 199, 228, 244, 257
social reproduction, 38, 39, 204. *See also* gender
spatial fix, 16, 19
Spinney, Justin, 40
Strava, 76
Streetsblog, 6, 123, 132, 179
Stuff White People Like, 7
subaltern, 6, 78, 105, 225, 233
suburbanization, xx, 9, 10, 16, 20, 22, 34, 114, 184
suburbanization of poverty, 4, 208
suburbs, xiii, xviii, 4, 11, 15–17, 19, 20, 24, 25, 27–29, 33, 34, 38, 42, 43, 45, 48, 51, 59, 65, 145, 147, 184, 213, 217
Sunday Streets, 70, 103, 221
Sunshine, Stuart, 93
sustainability, xii, xiii, xv, xvi, xxi, 5, 8, 11, 16, 17, 19, 20, 22, 23, 39, 40, 45, 53, 66, 74, 80, 81, 85, 87, 88, 93, 95, 107, 112, 133, 136, 143, 145, 152, 155, 159, 168, 170, 175, 184, 185, 187, 200

tactical urbanism, 55, 90, 105, 123, 144, 178
Tata, Jamii, 165
technocracy, 15, 18, 86, 89, 133, 148
technology, xvii, 12, 18, 21, 44, 45, 48, 55, 56, 75, 89, 104, 119, 130–32, 135, 143, 168, 179, 180, 200,

204, 210, 226, 237; high, xiv, 4, 11, 19, 25, 42, 46, 47, 108, 112, 159, 237
technopole, 40, 42, 51
Telegraph Bikeways Campaign, 133
Temescal Telegraph Business Improvement District (BID), 120–22, 252, 254
Temple University, 150, 162
Thailand, 75, 199
Theodore, Nik, 15, 108, 142, 147
Thornton, Adriel, 154, 165
Toole Design Group, 151
traffic, xiii, xx–xxii, 6, 10, 12, 14, 20, 23, 40, 42, 47, 49, 57, 61, 63, 71, 82, 83, 87, 91–93, 95–97, 100, 101, 106, 120, 122–24, 129–32, 140, 141, 173, 177–79, 184, 207, 239, 242, 250, 253; calming, 49, 95, 130; congestion, xix, 16, 20, 21, 35, 38, 40, 119, 128–31, 143, 171, 175, 178, 254
TransForm, 136, 167–69, 187
transit first policy, 41
Transportation Alternatives Program, 23
Transportation Research Board, 23
Tube Times, 94

Uber, 43, 105, 178, 182, 196
University City District, 45
University of California Berkeley, 13, 35, 115, 116, 159, 169, 267
University of Pennsylvania, 33, 45, 47
University of the Sciences, 45
Untokening, The, 7, 186, 277
urban acupuncture, 6, 8, 55, 90
urbanization, xv, xxii, 17, 20–22, 40, 50, 79, 109, 171, 183, 185, 187, 236
Urban Land Institute, 44

urban renewal, 108–9, 112, 114, 136, 138
Urry, John, 12

"Valencia epiphany," 87, 104, 110, 119, 126
vehicular cycling, 122, 130, 207
Velo Mondial, 102
Via Bicycle, xviii, 191
Vision Zero, xxii, 177–79, 186

Wagner, Julie, 40
Waite, Sarita, 252, 254
Walder, Jay, 166, 266
Walk Oakland Bike Oakland (WOBO), 6, 112, 118, 119, 125, 131, 251
Walk SF, 102–3
Washington, D.C., 7, 16, 86, 100, 102, 143, 151, 183
Wayne State University, 38, 48, 65, 153, 263
West Oakland Redevelopment Area, 140
West Oakland Specific Plan, 140
White Bike Plan, 143
whiteness, xviii, xix, 7, 16, 115, 186. *See also* race and racism
Whyte, William, 9, 24
William Penn Foundation, 151
Wladowski, Vlad, 133
World Bicycle Relief, xiv

Xerocracy, 57

Yellow Bike Project, 78, 167
Yes In My Back Yard (YIMBYism), 44, 246, 271

ZipCar, 168

JOHN G. STEHLIN, a former bicycle mechanic, is assistant professor in the Department of Geography, Environment, and Sustainability at the University of North Carolina at Greensboro. He received his PhD in geography and global metropolitan studies from UC Berkeley.